Frommer's®

Virgin Islands

11th Edition

by Darwin Porter & Danforth Prince

WILEY

John Wiley & Sons, Inc.

ABOUT THE AUTHORS

As a team of veteran travel writers, **Darwin Porter** and **Danforth Prince** have produced dozens of previous titles for Frommer's including many of their guides to Europe. They researched and wrote the first-ever guide for Frommer's on the Caribbean, including the Virgin Islands, as well as Bermuda and The Bahamas. Porter is also a Hollywood celebrity biographer, columnist, and radio broadcaster. He is joined by Danforth Prince, formerly of the Paris bureau of *The New York Times* and today the president of Blood Moon Productions.

Published by:
JOHN WILEY & SONS, INC.
111 River St.
Hoboken, NJ 07030-5774

ISBN 978-1-118-00426-5 (paper); ISBN 978-1-118-14044-4 (ebk); ISBN 978-1-118-14045-1 (ebk); ISBN 978-1-118-14046-8 (ebk)

Editor: Jennifer Polland
Production Editor: Eric T. Schroeder
Cartographer: Anton Crane
Photo Editor: Richard Fox
Production by Wiley Indianapolis Composition Services
Front Cover Photo: Tourists in water around large granite boulders at the Baths at Virgin Gorda, British Virgin Islands ©M. Timothy O'Keefe / Alamy Images.
Back Cover Photo: Typical buildings on Main Street, Road Town, British Virgin Islands ©SIME / eStock Photo.

For information on our other products and services or to obtain technical support, please contact our Customer Care Department within the U.S. at 877/762-2974, outside the U.S. at 317/572-3993 or fax 317/572-4002.

John Wiley & Sons, Inc. also publishes its books in a variety of electronic formats. Some content that appears in print may not be available in electronic formats.

Manufactured in the United States of America

5 4 3 2 1

CONTENTS

7 PLANNING YOUR TRIP TO THE VIRGIN ISLANDS 246

LIST OF MAPS

HOW TO CONTACT US

In researching this book, we discovered many wonderful places—hotels, restaurants, shops, and more. We're sure you'll find others. Please tell us about them, so we can share the information with your fellow travelers in upcoming editions. If you were disappointed with a recommendation, we'd love to know that, too. Please write to:

Frommer's Virgin Islands, 11th Edition
John Wiley & Sons, Inc. • 111 River St. • Hoboken, NJ 07030-5774
frommersfeedback@wiley.com

ADVISORY & DISCLAIMER

Travel information can change quickly and unexpectedly, and we strongly advise you to confirm important details locally before traveling, including information on visas, health and safety, traffic and transport, accommodation, shopping, and eating out. We also encourage you to stay alert while traveling and to remain aware of your surroundings. Avoid civil disturbances, and keep a close eye on cameras, purses, wallets, and other valuables.

While we have endeavored to ensure that the information contained within this guide is accurate and up-to-date at the time of publication, we make no representations or warranties with respect to the accuracy or completeness of the contents of this work and specifically disclaim all warranties, including without limitation warranties of fitness for a particular purpose. We accept no responsibility or liability for any inaccuracy or errors or omissions, or for any inconvenience, loss, damage, costs, or expenses of any nature whatsoever incurred or suffered by anyone as a result of any advice or information contained in this guide.

The inclusion of a company, organization, or Website in this guide as a service provider and/or potential source of further information does not mean that we endorse them or the information they provide. Be aware that information provided through some websites may be unreliable and can change without notice. Neither the publisher or author shall be liable for any damages arising herefrom.

FROMMER'S STAR RATINGS, ICONS & ABBREVIATIONS

Every hotel, restaurant, and attraction listing in this guide has been ranked for quality, value, service, amenities, and special features using a **star-rating system.** In country, state, and regional guides, we also rate towns and regions to help you narrow down your choices and budget your time accordingly. Hotels and restaurants are rated on a scale of zero (recommended) to three stars (exceptional). Attractions, shopping, nightlife, towns, and regions are rated according to the following scale: zero stars (recommended), one star (highly recommended), two stars (very highly recommended), and three stars (must-see).

In addition to the star-rating system, we also use **seven feature icons** that point you to the great deals, in-the-know advice, and unique experiences that separate travelers from tourists. Throughout the book, look for:

special finds—those places only insiders know about

fun facts—details that make travelers more informed and their trips more fun

kids—best bets for kids and advice for the whole family

special moments—those experiences that memories are made of

overrated—places or experiences not worth your time or money

insider tips—great ways to save time and money

great values—where to get the best deals

The following abbreviations are used for credit cards:

AE	American Express	DISC	Discover	V	Visa
DC	Diners Club	MC	MasterCard		

TRAVEL RESOURCES AT FROMMERS.COM

Frommer's travel resources don't end with this guide. Frommer's website, **www.frommers. com,** has travel information on more than 4,000 destinations. We update features regularly, giving you access to the most current trip-planning information and the best airfare, lodging, and car-rental bargains. You can also listen to podcasts, connect with other Frommers. com members through our active-reader forums, share your travel photos, read blogs from guidebook editors and fellow travelers, and much more.

THE BEST OF THE VIRGIN ISLANDS

Former stomping grounds of some of history's most famous sea marauders, the Virgin Islands are now invaded by visitors who arrive by the thousands daily either by plane or cruise ship. There about 100 of these green hilly islands, some governed by the United States and others by Great Britain, which rise from a clear blue sea—many of these islands are small and virtually uninhabited.

The major islands—and the most famous ones—are owned by the United States: St. Thomas (which attracts most visitors, many from cruise ships), St. Croix, and St. John, the smallest of the three. **St. Thomas** is the most accessible of all the islands, and likely to be your gateway. With the busiest cruise-ship harbor in the Caribbean, St. Thomas is constantly bustling with crowds, yet it also offers great shopping and first-class dining. **St. Croix** is far more laid-back than St. Thomas, and little **St. John** is positively sleepy.

Of the dozens of British Virgin Islands, **Tortola** is the best known, while **Virgin Gorda** is perhaps the most exclusive, attracting well-heeled visitors. The B.V.I. are not overly developed, evoking the relaxed feel of the 1950s' Caribbean. Former sailing grounds of some of history's most famous sea marauders, such as Sir Francis Drake, the B.V.I. offer the best sailing grounds in the Caribbean.

The Virgin Islands contain some of the best sandy beaches in the West Indies, including Magens Bay on St. Thomas, Trunk Bay on St. John, and Cane Garden Bay on Tortola. You'll find hidden beaches where you may be the only sunbather, as well as overdeveloped coves where too many bags of cement arrived before you did—this is especially true on the most populated island of St. Thomas. Throughout the archipelago there are also miles of idyllic hiking trails, especially in one of America's most beautiful national parks on St. John.

Because many of the Virgin Islands are so remote—some are mere rocky outcroppings—you'll feel like Robinson Crusoe while exploring these isolated, uninhabited islands. Yachties love it here, as the area rivals the Mediterranean (without the crowds) or the South Pacific with its steady winds and gin-clear waters. Swimming and snorkeling await you at every cove.

The Best of the Virgin Islands

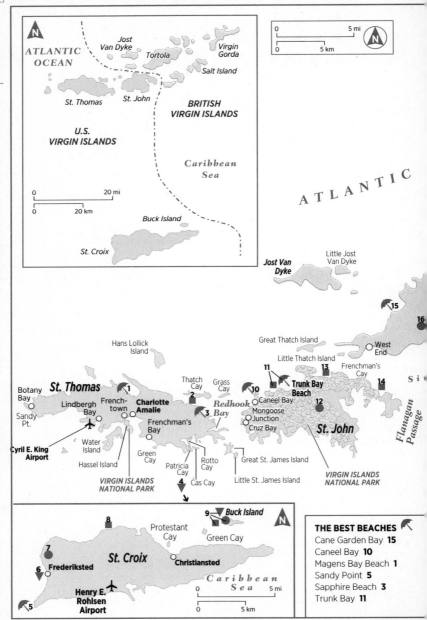

THE BEST BEACHES
Cane Garden Bay **15**
Caneel Bay **10**
Magens Bay Beach **1**
Sandy Point **5**
Sapphire Beach **3**
Trunk Bay **11**

British Virgin Islands
U.S. Virgin Islands

Anegada

The Settlement

O C E A N

Prickly Pear Island
Necker Island
Mosquito Island
Seal Dogs
North Sound
Eustatia
Great Camanoe
George Dog
West Dog
Guana Island
Scrub Island
Great Dog
South Sound
Little Camanoe
Marina Cay
Spanish Town
✈ *Virgin Gorda*
Tortola
East End ○ 17 ▼
Beef Island
Fallen Jerusalem
○ Road Town
Francis Drake Channel
Cooper Island
Round Rock
19
Salt Island Passage
Ginger Island
18 ▼
Salt Island
Peter Island
C a r i b b e a n   S e a
Norman Island

THE BEST SNORKELING ■ SPOTS	THE BEST DIVE SITES ▼	THE BEST NATURE WALKS ●
Buck Island **9**	Alice in Wonderland **19**	The Annaberg Historic Trail **12**
Cane Bay **8**	Buck Island **9**	Buck Island Walk **9**
Coki Point Beach **2**	Chikuzen **17**	The "Rain Forest" Hike **7**
Haulover Bay **14**	Cow and Calf Rocks **4**	Sage Mountain
Leinster Bay **13**	Frederiksted Pier **6**	National Park **16**
Trunk Bay **11**	The Wreck of the HMS Rhone **18**	

THE best BEACHES

Many Caribbean islands have only rocky beaches or beaches made of black volcanic sand (which heats up fast in the noonday sun), but those in the Virgin Islands are known for their fine white sand. Best of all, every beach in the Virgin Islands is free (except for Magens Bay in St. Thomas) and open to the public, although in some cases you'll have to walk across the grounds of a resort (or arrive by private boat) to reach them.

- **Magens Bay Beach** (St. Thomas): This half-mile loop of pebble-free sand, boasting remarkably calm waters, is by far the most popular and picturesque beach in the U.S. Virgin Islands. Two peninsulas protect the shore from erosion and strong waves, making Magens an ideal spot for swimming. Expect a lively crowd in the high season. See p. 81.
- **Sapphire Beach** (St. Thomas): This is one of the finest beaches on St. Thomas, and a favorite with windsurfers. Come here for some of St. Thomas's best shore snorkeling and diving (off Pettyklip Point). And don't worry about equipment—watersports concessions abound here. Take a moment to enjoy the panoramic view of St. John and other islands. See p. 82.
- **Trunk Bay** (St. John): This beach, which is protected by the U.S. National Park Service, is a favorite with cruise-ship passengers. It's famous for its underwater snorkeling trail and is consistently ranked in magazine polls as one of the top 10 Caribbean beaches. See p. 128.
- **Caneel Bay** (St. John): Site of a famous resort, Caneel Bay is a string of seven beaches stretching around Durloe Point to Hawksnest Caneel. Rosewood Hotels, which operates Caneel Bay Resort, admits day guests. See p. 128.
- **Sandy Point** (St. Croix): The biggest beach in the U.S. Virgin Islands, Sandy Point lies in the southwestern part of St. Croix, directly to the west of Alexander Hamilton Airport. Its waters are shallow and calm. Because the beach is a protected reserve and a nesting spot for endangered sea turtles, it's open to the public only on Saturdays and Sundays from 9am to 5pm. See p. 167.
- **Cane Garden Bay** (Tortola): The most popular beach in the British Virgin Islands, and a close rival to Magens Bay on St. Thomas (see above) for scenic beauty, is Cane Garden Bay. Its translucent waters and sugar-white sands are reason enough to visit Tortola. Happily, it's the closest beach to Road Town, the capital. See p. 192.

THE best SNORKELING SPOTS

The islands of St. Croix, St. John, and St. Thomas are among the finest places to snorkel in the Caribbean. Because of their historic shipwreck sites, the B.V.I. contain some of the best diving in the Caribbean, but their snorkeling spots can't quite compare to those in the U.S.V.I. Here are some of the best spots:

- **Coki Point Beach** (St. Thomas): On the north shore of St. Thomas, Coki Point offers superb year-round snorkeling. Especially enticing are the coral ledges near Coral World's underwater tower. See p. 85.
- **Leinster Bay** (St. John): Easily accessible Leinster Bay, on the northern shore of St. John, offers calm, clear, uncrowded waters teeming with sea life. See p. 130.
- **Haulover Bay** (St. John): A favorite with locals, this small bay is rougher than Leinster and is often deserted. The snorkeling, however, is dramatic, with ledges, walls, nooks, and sandy areas set close together. See p. 130.

- **Trunk Bay** (St. John): The self-guided, 675-foot-long snorkeling trail here has large underwater signs that identify species of coral and other marine life. Above water, the beach's freshwater showers, changing rooms, equipment rentals, and lifeguards make snorkeling downright convenient. See p. 130.
- **Cane Bay** (St. Croix): One of the island's best diving and snorkeling sites is off this breezy, north-shore beach. On a good day, you can swim out 450 feet to see the Cane Bay Wall, which drops dramatically off to the deep waters below. Multicolored fish, plus elkhorn and brain coral, flourish here. See p. 170.
- **Buck Island** (off St. Croix): This tiny island, whose land and offshore waters together are classified as a national monument, lies 2 miles off the north coast of St. Croix. More than 250 recorded species of fish swim through its reef system. A variety of sponges, corals, and crustaceans also inhabit the area. See p. 186.

THE best DIVE SITES

- **Cow and Calf Rocks** (St. Thomas): This site, off the southeast end of St. Thomas (about a 45-min. boat ride from Charlotte Amalie), is the island's best diving spot. It's also a good bet for snorkeling. You'll discover a network of coral tunnels filled with caves, reefs, and ancient boulders encrusted with coral. See p. 85.
- **Frederiksted Pier** (St. Croix): Those in the know have designated this pier, located in an old ramshackle town at the west end of St. Croix, the most interesting pier dive in the Caribbean. Plunge into a world of exotic creatures, including sponges, banded shrimp, plume worms, and sea horses. See p. 170.
- **Buck Island** (off St. Croix): This is one of the major diving meccas in the Caribbean, with an underwater visibility of some 100 feet. There are labyrinths and grottoes for more experienced divers, plus massive gardens of fiery coral inhabited by black sea urchins, barracudas, stingrays, and other creatures. See p. 186.
- **The Wreck of the HMS *Rhone*** (off Salt Island): The *Rhone* wreck is the premier dive site not only in the Virgin Islands, but also in the entire Caribbean. This royal mail steamer, which went down in 1867, was featured in the murky film *The Deep*. See p. 216.
- ***Chikuzen*** (off Tortola): Although it's not the *Rhone* (see above), this 269-foot steel-hulled refrigerator ship, which sank off the island's east end in 1981, is one of the British Virgin Islands' most fascinating dive sites. The hull—still intact under about 24m (79 ft.) of water—is now home to a vast array of tropical fish, including yellowtail, barracuda, black-tip sharks, octopus, and drum fish. See p. 216.
- **Alice in Wonderland** (Ginger Island, off Tortola): This brilliant coral wall, off the shore of a tiny island, slopes from 12m (39 ft.) to a sandy bottom at 30m (98 ft.). Divers often refer to the site as "a fantasy" because of its monstrous overhangs, vibrant colors, gigantic mushroom-shaped corals, and wide variety of sea creatures—everything from conch and garden eels to long-nose butterfly fish. See p. 216.

THE best NATURE WALKS

- **The Annaberg Historic Trail** (St. John): This paved walk is only .25 miles long, but it's a highlight of the 10,000-acre U.S. Virgin Islands National Park. The trail traverses the ruins of what was once the most important sugar-cane plantation on the island. Slaves' quarters, a windmill tower, and ballast-brick buildings are remnants of a long-vanished era. Stunning views look toward Tortola, Great Thatch Island, and Jost Van Dyke on the opposite side of Sir Francis Drake Passage. See p. 132.

- **The "Rain Forest" Hike** (St. Croix): At the northwestern end of St. Croix lies the 15-acre "rain forest," which is thick with magnificent plant life. The little-traveled four-wheel-drive roads through the area make great hiking paths. See p. 168.

- **The Buck Island Walk** (off St. Croix): A circumnavigation of this island, which is accessible by boat, takes about 2 hours and is rated moderate. Because the island is ringed with white-sand beaches, you can always take a break for a refreshing swim. There's also a trail that points inland. See p. 186.

- **The Sage Mountain National Park Hike** (Tortola): This 3- to 4-hour hike is one of the most dramatic in the British Virgins. It goes from Brewer's Bay to the top of Mount Sage, the highest peak in the Virgin Islands, at 523m (1,716 ft.). Along the way, you'll see intriguing ruins of old homes in addition to the beautiful flora and fauna of the park's primeval forest. See p. 216.

THE best HISTORIC SIGHTS

- **Fort Christian** (St. Thomas): This fort, which stands in the heart of Charlotte Amalie, was built in 1672 after the arrival of the first Danish colonists. The oldest building on the island, it has been vastly altered over the years and has housed a jail, a courthouse, a town hall, a church, and, most recently, a historical museum. Head to the roof for a stellar view. See p. 51.

- **Crown House** (St. Thomas): This 18th-century, stone-built mansion served as the home of two former governors. Among the many antiques here are memorabilia that belonged to Governor-General Peter von Scholten, who occupied the premises in 1827. A French chandelier in the mansion is said to have come from Versailles. See p. 90.

- **Annaberg Historic Trail** (St. John): The ruins of the Annaberg Sugar Plantation are the greatest reminder of St. John's plantation era. The remains of the building have been spruced up rather than restored, and the surrounding land is now filled with lush vegetation. Visitors can explore the former slave quarters. See p. 132.

- **Fort Christiansvaern** (St. Croix): This fort is one of the best preserved of its type in the West Indies, with a facade that hasn't changed much since the 1820s. It was constructed from ballast bricks imported from Denmark, the island's colonial guardian. The first fort on the spot was built between 1732 and 1749, and part of that structure remains. See p. 172.

- **Fort Frederik** (St. Croix): This fort, completed in 1760, is said to have been the first to salute the flag of the newly formed United States. It was also here, in 1848, that Governor-General Peter von Scholten read a proclamation freeing the island's slaves. A small museum sits on the site today. See p. 174.

THE best RESORTS

- **Frenchman's Reef & Morning Star Marriott Beach Resort** (St. Thomas; ✆ 888/236-2427 or 340/776-8500; www.marriott.com): The sprawling, luxe resort of Frenchman's Reef practically put St. Thomas on the tourist map. It's linked to its even better sibling next door, Marriott Morning Star Beach Resort, to make up one mega-resort. Guests at both properties share the same amenities, facilities, and restaurants. The resort stands on one of the best beaches on the island. See p. 64.

- **The Ritz-Carlton** (St. Thomas; ✆ 800/241-3333 or 340/775-3333; www.ritz carlton.com): There is no grander place to stay in the U.S. Virgin Islands. Fronted by white-sand beaches, this is the resort for those who want to escape to the Caribbean not like Robinson Crusoe, but as Bill Gates might if he showed up on a yacht. See p. 65.

o **The Buccaneer** (St. Croix; © **800/255-3881** or 340/712-2100; www.the buccaneer.com): Newer and glitzier competitors have sprouted up, but this large, luxurious, family-owned resort is still a class act. It lies on the island's best beaches, and has the best sports program, the best entertainment, and the best food of any hotel. See p. 146.

o **Caneel Bay** (St. John; © **888/767-3966** or 340/776-6111; www.caneelbay.com): There is no resort in the islands with a greater pedigree than this place. Laurance S. Rockefeller created Caneel Bay as the Caribbean's first eco-resort back in the days when no one knew what that word meant. Even though the resort isn't posh, it's an understated classic, an outpost of refinement without ostentation. See p. 113.

o **Westin St John Resort & Villas** (St. John; © **866/716-8108** or 340/693-8000; www.westinresortstjohn.com): The glitz and glitter missing at Caneel Bay can be found here. Architecturally dramatic and visually appealing, this resort sprawls across 34 landscaped acres, opening onto a 1,200-foot white-sand beach. It boasts a huge array of activities, including lots of watersports. See p. 114.

o **Biras Creek Resort** (Virgin Gorda; © **877/883-0756** or 248/494-3555; www. biras.com): A private and romantic retreat, this resort is built around an old hillside fortress. It's an escapist's hideaway, on a 60-hectare (148-acre) estate with its own marina. There are no phones and no TVs, but you can find the latest edition of the *Wall Street Journal*. See p. 226.

o **Bitter End Yacht Club** (Virgin Gorda; © **800/872-2392** or 284/494-2746; www. beyc.com): This is the best sailing and diving resort in all of the Virgin Islands, opening onto one of the most unspoiled and secluded deepwater harbors in the Caribbean. You'll live and dine here in style; you can even stay aboard a 30-foot yacht. See p. 226.

o **Long Bay Beach Resort & Villas** (Tortola; © **866/237-3491** or 284/495-4252; www.longbay.com): The finest resort in the capital of the B.V.I., this complex borders a 1.6km-long (1-mile) sandy beach. It's the only full-service resort in Tortola, and its deluxe beachfront rooms and cabanas are quite nice. See p. 202.

o **Peter Island Resort** (Peter Island; © **800/346-4451** or 284/495-2000; www. peterisland.com): This posh resort lies on its own 720-hectare (1,779-acre) tropical island. It opens onto Deadman's Beach, which, in spite of its name, is consistently voted one of the most romantic beaches in the world by various travel magazine reader polls. This is a true retreat—a hedonistic resort that's a monument to the good life. See p. 243.

THE most ROMANTIC RESORTS

Many hotels in the Virgin Islands will help you plan your wedding, doing everything from arranging the flowers and the photographer to applying for the marriage license (see "Getting Married in the Virgin Islands," in chapter 7, for more details). But even if you don't actually tie the knot here, the Virgin Islands offer some of the world's most romantic destinations for honeymooning couples (or those who just want to pretend they're honeymooning).

- **Elysian Beach Resort** (St. Thomas; ✆ 888/620-7994 or 340/775-1000; www.elysianbeachresort.net): For a great value, ask about the "Honeymoon Getaway" package, which includes a deluxe room or a one-bedroom suite, champagne on arrival, and use of the tennis courts, health club, and pool. See p. 66.

- **The Buccaneer** (St. Croix; ✆ 800/255-3881 or 340/712-2100; www.thebuccaneer.com): This resort boasts the most extensive facilities on St. Croix, including an 18-hole golf course, eight championship tennis courts, a spa and health club, a 2-mile jogging trail, and three beaches. The 1653 sugar mill on the grounds is the most popular wedding spot on the island. We recommend staying in one of the beachside rooms, which have fieldstone terraces that take you right down to the water. See p. 146.

- **Biras Creek Resort** (Virgin Gorda; ✆ 877/883-0756 or 284/494-3555; www.biras.com): This private and elegant hotel is located on a secluded 60-hectare (148-acre) promontory, accessible only by launch. Signposted nature trails cut through the lush tropical gardens. See p. 226.

- **Rosewood Little Dix Bay** (Virgin Gorda; ✆ 888/767-3966 or 284/495-5555; www.littledixbay.com): The understated elegance of this luxury resort is popular with older couples and honeymooners alike—in fact, the powerfully amorous atmosphere sometimes makes single guests feel like wallflowers. Spread out over 200 hectares (494 acres) on a secluded bay, this resort offers beautiful beaches and sporting activities galore, plus plenty of privacy, if that's what you're after. See p. 227.

THE best FAMILY RESORTS

- **Bolongo Bay Beach Resort** (St. Thomas; ✆ 800/524-4746 or 340/775-1800; www.bolongobay.com): The resort staff here offers a huge roster of family activities. In the off season, children 11 and under stay free in their parents' rooms, and eat free from a kids' menu. See p. 65.

- **Westin St. John Resort & Villas** (St. John; ✆ 866/716-8108 or 340/693-8000; www.westinresortstjohn.com): This contemporary mega-resort, set on 34 acres of landscaped grounds, offers the best children's programs on the island. Babysitting can be arranged, and children get reduced rates on everything. See p. 114.

- **The Buccaneer** (St. Croix; ✆ 800/255-3881 or 340/712-2100; www.thebuccaneer.com): This hotel, located on a 300-acre former sugar estate, is a long-time family favorite. It has on-site facilities for just about every sport you can think of, including tennis, golf, swimming, jogging, sailing, scuba diving, and snorkeling. Children's programs include a half-day sail to Buck Island Reef and nature walks through tropical foliage, where kids can taste local fruit in the wild. See p. 146.

- **Chenay Bay Beach Resort** (St. Croix; ✆ 866/226-8677 or 340/718-2918; www.chenaybay.com): Families staying in these West Indian–style cottages can keep their 3- to 12-year-olds busy with various organized activities, from swimming and snorkeling to nature walks and story hours. The friendly owners of this barefoot-casual hotel used their own offspring as test cases to design their children's program, which runs during the summer and over holiday periods. See p. 150.

- **Bitter End Yacht Club** (Virgin Gorda; ✆ 800/872-2392 or 284/494-2746; www.beyc.com): Most children's programs at this lively resort are geared toward those ages 6 and over, and involve all the typical watersports: sailing, windsurfing, snorkeling, swimming, and more. Ask about packages for families. See p. 226.

THE best SMALL HOTELS & BED & BREAKFASTS

- **Villa Blanca** (St. Thomas; ℂ **800/231-0034** or 340/776-0749; www.villablanca hotel.com): Small, intimate, and charming, this inn stands on 3 acres on a hill overlooking Charlotte Amalie. A homelike atmosphere prevails, and there's a fresh-water pool. The one con: You'll have to drive to the beach. See p. 64.

- **Villa Santana** (St. Thomas; ℂ **340/776-1311;** www.villasantana.com): At this country villa, originally built for a Mexican general, all rooms are suites. In honor of its previous occupant, the decor is Mexican. There's a pool, a sun deck, and a garden. See p. 57.

- **Garden by the Sea Bed & Breakfast** (St. John; ℂ **340/779-4731;** www.garden bythesea.com): Overlooking the ocean, this is a small but choice B&B on the least populated of the major U.S. Virgins. With easy access to beaches, it offers beautifully furnished bedrooms with elephant bamboo canopy beds and Japanese fountains. You get style and affordable prices—not bad. See p. 119.

- **Villa Greenleaf** (St. Croix; ℂ **888/282-1001** or 340/719-1958; www.villa greenleaf.com) is the best B&B on land, a snug family retreat in the style of New England inn-keeping. Personal service and an elegant ambience combine in this 1950s building, where life proceeds as in a private home. See p. 158.

- **Carringtons Inn** (St. Croix; ℂ **877/658-0508** or 340/713-0508; www.carringtons inn.com): This was once the grand home of a wealthy island family. It has since been converted into one of the most appealing B&Bs in the U.S. Virgin Islands. Personalized attention and comfortable surroundings are hallmarks. Some of the individually decorated bedrooms boast king-size canopy beds. See p. 157.

THE best PLACES TO GET AWAY FROM IT ALL

Although there are tranquil retreats on St. Croix, and even on St. Thomas, you'll find most of the remote oases on St. John and in the British Virgin Islands.

- **St. John:** This is one of the most secluded islands in the Caribbean. More than two-thirds of the land has been preserved as a national park. That means that unlike St. Thomas and St. Croix, St. John's landscape looks much like it did in the 1950s: white-sand beaches and verdant tropical forests. Day-trippers from St. Thomas come over in the morning and usually depart before 5pm. After that, St. John becomes a crowd-free paradise. **Caribbean Villas & Resorts** (p. 116; ℂ **800/338-0987;** www.caribbeanvilla.com) offers some of the best values for those who'd like to rent their own private villa. See chapter 4.

- **Sandcastle Hotel** (Jost Van Dyke; ℂ **284/495-9888;** www.soggydollar.com/ sandcastlehotel): This little island, reached by ferry from Tortola, is the ultimate escapist's dream. The island offers good hiking trails, uncrowded sandy beaches, and the ruins of an old military fort. People come to the Sandcastle in search of isolation and relaxation, and that's exactly what they get. See p. 236.

- **Anegada Reef Hotel** (Anegada; ℂ **284/495-8002;** www.anegadareef.com): This hotel is located some 32km (20 miles) north of Virgin Gorda's North Sound, on a flat mass of coral and limestone. It's one of the most remote spots in the entire

Virgin Islands chain. You may never meet any of the 250 local residents, although you'll occasionally see snorkelers, fishermen, and scuba divers. We recommend this unpolished hotel for devotees of deserted beaches and laid-back getaways. It's the kind of place where, if the bartender isn't around, you make your own cocktails and write down what you had. See p. 242.

o **Guana Island Club** (Guana Island; © **800/544-8262** or 284/494-2354; www.guana.com): This secluded, hilltop hideaway is the only development on a private, 344-hectare (850-acre) island off the coast of Tortola. The island is known for its six vacant, virgin beaches; rare species of plant and animal life (look for the roseate flamingo); and excellent nature trails. See p. 244.

o **Peter Island Resort** (Peter Island; © **800/346-4451** or 284/495-2000; www.peterisland.com): This exquisite resort inn sits on a 720-hectare (1,779-acre) private island, which comes complete with five pristine beaches, hiking trails, and gorgeous offshore reefs. Guests also enjoy first-rate watersports facilities, elegant candlelit dining, and secluded beachfront accommodations. See p. 243.

THE best RESTAURANTS

o **Tavern on the Waterfront** (St. Thomas; © **340/776-4328**): Every celebrity who visits the U.S.V.I. seems to turn up here. Opening onto harbor views at Charlotte Amalie, this restaurant serves some of the island's finest French and Caribbean cuisine. Imaginative dishes include such treats as espresso-and-cinnamon-encrusted pork medallions with passion fruit demi-glace. See p. 72.

o **Hervé Restaurant & Wine Bar** (St. Thomas; © **340/777-9703**): This establishment, next to the landmark Hotel 1829, has captured loads of attention. The panoramic view is great, but it's the cuisine that is the draw: a truly sublime repertoire of American and Caribbean cuisines. Nothing beats the black sesame–crusted tuna with a ginger-and-raspberry sauce. See p. 70.

o **Virgilio's** (St. Thomas; © **340/776-4920**): This cheerful, elegant spot boasts the best Italian food on the island. Virgilio's lovingly prepares all your favorite Italian classics (try the *osso buco* or chicken Parmigiana), in addition to more than 20 different homemade pasta dishes, and a few surprises, like *cioppino* (a kettle of savory seafood stew). Savvy diners always save room for one of the flambé desserts. See p. 72.

o **Asolare** (St. John; © **340/779-4747**): The most beautiful and elegant restaurant on St. John also features some of the island's best food. The chef produces a fusion of French and Asian cuisine that relies on the island's freshest seafood and produce. Try the prawn-and–coconut milk soup, or the spicy tuna tartare wrapped in noodles. The staff is the hippest and most attractive on the island. See p. 121.

o **Le Château de Bordeaux** (St. John; © **340/776-6611**): Both the view and the exquisite combination of Continental and Caribbean cuisine are winners. Wild game, and rack of lamb perfumed with rosemary and surrounded by a honey-Dijon nut crust, appear often on the ever-changing menu. The West Indian seafood chowder is a perfect blend of fish and spices. See p. 124.

o **The Terrace** (St. Croix; © **340/712-2100**): Housed in the Buccaneer, the most prestigious resort on St. Croix, this is the best hotel restaurant on the island. The first-class cuisine is prepared with quality ingredients. Wait until you try the grilled lobster cakes. See p. 160.

o **Kendrick's** (St. Croix; © **340/773-9199**): The married owners at Kendrick's bring a light Continental touch to richly flavored dishes. You might begin with baked brie smothered in perfectly seasoned wild mushrooms, then move on to coconut shrimp in a chive-studded, peppery aïoli. Some of this culinary couple's recipes have been featured in *Bon Appétit* magazine. See p. 161.

THE best DISHES IN THE VIRGIN ISLANDS

- **Conch Chowder at Molly Malone's** (St. Thomas; ✆ **340/775-1270**): Island chefs pride themselves on their conch chowder, but Molly has got the other cooks beat. Savory, spicy, perfectly flavored conch chowder is served nightly. See p. 79.

- **Creative Salads at Robert's American Grille** (St. Thomas; ✆ **340/714-3663**): The homemade salads here are the freshest on the island. A delightful treat is the Elysian salad, made with mesclun tossed with roasted walnuts, Bermuda onions, chopped tomatoes, and a house-made dried cranberry–and–poppy seed dressing. See p. 79.

- **Callaloo Soup at Miss Lucy's** (St. John; ✆ **340/693-5244**): Callaloo is a spinach-like vegetable native to the West Indies, and local chefs know how to make one of the island's most satisfying soups from this humble plant. Self-taught Miss Lucy seems to impart a magic touch to her kettle. We always go for a second bowl. See p. 126.

- **Garlic Chicken at Vie's Snack Shack** (St. John; ✆ **340/693-5033**): Some residents of St. Thomas cross the bay just to sample some of Vie's fabled garlic chicken. We don't know exactly what she does with the bird, but it's such a savory concoction that the dish becomes addictive. See p. 127.

- **Succulent Pastas at ZoZo's Ristorante** (St. John; ✆ **340/693-9200**): You can enjoy an array of appetizing pastas at one of the finest Italian restaurants in the Virgins. It doesn't get much better than the lobster ravioli with wild mushrooms and toasted pine nuts. See p. 125.

- **Seafood Chowder at Le Château de Bordeaux** (St. John; ✆ **340/776-6611**): Even if you're from New England, you'll savor the West Indian seafood chowder here. The chef uses the freshest fish and just the right spices. See p. 124.

- **Margaritas at Morgan's Mango** (St. John; ✆ **340/693-8141**): Thursday is officially Margarita Night, but on any night the bartenders will whip up your favorite margarita. Only Jimmy Buffet knows how to do it better. See p. 126.

- **Tantalizing Curries at Savant** (St. Croix; ✆ **340/713-8666**): The spicy dishes of Thailand and Mexico are served at this Christiansted eatery. We always go for the Thai curries, which are as good as some of those served in the mother country. The red-coconut-curry sauce is among the finest we've ever sampled. See p. 162.

- **Lobster Pasta at the Bombay Club** (St. Croix; ✆ **340/773-1838**): We've never been able to work our way through the menu here, because we always like to fill up on the fresh lobster pasta, which is cooked to perfection and well seasoned with delectable hunks of fresh lobster. See p. 162.

- **Mahimahi at Round Hill Vacation Villa** (Tortola; ✆ **284/495-9353**): Joycelyn and Allan Rhymer perform wonders with one of our favorite fishes, mahimahi, serving it with a savory garlic-butter sauce. See p. 211.

- **Home-Cooked West Indian Meals at Mrs. Scatliffe's Restaurant** (Tortola; ✆ **284/495-4556**): Mrs. Scatliffe's Restaurant is the domain of everyone's favorite B.V.I. grandmother. She'll feed you the most authentic West Indian cuisine in the B.V.I., including spicy conch soup, curried goat, a whitefish called "old wife," and more. See p. 211.

o **The Spareribs at Pusser's East** (Tortola; ✆ 284/495-1010): Even if you're from the South, you'll salivate over the ribs served here. Like all barbecue chefs, the cooks here keep their sauce a secret—and is it ever tasty. See p. 212.

o **Mud Pie at Pusser's Landing** (Tortola; ✆ 284/495-4554): Mud pie may appear on many menus, but it's a classic at Pusser's, home of "the rum people." It's so rich that no one ever asks for a second helping. Don't like mud pie? Dig into the mango soufflé. See p. 213.

o **Conch Fritters at Top of the Baths** (Virgin Gorda; ✆ 284/495-5497): From the Bahamas to Key West, hundreds of chefs proclaim that they make the best conch fritters. We'd like to nominate the cooks at this little eatery for their spicy, delectable fritters, which are meals unto themselves. See p. 232.

o **The Painkiller at the Soggy Dollar Bar** (Jost Van Dyke; ✆ 284/495-9888): We can't compete with the yachtsman who drank 10 Painkillers in 1 night, leaving him feeling no pain indeed. But this delectable rum-based drink, whose recipe is a closely guarded secret, gets our vote for the best-tasting rum punch in the B.V.I. Its home is the bar at the Sandcastle. See p. 238.

o **Grilled Swordfish at the Cow Wreck Beach Bar & Grill** (Anegada; ✆ 284/495-8047): This elegant fish is grilled and flavored to perfection here. "It gets no better," proclaimed one happy diner at the table next to us, and we agree. Our dish was so fresh that the fish must have been just "harvested" from the sea. See p. 242.

THE best SHOPPING BUYS

The U.S. Virgin Islands are the shopping mecca of the Caribbean, mostly because there's no sales tax and because shoppers can take advantage of the $1,600 duty-free allowance. St. Thomas's capital, Charlotte Amalie, is the nerve center of the shopping activity here. Look for two local publications, *This Week in St. Thomas* and *Best Buys*—either will steer you toward the goods you want.

Before you leave home, try to check out the price of comparable items you hope to buy; that way, you'll know if you are really getting a bargain. With that said, your best deals will most likely be found in the following categories:

o **Arts and Crafts:** Though arts and crafts are not the high-priority items that they are on such islands as Haiti and Jamaica, you can certainly find them in the Virgin Islands. The **Tillett Gardens Center for the Arts** in St. Thomas (p. 102) is the premier art gallery and craft studio in the U.S. Virgin Islands. In St. John, **Mongoose Junction** (see "Shopping," in chapter 4), in a woodsy roadside area right at Cruz Bay, offers the best assortment of locally produced arts and crafts (all tax-free for U.S. citizens). Handmade pottery, sculpture, and glass are sold here, along with locally made clothing. If you're looking for handicrafts exclusive to the U.S. Virgin Islands, head for **Many Hands** (p. 184), also in Christiansted.

o **Fine China & Crystal:** Sometimes (not always) you can find great deals on these wares—many shoppers report savings of 30% to 50%. We noted that Baccarat goblets sold on St. Thomas went for about a third of the price quoted in the U.S. catalog. Again, know your prices before you land on St. Thomas. The best outlet for fine china and crystal is in St. Thomas at the **Crystal Shoppe** (p. 103).

○ **Jewelry:** Watches and gold jewelry are often heavily discounted in St. Thomas and St. Croix, especially during the off season (mid-Apr to mid-Oct), when there isn't a traffic jam of cruise ships in the harbors. The sheer volume of jewelry offered in St. Thomas is stunning—diamonds, emeralds, rubies, opals, gold, and platinum. Options include works by world-famous designers as well as one-of-a-kind pieces created by local artists. The best outlet for jewelry is in St. Thomas at **Cardow Jewelers** (p. 104).

○ **Liquor:** A recent spot survey showed that prices for liquor in St. Thomas and St. Croix were 50% to 60% less than in New York City. You're allowed to bring 5 liters of liquor back to the United States, or 6 liters if the sixth is locally produced. Local liquor nearly always means rum in the Virgin Islands, but it could also include Southern Comfort, which is bottled on the island (check the label). Because of the generous U.S. Customs allowances in the Virgin Islands, St. Thomas or St. Croix might be the best places to purchase expensive French brandy, champagne, or liqueurs. The widest selection of discount liquor for sale is found on the island of St. Thomas, at **Al Cohen's Discount Liquors** and **A. H. Riise Gift & Liquor Stores** (p. 104 and 103). You can also buy Cruzan Rum straight from the source, at the **Cruzan Rum Factory** on St. Croix (p. 179).

○ **Perfumes and Cosmetics:** Be on the lookout for bargains on imported perfumes and beauty products such as bath gels and makeup. How much you save depends on the product. **Tropicana Perfume Shoppe,** in St. Thomas, has the largest selection of fragrances (for both women and men) in the U.S. Virgin Islands (p. 103).

THE best NIGHTLIFE

If you're a serious party animal, you'll want to avoid St. John and most places in the British Virgin Islands, and concentrate on St. Thomas and St. Croix. Below are the latest hot spots:

○ **Reichhold Center for the Arts** (St. Thomas; ℭ **340/693-1559;** www.reichhold center.com): This artistic center is the premier performing arts venue in the Caribbean. Some of the world's greatest companies, such as the Alvin Ailey American Dance Theater, perform here. Check locally to see what's happening. See p. 106.

○ **Turtle Rock Bar** (St. Thomas; ℭ **340/777-7100**): This place, near Red Hook, is known for its burgers and bar scene. There's always something going on, whether it's karaoke or live shows by steel bands or other local talent. Happy hour, from 4 to 6pm, means half-price cocktails. See p. 108.

○ **Morgan's Mango** (St. John; ℭ **340/693-8141**), across from the national park dock, is the hottest watering hole at Cruz Bay, or for the entire island. Look for special nights such as Margarita Night or Lobster Night. See p. 138.

○ **The Buccaneer** (St. Croix; ℭ **800/255-3881** or **340/773-2100**): This deluxe hotel has the best nightlife on the island. Call to see what's going on during your visit; it could be anything from a limbo show to live reggae. See p. 146.

○ **Blue Moon** (St. Croix; ℭ **340/772-2222**): On Thursday and Friday nights, this little dive/bistro is the hottest spot in Christiansted. The crowd here is predominantly local, with a few savvy visitors thrown into the mix. See p. 185.

- **Divi Carina Bay Casino** (St. Croix; © 340/773-7529): At the Divi Carina Bay Resort, this glittering casino has introduced gambling to the U.S. Virgin Islands for the first time (if you don't count the island's buccaneering days). Built in the midst of a raging controversy over gambling, it boasts 12 gaming tables and 275 slot machines. Even though it's very touristy, the casino has become a hot spot for locals and visitors alike. See p. 186.

- **Bomba Surfside Shack** (Tortola; © 284/495-4148): This is one of the most famous bars in the West Indies and the most interesting hangout in the British Virgin Islands. Bomba's decor consists of junk and neon graffiti. The rum punches are always flowing, and the hippest people in town show up here, especially for the notorious all-night full-moon parties. See p. 221.

THE VIRGIN ISLANDS IN DEPTH

The golden beaches shaded by palm trees and crystal-line waters teeming with rainbow-hued sea creatures are undoubtedly the main attractions in both the U.S. and British Virgin Islands. Most visitors are more than happy to spend their mornings on the beach, their afternoons browsing the boutiques, and their evenings savoring a fresh-caught dinner. But the history of the Virgin Islands encompasses much more than the history of resort tourism. Like so many other islands in the Caribbean, the Virgin Islands were deeply involved in the colonial ambitions of Western Europe and the slave trade with North America. This chapter gives a peek at the cultural and historical influences coursing just beneath the surface of any modern-day escape to the Virgin Islands.

This chapter will also give you some information about the scenes of the various islands today, and will help you select which islands to visit during your Caribbean vacation. In this chapter, we explore the lay of the land, and provide information on the myriad outdoor activities available to you. We'll also give you tips about when to go (or not to go in the hurricane season), and what to eat and drink while there.

CHOOSING THE PERFECT ISLAND

Peering at the tiny Virgin Islands chain on a world map, you may find it difficult to distinguish the different islands. They vary widely, however, in looks and personality, and so will your vacation, depending on which island or islands you choose. It's important to plan ahead. For example, if you're an avid golfer, you won't want to spend a week on a remote British Virgin Island with only a rinky-dink 9-hole course or no course at all. But that same island might be perfect for a young couple contemplating a romantic honeymoon. By providing detailed information about the character of each inhabited island in both the U.S. Virgin Islands and the British Virgin Islands, we hope to guide you to your own idea of paradise.

The Virgin Islands

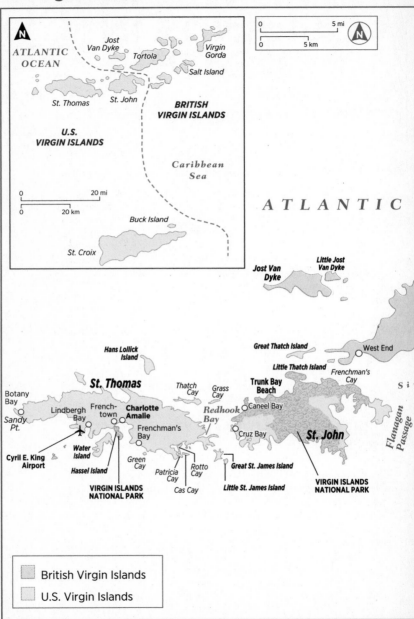

British Virgin Islands

U.S. Virgin Islands

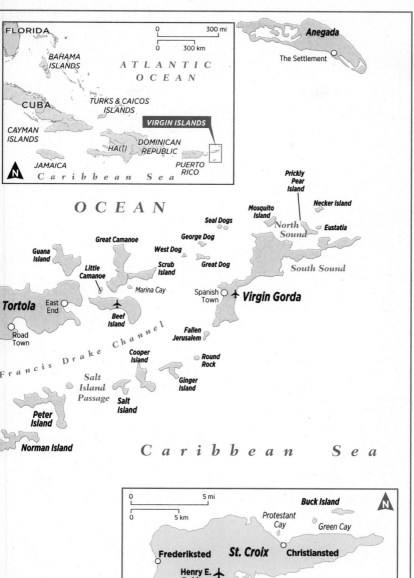

FLORIDA

BAHAMA
ISLANDS

ATLANTIC
OCEAN

0   300 mi
0   300 km

CUBA

TURKS & CAICOS
ISLANDS

VIRGIN ISLANDS

CAYMAN
ISLANDS

HAITI

DOMINICAN
REPUBLIC

JAMAICA

PUERTO
RICO

N

Caribbean   Sea

Anegada

The Settlement

OCEAN

Prickly
Pear
Island

Mosquito
Island

Necker Island

Seal Dogs

North
Sound

Eustatia

Great Camanoe

George Dog

Guana
Island

West Dog

South Sound

Little
Camanoe

Scrub
Island

Great Dog

Marina Cay

Spanish
Town

Virgin Gorda

Tortola

East
End

Beef
Island

Road
Town

Fallen
Jerusalem

Francis Drake Channel

Cooper
Island

Round
Rock

Salt
Island
Passage

Ginger
Island

Peter
Island

Salt
Island

Norman Island

Caribbean   Sea

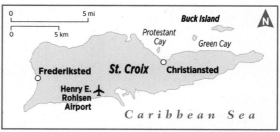

0   5 mi
0   5 km

Buck Island

N

Protestant
Cay

Green Cay

Frederiksted

St. Croix

Christiansted

Henry E.
Rohlsen
Airport

Caribbean   Sea

U.S. vs. British Virgin Islands

American and British cultures have left different imprints on the Virgin Islands. The **U.S. Virgin Islands,** except for St. John, offer much of the commercial hustle-and-bustle of the mainland United States, including supermarkets and fast-food chains. In contrast, the British islands are sleepier. Except for a few deluxe hotels (mostly on Virgin Gorda), they recall the way the Caribbean was before the advent of high-rise condos, McDonald's restaurants, and fleets of cruise ships.

If you want shopping, a wide selection of restaurants and hotels, and nightlife, head to the U.S. Virgin Islands, particularly **St. Thomas** and **St. Croix.** With a little research and effort, you can also find peace and quiet on these two islands, most often at outlying resorts. But overall, among the U.S. Virgin Islands, only **St. John** matches the British Virgins for tranquillity. St. John is a rugged mixture of bumpy dirt roads, scattered inhabitants, and a handful of stores and services. It's protected by the U.S. Forest Service, and remains the least developed of the U.S. islands.

The **British Virgin Islands** seem to be lingering in the past, although change is in the air. **Tortola** is the most populated British isle, but its shopping, nightlife, and dining are still limited. It's more of a spot for boaters of all stripes—it's considered the cruising capital of the Caribbean. To the east, **Virgin Gorda** claims most of the B.V.I.'s deluxe hotels. There are also attractive accommodations and restaurants on the smaller islands, such as Jost Van Dyke, Anegada, and Peter Island.

If you'd like to meet and mingle with locals, and get to know the islanders and their lifestyle, it's much easier to do so in the sleepy B.V.I. than in all the comings and goings of St. Thomas or even St. Croix. Again, the only U.S. Virgin Island that has the laid-back quality of the B.V.I. is St. John—except that the "local native" you are likely to meet on St. John is often an expat from the U.S. mainland, not a Virgin Islander born and bred.

There are frequent ferry connections between St. Thomas and St. John, but traveling among the other islands is a bit difficult, requiring private boats in some cases or airplane flights in others. The day will surely come when transportation from island to island will be made more convenient and frequent, but that day hasn't arrived yet.

The Major Islands in Brief

The islands previewed below are chock-full of quality shopping, hotels, restaurants, attractions, and nightlife, and are the most frequently visited in the V.I. A few words about islands that aren't mentioned below: For those who want to avoid the masses, the British Virgin Islands have a number of escapist-friendly islands such as Peter Island, Mosquito Island, and Guana Island. These are virtually private hideaways, often with expensive resorts (which are the main reason for going there in the first place). Two remote British Virgin Islands with more democratically priced hotels are Anegada and Jost Van Dyke. Even if you're staying at a resort on Virgin Gorda or Tortola, you might want to join a boat excursion to visit some of the lesser-known islands as part of a sightseeing excursion (with time devoted to R & R on a nearly deserted beach, of course).

ST. THOMAS

The most developed of the U.S. Virgin Islands, St. Thomas resembles a small city at times. There are peaceful retreats here, but you must seek them out. The harbor at **Charlotte Amalie,** the capital, is one of the largest cruise-ship magnets in the Caribbean. Many locals try to avoid Charlotte Amalie when the greatest concentration of vessels is in port (usually Dec–Apr). Charlotte Amalie offers the widest selection of duty-free shopping in the Caribbean. However, you must browse carefully through the labyrinth of bazaars to find the real bargains.

St. Thomas, like most of the Virgin Islands, gives you plenty of opportunity to get outside and get active, although many visitors come here simply to sit, sun, and maybe go for a swim. **Magens Bay Beach,** with its tranquil surf and sugar-white sand, is one of the most beautiful beaches in the world, but it is likely to be packed, especially on heavy cruise-ship days. More-secluded beaches include **Secret Harbour** and **Sapphire Beach** in East End.

St. Thomas has only one golf course, **Mahogany Run,** but it's a real gem. The three trickiest holes (13, 14, and 15) are known throughout the golfing world as the "Devil's Triangle."

Yachts and boats anchor at **Ramada Yacht Haven Marina** in Charlotte Amalie and at **Red Hook Marina** on the island's somewhat isolated eastern tip, though the serious yachting crowd gathers at Tortola in the British Virgin Islands (see "Tortola," below). Sportsfishers angle from the **American Yacht Harbor** at Red Hook. The island also attracts snorkelers and scuba divers—there are many outfitters offering equipment, excursions, and instruction. Kayaking and parasailing also draw beach bums away from the water's edge.

St. Thomas has the most eclectic and sophisticated restaurant scene in the Virgin Islands. Emphasis is on French and Continental fare, but the wide selection of restaurants also includes options from Mexican, West Indian, and Italian to Asian and American. St. Thomas pays more for its imported (usually European) chefs and secures the freshest of ingredients from mainland or Puerto Rican markets.

 A Famous Virgin Islander

Kelsey Grammer, a native of St. Thomas, is known to TV audiences around the world as Dr. Frasier Crane, the egghead/psychiatrist at the bar in the long-running TV series *Cheers* and *Frasier*.

There's also a wide variety of accommodations on St. Thomas, from the small, historic **Hotel 1829** in Charlotte Amalie, to more modern beachfront complexes in the East End, including the manicured **Elysian Beach Resort.** Apartment and villa rentals abound, and you can also find a handful of old-fashioned B&B-style guesthouses.

ST. JOHN

Our favorite of the U.S. Virgin Islands, St. John has only two deluxe hotels, but you'll find several charming inns and plenty of campgrounds. The island's primary attraction is the **U.S. Virgin Islands National Park,** which covers more than half the island. Guided walks and safari bus tours are available to help you navigate the park, which is full of pristine beaches, secret coves, flowering trees, and ghostly remains of sugar-cane plantations. An extensive network of trails invites hiking. A third of the park is underwater. **Trunk Bay,** which also boasts the island's finest beach, has an amazing underwater snorkeling trail. As you can imagine, scuba diving is another major attraction on St. John.

St. John has a handful of posh restaurants, as well as a number of colorful, West Indian eateries. Many residents and long-term visitors like to bring ingredients over on the ferry from St. Thomas, where prices are lower and the selection is broader.

Nightlife isn't a major attraction here; it usually consists of sipping rum drinks in a bar in **Cruz Bay,** and maybe listening to a local calypso band. After spending a day outdoors, most visitors on St. John are happy to turn in early.

ST. CROIX

This island is the second-most-visited destination in the U.S. Virgin Islands. Like St. Thomas, St. Croix is highly developed. Cruise-ship passengers continue to flood **Frederiksted** and the capital, **Christiansted,** looking for duty-free goods and a handful of white sand to take home in a plastic bag. St. Croix is also the only island that has a casino. Although parts of the island resemble American suburbia, some of St. Croix's true West Indian–style buildings have been preserved, along with many of its rich cultural traditions.

One of the best reasons to take a trip to St. Croix, even if only for a day, is to visit **Buck Island National Park,** just 1½ miles off St. Croix's northeast coast. The park's offshore reef attracts snorkelers and divers from around the world. Signs posted along the ocean floor guide you through a forest of staghorn coral swarming with flamboyant fish.

St. Croix is the premier golfing destination in the Virgin Islands, mainly because it boasts **Carambola,** the archipelago's most challenging 18-hole course. St. Croix is also a tennis mecca of sorts: The **Buccaneer Hotel** has some of the best courts in the Virgin Islands and hosts several annual tournaments. Other sports for active vacationers include horseback riding, parasailing, sportsfishing, and water-skiing.

The restaurants on St. Croix are generally not as good as those on St. Thomas, although they claim to be. You will find plenty of small, local eateries serving up dishes and snacks ranging from West Indian curries to French croissants. Life after dark is mostly confined to a handful of bars in Christiansted.

As for accommodations, St. Croix has only a few real luxury hotels, but there are a lot of small, attractive inns. And, as on St. Thomas, it's easy to find villas and condos for rent at reasonable weekly rates.

TORTOLA

Tortola is the hub of the British Virgin Islands, but not always the best place for visitors, especially if you're planning to spend more than a couple of days here; we think Virgin Gorda (see below) has better hotels and restaurants. **Road Town,** the capital, with its minor shopping, routine restaurants, and uninspired architecture, requires a

---

   Another Famous Virgin Islander

One of the most popular basketball players in the NBA, San Antonio Spur Tim Duncan, is St. Croix born and bred. Growing up on the island, he wanted to be a swimmer, and while still a teenager he became one of the top-ranked swimmers in the United States in his age group. When Hurricane Hugo swept away his team's swimming pool in 1989, Tim gave up swimming and started playing basketball. After graduating from Wake Forest University in 1997—and being named NCAA Player of the Year while there—he went on to play for the San Antonio Spurs. Since then, he has gone on to become the team captain and has helped the Spurs win four NBA championships. In St. Croix, "Little Timmy Duncan" is a local hero, and his portrait stands across from the airport.

couple of hours at the most. Once you leave Road Town, however, you'll find Tortola more alluring. The island's best and most unspoiled beaches, including **Smuggler's Cove** (with its collection of snorkeling reefs), lie at the island's western tip. Tortola's premier beach is **Cane Garden Bay,** a 2.4km (1½-mile) stretch of white sand. Because of the gentle surf, it's one of the safest places for families with small children. For hikers on Tortola, exploring **Sage Mountain National Park,** where trails lead to a 543m (1,781-ft.) peak that offers panoramic views, is a definite highlight. The park is rich in flora and fauna, from mamey trees to mountain doves.

Although many visitors to the Caribbean look forward to fishing, hiking, horseback riding, snorkeling, and surfing, what makes Tortola exceptional is boating. It is *the* boating center of the British Virgin Islands, which are among the most cherished sailing territories on the planet. The island offers some 100 charter yachts and 300 bareboats, and its marina and shore facilities are the most up-to-date and extensive in the Caribbean Basin.

The crystal-clear waters compensate for the island's lackluster bars and restaurants. You can count on simple and straightforward food here; we suggest any locally caught fish grilled with perhaps a little lime butter.

VIRGIN GORDA

Our favorite British Virgin Island is Virgin Gorda, the third-largest member of the archipelago, with a permanent population of about 1,400 lucky souls. Many visitors come over just for a day to check out the **Baths,** an astounding collection of gigantic rocks, boulders, and tide pools on the southern tip. Crafted by volcanic pressures millions of years ago, the boulders have eroded into shapes reminiscent of a Henry Moore sculpture. With more than 20 uncrowded beaches, the best known of which are **Spring Beach** and **Trunk Beach,** Virgin Gorda is a sun worshiper's dream come true.

Unlike Tortola, Virgin Gorda has some of the finest hotels in the Virgin Islands, including **Little Dix Bay** and **Biras Creek.** One caveat: You must be willing to pay a high price for the privilege of staying at one of these regal resorts. There are also more reasonably priced places to stay, such as **Virgin Gorda Village.** Outside the upscale hotels, restaurants tend to be simple places serving local West Indian cuisine. No one takes nightlife too seriously on Virgin Gorda, so there isn't very much of it.

THE VIRGIN ISLANDS TODAY

The American way of life prevails today in the U.S. Virgin Islands, and it has swept across to the British Virgin Islands as well. The region's traditional recipes and remedies, as well as the self-reliant arts of fishing, boat building, farming, and even hunting, are all but gone. When islanders need something, they have it shipped from Miami. In clothes, cars, food, and entertainment, America, not Great Britain, rules the seas around both archipelagos. The British Virgins even use the U.S. dollar as their official currency, instead of British pounds.

Like the rest of the world, the Virgin Islands have felt the effects of the recent global recession. Because so much of the islands' economy depends on tourism, both the U.S.V.I. and the British Virgin Islands were hit hard when the recession started in about 2008, and they are still continuing to feel the effects of the recession to this day. The bad economy has touched nearly everyone in the Virgin Islands. Many people are employed in offshoots of the tourism industry: food suppliers, laundry services that wash hotel sheets, liquor dealers, shop keepers, and more. Jobs are a

A 51ST state?

U.S. Virgin Islanders are not allowed to vote in national elections, a sore spot among some of the local residents. Many hope to see another star added to the American flag in the near future, but others prefer not to rock the boat.

When the 1936 Organic Act of the Virgin Islands was passed under the Roosevelt administration, residents ages 21 and over were granted suffrage and could elect two municipal councils and a legislative assembly for the islands. In 1946, the first black governor of the islands, William Hastie, was appointed. By 1970, the U.S. Virgin Islanders had the right to elect their own governor and lieutenant governor.

Today, the U.S. Virgin Islands remain an unincorporated territory administered by the U.S. Department of the Interior. Politically speaking, the Virgin Islands, like Puerto Rico, remain outside the family of the United States. They are only permitted to send a nonvoting delegate to the U.S. House of Representatives.

Some islanders are beginning to demand more representation. They feel that only full statehood will provide the respect, power, and influence needed to turn the islands into more than just a "colony." But as of yet, it seems unlikely. The question of statehood is raised at each new election of Congress or of a president, but progress in this direction moves sluggishly along, if at all.

primary concern. The U.S. Virgin Islands were awarded $364 million in U.S. federal stimulus funding in 2009, and the funding is being used to stimulate the local economy during the recession. One of the major and predictable goals of the stimulus package is in job creation.

Although there has been a slight increase in tourism since the recession initially hit, the Virgin Islands have not seen the same number of visitors as they had prior to the recession. However, tourism officials are hopeful that the number of visitors will increase over the next few years. To attract visitors, the local tourist industry has been aggressively promoting itself, offering discounted hotel deals, cut-rate airfares, and promotions for destination weddings. Corporate travelers are increasingly being wooed, and sweet deals are being made with American companies to have their conventions in the islands.

To attract tourists, the government officials—rather belatedly in some cases—have come to realize that the natural environment must be protected. During the 1980s, the islands, especially St. Thomas, experienced a real estate boom, and much of the island's natural terrain was converted into shopping malls and condo complexes. Today, protecting the environment—and curbing overdevelopment—has become a primary concern in the Virgin Islands. The B.V.I., for example, has done more than the U.S.V.I., adding 10 new parks, including the Anegada Nature Reserve, to its existing national park system, which includes the Gorda Peak National Park and the Devil's Bay National Park on Virgin Gorda and the Sage Mountain National Park on Tortola. St. John, the smallest of the U.S. Virgin Islands, is the most protected landmass in the Caribbean, with some 60% of its acreage directly controlled by the U.S. National Park Service.

On the other hand, St. Thomas has been so overly developed that a battle is going on over the future of the 360 acres surrounding Botany Bay, on the western end of

Roll the Dice

In 1996, U.S. senators agreed to allow the opening of gambling casinos in the U.S. Virgin Islands, granting permission for the building of two casino hotels on St. Croix. In a bow to the islanders, senators agreed that majority ownership of the casino hotels will be reserved for locals. The arrival of gambling conflicts with the desire of many islanders to preserve the scenic beauty of their land. Nonetheless, the gambling wheels are spinning at St. Croix's **Divi Carina Bay Casino.** The establishment of a second casino on St. Croix was approved at a building site in Robin Bay several years ago, but ground has not been broken yet as of 2011. Local governments are struggling to balance the preservation of the islands' number-one resource—scenic beauty—with modern economic realities.

St. Thomas, long a refuge from the bustle of Charlotte Amalie, the capital. Locals claim this controversy over Botany Bay may not be settled before 2020, if then.

The area is a final refuge for deer and a nesting ground for sea turtles, with some of the healthiest coral reefs around St. Thomas. Some developers want to turn this pristine area into a resort complex with hotel rooms, timeshare apartments, and condos. The island is more than $1 billion in debt—and it needs the cash that development could bring. Caroline Brown, of the Environmental Association of St. Thomas, has issued a dire warning that islanders may find themselves "living in a concrete jungle." Because protection of the environment is at issue here, this is a hot-button political topic, and much of the future of the islands is riding on what the eventual plan will be for Botany Bay.

LOOKING BACK: VIRGIN ISLANDS HISTORY

A Brief History

Christopher Columbus is credited with "discovering" the Virgin Islands in 1493, but, in fact, they had already been inhabited for 3,000 years. It is believed that the original settlers were the nomadic Ciboney Indians, who migrated from the mainland of South America and lived off the islands' fish and vegetation. The first real homesteaders were the peaceful Arawak Indians, who arrived from Venezuela, presumably in dugout canoes with sails.

For about 500 years, the Arawaks occupied the Virgin Islands, until the arrival of the cannibalistic Carib Indians in the 15th century. The Caribs destroyed the Arawaks, either by working them to death as slaves or by eating them. With the advent of European explorers and their diseases, these tribes were completely wiped out.

The Age of Colonization

In November 1493, on his second voyage to the New World, Columbus spotted the Virgin Islands, naming them *Las Once Mil Virgenes,* after the Christian St. Ursula and her martyred maidens. Short of drinking water, he decided to anchor at what is now Salt River on St. Croix's north shore. His men were greeted by a rainfall of arrows.

Looking Back at the Virgin Islands

0 | 5 mi
0 | 5 km

☐ British Virgin Islands
☐ U.S. Virgin Islands

1 **1493.** Short of drinking water, explorer Christopher Columbus anchors outside St. Croix and is greeted by a rainfall of arrows from the natives. Embittered, Columbus calls that part of the island Cabo de Flechas, or "Cape of the Arrows," and sails toward Puerto Rico.

2 **1674.** French troops take control of Christiansted, as King Louis XIV proclaims the island part of the Kingdom of France.

3 **Early 1700s.** Edward Teach, the notorious English pirate called "Blackbeard," anchors his feared *Queen Anne's Revenge* outside Charlotte Amalie during the "Golden Age of Piracy."

4 **1733.** Slaves imported from Africa to work some 100 plantations on St. John rise in rebellion against their masters. The slaves take control of the island for about 6 months, killing many Europeans. It takes hundreds of French troops to quell the rebellion.

5 **1883.** The adventure novel *Treasure Island* publishes. Author Robert Louis Stevenson is said to have used Norman Island as the setting for his classic novel.

6 **1916.** Fearing that the Virgin Islands might be seized by Germany as a submarine base in World War I, the United States purchases the Virgin Islands from Denmark for only $25 million.

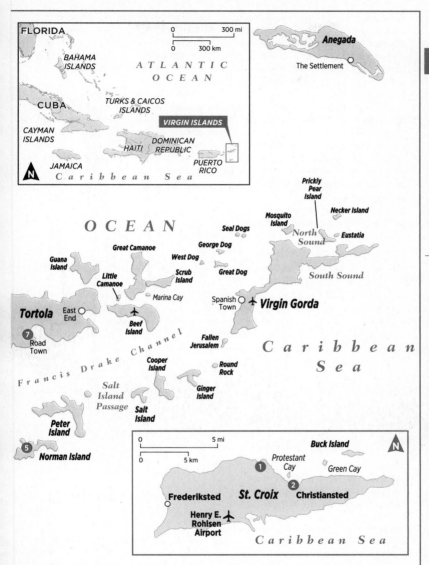

⑦ **1967.** The government of the British Virgin Islands adopts a new constitution which provides for a ministerial system of government headed by a Chief Minister.

⑧ **Post-2000.** An environmental debate rages among residents of St. Thomas on whether to develop Botany Bay, a scenic refuge for deer and a nesting ground for sea turtles, or leave it green.

Christian Worship Meets the Obeah

The native Virgin Islanders have strong spiritual beliefs. The early Christian missionaries were zealous. The slaves, who were brought over from Africa, took quickly to the Christian religion, but the way they practiced it was unique. Many times they incorporated a belief in magic powers and a host of superstitions that they brought over from Africa.

The most famous mythological figure of the Virgin Islands is the Obeah. Originally, belief in the Obeah was not strong among native Virgin Islanders, but it did enjoy cult status "down island," a reference to the islands that sweep downward toward South America. With the influx of so many immigrant islanders into the Virgin Islands looking for work and better economic opportunities, the Obeah arrived.

Basically, the Obeah is a "superstitious force" that natives believe can be responsible for both good and evil. It is considered prudent not to get on the bad side of this force, which might reward you or make trouble for you. If you encounter an old-timer islander and ask, "How are you?" the answer is likely to be, "Not too bad." The person who may actually feel great says this so as not to tempt the force, which might be listening.

Embittered, Columbus called that part of the island *Cabo de Flechas*, or "Cape of the Arrows," and sailed toward Puerto Rico.

As the sponsor of Columbus's voyage, Spain claimed the Virgin Islands; however, with more interest in the Greater Antilles, Spain chose not to colonize the Virgins, leaving the door open to other European powers. In 1625, both the English and the Dutch established opposing frontier outposts on St. Croix. Struggles between the two nations for control of the island continued for about 20 years, until the English prevailed (for the time being).

As the struggle among European powers widened, the islands continued to function as a battleground. In 1650, Spanish forces from Puerto Rico overran the British garrison on St. Croix. Soon after, the Dutch invaded; in 1653, the island fell into the hands of the Knights of Malta, who gave St. Croix its name.

Impressions

There could never be lands any more favorable in fertility, in mildness and pleasantness of climate, in abundance of good and pure water. A very peaceful and hopeful place that should give all adventurers great satisfaction.
—Captain Nathaniel Butler, HM Frigate *Nicodemus*, 1637

However, these aristocratic French cavaliers weren't exactly prepared for West Indian plantation life, and their debts quickly mounted. By 1674, King Louis XIV of France took control of St. Croix and made it part of his kingdom.

The English continued to fight Dutch settlers in Tortola, which was considered the most important of the British Virgin Islands. It wasn't until 1672 that England added the entire archipelago to its growing empire.

A year before, in March 1671, the Danish West India Company made an attempt to settle St. Thomas. The company sent two ships, but only one, the *Pharaoh*, completed the voyage, with about a third of its crew. Eventually, reinforcements arrived, and by 1679, at least 156 Europeans were reported living on St. Thomas, along with their slaves. Captain Kidd, Sir Francis Drake, Blackbeard, and other legendary pirates of the West Indies continued to use St. Thomas as their base for maritime raids in the area. Its harbor also became famous for its slave market.

In 1717, Danish planters sailed to St. John from St. Thomas to begin cultivating plantations. By 1733, an estimated 100 sugar, tobacco, and cotton plantations were operating on the island. That same year, the slaves rebelled against their colonial masters, taking control of the island for about 6 months and killing many Europeans. It took hundreds of French troops to quell the rebellion.

THE DANES ARE GONE BUT their architecture STILL STANDS

Some of the architectural legacy left by the colonizing Danes still remains in the islands, especially in Christiansted and Frederiksted on St. Croix, and in Charlotte Amalie on St. Thomas.

Many of the commercial buildings constructed in downtown Charlotte Amalie are restrained in ornamentation. Pilasters and classical cornices were commonplace on many buildings. Most door arches and windows were framed in brick. To "dress up" a building, ornamentation, such as cornices, was added in the final stages. The walls were covered with plaster and stucco, but in recent decades have been stripped from the walls. Underneath the rubble, well-designed shapes and patterns of old brick and blue bitch—a stone made of volcanic tuff—were discovered. The old masons may have known what they were doing. Once stripped of their plaster coating, the walls don't stand up well in the Caribbean sun and salt air. Cast-iron grillwork on some of the second-floor overhanging balconies displays a certain architectural flair. Many of the buildings in St. Thomas originally had courtyards, or still do. These added to the living space on the second floor. In the courtyard were kitchens and, almost more vital, cisterns to capture the precious rainwater.

Similar building techniques were used on structures that went up on St. Croix.

Christiansted remains one of the most historically authentic towns in the West Indies, true to its original Danish colonial flavor. The basic style was a revival of the European classic look of the 18th century, but with variations to accommodate the tropical climate. As early as 1747, the Danes adopted a strict building code, which spared Christiansted from some of the violent fires that virtually wiped out Charlotte Amalie. Frederiksted, the other major town of St. Croix, has a well-designed waterfront, with blocks of arcaded sidewalks. The quarter is protected by the government as part of Frederiksted's National Historic District.

Great architecture was never the forte of the British Virgin Islands. During a time when major buildings might have been created, the B.V.I. were too economically depressed to find the funds for major structures of lasting significance. Therefore, for much of its history, its people have lived in typical West Indies shanties, with an occasional public building constructed that vaguely imitated 18th-century Europe in style. Curiously enough, although the B.V.I. didn't leave the world any lasting architectural heritage, it did produce a native son, William Thornton, whose designs were used for the U.S. Capitol building in Washington.

Impressions

Viewed from every point except remote naval contingencies, it was unfortunate we ever acquired these islands.
—**President Herbert Hoover, 1931**

In that same year, France sold St. Croix to the Danish West India Company, which divided the island into plantations, boosting the already flourishing slave trade. Some historians say that nearly 250,000 slaves were sold on the auction blocks at Charlotte Amalie before being sent elsewhere, often to America's South. By 1792, Denmark changed its tune and announced that it officially planned to end the slave trade. It was not until 1848, however, that it did so. The British had freed their 5,133 slaves in 1834.

The great economic boom that resulted from the Virgin Islands plantations began to wilt by the 1820s. The introduction of the sugar beet virtually bankrupted plantation owners, as the demand for cane sugar drastically declined. Cuba eventually took over the sugar market in the Caribbean. By 1872, the British had so little interest in the British Virgins that they placed them in the loosely conceived and administered Federation of the Leeward Islands.

Enter the United States

In 1867, the United States attempted to purchase the islands from Denmark, but the treaty was rejected by the U.S. Senate in 1870; the asking price was $7.5 million. Following its acquisition of Puerto Rico in 1902, the United States expressed renewed interest in acquiring the Danish islands. This time, the United States offered to pay only $5 million, and the Danish parliament spurned the offer.

On the eve of its entry into World War I, the U.S. Navy began to fear a possible German takeover of the islands. The United States was concerned that the Kaiser's navy, using the islands as a base, might prey on shipping through the Panama Canal. After renewed attempts by the United States to purchase the islands, Denmark agreed to sell them in 1916 for $25 million, a staggering sum to pay for island real estate in those days.

DATELINE

- **1493** Columbus sails by the Virgin Islands, lands on St. Croix, and is attacked by Carib Indians.
- **1625** Dutch and English establish frontier outposts on St. Croix.
- **1650** Spanish forces from Puerto Rico overrun English garrison on St. Croix.
- **1653** St. Croix taken over by the Knights of Malta.
- **1671** Danes begin settlement of St. Thomas.
- **1672** England adds British Virgin Islands to its empire.
- **1674** King Louis XIV of France makes St. Croix part of his empire.
- **1717** Danish planters from St. Thomas cultivate plantations on St. John.
- **1724** St. Thomas is declared a free port.
- **1733** Danish West India Company purchases St. Croix from France; slaves revolt on St. John.
- **1792** Denmark announces plans to abandon the slave trade.
- **1807–15** England occupies Danish Virgin Islands.
- **1820s** Sugar plantations on the Virgin Islands begin to see a loss in profits.

By 1917, the United States was in full control of the islands, and Denmark retreated from the Caribbean after a legacy of nearly 2½ centuries. The U.S. Navy looked after the islands for 14 years, and in 1954, they came under the sovereignty of the U.S. Department of the Interior.

Some money was diverted to the area during the Prohibition era, as some islanders made rum and shipped it illegally to the United States, often through Freeport, the Bahamas. In 1927, the United States granted citizenship to the island residents. In 1936, under Franklin Roosevelt, the first Organic Act was passed, giving the islanders voting rights in local elections. This act was revised in 1954, granting them a greater degree of self-government.

Jobs generated by World War II finally woke the islands from their long economic slumber. The U.S.V.I. were used as a port during the war and visitors first started to appear on the islands. In the postwar economic boom that swept across America, the Virgin Islands at long last found a replacement for sugar cane.

The British Virgin Islands Develop

The British Virgin Islands were finally freed from the Leeward Islands Federation in 1956, and in 1966, Queen Elizabeth II visited this remote colonial outpost. By 1967, the British Virgin Islands had received a new constitution. Tourism was slower to come to the British Virgins than to the U.S. Virgin Islands, but it is now the mainstay of the economy.

In 2000, the British government issued a report that found that nearly 41% of offshore companies in the world were formed in the British Virgin Islands. By 2011, the B.V.I. was one of the world's leading offshore financial centers, and the local population boasted one of the highest incomes per capita in the Caribbean—at around $40,000 per family.

Tourism & the Economy Today

The economy of both the British and the U.S. Virgins has been one of the most stable and prosperous in the Caribbean. But with the worldwide economic slump, all of the

1834 England frees 5,133 slaves living in British Virgin Islands.

1848 Under pressure, the governor of St. Croix grants slaves emancipation.

1867 First attempt by the United States to purchase the Virgin Islands from the Danish.

1872 British Virgin Islands put under administration of the Federation of the Leeward Islands.

1916 Denmark signs treaty with the U.S. and sells islands for $25 million.

1917 Virgin Islands fall under the control of the U.S. Navy for 14 years.

1927 United States grants citizenship to island residents.

1936 Under Franklin Roosevelt, the first Organic Act is passed, granting voting rights to U.S. Virgin Islanders.

1940 Population of U.S. Virgin Islands increases for the first time since 1860 because of its use as a port during World War II.

1946 First black governor of the U.S.V.I., William Hastie, is appointed.

1954 Revised Organic Act passed; the U.S.V.I. fall under jurisdiction of Department of the Interior.

continues

islands are feeling the impact, with a falloff in tourism and revenues. There has also been a drop in investments in the private sector aimed at expanding tourist facilities.

In the meantime, the governments of both the British Virgins and the U.S. Virgins continue to struggle with unemployment as they mount ongoing struggles to reduce crime and to protect the environment.

In 2010, officials in the U.S. Virgin Islands developed closer contact with the U.S. Environmental Protection Agency. The aim is to help the territory solve some of its long-standing problems, such as the best way to address the solid waste problem and how to preserve healthy air standards.

The U.S. Virgin Islands were awarded $364 million in federal stimulus funding in 2009, and the funding is being used to stimulate the local economy during the recession. One of the major and predictable goals of the stimulus package is in job creation. Some of the money has been earmarked for upgrading the ferry service between Cruz Bay on St. John and Red Hook on St. Thomas. Other programs will be announced at some point in the future.

THE VIRGIN ISLANDS IN POP CULTURE

Books

FICTION

Herman Wouk's *Don't Stop the Carnival* (Little Brown & Co., 1992) is "the Caribbean classic," and all readers contemplating a visit to the Virgin Islands might want to pick it up. It's great airport lounge reading. Wouk lived in St. Thomas in the 1950s, and his novel is based on actual people he met during that time. Bob Shacochis's *Easy in the Islands* (Grove, 2004) giddily re-creates the flavor of the West Indies with short stories. *Tales of St. John & the Caribbean,* by Gerald Singer (Sombrero Publishing Co., 2001), is an easy read: a collection of amusing and insightful stories, and the best

1956	British Virgins released from the Federation of the Leeward Islands.
1966	Queen Elizabeth II visits the British Virgin Islands.
1967	B.V.I. get a new constitution.
1980s	U.S.V.I. see major development and construction, putting natural resources at risk.
1989	Hurricane Hugo rips through the islands, hitting St. Croix especially hard.
1995	Hurricane Marilyn causes millions of dollars of damage and leaves thousands homeless.
1996	Water Island, off the coast of St. Thomas, is officially declared the fourth U.S. Virgin Island; U.S. Senate grants permission for two casino hotels to be built on St. Croix.
2000	St. Croix becomes the first "casino island" in the Virgin Islands.
2005	Plans stall for grand development of St. Thomas.
2008	B.V.I. become one of the world's leading offshore financial centers.
2009	Islands experience drop-off in tourism as U.S. economy goes into recession.
2010	U.S.V.I. officials tackle environmental problems.

The Mother of Folklore

One person who wants to keep alive the stories of the old days in the Virgin Islands is Arona Peterson, author of *The Food & Folklore of the Virgin Islands*. This St. Thomas food writer and folklorist is also the author of *Herbs and Proverbs* and *Kreole Ketch 'N' Keep*. Many people consider her the authority on the history and culture of the Virgin Islands. *Kreole Ketch 'N' Keep* is a collection of West Indian stories. Ms. Peterson has a keen ear and recaptures the flavor of old island days, interspersing stories with recipes.

In her stories she remembers the sound and the idiom of the old days and the island's colorful language. In her story "What Does Tomorrow Mean? In any Language, Wait" appears this passage: "Wat I trying to say is dat waitin is wat life is about. Everybody waitin fo something or udder, mannin or nite. Tain get wan purson wat, livin ain waitin-fo a bus, fo a taxi, fo a airplane, fo a steamer, fo a letter to come back. Some doan even know wat dey waiting for but dey still waitin." Her books are sold in local shops.

volume if you'd like a behind-the-scenes look at St. John after the tourists have taken the ferry back to St. Thomas for the night.

My Name Is Not Angelica, by Scott O'Dell (Yearling Books, 1990), is a young-adult historical novel based in the Virgin Islands in the early 18th century. It tells the saga of a slave girl, Raisha, who escapes bondage; the rather grim realities of slavery are depicted here.

Robert Louis Stevenson is said to have used Norman Island, in the B.V.I., as a fictional setting for his 1883 classic *Treasure Island*. This swashbuckling adventure has intrigued readers for years with such characters as the immortal Long John Silver. The book, which gave rise to such memorable lines as "shiver me timbers," continues to find new generations of readers.

COOKBOOKS

A number of books are devoted to recipes of the Caribbean, including *The Sugar Mill Caribbean Cookbook: Casual and Elegant Recipes Inspired by the Islands,* by Jinx and Jefferson Morgan (Harvard Common Press, 1996). The Morgans run the Sugar Mill on Tortola. With this book, you can learn the secrets of their signature dishes, including Rasta Pasta, rum-glazed chicken wings, and lobster and christophine curry.

Food & Folklore of the Virgin Islands (Romik, 1990) is penned by Arona Petersen, a well-known St. Thomas writer and folklorist. The regional flavor of Virgin Islands fare is captured in her recipes, and the idiomatic dialogues of island people are perfectly re-created as she spins old island tales and wisdom.

HISTORY BOOKS

The concise *History of the Virgin Islands* (University Press of the West Indies, 2000) is a bit scholarly for some tastes, but if you're seriously interested in the islands, this is the best-researched survey of what was going on before your arrival. *Caribbean Pirates,* by Warren Alleyne (Macmillan-Caribbean, 1986), is a good read for preteen travelers and attempts to separate fact from fiction in the sagas of the most notorious pirates in history. Some of the material is based on published letters and documents.

OUTDOOR ADVENTURE BOOKS

Sailing enthusiasts say you shouldn't set out to explore the islets, cays, coral reefs, and islands of the B.V.I. without John Rousmanière's well-researched *The Sailing Lifestyle* (Fireside, 1988).

Exploring St. Croix, by Shirley Imsand and Richard Philobosian (Travelers Information Press, 1987), is a very detailed guide of this island. The authors take you to 49 beaches, 34 snorkeling and scuba-diving sites, and 22 bird-watching areas, and lead you on 20 different hikes.

A Guide to the Birds of Puerto Rico & the Virgin Islands, by Herbert A. Raffaele, Cindy J. House, and John Wiessinger (Princeton University Press, 1989), is for bird-watchers. The illustrations alone are worth a look, with 273 depictions of the 284 documented species on the islands.

Film

St. Thomas was one of the sites selected for background shots on the Brad Pitt film *The Curious Case of Benjamin Button* (2008). Islanders hope that the success of the film will inspire other movie companies to come to St. Thomas to revive fading film production that reached its heyday in the '70s and '80s, when major TV shows such as *Charlie's Angels, The Love Boat,* and *All My Children* were shot here.

Many films have been shot in the Virgin Islands, including *Open Water* (2003), the adventure story of a couple stranded in shark-infested waters; *Weekend at Bernie's II* (1993), shot in both St. John and St. Thomas; and the final scene of *The Shawshank Redemption* (1994), when Andy Dufresne escapes the harsh Shawshank Prison for a tropical island. The final island scene in *Trading Places* (1983), starring Eddie Murphy and Jamie Lee Curtis, was shot in St. Croix. A 1980s film classic, *The Four Seasons* (1981), was filmed in part in the Virgin Islands; the film is a tender-sweet melodrama that stars Carol Burnett and Alan Alda. Three middle-aged couples take vacations together in spring, summer, fall, and winter.

The true classic of the archipelago is *Virgin Island* (1958), starring John Cassavetes and Sidney Poitier. Filmed in the beautiful British Virgin Islands, it is a fairy-tale type of story about a young man and woman, who buy a small, uninhabited island and go there to find their dream. The film was based on the actual experiences of novelist Robb White, who, along with his wife, decided to pursue a Robinson Crusoe existence on the islands.

 Don't Let the Jumbies Get Ya!

"Don't let the Jumbies get ya!" is an often-heard phrase in the Virgin Islands, particularly when people are leaving their hosts and heading home in the dark. Jumbies, capable of good or evil, are supernatural beings that are believed to live around households. It is said that new settlers from the mainland of the United States never see these Jumbies and, therefore, need not fear them. But many islanders believe in their existence and, if queried, may enthrall you with tales of sightings.

No one seems to agree on exactly what a Jumbie is. Some claim it's the spirit of a dead person that didn't go where it belonged. Others disagree. "They're the souls of live people," one islander told us, "but they live in the body of the dead." The most prominent Jumbies are "Mocko Jumbies," carnival stilt walkers seen at all parades.

○**Christopher Fleming (1851–1935):** Born in the East End of Tortola, Fleming spent most of his life at sea, and may even have been a smuggler. In 1890, a B.V.I. Customs officer seized a native boat, and in protest, Fleming led a group of armed men to the commissioner's house. Danish soldiers from St. Thomas put down the rebellion, and Fleming was sentenced to 6 months in jail. Today, islanders look upon Fleming as a hero who protested against poverty and unfair economic conditions.

○**John Coakley Lettsom (1744–1815):** Born into a Quaker family on Jost Van Dyke, he was educated in England and completed his medical education in Edinburgh, Scotland. Rising rapidly and brilliantly, he founded the Royal Human Society of England, the Royal Seabathing Hospital at Margate, and the London Medical Society. Regrettably, he is mainly remembered today for this famous but libelous doggerel: "I John Lettsom . . . Blisters, bleeds,

and sweats 'em. If, after that, they please to die . . . I, John Lettsom."

○**Frederick Augustus Pickering (1835–1926):** Born in Tortola, he became a civil service worker who, by 1884, had risen to become the first black president of the British Virgin Islands. He held the post until 1887, and was the last man to be known as president, as the job description after his presidency was changed to commissioner.

○**John Pickering (1704–68):** Born into a fervent Quaker family in Anguilla, Pickering moved in the 1720s to Fat Hogs Bay in Tortola. In 1736, he became the leader of a congregation of Quakers, and by 1741 he was named first lieutenant governor of the island. Fearing the Virgin Islands would be drawn into war between Spain and Britain, he resigned his post because of his Quaker beliefs. Apparently, he was an "enlightened" plantation owner, as hundreds of slaves, islandwide, mourned his death—or perhaps they feared their new master.

Music

As the Caribbean rhythms go, the Virgin Islands encompass it all, from reggae to classical to steel drums to spiritual hymns, but soca, reggae, calypso, and steel-pan beats seem to dominate the night.

Calypso, though originating in Trinidad, has its unique sounds in the Virgins. It is famously known for expressing political commentary through satire.

If you add a little soul music to calypso, you have **soca,** a music form that also originated in Trinidad, but made its way north to the Virgin Islands. **Reggae** originated on another island, Jamaica, but also made its way to the Virgins. As reggae is sung in the Virgin Islands, it usually focuses on redemption. Virgin Islanders have put a unique stamp on reggae, making it their own.

Scratch bands are popular in the British Virgins, in the musical form known as **fungi. Merengue** is also heard in the Virgins, having "floated over" from Puerto Rico and the Dominican Republic.

Throughout the year in various clubs, you can hear the music of the islands, including **zouk,** dance music from Martinique. Music is most popular at frequent reggae concerts, steel-pan shows, and jazz concerts. Find out what's happening by reading the local newspapers.

Of course, the leading musicians of the islands make recordings, including the hypnotic and tantalizing vocals from Dezarie, which can be heard in the album *Gracious Mama Africa*. This album, among others, has earned her the title of St. Croix's Roots Empress. Another empress is Mada Nile, known for her poignant lyrics. Our favorites of her selections are "Senseless Killing" and "Righteously."

A vocal rival of both Dezarie and Mada Nile is Sistah Joyce, who is acclaimed for her hard-hitting lyrics as evoked by her recording of "Remembah." She scored a hit with her debut album, *H.Y.P.O.C.R.I.C.Y.*

Since the new millennium, island music has reached an international following for the first time. Reggae bands, such as Midnite and Inner Visions have found renewed popularity, although they've been around since the '80s. *Midnite Intense Pressure*, Midnite's debut album, firmly established them as a force in roots music; the group is known for its fiery lyrics. Midnite's rival group is Inner Visions; their album *Spiritual Dancer* demonstrates the group's refined musical abilities, which distinguish them from the more "raw roots" style of other rival artists. The band is made up of first- and second-generation members of the Pickering family, with names like Grasshopper and Jupiter. The voices of two generations blend harmoniously as they "Blow Down Babylon."

EATING & DRINKING

Just as food critics were composing eulogies for traditional cooking in the Virgin Islands, there was a last-minute resurgence. Many of the old island dishes have made a comeback, and little taverns and shanties offering regional specialties are popping up everywhere. You can now escape hamburger hell and taste some real Caribbean flavors.

When dining in the Virgins, try **fresh fish,** especially mahimahi, wahoo, yellowtail, grouper, and red snapper. These fish, accompanied by a hot lime sauce, are among the tastiest island specialties. Watch out for the sweet Caribbean lobster: It's likely to be overpriced and overcooked, and many diners, especially those from Maine, feel that it's not worth the price.

The major resort hotels often feature elaborate **buffets,** which inevitably include some West Indian dishes along with more standard Continental fare. They're almost always reasonable in price, and you'll most likely enjoy the sounds of a West Indian fungi band while you eat (fungi music is a melodious, usually improvised blend of African and Spanish sounds). You don't have to be a hotel guest to indulge, but you often need to make a reservation.

Tips on Dining

Dining in the Virgin Islands is generally more expensive than it is in North America because, except for locally caught seafood, many of the ingredients have to be imported. This also means that sometimes they aren't as fresh as they could be. Whenever possible, stick to regional food, which is fresher.

Overall, the food on the islands is better than ever. Many fine talents, including some top-notch chefs, now cook here. These chefs often combine mainland recipes with local ingredients to come up with a Caribbean/American cuisine. Try to eat at some of the local places as well. The prices there are more reasonable, and the fare is more adventurous.

TIPPING A 10% to 15% service charge is automatically added to most restaurant tabs. If the service has been good, you should tip a bit extra.

WHAT TO WEAR In some of the posh resorts, such as Caneel Bay on St. John, it is customary for men to wear a jacket, but in summer, virtually no establishment requires it. If in doubt, ask the restaurant beforehand. At the better places, women's evening attire is casual-chic. During the day it is proper to wear something over your bathing suit if you're in a restaurant.

RESERVATIONS Check to see if reservations are required before heading out to eat. In summer, you can almost always get in, but in winter, all the tables may be taken at some of the famous but small places.

The Cuisine

Be sure to read "The Best Dishes in the Virgin Islands," in chapter 1, for our recommendations on where to find the finest examples of some of the dishes discussed below.

APPETIZERS The most famous soup in the islands is *kallaloo,* or **callaloo,** made in an infinite number of ways with a leafy green vegetable similar to spinach. It's often flavored with any combination of the following: salt beef, pig mouth, pig tail, hot peppers, ham bone, fresh fish, crab, corned conch, okra, onions, and spices.

Sustainable Eating

Because of the decline of local species, such as Caribbean lobster and conch, you may want to eschew ordering reef fish, such as grouper, snapper, and grunt, and opt for equally tasty and more sustainable alternatives that live out in open water such as dorado, wahoo, and barracuda.
—Christina P. Colón

Many **soups** are sweetened with sugar and often contain fruit; for example, the classic red-bean soup—made with pork or ham, various spices, and tomatoes—is sugared to taste. *Tannia* soup is made with its namesake, a starchy root known as the "purple elephant ear" because of its color and shape; it's combined with salt-fat meat and ham, tomatoes, onions, and spices. Souse is an old-time favorite made with the feet, head, and tongue of a pig, and flavored with a lime-based sauce.

Saltfish salad is traditionally served on Maundy Thursday or Good Friday in the Virgin Islands. It consists of boneless salt fish, potatoes, onions, boiled eggs, and an oil-and-vinegar dressing.

Herring gundy is another old-time island favorite; it's a salad made with salt herring, potatoes, onions, green sweet and hot peppers, olives, diced beets, raw carrots, herbs, and boiled eggs.

SIDE DISHES Rice—seasoned, not plain—is popular with Virgin Islanders, who are fond of serving several starches at one meal. Most often rice is flavored with ham or salt pork, tomatoes, garlic, onion, and shortening.

Fungi is a simple cornmeal dumpling, made more interesting with the addition of okra and other ingredients. Sweet *fungi* is served as a dessert, with sugar, milk, cinnamon, and raisins.

Okra (often spelled *ochroe* in the islands) is a mainstay vegetable, usually accompanying beef, fish, or chicken. It's often fried and flavored with hot peppers, tomatoes, onions, garlic, and bacon fat or butter. *Accra,* a popular dish, is made with okra, black-eyed peas, salt, and pepper, all fried until they're golden brown.

The classic vegetable dish, which some families eat every night, is **peas and rice.** It usually consists of pigeon peas flavored with ham or salt meat, onion, tomatoes, herbs, and sometimes slices of pumpkin. Pigeon peas, one of the most common vegetables in the islands, are sometimes called congo peas or *gunga.*

FISH & MEAT Way back when, locals gave colorful names to the various fish brought home for dinner, everything from "ole wife" to "doctors," both of which are whitefish. "Porgies and grunts," along with yellowtail, kingfish, and bonito, also show up on many Caribbean dinner tables. Fish is usually boiled in a lime-flavored brew seasoned with hot peppers and herbs, and is commonly served with a Creole sauce of peppers, tomatoes, and onions, among other ingredients. **Salt fish and rice** is an excellent low-cost dish; the fish is flavored with onion, tomatoes, shortening, garlic, and green peppers.

Conch Creole is a savory brew, seasoned with onions, garlic, spices, hot peppers, and salt pork. Another local favorite is chicken and rice, usually made with Spanish peppers. More adventurous diners might try **curried goat,** the longtime classic West Indian dinner prepared with herbs, cardamom pods, and onions.

The famous **johnnycakes** that accompany many of these fish and meat dishes are made with flour, baking powder, shortening, and salt, then fried or baked.

DESSERTS **Sweet potato pie** is a Virgin Islands classic, made with sugar, eggs, butter, milk, salt, cinnamon, raisins, and chopped raw almonds. The exotic fruits of the islands lend themselves to various **homemade ice creams,** including mango, guava (our favorite), soursop (a tangy fruit), banana, and papaya. Sometimes **dumplings,** made with guava, peach, plum, gooseberry, cherry, or apple, are served for dessert.

Drinks

The islands' true poison is **Cruzan rum.** To help stimulate the local economy, U.S. Customs allows you to bring home an extra bottle of Cruzan rum, in addition to your usual 5-liter liquor allowance.

Long before the arrival of Coca-Cola and Pepsi, many islanders concocted their own drinks with whatever was available, including local fruit. Fresh fruit concoctions are still available today.

Water is generally safe to drink on the islands. Much of the water is stored in cisterns and filtered before it's served. Delicate stomachs should stick to mineral water or club soda. American sodas and beer are sold in both the U.S. Virgin Islands and the British Virgin Islands. Wine is sold, too, but it's usually quite expensive.

WHEN TO GO
Weather

Sunshine is practically an everyday affair in the Virgin Islands. Temperatures climb into the 80s (high 20s Celsius) during the day, and drop into the more comfortable 70s (low 20s Celsius) at night. Winter is generally the dry season in the islands, but rainfall can occur at any time of the year. You don't have to worry too much, though—tropical showers usually come and go so quickly you won't even really notice. If you're out exploring for the day, you may want to bring rain gear.

HURRICANES The hurricane season, the dark side of the Caribbean's beautiful weather, officially lasts from June to November. The Virgin Islands chain lies in the main pathway of many a hurricane raging through the Caribbean, and the islands are often hit. If you're planning a vacation in hurricane season, stay abreast of weather conditions. It may pay to get trip-cancellation insurance because of the possibility of hurricanes.

Islanders certainly don't stand around waiting for a hurricane to strike. Satellite forecasts generally give adequate warning to both residents and visitors. And of course, there's always prayer: Islanders have a legal holiday in the third week of July called Supplication Day, when they ask to be spared from devastating storms. In late October, locals celebrate the end of the season on Hurricane Thanksgiving Day.

Average Temperatures & Rainfall (in.) for St. Thomas

	JAN	FEB	MAR	APR	MAY	JUNE	JULY	AUG	SEPT	OCT	NOV	DEC
Temp (°F)	77	77	77	79	79	82	82	83	82	83	81	77
Temp (°C)	25	25	25	26	26	28	28	28	28	28	27	25
Precip.	1.86	.95	.97	8.32	9.25	1.62	2.25	3.6	2.04	4.43	7.77	2.46

The High Season & the Off Season

High season (or winter season) in the Virgin Islands, when hotel rates are at their peak, runs roughly from mid-December to mid-April. However, package and resort rates are sometimes lower in January, as a tourist slump usually occurs right after the Christmas holidays. February is the busiest month. If you're planning on visiting during the winter months, make reservations as far in advance as possible.

Off season begins when North America starts to warm up, and vacationers, assuming that temperatures in the Virgin Islands are soaring into the 100s (upper 30s Celsius), head for less tropical local beaches. However, it's actually quite balmy year-round in the Virgin Islands—thanks to the fabled trade winds—with temperatures varying little more than 5° between winter and summer.

There are many advantages to off-season travel in the Virgin Islands. First, from mid-April to mid-December, hotel rates are slashed a startling 25% to 50%. Second, you're less likely to encounter crowds at swimming pools, beaches, resorts, restaurants, and shops. Especially in St. Thomas and St. Croix, a slower pace prevails in the off season, and you'll have a better chance to appreciate the local culture and cuisine. Of course, there are disadvantages to off-season travel, too: Many hotels use the slower months for construction and/or restoration, fewer facilities are likely to be open, and some hotels and restaurants may close completely when business is really slow.

Additionally, if you're planning a trip during the off season and traveling alone, ask for the hotel's occupancy rate—you may want crowds. The social scene in both the B.V.I. and the U.S.V.I. is intense from mid-December to mid-April. After that, it slumbers a bit. If you seek escape from the world and its masses, summer is the way to go, especially if you aren't depending on meeting others.

Holidays

In addition to the standard legal holidays observed in the United States, **U.S. Virgin Islanders** also observe the following holidays: Three Kings' Day (Jan 6); Transfer Day, commemorating the transfer of the Danish Virgin Islands to the Americans (Mar 31); Organic Act Day, honoring the legislation that granted voting rights to the islanders (June 20); Emancipation Day, celebrating the freeing of the slaves by the Danish in 1848 (July 3); Hurricane Supplication Day (July 25); Hurricane Thanksgiving Day

(Oct 17); Liberty Day (Nov 1); and Christmas Second Day (Dec 26). The islands also celebrate 2 carnival days on the last Friday and Saturday in April: Children's Carnival Parade and the Grand Carnival Parade.

In the **British Virgin Islands,** public holidays include the following: New Year's Day, Commonwealth Day (Mar 12), Good Friday, Easter Monday, Whitmonday (sometime in July), Territory Day Sunday (usually July 1), Festival Monday and Tuesday (during the first week of Aug), St. Ursula's Day (Oct 21), Birthday of the Heir to the Throne (Nov 14), Christmas Day, and Boxing Day (Dec 26).

The Virgin Islands Calendar of Events

For an exhaustive list of events beyond those listed here, check http://events.frommers. com, where you'll find a searchable, up-to-the-minute roster of what's happening in cities all over the world.

FEBRUARY

Annual St. Croix International Regatta, St. Croix. Held at the St. Croix Yacht Club on Teague Bay, this 3-day regatta celebrates its 19th year in 2012. Although a rather minor regatta, it draws serious yachties from the B.V.I., the U.S.V.I., and Florida. Call St. Croix Yacht Club at ⒸⒸ **340/773-9531,** or visit www.stcroixyc.com for details. Mid-February.

MARCH

Mardi Gras Annual Parade, St. Croix. The scenic north shore of St. Croix becomes one big colorful party at Mardi Gras, with a parade to Cane Bay. For information, check www.stcroixtourism.com. First Saturday before Fat Tuesday, usually early March.

International Rolex Cup Regatta, St. Thomas. This is one of three regattas in the Caribbean Ocean Racing Triangle (CORT) series. Top-ranked international racers come to St. Thomas to compete in front of the world's yachting press. The St. Thomas Yacht Club hosts the 3-day event. Call ⒸⒸ **340/775-4701,** or visit www.rolexcup regatta.com. Late March.

Transfer Day, U.S. Virgin Islands. This holiday commemorates the day the U.S. Virgins were transferred from Denmark to the United States. On this day, vendors sell Danish products, and visits to the remains of Danish ruins and forts are arranged. Call ⒸⒸ **340/772-0598,** or visit www.stcroix landmarks.com. March 31.

APRIL

B.V.I. Spring Regatta, Tortola. This is the third of the CORT events (see International Rolex Cup Regatta, above). A range of talents, from the most dedicated racers to bareboat crews out for "rum and reggae," participate in the 4-day race. Contact the B.V.I. Spring Regatta Committee in Tortola at ⒸⒸ **284/541-6732,** or sail over to www. bvispringregatta.org for information. Early April.

Virgin Gorda Easter Festival, Virgin Gorda. Easter weekend is a big event on Virgin Gorda, featuring street parades, a beauty pageant, and nonstop partying. Arrive on Good Friday, Holy Saturday, or Easter Sunday, and you should have no trouble finding the party. Easter weekend.

Virgin Islands Carnival, St. Thomas. This annual celebration on St. Thomas, with origins in Africa, is the most spectacular and fun carnival in the Virgin Islands. "Mocko Jumbies," people dressed as spirits, parade through the streets on stilts nearly 20 feet high. Steel and fungi bands, "jumpups," and parades are part of the festivities. Over the years, interestingly, the festivities have become more and more Christianized. Events take place islandwide, but most of the action is on the streets of Charlotte Amalie. For information, call ⒸⒸ **340/776-3112,** or visit www.vicarnival.com for a schedule of events. After Easter.

MAY

B.V.I. Music Festival, Tortola. Music—mostly reggae—drowns out the sea at this music festival on Cane Garden Bay in Tortola, the island's best beach. Musicians come from all over the West Indies to perform. For more information, visit www.bvimusic festival.com. Late May.

JUNE

Mango Melee and Tropical Fruit Festival, St. Croix. Mango aficionados and devotees of other tropical fruit converge here for tastings, cooking demonstrations, and contests. For more information, call (✆ **340/692-2874,** or visit www.sgvbg.org. Late June.

Virgin Islands Bartender Olympics, St. Croix. Inspired by the Tom Cruise movie *Cocktail,* bartenders and servers throughout the Virgin Islands come together to show off their skills in mixing fruit punches and other drinks. The best bartender and best server are named, and there's plenty to drink. For more information, call (✆ **340/514-8226.** Usually late June.

St John Festival, St. John. Known also as "Carnival," this month-long cultural event takes place on St. John, with steel-pan concerts, calypso shows, parades, beauty pageants, and fireworks displays. For more information, call (✆ **800/372-USVI** [8784]. The carnival begins the first week of June and lasts until July 4.

JULY

Independence Day, St. John. The elements of Carnival are combined with emancipation and independence celebrations in this festive event, which culminates on July 4 with a big parade. Thousands of St. Thomas residents flock to St. John for the parades, calypso bands, colorful costumes, and events leading up to the selection of Ms. St. John and the King of the Carnival. Call the St. John tourist office at (✆ **340/776-6201** for more details. July 4.

AUGUST

B.V.I. Emancipation Celebrations, Tortola. Many visitors from other Caribbean islands hop over to Road Town, in Tortola, for this 2-week party. Join locals as they dance to fungi and reggae bands, and take part in the Emancipation Day Parade and other carnival activities and festivities. For information, call the B.V.I. Tourist Board Office at (✆ **284/494-3701.** Early August.

U.S. Virgin Islands Open/Atlantic Blue Marlin Tournament, St. Thomas. This prestigious St. Thomas–centered charity event (proceeds go to the Boy Scouts) is also eco-friendly—trophies are based on the number of blue marlin caught, tagged, and released. The tournament is open to anyone who's interested, and sportsfishers come from around the world to participate. For more information, call the VI Council of the Boy Scouts of America at (✆ **888/234-7484** or 340/775-9500; www.abmt.vi. Late August (weekend closest to the full moon).

OCTOBER

Virgin Islands Fashion Week, St. Thomas. Aspiring designers from across the Caribbean, the United States, and even West Africa fly into St. Thomas to showcase their latest fashion designs. At the Caribbean Catwalk Runway show, beach and casual fashions are the draw. Nearly all events, including rap party, are open to the public. For more information, call (✆ **340/344-6078.** Five days in October, dates vary.

NOVEMBER

Annual Holiday Arts, Crafts & Music Festival, St. Thomas. This annual festival, which takes place in Tillett Gardens in St. Thomas, includes displays from over 30 local artists, along with live music and entertainment. There are even free activities for kids. For information, visit www.tillettfoundation.org.

DECEMBER

Christmas in St. Croix. This major event launches the beginning of a 12-day celebration that includes Christmas Day, Christmas Second Day (Dec 26), New Year's Eve (called "Old Year's Day"), and New Year's Day. It ends on January 6, the Feast of the Three Kings, with a parade of flamboyantly attired merrymakers. For information, call the U.S. Virgin Islands Department of Tourism office in Christiansted at (✆ **340/773-0495.**

THE LAY OF THE LAND

The U.S. Virgin Islands

Lying some 90 miles east of Puerto Rico, the U.S. Virgin Islands consist of three main resort islands: St. Thomas, St. John, St. Croix, plus a little islet called Water Island and several smaller islets. Their combined landmass is roughly twice the size of Washington, D.C.

The largest of the islands is St. Croix, with 82 square miles, which is structurally akin to the Lesser Antilles. It has the same flora and fauna as Puerto Rico.

At its widest point, St. Croix is 6 miles wide; it is also 22 miles long. Its highest peak is Mount Eagle at 1,088 feet. The western end of the island is lush with towering fruit trees and ferns growing on the mountainside, but the eastern terrain is rocky and arid.

A few natural harbors and protected bays grace St. Croix. In the middle of the island are beautiful white sandy beaches. The distance between St. Thomas and St. Croix is 40 miles.

The coasts of St. Croix are generally flat and uniform, but St. Thomas and St. John have very irregular coastlines, broken by bays and rugged headlands. Both St. John and St. Thomas have excellent natural harbors that provide shelter for boats against the many hurricanes that strike the area.

The highest elevation on St. Thomas is Crown Mountain at 1,550 feet. Unlike St. Croix, there are relatively few flat areas on St. Thomas. The island is virtually one long ridge of hills running east and west. Its landmass is 31 square miles, and St. Thomas is about 4 miles wide and 13 miles long. Both St. Thomas and St. John are volcanic in origin, whereas St. Croix was formed by a coral reef, which explains why it is flatter.

Lying 4 miles off St. Thomas's East End, the small island of St. John, 7 miles long and 3 miles wide, is virtually a national park. More than two-thirds of the island is protected by the National Park Service. Its highest point is Bordeaux Mountain at a modest 1,277 feet. Cruz Bay is the main town and natural harbor, but the island's coastal areas have many fine protected bays, especially the natural harbor of Coral Bay.

The fourth island of any significant size is Water Island, less than 500 acres. It is 2½ miles long and 1 mile wide, and is irregular in shape, studded with many bays and peninsulas. The highest point on Water Island is only 300 feet above sea level. The island lies just half a mile off the southern shore of St. Thomas.

The British Virgin Islands

Lying 97km (60 miles) to the east of Puerto Rico, the British Virgin Islands comprise 16 inhabited and more than 20 uninhabited islands. The total landmass of the B.V.I. is 153 sq. km (59 sq. miles), a little smaller than Washington, D.C. This subtropical archipelago at its highest point reaches only 534m (1,752 ft.) at Mount Sage on Tortola, also home to Road Town, the capital of the B.V.I. The other principle islands are Virgin Gorda, Anegada, and Jost Van Dyke.

The volcanic British Virgins are the easternmost extension of the Greater Antilles, representing peaks of submerged mountains that rise up from the ocean floor.

Virgin Gorda lies 13km (8 miles) to the east of Tortola. To its north are the islands of Mosquito and Prickly Pear. Anegada lies 24km (15 miles) to the north of Virgin Gorda.

To the north of Tortola are Jost Van Dyke (with tourist facilities) and both Great Tobago and Little Tobago. Other islands south of Drake Channel include Norman (of Robert Louis Stevenson fame) and Peter Island (site of a luxurious resort).

The most northerly of the B.V.I. is Anegada, flat, dry, and bare of foliage, its highest elevation reaching only 8.5m (28 ft.). It is not volcanic in origin, like the other islands, but is a coral atoll fringed by dangerous horseshoe-shaped reefs. The island is home to the endangered rock iguana.

South of Tortola, Salt Island is known as the site of the wreck of the *Rhone*, the most famous dive site in the Caribbean. The vessel sank in 1867 in one of the most devastating hurricanes ever to strike the B.V.I.

With its white sandy beaches and scalloped coastlines of tiny coves, the B.V.I. remains the most secluded spot in the Virgin Island archipelago, a retreat of yachties seeking safe havens and visitors who want to escape from modern civilization.

RESPONSIBLE TRAVEL

Eco-tourism is a relatively new concept to the Virgin Islands. Many of the islands were clear-cut in the 1700s to make way for sugar plantations, destroying much of the natural landscape. All through the 1900s, while real estate developments on St. Thomas continued to grow, little concern was given to preserving and sustaining the natural resources of the U.S.V.I. Today, there is a very different attitude toward the ecosystem of the Virgin Islands among permanent residents and visitors alike.

While the eco-tourism infrastructure is still underdeveloped, and the terms "eco-friendly" and "sustainable" can be misused, it is still possible to find truly eco-friendly lodgings on the islands. Camping is always an option. St. John, which is almost entirely a national park, has numerous campsites. Aside from those run by the National Park Service, there is the **Maho Bay Camp** (p. 121), which is an umbrella name for two different campsites with several types of eco-friendly lodgings ranging from bare cottages to comfortable studios. On St. Croix, there is **Mount Victory Camp** (p. 158), which relies on renewable energy to power its cottages. The British Virgin Islands are less developed than their American cousins, so lodgings tend to be more eco-friendly by nature. You don't have to camp out to stay in eco-sensitive lodging. The **Cooper Island Beach Club** (p. 203) meets the middle ground between luxury and roughing it. **Guana Island** (p. 244) is a private island with only one hotel. The entire island is a wildlife sanctuary watched over by the attentive owners.

Low-impact activities like hiking, snorkeling, and kayaking abound in the Virgin Islands. While on St. Croix, contact the **St. Croix Environmental Association** (p. 158), which hosts hikes, tours of research facilities, and events based around the hatching of baby sea turtles. Aside from the many companies that offer tours, the St. Thomas–based **Virgin Islands Ecotours/Mangrove Adventures** (p. 84) offers tours with professional naturalists of the mangrove lagoon and nature reserve at Cas Cay.

St. Thomas, with all its development and modern conveniences, faces the biggest challenges in regard to sustainable development. To learn more about recent land-use debates, see the section "The Virgin Islands Today," earlier in this chapter.

TOURS

The Virgin Islands are small and easy to navigate, so most people opt to visit these islands independently. Tours are not vital to a vacation here, but if you'd like to be taken around on a tour, a limited number of excursions are offered. *Note:* During the low summer season, these tours may not run regularly unless enough people book, so always call in advance to make arrangements.

Air Tours

It's a pricey option, but well-heeled visitors may want to see the Virgin Islands as the birds do. Helicopter tours are available through **Air Center Helicopters,** Cyril E. King Airport, in St. Thomas (© **340/775-7335;** www.aircaenterhelicopters.com). Parties can rent the entire helicopter for a 17-minute tour of St. Thomas and St. John for $385; a 25-minute tour that flies over both of these islands as well as Jost van Dyke in the B.V.I. costs $565. Helicopters seat five passengers and a pilot.

Air Ventures in Paradise (© **340/719-5529;** www.airventuresinparadise.com), based in St. Croix's Henry Rohlsen Airport, offers "flightseeing" tours of St. Thomas and St. Croix in small private airplanes. They also offer charter flights to nearby islands and private flight lessons.

If you can't afford such a luxury, you can get a panoramic aerial view from Paradise Point on St. Thomas. See **Paradise Point St. Thomas Skyride** (p. 92).

Adventure Trips

See the "Active Vacation Planner," below, for information on biking, boating, hiking, scuba-diving, and snorkeling tours.

Guided Tours

One of the best tour operators in the U.S.V.I. is **Adventure Center,** in the Marriott Frenchman's Reef Resort, Flamboyant Point, St. Thomas (© **340/774-2992;** www.adventurecenters.net). They offer a wide variety of tours, on both land and sea, and many tours of both St. Thomas and St. John depart right from the hotel's dock. Their 2½ hour "Scenic Island Drive" tour explores St. Thomas's highlights, including the Botanical Gardens, Drake's Seat, and Charlotte Amalie; this tour costs $49 per person. Their "St. John Land and Snorkel Safari" is a full-day tour that takes visitors through the beaches and national parks in St. John, including a snorkel stop in Trunk Bay, in open-air buses; it costs $95 per person. Adventure Center offers an array of other quality guided tours throughout the Virgin Islands.

Tan Tan Tours (© **340/773-7041;** www.stxtantantours.com) is a tour operator based in St. Croix that offers off-the-beaten-path jeep tours of the island. A 2½-hour tour of the tide pools costs $70 per person, while a full-day (8-hr.) tour of the island costs $140 per person; custom tours are also available.

B.V.I. Eco-Tours (© **284/495-0271;** www.bvi-ecotours.com) offers a variety of guided tours, including snorkeling, hiking, bird watching, sightseeing, diving, and general tours of the British Virgin Islands. **Virgin Gorda Tours** (© **284/495-5240;** www.virgingordatours.com) offers guided taxi tours of Virgin Gorda, including stops at Savannah Bay, Gorda Peak, the historical Copper Mine ruins, and the famous Baths; tours vary, but a 1-hour tour (for 2 people) costs $55.

THE ACTIVE VACATION PLANNER

There's no rule that says you have to confine yourself to a beach chair within arm's length of the bar while visiting the Virgin Islands (though there's no rule against it, either). You will have endless opportunities to sit by the surf sipping rum drinks, but remember that these islands offer more than just a coastline. Coral reefs and stunning beaches provide breathtaking backdrops for a variety of watersports, from snorkeling to sea kayaking and sailing, and there's also plenty of golf, tennis, hiking, and even horseback riding. This section presents an overview of the outdoor activities on the Virgin Islands. See individual chapters for more specific information on locations and outfitters.

Activities A to Z

BICYCLING   It is possible to rent bikes on some of the islands, and bike riding can be a wonderful way to explore the islands. **Water Island Adventures** (© 340/775-5770; www.waterislandadventures.com) offers guided bike tours on Water Island, off of St. Thomas. Tours depart from St. Thomas, where you'll take a ferry to Water Island—from there the biking tour begins. On St. Croix, contact **Freedom City Cycles** (© 340/227-2433; www.freedomcitycycles.com), which, in addition to offering bike rentals, can arrange guided bike tours of the island. A 2- to 3-hour mountain biking tour begins at sea level and climbs through the rain forest on both paved and unpaved roads, costing $50 per person.

CAMPING   The best campsites in the Virgin Islands are on St. John, at **Maho Bay** and **Cinnamon Bay** (the Cinnamon Bay campground is considered one of the finest campgrounds in the Caribbean). Both facilities are open year-round and are so popular that reservations need to be made far in advance during the winter months. In the British Virgin Islands, the best campsite is Tortola's **Brewers Bay Campground,** which rents tents and basic equipment and is open year-round.

FISHING   In the past 25 years or so, more than 20 sportsfishing world records have been set in the Virgin Islands, mostly for the mega blue marlin. Other abundant fish in these waters are bonito, tuna, wahoo, sailfish, and skipjack. Sport-fishing charters, led by experienced local captains, abound in the islands; both half-day and full-day trips are available. But you needn't go out to sea to fish. On St. Thomas, St. John, and St. Croix, the U.S. government publishes lists of legal shoreline fishing spots (contact local tourist offices for more information). Closer inshore, you'll find kingfish, mackerel, bonefish, tarpon, amberjack, grouper, and snapper.

On St. Thomas, many people line-fish from the rocky shore along Mandahl Beach, which is also a popular spot for family picnics. The shore here is not the best place for swimming, because the seafloor drops off dramatically and the surf tends to be rough. On St. John, the waters in Virgin Islands National Park are open to fishermen with hand-held rods. No fishing license is required for shoreline fishing, and government pamphlets available at tourist offices list some 100 good spots. Call © 340/774-8784 for more information.

GOLF   The golfing hub of the Virgin Islands is the challenging **Carambola Golf & Country Club** (© 340/778-5638; www.golfcarambola.com) in St. Croix. Also on St. Croix is the excellent course at the **Buccaneer** (© 340/712-2100), just outside Christiansted. The highlight on St. Thomas is the **Mahogany Run**

(© **800/253-7103** or 340/777-6006; www.mahoganyrungolf.com). There aren't any courses on St. John or the British Virgin Islands.

HIKING   The best islands for hiking are **Tortola** and **St. John.** In Tortola, the best hiking is through Sage Mountain National Park, spread across 37 hectares (91 acres) of luxuriant flora and fauna. On St. John, the most intriguing hike is the Annaberg Historic Trail, which takes you by former plantation sites. Most of St. John is itself a National Park, so there are dozens of opportunities for hiking. **St. Croix** also has good hiking in its "Rain Forest" area. **Buck Island,** off the coast of St. Croix, is beloved by snorkelers and scuba divers but also fascinating to hike. You can easily explore the island in a day, as it is only half a mile wide and a mile long. While hiking in the Virgin Islands, you'll encounter many birds and flowers—but no poisonous snakes. Be sure to look for the trumpet-shaped Ginger Thomas, the U.S. Virgin Islands' official flower.

To reach some of the most remote but scenic places on St. Croix, take a hiking trip with **Ay Ay Eco Tours & Hikes** (© 340/772-4079), which offers a variety of hiking trips ranging from 3 hour-tours to half-day tours. Tours vary based on the hikers' ability and stamina. A half-day tour, lasting about 4 to 5 hours, may take hikers to explore northeast St. Croix, with its forest glades, secluded coastline, and panoramic vistas; this tour costs $80 per person.

HORSEBACK RIDING   Equestrians should head for St. Croix. **Paul and Jill's Equestrian Stables** (© 340/772-2880; www.paulandjills.com), at Sprat Hall Plantation, are the best stables not only in the Virgin Islands but also in all the Caribbean. The outfit is known for the quality of both its horses and its riding trails. Neophytes and experts are welcome.

SAILING & YACHTING   The Virgin Islands are a sailor's paradise, offering crystal-clear turquoise waters, secluded coves and inlets, and protected harbors for anchoring.

For details on chartering your own boat, see the box on p. 46. Most visitors, however, are content with **day sails,** which are easy to organize, especially at the harbors in St. Thomas, Tortola, and Virgin Gorda. Regardless of where you decide to cruise, you really shouldn't leave the islands without spending at least 1 day on the water, even if you have to load up on Dramamine or snap on your acupressure wristbands before you go.

The most popular cruising area around the Virgin Islands is the deep and incredibly scenic **Sir Francis Drake Channel,** which runs from St. John to Virgin Gorda's North Sound. The channel is surrounded by mountainous islands, and boasts crisp breezes year-round. In heavy weather, the network of tiny islands shelters yachties from the brute force of the open sea. The waters surrounding St. Croix to the south are also appealing, especially near Buck Island.

Outside the channel, the Virgin Islands archipelago contains reefy areas that separate many of the islands from their neighbors. To navigate these areas, you need to use a depth chart (available from charter companies or any marine supply outlet) and have some local knowledge. *Tip:* Locals and temporarily shore-bound sailors willingly offer free advice, often enough to last a couple of drinks, at almost any dockside watering hole.

For more than a quarter of a century, *The Yachtsman's Guide to the Virgin Islands* has been the classic cruising guide to this area (it's updated periodically). The detailed, 240-page text is supplemented by 22 sketch charts, more than 100 photographs and

The Best Boating Outfitters

Boating is big in the U.S. Virgin Islands, and it's even bigger in the British Virgins, which are said to have the best cruising in the Caribbean. Here are the best boat operators:

- **American Yacht Harbor Marina** (St. Thomas): This is one of the best bareboat and full-crew charter companies on St. Thomas, located in Red Hook. Whatever craft you're looking for, you're bound to find it here. See p. 83.

- **The Moorings** (Tortola): This is the finest charter service in the Virgin Islands. It has done more than any other outfitter to make the British Virgin Islands the destination of choice among the world's yachters. Its fleet of yachts and boats is staggering—everything from bareboat rentals to fully crewed vessels with a skipper, crew, and cook. See p. 197.

illustrations, and numerous landfall sketches showing harbors, channels, landmarks, and such. Subjects covered include piloting, anchoring, communication, weather, fishing, and more. The guide also covers the eastern end of Puerto Rico, Vieques, and Culebra. Copies are available at major marine outlets, bookstores, and direct from **Yachtman's Guide** (© 877/923-9653; www.yachtsmansguide.com).

Except for **Anegada,** which is a low-lying atoll of coral limestone and sandstone, all the Virgin Islands are high and easily spotted. The water here is very clear. The shortest distance between St. Thomas and St. Croix is 35 nautical miles; from St. John to St. Croix, 35 nautical miles; from St. Thomas to St. John, 2 nautical miles; from Tortola to St. Thomas, 10 nautical miles; from Virgin Gorda to Anegada, 13 nautical miles; and from St. John to Anegada, 30 nautical miles. Virgin Gorda to St. Croix is about the longest run, at 45 nautical miles. (Specific distances between the islands can be misleading, though, because often you may need to take roundabout routes from one point to another.)

If you don't know how to sail but would like to learn, contact one of the sailing schools on St. Croix. **Jones Maritime Sailing School,** 1215 King Cross St., Christiansted, St. Croix, U.S.V.I. 00820 (© 340/773-4709; www.jonesmaritime.com), has three 24-foot day-sailors and charges $295 per person for a 2-day course, held on Saturdays and Sundays.

Womanship, 137 Conduit St., Annapolis, MD 21401 (© 800/342-9295 in the U.S.; www.womanship.com), offers a sailing program for women of all ages and levels of nautical expertise in the British Virgin Islands. Groups consist of a maximum of six students with two female instructors. Participants sleep aboard the boat, meals included. Courses normally last a week. The cost is $2,065 to $2,795 from January to May and $1,995 to $2,695 from October to December.

The British Virgin Islands are also the headquarters of the **Offshore Sailing School,** Prospect Reef Resort, Road Town (© 284/494-5119). This school offers sailing instruction year-round. For information before you go, write or call Offshore Sailing School, 16731 McGregor Blvd., Ft. Myers, FL 33908 (© 888/454-7015 or 239/454-1700; www.offshore-sailing.com).

SEA KAYAKING **Arawak Expeditions,** Cruz Bay, St. John (© 800/238-8687 or 340/693-8312 in the U.S.; www.arawakexp.com), is the only outfitter in the Virgin

CHARTERING YOUR OWN boat

There may be no better way to experience the Virgin Islands than on the deck of your own yacht. Impossible? Not really. No one said you had to *own* the yacht.

Experienced sailors and navigators with a sea-wise crew might want to rent a **bareboat charter**—a fully equipped boat with no captain or crew. You'll have to prove that you can handle the boat before you're allowed to set sail; even then, you may want to take along an experienced local sailor who's familiar with the sometimes tricky waters. If you're not an expert sailor but you still yearn to hit the high seas, consider a **fully crewed charter,** with a crew that includes a captain and cook. The cost of a crewed boat is obviously more than that of a bareboat, and varies according to crew size and experience.

Four to six people (and sometimes more) charter yachts measuring from 50 to 100 feet. Most are rented on a weekly basis and come with a fully stocked kitchen (or a barbecue) and bar, fishing gear, and watersports equipment. More and more bareboaters are saving money on charters by buying their own provisions, rather than relying on the charter company.

The best outfitter in the Virgin Islands is the **Moorings,** P.O. Box 139, Wickham's Cay, Road Town, Tortola, B.V.I. (*©* **888/952-8420;** www.moorings. com), which offers both bareboat and fully crewed charters equipped with a barbecue, snorkeling gear, a dinghy, and linens. The company even supplies windsurfing equipment for free with crewed boats (and for an extra cost with bareboats). The experienced staff of mechanics, electricians, riggers, and cleaners is extremely helpful, especially if you're going out on your own. They'll give you a thorough briefing about Virgin Islands waters and anchorages. Seven-night, six-person combined hotel-and-crewed-yacht packages run $1,750 to $3,500 per person.

Islands offering multiple-day sea-kayaking/island-camping excursions, although numerous outfitters and hotels throughout the chain provide kayaks for day trips. The vessels with Arawak Expeditions are in two-person fiberglass kayaks, complete with foot-controlled rudders. The outfit provides all the kayaking gear, healthy meals, camping equipment, and experienced guides. The cost of a full-day trip is $110, half-day, $65; you can also book longer expeditions, such as a 5-day excursion costing $1,195 per person or a 7-day trip going for $2,495 per person.

SNORKELING & SCUBA DIVING   On St. Croix, the best site for both is **Buck Island,** easily accessible by day sails from the harbor in Christiansted. St. Croix is also known for its dramatic "drop-offs," including the famous Puerto Rico Trench.

On St. Thomas, all major hotels rent fins and masks for snorkelers, and most day-sail charters have equipment on board. Many outfitters, like the **St. Thomas Diving Club** (*©* **340/776-2381;** www.stthomasdivingclub.com), also feature scuba programs.

As for the British Virgin Islands, the best snorkeling is around the **Baths,** Virgin Gorda's major attraction. **Anegada Reef,** which lies off Anegada Island, has been a "burial ground" for ships for centuries; an estimated 300 wrecks, including many pirate ships, have perished here. The wreckage of the **HMS *Rhone,*** near the westerly tip of Salt Island, is the most celebrated dive spot in the B.V.I. This ship went under in 1867 in one of the most disastrous hurricanes ever to hit the Virgin Islands.

Diving cruises are packaged by **Oceanic Society Expeditions,** Fort Mason Center, San Francisco, CA 94123 (✆ **800/326-7491** or 415/441-1106 in San Francisco; www. oceanicsociety.org), which also offers whale-watching and some research-oriented trips. **Caradonna Dive Adventures** (✆ **800/330-6611;** www.caradonna.com) offers all sorts of diving packages. See individual destination chapters for information on snorkeling and scuba outfitters and lessons.

TENNIS Tennis is becoming a major sport in the Virgin Islands. Most courts are all-weather or Laykold. Because of intense midday heat, many courts are lit for night games. Pro shops, complete with teaching pros, are available at the major tennis resorts, especially on St. Croix and St. Thomas.

St. Thomas has six public (and free) tennis courts that operate on a first-come, first-served basis. If the courts at the major hotels aren't booked by resident guests, you can usually play there for a minimal fee as long as you call a day in advance. Both **Bolongo Bay** and **Frenchman's Reef & Morning Star Marriott Beach Resort** have four courts.

The best tennis facilities in the Virgin Islands are on St. Croix at the **Buccaneer,** which has eight meticulously maintained courts and a state-of-the-art pro shop. The island also has seven public courts, but they're rather rough around the edges.

On Tortola, there are six courts at **Prospect Reef;** they're often open to nonguests for a fee. If you're a serious tennis buff and are planning to stay on Virgin Gorda, consider **Little Dix Bay,** which has seven beautiful courts reserved for guests only.

ST. THOMAS

Called the most "unvirgin" of the Virgin Islands, St. Thomas is for those who want action. It is the shopping mart of the Caribbean, centered on the bustling capital of Charlotte Amalie. The port is also the busiest cruise-ship harbor in the West Indies. To escape the crowds, retreat to the island's famous beaches, including Magens Bay, hailed as one of the most beautiful beaches in the world. The surrounding turquoise sea attracts yachties and fishermen with such trophy-worthy catches as the blue Marlin.

Things to Do Pretty 18th-century buildings surround the harbor of the active port of **Charlotte Amalie,** where warehouses once filled with pirate booty still stand. See the colorful Caribbean water world from an *Atlantis* submarine dive. Explore island history in the redbrick **Fort Christian.** Laze in the white sands at **Magens Bay,** or seek shade under the coconut palms of **Secret Harbour** on the East End. For a little seclusion, try **Limetree Beach** or **Vessup Bay.**

Shopping Spend freely at the designer boutiques and jewelry stores of **Charlotte Amalie.** Sift through pottery, silk-screened fabrics, candles, and watercolors at **Tillett Gardens,** or duck into the warehouses on **Main Street** for island trinkets and clothing. When you tire of French perfumes and Swiss watches, head for **Market Square** for ackee, cassava, and breadfruit, or buy local crafts and souvenirs from nearby **Havensight Mall. Duty-free shopping** bargains include china, crystal, perfumes, jewelry (especially emeralds), Haitian art, clothing, watches, and items made of wood.

Nightlife & Entertainment St. Thomas sizzles with the most extensive nightlife in the U.S. or British Virgin Islands. **Charlotte Amalie** still swings with Waterfront pubs and bars, but much of the action has shifted to the bars and restaurants of **Frenchtown.** The big hotels have the most lively options, and after a day in the hot sun, you can wind down with a cocktail and local fungi band playing traditional music on homemade instruments.

Restaurants & Dining St. Thomas adds an eclectic mix of cuisines—including American, Italian, Mexican, and Asian—to its spicy Caribbean palate. **Charlotte Amalie** is dense with restaurants, but the **East End** has a variety of spots as well. Seafood specialties abound, such as "ole wife" and yellowtail at Waterfront dining rooms, or splurge on Coral Bay crab cakes served with island rémoulade on an elegant terrace. Most local restaurants serve **johnnycake,** a popular fried, unleavened bread.

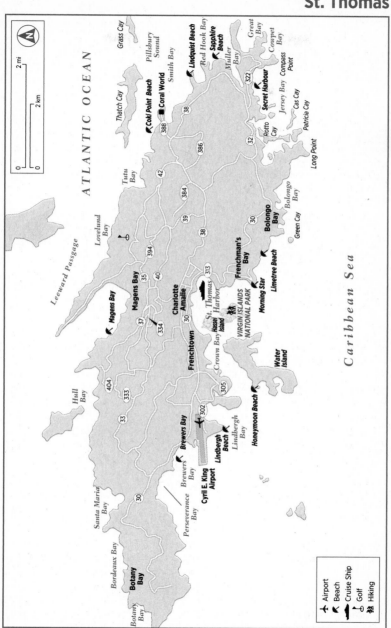

ESSENTIALS
Getting There
BY PLANE

If you're flying to St. Thomas, you will land at the **Cyril E. King Airport** (© **340/ 774-5100;** www.viport.com/airports.html; airport code STT), to the west of Charlotte Amalie on Route 30. From here, you can easily grab a taxi to your hotel or villa. Chances are you will be staying east of Charlotte Amalie, so keep in mind that getting through town often involves long delays and traffic jams.

Nonstop flights to the U.S. Virgin Islands from New York City take 3¾ hours. Flight time from Miami is about 2½ hours. Flight time between St. Thomas and St. Croix is only 20 minutes. Flying to San Juan, Puerto Rico, from mainland cities and connecting to St. Thomas may cost less than regular nonstop fares.

American Airlines (© **800/433-7300** in the U.S.; www.aa.com) offers frequent service to St. Thomas and St. Croix from the U.S. mainland, with two daily flights from New York to St. Thomas in high season. Passengers flying from other parts of the world are usually routed to St. Thomas through American's hubs in Miami or San Juan, both of which offer nonstop service (often several times a day) to St. Thomas. (American Eagle alone has 12 nonstop flights daily from San Juan to St. Thomas.)

Delta (© **800/241-4141** in the U.S.; www.delta.com) offers two daily nonstop flights between Atlanta and St. Thomas in winter. **US Airways** (© **800/428-4322** in the U.S.; www.usairways.com) has one nonstop daily flight from Philadelphia to St. Thomas, and an additional flight on Saturday.

Cape Air (© **800/352-0714** in the U.S.; www.flycapeair.com) has service between St. Thomas and Puerto Rico. This Massachusetts-based airline offers 5 to 12 flights daily. Cape Air has expanded its service to include flights from San Juan to St. Croix and Tortola, and flights between St. Croix and St. Thomas.

United Airlines (© **800/538-2929** in the U.S.; www.united.com) has nonstop service on Saturday to St. Thomas from Chicago and Washington, D.C.

Continental Airlines (© **800/231-0856** in the U.S.; www.continental.com) has daily flights from Newark International Airport, in New Jersey, to St. Thomas.

Tip: Bargain seekers should ask their airline representative to connect them with the tour desk, which can often arrange discounted hotel rates if a hotel reservation is booked simultaneously with airline tickets.

BY BOAT

If you're in the British Virgin Islands, you can take a boat to Charlotte Amalie from Tortola. Trip time is only 45 minutes between these two capitals, and a one-way ticket is $30 ($50 round-trip). The major carriers to and from Tortola are **Smith's Ferry** (© **340/775-7292;** www.smithsferry.com) and **Native Son** (© **340/774-8685;** www.nativesonferry.com), which are both based in Charlotte Amalie. Boats arrive in and depart from Tortola's West End.

St. Thomas is also linked by boat to St. John, about 3 to 5 miles away. Ferries depart Red Hook Marina on the East End of St. Thomas and arrive at Cruz Bay on St. John. Trip time is about 15 to 20 minutes; the cost is $6.10 one-way for adults ($1 for kids 2 to 10). For complete ferry schedules, call **Transportation Services** at © **340/776-6282.**

It's also possible to take a ferry service from Puerto Rico to St. Thomas, with a stop in St. John. The service, however, is available only during Carnival. Trip time between

Fajardo and Charlotte Amalie (St. Thomas) is about 1¾ hours, with the departure Saturday morning and the return Sunday afternoon. The cost is $100 one-way, $125 round-trip. For more information, call **Transportation Services** at ✆ **340/776-6282.**

Visitor Information

The **visitor center,** 78 1-2-3 Estate Constant, across from the Nisky Shopping Center, on the Waterfront in downtown Charlotte Amalie (✆ **340/774-8784;** www.visit usvi.com), is open Monday to Friday 8am to 5pm and Saturday 8am to 2pm. You can get maps and a list of legal shoreline fishing sites throughout the islands here. There's also an information desk at the cruise-ship terminal.

Island Layout

CHARLOTTE AMALIE

For a map of the landmarks and attractions discussed below, see "Walking Tour: Charlotte Amalie," on p. 87.

Charlotte Amalie, the capital of St. Thomas, is the only town on the island. Its seaside promenade is called **Waterfront Highway,** or simply, the **Waterfront.** From here, you can take any of the streets or alleyways into town to **Main Street** (also called Dronningens Gade). Principal links between Main Street and the Waterfront include **Raadets Gade, Tolbod Gade, Store Tvaer Gade,** and **Strand Gade.**

Main Street is home to all of the major shops. The western end (near the intersection with Strand Gade) is known as **Market Square.** Once the site of the biggest slave market auctions in the Caribbean Basin, today it's an open-air cluster of stalls where native farmers and gardeners gather daily (except Sun) to sell their produce. Go early in the morning to see the market at its best.

Running parallel to and north of Main Street is **Back Street** (also known as Vimmelskaft Gade), which is also lined with stores, including some of the less expensive choices. *Beware:* It can be dangerous to walk along Back Street at night, but it's reasonably safe for daytime shopping.

In the eastern part of town, between Tolbod Gade and Fort Pladsen (northwest of Fort Christian), lies **Emancipation Park,** commemorating the liberation of the slaves in 1848. Most of the major historic buildings, including the Legislature, Fort Christian, and Government House, lie within a short walk of this park.

Southeast of the park looms **Fort Christian.** Crowned by a clock tower and painted rusty red, it was constructed by the Danes in 1671. The **Legislative Building,** seat of the elected government of the U.S. Virgin Islands, lies on the harbor side of the fort.

Kongens Gade (or King's St.) leads to **Government Hill,** which overlooks the town and St. Thomas Harbor. **Government House,** a white brick building dating from 1867, stands atop the hill.

Between **Hotel 1829** (a mansion built that year by a French sea captain) and Government House is a staircase known as the **Street of 99 Steps.** Actually, someone miscounted: It should be called the Street of 103 Steps. Regardless, the steps lead to the summit of Government Hill.

WEST OF CHARLOTTE AMALIE

The most important of the outlying neighborhoods to the west of Charlotte Amalie is **Frenchtown.** Some of the older islanders still speak a distinctive Norman-French dialect here. Because the heart of Charlotte Amalie is dangerous at night, Frenchtown, with its finer restaurants and interesting bars, has become the place to go after dark. To reach Frenchtown, take Veterans Drive west of town along the Waterfront, turning left (shortly after passing the Windward Passage Hotel on your right) at the sign pointing to the Villa Olga.

The middle-grade hotels which lie to the immediate west of Charlotte Amalie attract visitors who are seeking more moderate hotel rates than those charged at the mega-resorts that lie along the gold-plated South Coast. The disadvantage is that you may have to depend on public transportation to reach the sands. The biggest attraction is that you're on the very doorstep of Charlotte Amalie, with all its amusements.

EAST OF CHARLOTTE AMALIE

Traveling east from Charlotte Amalie, along a traffic-clogged highway, you'll see St. Thomas Harbor on your right. If you stay in this area, you'll be in a tranquil setting just a short car or taxi ride from the bustle of Charlotte Amalie. The major disadvantage is that you must reach the sands by some form of transportation; if you want to run out of your hotel-room door onto the beach, look elsewhere.

THE SOUTH COAST

This fabled strip, with its good sandy beaches, has put St. Thomas on the tourist maps of the Caribbean. If you don't mind paying the big bucks, you can stay here in grand style. Many visitors prefer the resorts on the South Coast because they want to be far removed from the hustle and bustle of Charlotte Amalie, especially during the day, when it's overrun by cruise-ship passengers and others. But if you feel the need for a shopping binge, cars, buses, hotel shuttles, and taxis can quickly deliver you to Charlotte Amalie if you wish.

THE EAST END

The East End is reached by traversing a long, difficult, traffic-clogged road. Once you're here, you can enjoy sea, sand, and sun with little to disturb you (the East End offers even more isolation than the South Coast). This is the site of great beaches such as Sapphire Beach and Lindquist Beach. This section of bays and golden sands offers some ritzy, expensive properties that compete with the mega-resorts of the South Coast, but smaller, less-expensive gems also exist. The little settlement at **Red Hook** is a bustling community with raffish charm and lots of loud bars and affordable eateries. It is also the departure point for ferries to St. John.

THE NORTH COAST

The renowned beach at **Magens Bay,** celebrated as one of the finest strips of sands in the Caribbean, lies on the lush North Coast. Be aware, though, that the beach is often overrun with visitors, especially when cruise-ship arrivals are heavy. The North Coast has few buildings and not much traffic, making it a destination for those who'd like to dine in a less heavily visited area of the island. The vistas here are among the most panoramic on the island, though traveling the roads is like a ride on a roller coaster—the roads have no shoulders and are especially scary for those not familiar with driving on the left. A lot of the northwest coast, especially at Botany Bay, Bordeaux Bay, and Santa Maria Bay, isn't linked to any roads.

Getting Around

BY CAR

St. Thomas has many leading North American **car-rental firms** at the airport, and competition is stiff. Before you go, compare the rates of the "big three": **Avis** (© **800/331-1212** or 340/774-1468; www.avis.com), **Budget** (© **800/626-4516**

○ In 1825, the last pirate was hanged at St. Thomas.

○ St. Thomas was a base for blockade runners and privateers sympathetic to the Confederate cause in the Civil War.

○ The U.S. Senate in 1870 rejected a treaty signed with Denmark agreeing to pay $7.5 million for the U.S. Virgins.

○ The U.S. Virgin Islanders celebrate more holidays than anywhere else in the U.S., 23 in all.

○ Charlotte Amalie was named after a queen of Denmark.

○ A Jewish synagogue in Charlotte Amalie is the oldest in the U.S., and still maintains its sand floors.

○ Locally made products from St. Thomas are not taxable.

○ For centuries, St. Thomas had the largest slave auctions in the Caribbean Basin.

or 340/776-5774; www.budgetstt.com), and **Hertz** (© **800/654-3131** or 340/774-1879; www.hertz.com). You can often save money by renting from a local agency, although vehicles sometimes aren't as well-maintained. Try **Dependable Car Rental,** 3901 B Altona, Welgunst, behind the Bank of Nova Scotia and the Medical Arts Complex (© **800/522-3076** or 340/774-2253; www.dependablecar.com), which will pick up renters at the airport or their hotel; or the aptly named **Discount Car Rental,** 14 Harwood Hwy., outside the airport on the main highway (© **877/478-2833** or 340/776-4858; www.discountcar.vi), which grants drivers a 12% discount on rivals' rates. *Note:* There is no tax on car rentals in the Virgin Islands.

DRIVING RULES *Always drive on the left.* The speed limit is 20 mph in town, 35 mph outside town. Remember, there is often a lot of traffic on the roads going east out of Charlotte Amalie. Take extra caution when driving in St. Thomas, especially at night. Many roads are narrow, curvy, and poorly lit.

PARKING Because Charlotte Amalie is a labyrinth of congested one-way streets, don't try to drive within town looking for a parking spot. If you can't find a place to park along the Waterfront (free), go to the sprawling lot to the east of Fort Christian, across from the Legislature Building. Parking fees are nominal here, and you can park your car and walk northwest toward Emancipation Park, or along the Waterfront, until you reach the shops and attractions.

BY TAXI

Taxis are unmetered, but fares are controlled and widely posted; however, we still recommend that you negotiate a fare (usually per person) with the driver before you get into the car. A typical fare from Charlotte Amalie to Sapphire Beach is $13 per person; to the East End, it's about $25 per person. Surcharges, one-third of the price of the excursion, are added after midnight. You'll pay $2 to $4 per bag for luggage. You can easily hail a taxi in Charlotte Amalie, although it's not so easy throughout the island. Reason? The taxis are all waiting for cruise passengers at the dock in Charlotte Amalie. You will more than likely have to call a taxi to pick you up while out on the island. Of course, your hotel can always call one for you. For 24-hour radio-dispatch taxi service, call © **340/774-7457.** If you want to hire a taxi and a driver (who just may be a great tour guide) for a day, expect to pay about $40 per person for 2 hours of sightseeing in a shared car, or $55 to $80 per hour for two to four people.

Taxi vans transport 8 to 12 passengers to multiple destinations on the island. It's cheaper to take a van instead of a taxi if you're going between your hotel and the airport. The cost for luggage ranges from $1 to $2 per bag. Call ☏ **340/774-7457** to order a taxi van.

BY BUS

Buses, called **Vitrans,** leave from street-side stops in the center of Charlotte Amalie, fanning out east and west along all of the most important highways. They run between 5:30am and 9pm daily, but waits can be very long and this is a difficult way to get about. A ride within Charlotte Amalie is 75¢; a ride to anywhere else is $1. The Fortuna buses are run by Vitrans and have no set schedule. A ride from Charlotte Amalie to Brewers Bay or Lindbergh Beach is $6 to $8 per person. For schedule and bus-stop information, call ☏ **340/774-5678** or www.vinow.com.

ON FOOT

Trust us: This is the *only* way to explore the heart of Charlotte Amalie. All the major attractions and main stores are within easy walking distance. However, other island attractions, like Coral World and Magens Bay, require you to take a bus or taxi.

[FastFACTS] ST. THOMAS

Banks Several major U.S. banks are represented on St. Thomas, including **First-Bank,** 11A Curaçao Gade, Charlotte Amalie (☏ **340/775-7777**). Most island banks are open Monday to Thursday 8:30am to 3pm, and Friday 8:30am to 4pm. The banks are your only option if you need to exchange currency. More than 50 ATMs are available on the island.

Bookstores Dockside Bookshop, Havensight Mall, Charlotte Amalie (☏ **340/774-4937**), where the cruise ships dock, sells books, cards, maps, and board games.

Business Hours Typical business and store hours are Monday to Friday 9am to 5pm and Saturday 9am to 1pm. Some shops open Sunday for cruise-ship arrivals. Bars are usually open daily 11am to midnight

or 1am, although some hot spots stay open later.

Dentists The **Smile Center** (☏ **340/775-9110**) is a member of the American Dental Association and is also linked with various specialists. Call for information or an appointment.

Doctors Roy Lester Schneider Hospital, 9048 Sugar Estate, Charlotte Amalie (☏ **340/776-8311;** www.rlshospital.org), provides services for locals and visitors.

Drugstores Go to **Drug Farm,** 2–4 Ninth St., Charlotte Amalie (☏ **340/776-7098**), or **Havensight Pharmacy,** Havensight Mall, Building 4, Charlotte Amalie (☏ **340/776-1235**).

Emergencies For the police, call ☏ **911;** ambulance, **911;** fire, **921.**

Hospitals The **Roy Lester Schneider Hospital** is at 9048 Sugar Estate,

Charlotte Amalie (☏ **340/776-8311**).

Hot Lines Call the **police** at ☏ **911** in case of emergency. If you have or witness a boating mishap, call the **U.S. Coast Guard Rescue** (☏ **787/729-6800**), which operates out of San Juan, Puerto Rico. Scuba divers should note the number of a **decompression chamber** (☏ **340/776-8311**) at the Roy Schneider Community Hospital on St. Thomas.

Internet The best cyber-cafe is **Beans, Bytes, and Websites** at the Royal Dane Mall (☏ **340/777-7089;** www.beansbytesandweb sites.com), in the center of Charlotte Amalie. It is open Monday to Saturday 7am to 4pm, charging 15¢ a minute with a $2 minimum. Not only do you face a myriad of options for your computer needs, but you can

54

enjoy rich coffee, tropical juices, fruit smoothies, and pastries as well.

Laundry & Dry Cleaning The major hotels provide laundry service, but it's more expensive than a Laundromat. For dry cleaning, go to **One-Hour Martinizing,** Barbel Plaza, Charlotte Amalie (✆ **340/774-5452**).

Mail Postage rates are the same as on the U.S. mainland: 28¢ for a postcard and 44¢ for a letter to U.S. addresses. For international mail, a first-class letter of up to 1 ounce costs 98¢ (75¢ to Canada and 79¢ to Mexico); a first-class postcard costs the same as a letter.

Maps See "Visitor Information," earlier in this chapter.

Newspapers & Magazines Copies of U.S. mainland newspapers, such as the *New York Times, USA Today,* and the *Miami Herald,* arrive daily in St. Thomas and are sold at hotels and newsstands. The latest copies of *Time* and *Newsweek* are also for sale. *St. Thomas Daily News*

covers local, national, and international events. *Virgin Islands Playground* and *St. Thomas This Week,* both of which are packed with visitor information, are distributed free on the island.

Police The main police headquarters is at the **Alexander A. Farrelly Justice Center,** 8172 Sub Base, Charlotte Amalie (✆ **340/774-2211**).

Post Office The main post office is at 9846 Estate Thomas, Charlotte Amalie (✆ **340/774-1950**), and is open Monday to Friday 7:30am to 5pm and Saturday 7:30am to noon.

Safety St. Thomas has an unusually high crime rate, particularly in Charlotte Amalie. Don't wander around town at night, particularly on Back Street. Single women should avoid frequenting Charlotte Amalie's bars alone at night. Guard your valuables. Store them in hotel safes if possible, and make sure you keep your doors and windows shut at night.

Taxes The only local tax is an 8% surcharge added to all hotel rates.

Telephone All island phone numbers have seven digits. It is not necessary to use the 340 area code when dialing within St. Thomas. Numbers for all three islands, including St. John and St. Croix, are found in the U.S. Virgin Islands phone book.

Tipping Tip as you would on the U.S. mainland—15% to 20% or so on a restaurant check, and a few dollars a day for housekeeping services in a hotel.

Toilets You'll find public toilets at beaches and at the airport, but they are limited in town. Most visitors use the facilities of a bar or restaurant.

Transit Information Call ✆ **340/774-7457** to order a taxi 24 hours a day. Call ✆ **340/774-5100** for airport information and ✆ **340/776-6282** for information about ferry departures for St. John.

Weather For emergency (hurricane and disaster) weather reports, call **Vietema** at ✆ **340/774-2244.**

WHERE TO STAY

Nearly every beach on St. Thomas has its own hotel, and the island also has more quaint inns than any other place in the Caribbean. The choice of hotels on St. Thomas divides almost evenly between places to stay in Charlotte Amalie, and grand resorts along the East End that front the fabulous beaches. There are advantages and disadvantages to both, and your choice becomes a matter of personal taste.

Say you're in St. Thomas for shopping and you want to be near the best stores, the widest choice of restaurants and bars, and nearly all the historic attractions. Chances are you'll elect to stay in Charlotte Amalie. And if you're looking for budget accommodations, or a choice of moderately priced inns, you'll need to be in or near Charlotte Amalie. The downside to staying here is that you'll have to take a shuttle over to

St. Thomas Hotels at a Glance

	Wheelchair access	A/C in bedrooms	Child-care facilities	Children are welcome	Convention facilities	Credit cards accepted	Directly beside beach	Health club
At Home in the Tropics		✓				✓		
Bellavista Bed & Breakfast		✓				✓		
Best Western Carib Beach Resort	✓	✓		✓	✓	✓	✓	
Best Western Emerald Beach Resort		✓		✓		✓	✓	✓
Bolongo Bay Beach Resort	✓	✓	✓	✓	✓	✓	✓	✓
Bunker Hill Hotel		✓		✓		✓		✓
The Crystal Palace		✓		✓		✓		
Elysian Beach Resort		✓		✓	✓	✓	✓	✓
Frenchman's Reef & Morning Star Marriott Beach Resort	✓	✓	✓	✓	✓	✓	✓	✓
Galleon House		✓		✓		✓		
The Green Iguana		✓				✓		
Hotel 1829		✓				✓		
Island Beachcomber Hotel		✓		✓		✓		
Mafolie Hotel		✓		✓		✓		
Pavilions and Pools	✓	✓		✓		✓	✓	
Point Pleasant Resort	✓	✓		✓		✓		
The Ritz-Carlton, St. Thomas	✓	✓	✓	✓	✓	✓	✓	✓
Secret Harbour Beach Resort	✓	✓	✓	✓		✓	✓	✓
Villa Blanca		✓		✓		✓		
Villa Santana						✓		
Windward Passage Hotel		✓				✓		✓
Wyndham Sugar Bay Resort & Spa	✓	✓	✓	✓	✓	✓	✓	✓

a good beach, a ride of no more than 10 to 15 minutes from most Charlotte Amalie properties. If you want the isolation of a resort along with proximity to Charlotte Amalie, with all the attractions and shops, you can book into the Marriott property directly to the east of Charlotte Amalie at Flamboyant Point.

If your dream is to arrive in St. Thomas and anchor yourself directly on a beach, then the East End is your best bet. All the properties here are grand, luxurious resorts with many attractions, including watersports and nightlife. The downside is that if you don't want to take expensive transportation, or drive along narrow, dark, and unfamiliar roads at night, you'll be resort-bound for the evening, as commutes to some of the island's best restaurants are difficult after sunset. You'll also have to spend time and money if you want to get into Charlotte Amalie for shopping. Almost without exception, the East End beachfront resorts are very expensive. In spite of the high

Golf course nearby	Live entertainment	Marina facilities	Restaurant and/or bar	Spa facilities	Swimming pool	Tennis courts	TV in bedroom	Watersports
					✓			
					✓		✓	
✓		✓		✓			✓	
✓		✓		✓	✓	✓	✓	✓
✓	✓	✓	✓	✓	✓	✓	✓	✓
		✓	✓					✓
						✓		
✓		✓		✓	✓	✓	✓	
✓		✓	✓	✓	✓	✓	✓	
				✓		✓	✓	
					✓			
		✓		✓		✓		
		✓					✓	
		✓		✓		✓		
		✓		✓		✓	✓	
	✓		✓		✓	✓	✓	✓
✓		✓	✓	✓	✓	✓	✓	
		✓		✓	✓	✓	✓	
		✓		✓	✓			
				✓		✓		
					✓		✓	
		✓	✓	✓	✓	✓	✓	

costs, these hotels attract customers who want the decadent resort life that is impossible to find at the smaller inns of Charlotte Amalie.

Hotels in the Virgin Islands slash their prices in summer by 20% to 60%. Unless otherwise noted, the rates listed below *do not* include the 8% government tax.

In Charlotte Amalie
EXPENSIVE
Villa Santana ★   Locals call this all-suite property "The General's Place." It was originally built by General Antonio Lopez de Santa Anna of Mexico in the 1850s. Offering a panoramic view of Charlotte Amalie and the St. Thomas harbor, this villa is more luxurious than its closest competitor, **Villa Blanca** (which is also good; p. 64). The shopping district in Charlotte Amalie is just a 5-minute walk away;

renting A CONDO, APARTMENT, OR VILLA

For those who don't care for the resort or hotel life, renting a condo, apartment, or villa is an excellent option. Sometimes you can get a great deal. We've found that **Calypso Realty** (© **800/ 747-4858** or 340/774-1620; www. calypsorealty.com) has the best offers, especially on rentals from April to mid-December. A condo goes for $1,200 to $4,000 per week, with a 7-day minimum stay.

Another source to check is **McLaughlin Anderson Luxury Caribbean Villas** (© **800/537-6246** or 340/776-0635; www.mclaughlinanderson.com), which has rentals not only on St. Thomas but also on St. John, St. Croix, and various other Caribbean isles. A two-bedroom villa begins at $2,000 per week in winter, with off-season rates beginning at $1,449.

You can also contact **Paradise Properties** (© **800/524-2038** or 340/775-0111; www.paradisepropertiesvi. com), which currently represents five condo complexes. Rental units range from studio apartments to two-bedroom villas suitable for up to eight people; each has a fully equipped kitchen. A minimum stay of 3 days is required in any season, and 7 nights are required around Christmas. The prices range from $225 to $400 per day in winter and from $135 to $260 per day in the off season.

Antilles Resorts (© **800/874-7897** or 340/775-6100; www.antillesresorts. com) is a hit among habitual islandgoers, enjoying a repeat business of some 60%. Among other offerings, it rents condo suites that are a short walk from the beach and feature private balconies with ocean views. These suites start at $250 a night in winter, reduced to $185 a night in summer.

Magens Bay Beach is a 15-minute drive north. Each guest room is located in a different part of the villa. You might go for La Mansion, the former library; La Casa de Piedra, a former bedroom; or La Torre, the old pump house, which has been converted into a modern lookout tower. Most of the general's personal effects were looted over the years, but guests can still sleep in his four-poster Mahogany bed where he bedded his many mistresses. The Mexican-style decor features clay tiles, rattan furniture, and stonework. There is also a sun deck and small garden with hibiscus and bougainvillea.

2602 Bjerre Gade, No. 2D, Denmark Hill, Charlotte Amalie, St. Thomas, U.S.V.I. 00802. www.villasantana. com. ©/fax **340/776-1311.** 6 units. Winter $234 suite for 2; off season $174 suite for 2. AE, MC, V. **Amenities:** Outdoor pool. *In room:* Ceiling fan, TV, kitchen, Wi-Fi (free).

Windward Passage Hotel ★ This hotel was created as a Holiday Inn, designed around a courtyard with nightly entertainment. Even though its charm is not immediately apparent, this well-managed and upgraded hotel enjoys the highest number of repeat guests in St. Thomas. It is favored by business travelers and sports teams, as many of its rooms with balconies overlook the adjacent Emile Griffith Park, a venue for many baseball games. Rooms are well-furnished and contemporary. You might opt for the oceanfront rooms, even though they have more noise from traffic, because you get a panoramic sweep of the cruise ships in harbor. There is a shuttle to Magens Bay Beach.

Veterans Dr., P.O. Box 640, St. Thomas, U.S.V.I. 00804. www.windwardpassage.com. © **888/465-4239** or 340/774-5200. Fax 340/774-1231. 151 units. Winter $275–$325 double, $300–$375 suite; summer

St. Thomas Hotels

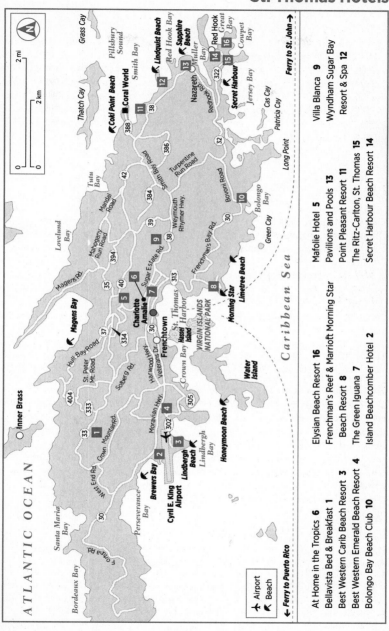

At Home in the Tropics **6**
Bellavista Bed & Breakfast **1**
Best Western Carib Beach Resort **3**
Best Western Emerald Beach Resort **4**
Bolongo Bay Beach Club **10**

Elysian Beach Resort **16**
Frenchman's Reef & Marriott Morning Star
   Beach Resort **8**
The Green Iguana **7**
Island Beachcomber Hotel **2**

Mafolie Hotel **5**
Pavilions and Pools **13**
Point Pleasant Resort **11**
The Ritz-Carlton, St. Thomas **15**
Secret Harbour Beach Resort **14**

Villa Blanca **9**
Wyndham Sugar Bay
   Resort & Spa **12**

$172–$223 double, $225–$265 suite. AE, DC, MC, V. **Amenities:** Restaurant; bar; babysitting; off-site health club ($25 per day); watersports equipment/rentals. *In room:* A/C, TV, fridge, hair dryer, Wi-Fi (free).

MODERATE

At Home in the Tropics ★ 💼   This is one of the best-run and most comfortable B&Bs in Charlotte Amalie. Because it is a traditional West Indian house that is only one room deep, each accommodation opens onto a panoramic view of Charlotte Amalie harbor. The structure dates from 1803, when it was the barracks for the personal guard of the Danish governor. Handsomely restored, the bedrooms are attractively furnished in an airy Caribbean motif. The setting is in the midst of many of the island's elegant mansions and gardens. Guests are given their own keys to the locked gate for the courtyard property. The property is small and the swimming pool is deep, so kids younger than 13 are discouraged.

Blackbeard's Hill, Charlotte Amalie, St. Thomas, U.S.V.I. 00804. www.athomeinthetropics.com. © **340/777-9857.** Fax 340/774-3890. Winter $225–$245 double; off season $205–$225 double. Rates include breakfast. AE, MC, V. **Amenities:** Outdoor swimming pool. *In room:* A/C, ceiling fan, hair dryer, Wi-Fi (free).

Bellavista Bed & Breakfast ★★ 💼   This B&B is about as luxurious as it gets in Charlotte Amalie. Nestled on Denmark Hill, the restored island estate overlooks Charlotte Amalie and its historic harbor. It is only a 5-minute walk into town or a 7-minute drive to the premiere beach of Magens Bay. The romantic bedrooms have an architectural charm with an eclectic tropical decor, and have names such as Bambooshay or J'ouvert Gardens. The former master bedroom, for example, is decorated with jewel-toned fabrics and bamboo accents, the bed adorned with a demi-canopy trimmed in mosquito netting. The choice rooms open onto private balconies with views.

2713 Murphy Gade 12-14, St. Thomas U.S.V.I. 00802. www.bellavista-bnb.com. © **888/333-3063** or 340/714-5706. 4 units. Winter $195–$245 double; summer $175–$235 double. Rates include breakfast. MC, V. **Amenities:** Concierge; outdoor pool. *In room:* A/C, TV, ceiling fan, fridge, hair dryer, Wi-Fi (free).

INEXPENSIVE

Bunker Hill Hotel   The "bunk" in the name Bunker Hill is apt. This affordable choice is suggested only if the other recommended inexpensive hotels are fully booked, as is often the case. Bunker Hill Hotel is not in the safest district in St. Thomas, so caution is advised, especially at night. But this centrally located lodge is suitable for anyone who will sacrifice some comfort (you'll have to put up with some street noise) for their budget's sake. Four rooms have balconies, and some offer a view of the lights of Charlotte Amalie and the sea. The rooms are small, with simple furnishings. One room has a microwave and sink, giving it a slight advantage over the others.

2307 Commandant Gade, Charlotte Amalie, St. Thomas, U.S.V.I. 00802. © **340/774-8056.** Fax 340/774-3172. www.bunkerhillhotel.com. 20 units. Winter $99–$125 double; off season $79–$105 double. Rates include continental breakfast. Children 5 and under stay free in parent's room. AE, MC, V. **Amenities:** 2 pools (outdoor); Wi-Fi (free in lobby). *In room:* A/C, TV, fridge (in some).

The Crystal Palace   At this B&B you get the feeling of living in someone's grand old private home. It occupies a structure that was rebuilt in 1932 on early-19th-century foundations after a series of fires and hurricanes that left other parts of the island homeless. Today, its owner is the kindly but crusty Ronnie Lockhart, president of the St. Thomas & St. John Friends of Denmark Society, Inc., who showcases the

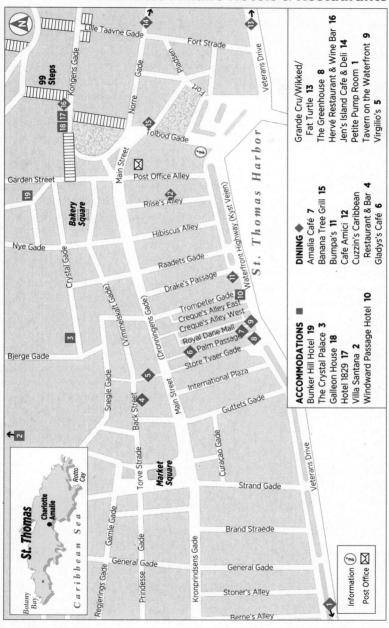

Charlotte Amalie Hotels & Restaurants

ACCOMMODATIONS ■

Bunker Hill Hotel **19**
The Crystal Palace **3**
Galleon House **18**
Hotel 1829 **17**
Villa Santana **2**
Windward Passage Hotel **10**

DINING ◆

Amalia Café **7**
Banana Tree Grill **15**
Bumpa's **11**
Cafe Amici **12**
Cuzzin's Caribbean
  Restaurant & Bar **4**
Gladys's Café **6**
Grande Cru/Wikked/
  Fat Turtle **13**
The Greenhouse **8**
Hervé Restaurant & Wine Bar **16**
Jen's Island Cafe & Deli **14**
Petite Pump Room **1**
Tavern on the Waterfront **9**
Virgilio's **5**

Information ⓘ
Post Office ☒

99 Steps

Lille Taavne Gade
Fort Strade
Kongens Gade
Norre Gade
Fort
Papsen
Veterans Drive

Garden Street
Post Office Alley
Main Street
Tolbod Gade
Bakery Square
Riise's Alley
Hibiscus Alley
Nye Gade
Raadets Gade
Crystal Gade
Drake's Passage
Trompeter Gade
Creque's Alley East
Creque's Alley West
Royal Dane Mall
Palm Passage
Store Tvaer Gade
Bjerge Gade
International Plaza
Snegle Gade
(Vimmelskaft Gade)
(Dronningens Gade)
Guttets Gade
Back Street
Main Street
Curaçao Gade
Torve Strade
Market Square
Strand Gade
Ganle Gade
Brand Straede
General Gade
Gade
General Gade
Prindesse
Regjerings Gade
Kronprindsens Gade
Stoner's Alley
Berne's Alley
Veterans Drive
Waterfront Highway (Kyst Vejen)

St. Thomas Harbor

St. Thomas
Charlotte Amalie
Botany Bay
Rotto Cay
Caribbean Sea

home he was raised in as a genuinely historical but somewhat battered mansion. There's a stateliness to this elegant antique building with its treasure trove of West Indian relics, including tray ceilings, hardwood floors, hand-painted tiles, and wrought-iron gates. Views from the covered balconies sweep out over the city and the harbor. Furnishings include a mixture of the modern, prosaic, and serviceable and the genuinely antique, scattered rather formally amid souvenirs from the Lockhart family of long ago. Only two of the building's five accommodations contain private bathrooms—the others are shared facilities in the corridors.

12 Crystal Gade, Synagogue Hill, St. Thomas, U.S.V.I. 00802. www.crystalpalaceusvi.com. ✆ **866/502-2277** or 340/777-2277. 4 units, 2 with bathrooms. Winter $119 double without bathroom, $149 double with bathroom; off season $99 double without bathroom, $119 double with bathroom. Rates include breakfast. AE, DISC, MC, V. *In room:* A/C, TV, no phone, Wi-Fi (free).

Galleon House At the east end of Main Street, about a block from the main shopping area, Galleon House is accessible via a difficult climb, especially in sweltering heat. Nevertheless, its rates are among the most competitive in town. Although it may not be for everyone, there is a laid-back, casual atmosphere and friendly welcome here that pleases many visitors on a budget. The small rooms, located in scattered hillside buildings, each have a ceiling fan and so-so air-conditioning, plus a cramped bathroom. If you want character, check into the older rooms in the main building. More spacious units with better views lie up the hill in a pair of dull apartment buildings. Breakfast is served on a veranda overlooking the harbor, and Magens Bay Beach is 15 minutes by car or taxi from the hotel. If you check in, say hi to the iguanas for us.

Government Hill (P.O. Box 6577), Charlotte Amalie, St. Thomas, U.S.V.I. 00804. www.galleonhouse.com. ✆ **800/524-2052** or 340/774-6952. Fax 340/774-6952. 13 units, 11 with bathrooms. Winter $85 double without bathroom, $109–$159 double with bathroom; off season $75 double without bathroom, $89–$125 double with bathroom. Rates include full breakfast. AE, MC, V. **Amenities:** Pool (outdoor); snorkeling equipment. *In room:* A/C, ceiling fan, TV, Wi-Fi ($5 per hr.).

Hotel 1829 ★ 🦀 Stylish, yet affordable, this national historic site is one of the leading small hotels in the Caribbean. It was designed in a Spanish motif, with French grillwork, Danish bricks, and sturdy Dutch doors. Danish and African labor completed the structure in 1829 (hence the name), and since then it has entertained the likes of Edna St. Vincent Millay and Mikhail Baryshnikov. The place stands right in the heart of town, on a hillside 3 minutes from Government House. Magens Bay Beach is about a 10-minute drive. It's a bit of a climb to the top of this multitiered structure—there are many steps, but no elevator. Amid a cascade of flowering bougainvillea are the upper rooms, which overlook a central courtyard with a miniature pool. The rooms in the main house are well designed and attractive, and most face the water. All have wood beams and stone walls. The smallest units, in the former slave quarters, are the least comfortable. Children 11 and under aren't really encouraged here.

Kongens Gade (P.O. Box 1567), Charlotte Amalie, St. Thomas, U.S.V.I. 00804. www.hotel1829.com. ✆ **800/524-2002** or 340/776-1829. Fax 340/776-4313. 14 units. Winter $105–$155 double, from $190 suite; off season $80–$125 double, from $145 suite. Rates include continental breakfast. DISC, MC, V. **Amenities:** Bar; small outdoor pool. *In room:* A/C, TV, fridge, hair dryer, no phone, Wi-Fi (free).

West of Charlotte Amalie

EXPENSIVE

Best Western Emerald Beach Resort ★ ☺ Its big draw? This miniresort is on a white-sand beach that is one of the best in St. Thomas. Its major drawback? It lies just across from the busy airport, 2 miles to the west of Charlotte Amalie, to which it is linked by free shuttle service. Emerald Beach attracts businesspeople (for its location) and families (for its resort-like feel) alike. All of the tastefully furnished rooms face the sands, and each unit opens onto its own patio or oceanfront balcony. The Sunday brunch here is one of the best in the area.

8070 Lindbergh Bay, St. Thomas, U.S.V.I. 00802. www.emeraldbeach.com. ✆ **800/233-4936** in the U.S., or 340/777-8800. Fax 340/776-3426. 90 units. Winter $309 double; off season $159 double. Children 11 and under stay free in parent's room. AE, DC, DISC, MC, V. **Amenities:** Restaurant; bar; exercise center; Internet (free in lobby); limited watersports equipment/rentals; tennis court (lit). *In room:* A/C, TV, fridge, hair dryer.

MODERATE

Best Western Carib Beach Resort This Best Western is recommended for its location (only about a 3-min. walk from the good beach at Lindbergh Bay) and its affordable oceanview rooms with private terraces. It's not the fanciest place on the island, and it's not as good as Emerald Beach Resort (see review above), although the two properties are only a 5-minute walk apart and guests can use the facilities there. (A free shuttle runs between here and Emerald Beach.) Carib Beach is a favorite with business travelers as well as some vacationers. The accommodations are housed in pink-and-blue concrete structures, plus five cottages closer to the sea. The bedrooms are comfortable, but not large. Room nos. 207 through 216 are the best. Ask for one of the "Sea Wing" bedrooms, which open onto the ocean.

70-C Lindbergh Bay, St. Thomas, U.S.V.I. 00801. www.caribbeachresort.com. ✆ **800/792-2742** in the U.S., or 340/774-2525. Fax 340/777-4131. 51 units. Winter $180–$210 double; off season $120–$150 double. Children 12 and under stay free in parent's room. AE, DC, DISC, MC, V. **Amenities:** Restaurant; bar; pool (outdoor). *In room:* A/C, TV, fridge, Wi-Fi (free).

Island Beachcomber Hotel ✍ When this hotel opened back in 1956 it was the first beachfront hotel in St. Thomas. In those days, everyone from Cecil B. DeMille to Vivian Vance (Ethel Mertz from "I Love Lucy") checked in. Much renovated and expanded over the years, it has kept up with the times. This rather standard inn near the airport is known for its affordable rates and its beautiful location near one of the island's best sandy beaches, on Lindbergh Bay. Many guests are 1-nighters, staying over between yacht charters. A beach-party atmosphere prevails here, and there's a Tahitian aura to the place, created by tropical foliage, bird cages, bridges, and thatched umbrellas. The well-maintained rooms are medium in size, with louvered doors and jalousies, excellent lighting, and ceiling fans, plus a patio or porch. Accommodations face either the garden or the beach; those opening onto the water are grabbed up first, so if you're interested, call well ahead.

8071 Lindbergh Beach Rd., Lindbergh Bay, St. Thomas, U.S.V.I. 00802. www.islandbeachcomber.net. ✆ **340/774-5250.** Fax 340/774-5615. 48 units. Winter $199–$225 double; off season $130–$169 double. Extra person $15. AE, DC, DISC, MC, V. **Amenities:** Restaurant; bar. *In room:* A/C, ceiling fan, TV, fridge, hair dyer, Wi-Fi (free).

East of Charlotte Amalie

MODERATE

The Green Iguana ★ ✍ Crowning Blackbeard's Hill, in the center of Charlotte Amalie, this is one of the best run inns on the island. There's a remnant within the construction from a much older building, but much of what you'll see today is an unpretentious concrete structure from the 1970s and 1980s. Bedrooms have panoramic views of the harbor, the constantly arriving cruise ships, and the other Virgin

Islands. The little inn lies only a 5-minute walk from the town's shops, restaurants, and bars; and Magens Beach is a 10-minute drive over the hill. Bedrooms are midsize and done in a tropical motif with wicker.

37-B Blackbeard's Hill, Charlotte Amalie, St. Thomas, U.S.V.I. 00802. www.thegreeniguana.com. *☎* **800/484-8634** or 340/776-7654. Fax 340/777-4312. 9 units. Winter $140–$170 double; off season $125 double. AE, MC, V. *In room:* A/C, ceiling fan, hair dryer, kitchenette, Wi-Fi (free).

Mafolie Hotel ★ ✿ A unique gem among many bland cookie-cutter hotels, this top value guesthouse is perched 800 feet above Charlotte Amalie's harbor. Its proprietor, Michael Sigler, and his wife, Helga, provide very friendly service at the hotel, while their daughter Natasha and son-in-law AJ take care of the superb restaurant, where you can feast on tender Angus steaks, succulent pastas, and freshly caught seafood dishes. Each room is unique and decorated with personal touches. There is a free shuttle to the beach.

7091 Estate Mafolie, Mafolie Hill, Charlotte Amalie, St. Thomas, U.S.V.I. 00802. www.mafolie.com. *☎* **800/225-7035** or 340/774-2790. Fax 340/774-4091. 22 units. Winter $134–$154 double, $164 junior suite; off season $108–$124 double, $144 junior suite. Rates include continental breakfast. Up to 2 children 12 and under stay free in parent's room. Extra person $15. AE, MC, V. **Amenities:** Restaurant; bar; concierge. *In room:* A/C, TV, fridge, Wi-Fi (free).

Villa Blanca ★ ✿ This hotel, located on a lush hilltop 1½ miles east of Charlotte Amalie, offers the most panoramic views on the island, looking out over the harbor and the green rolling hills. The grounds are beautifully landscaped, with such flowering plants and shrubs as oleander, firecracker, hibiscus, spider lily, yellow trumpet, and more. Once the home of owner Blanca Terrasa Smith, today, a homey and caring ambience prevails. Each room has air-conditioning, a well-equipped kitchenette, a good bed with a firm mattress, and a private balcony or terrace with sweeping views either eastward to St. John or westward to the harbor of Charlotte Amalie and Puerto Rico. While there's no restaurant, the rates include a light continental breakfast, and each room has a kitchenette, so you can easily prepare modest meals. On the premises are a freshwater pool and a large covered patio where you can enjoy the sunset. The closest beach is Morningstar Bay, about 4 miles away.

4 Raphune Hill, Rte. 38, Charlotte Amalie, St. Thomas, U.S.V.I. 00801. www.villablancahotel.com. *☎* **800/231-0034** or 340/776-0749. Fax 340/779-2661. 14 units. Winter $135–$155 double; off season $95–$105 double. Rates include continental breakfast. Children 9 and under stay free in parent's room. AE, DISC, MC, V. **Amenities:** Pool (outdoor); Wi-Fi (free in lobby). *In room:* A/C, ceiling fan, TV, kitchenette.

The South Coast

VERY EXPENSIVE

Frenchman's Reef & Morning Star Marriott Beach Resort ★★★ If you like a grand hotel, with lots of facilities, entertainment, and dining choices, this resort is for you. Guests have compared its nonstop activities to sailing the Caribbean on a mammoth cruise ship. Lying 3 miles east of Charlotte Amalie on the south shore, this is the largest hotel in the U.S. Virgin Islands; but since the opening of the Ritz-Carlton, it is no longer the most plush or most glamorous. In 2005, the two separate parts of this hotel, Frenchman's Reef and Morning Star, were officially conglomerated into one mega-resort with an excellent location on a bluff overlooking both the harbor and the Caribbean.

This is a full-service, American-style resort. Facilities devoted to the good life are everywhere: To reach the secluded beach, for example, you take a glass-enclosed elevator. The accommodations here have all you'll need for comfort, including generally spacious bathrooms. The bedrooms at Frenchman's Reef are traditionally furnished and quite comfortable, while those at the Morning Star are more luxurious. All units have private balconies with sea views.

There is enough variety in dining to keep you on the premises at night, and the cuisine has become better and better. In general, we prefer the seafood to the frozen meat imported from the U.S. mainland. The complex boasts the hip **Havana Blue** (p. 78), a cocktail/cigar lounge with a truly inspired menu.

No. 5 Estate Bakkeroe, Flamboyant Point (P.O. Box 7100), St. Thomas, U.S.V.I. 00801. www.marriott.com. ⓒ **888/236-2427** or 340/776-8500. Fax 340/715-6193. 478 units. Winter $360–$745 double, from $760 suite; off season $300–$630 double, from $600 suite. Children 12 and under stay free in parent's room. AE, DC, DISC, MC, V. **Amenities:** 6 restaurants; 3 bars; babysitting; health club and spa; room service; 2 tennis courts (lit); watersports equipment/rentals. *In room:* A/C, TV, fridge, hair dryer, Wi-Fi ($7 per day).

The Ritz-Carlton, St. Thomas ★★★ ☺   This resort is as posh as it gets on St. Thomas. It's great for either a honeymoon or an off-the-record weekend (the staff is very discreet). Fronted by white-sand beaches, the Ritz-Carlton stands on 30 acres of oceanfront at the island's southeastern tip, 4 miles from Charlotte Amalie. The hotel's architecture evokes a *palazzo* in Venice, as befitting of a Ritz property, and is set amid landscaped gardens, with bubbling fountains and hidden courtyards evoking the feel of a truly sprawling villa.

Also befitting of the Ritz is the special, key-activated Club Lounge featuring 75 well-appointed units, each with views of the Caribbean and a private balcony. Some of the rooms also contain separate bathtubs and "rain-shower stalls." The resort features an extensive spa with 11 luxurious treatment rooms and more open-air cabanas. Of the restaurants, **Bleuwater** (p. 77) is highly recommended and has the best chef on the island; the **Great Bay Lounge** (p. 79) is a chic place for cocktails, tapas, and sushi. The Ritz Kids program is one of the best on the island, with such features as snorkeling and scuba diving. Finally, the property has its own scuba-diving school and private yacht, readily available for guests.

6900 Great Bay, St. Thomas, U.S.V.I. 00802. www.ritzcarlton.com. ⓒ **800/241-3333** or 340/775-3333. Fax 340/775-4444. 180 units. Winter $660–$880 double, from $1,290 suite; off season $380–$570 double, from $700 suite. AE, DC, DISC, MC, V. **Amenities:** 4 restaurants; 3 bars; babysitting; children's programs; concierge; health club and spa; 2 pools (outdoor); room service; 2 tennis courts (lit); watersports equipment/rentals. *In room:* A/C, TV, Internet (free), minibar.

EXPENSIVE

Bolongo Bay Beach Resort ★ ☺   This family-run resort is an unpretentious, barefooted-welcome kind of place. You'll find a half-moon-shaped white-sand beach and a cluster of pink two- and three-story buildings, plus some motel-like units closer to the sands. There's also a social center consisting of a smallish pool and a beachfront bar, replete with palm fronds. It's a relatively small property, but it offers all the facilities of a big resort. Many guests check in on the European Plan, which includes watersports activities and even a scuba-diving lesson; others opt for all-inclusive plans that include all meals, drinks, a sailboat excursion to St. John, and use of scuba equipment. Rooms are simple, summery, and filled with unremarkable but comfortable furniture. Each unit has a balcony or patio, a refrigerator, and one king-size or two double beds. Some of the units on the beach come with kitchenettes; and the apartment-style condos, in a three-story building, have full kitchens.

7150 Bolongo, St. Thomas, U.S.V.I. 00802. www.bolongobay.com. © **800/524-4746** or 340/775-1800. Fax 340/775-3208. 65 units. Winter $210–$335 double; off season $185–$310 double. Ask about other packages and various meal plans. AE, MC, V. **Amenities:** 2 restaurants, including Iggies Beach Bar & Grill (p. 76); 2 bars; babysitting; children's programs (ages 4–12); exercise room; 2 pools (outdoor); 2 tennis courts (lit); watersports equipment/rentals; Wi-Fi by pool (free). *In room:* A/C, ceiling fan, TV, fridge, hair dryer, kitchenette (in some).

The East End

VERY EXPENSIVE

Wyndham Sugar Bay Resort & Spa ★★ ☺   If on a holiday you want a big full service resort, with everything from beauty parlors to a doctor on call, this is a formidable candidate. At the eastern end of the island, on a desirable 32-acre plot of steeply sloping terrain, within a 5-minute ride from Red Hook, this well-maintained, high-rise hotel caters very clearly to a conservative, mainstream clientele who often opt to bring their families and young children along with them on holiday. Because about 60% of the guests who stay here opt for a full-board plan, it is the largest all-inclusive hotel on St. Thomas. It has panoramic views that sweep out over the sea from its position atop a rocky headland, although its secluded beach is really too small for a resort of this size. Many of the attractive rooms are decorated with rattan pieces and pastels. This is not the most cutting-edge or stylish hotel on the island, but guest rooms have modern carpeting, Balinese furnishings, electronics, wall treatments, and state-of-the-art plumbing. The hotel has one of only two casinos (slot machines only) on the island, and the hotel's spa, Journeys, is the largest full-service spa in the U.S. Virgins.

6500 Estate Smith Bay, St. Thomas, U.S.V.I. 00802. www.wyndham.com. © **877/999-3223** or 340/777-7100. Fax 340/777-7300. 294 units. Winter $590–$690 double, from $1,250 suite; off season $500–$615 double, from $1,050 suite. Ask about packages and various meal plans. AE, DC, DISC, MC, V. **Amenities:** 3 restaurants; 2 bars; babysitting; casino (slot machines only); children's programs; exercise room; Internet (70¢ per minute); 4 tennis courts (lit). *In room:* A/C, ceiling fan, TV, fridge, hair dryer, Internet ($15 per day).

EXPENSIVE

Elysian Beach Resort ★   The setting is a Caribbean cliché, overlooking its own secluded yacht-filled cove and private white-sand beach. This timeshare resort on Cowpet Bay, a 30-minute drive from Charlotte Amalie, is imbued with a certain European resort chic. If you seek tranquillity and seclusion without all the razzle-dazzle of other East End competitors, stay here. The beautiful white-sand beach is another compelling reason to choose this place. There are free shuttles to Charlotte Amalie and Magens Bay Beach, should you decide to leave. The thoughtfully planned bedrooms contain balconies, and 14 offer sleeping lofts that are reached by a spiral staircase. The decor is tropical, with rattan and bamboo furnishings, ceiling fans, and natural-wood ceilings. Try to avoid rooms in buildings V to Z, as they are some distance from the beach. The hotel also boasts **Robert's American Grille** (p. 79), a peaceful spot to enjoy creative American and West Indian cuisine.

6800 Estate Nazareth, Cowpet Bay, St. Thomas, U.S.V.I. 00802. www.elysianbeachresort.net. © **866/620-7994** or 340/775-1000. Fax 340/776-0910. 180 units. Winter $220–$265 double, $459 suite; off season $215–$260 double, $399 suite. AE, DC, DISC, MC, V. **Amenities:** 2 restaurants; 2 bars; exercise room; pool (outdoor); small spa; tennis court (lit); watersports equipment/rentals. *In room:* A/C, TV, hair dryer, kitchenette, Wi-Fi ($10 per day).

FAMILY-FRIENDLY hotels

Best Western Emerald Beach Resort (p. 62)   In spite of its major drawback (it's located across from the airport), this is a safe, family-friendly place for those with kids. Children age 11 and under stay free in their parent's room, and the resort opens onto one of the best beaches on the island. The price is right, too.

Bolongo Bay Beach Resort (p. 65) On a half-moon-shaped, white-sand beach, this resort attracts families with its hospitality and children's programs. Many of its rooms have extra beds for children. Plenty of activities—such as sand-castle building, water volleyball, and bag hopping—keep the kids busy.

Island Beachcomber Hotel (p. 63) For the family on a budget, this hotel near the airport is appealing. It's not grand in any way, but it's clean and decent. Many of its rooms have two double beds. A beach-party atmosphere prevails, and kids and their families find the place festive, if a little worn.

Secret Harbour Beach Resort (p. 68) Children age 11 and under stay free in their parent's room at this Nazareth Bay hotel. Many units have kitchenettes where families can prepare light meals. Beach facilities are right at your doorstep.

The Ritz-Carlton, St. Thomas (p. 65) With 30 acres of oceanfront property and a white sand beach, this palazzolike resort puts on the Ritz for kids as well as adults. The children's program is one of the island's best, with snorkeling and scuba-diving activities, a scuba school, and a private yacht for guests.

Wyndham Sugar Bay Resort & Spa (p. 66)   Most guests opt for full board at this traditional all-inclusive that caters to travelers with kids. The secluded beach is small, but the location affords panoramic views of the sea. Rooms are attractive enough, but parents won't need to fret about the utilitarian furnishings.

Pavilions and Pools ★   This is the premier choice for a romantic getaway. Ideal for a honeymoon, this resort lets you have your own villa, with floor-to-ceiling glass doors opening onto your own private swimming pool. It's perfect for those who want to run around nude as Adam and Eve, Eve and Eve, or Adam and Adam. The resort, 7 miles east of Charlotte Amalie, is actually just a string of condominium units, tastefully furnished according to the tastes of each individual owner. After checking in and following a landscaped pathway to your villa, you don't have to see another soul until you leave, if you so wish—the fence and gate around your space are that high. Your swimming pool is encircled by a deck and plenty of tropical greenery. Inside, a room divider screens a well-equipped kitchen. The place is not posh, and an average good motel in the States will have better-quality furniture. The resort is a steep uphill walk from Sapphire Bay, which boasts one of the island's best beaches and many watersports concessions. Honeymooning couples should inquire about packages.

6400 Estate Smith Bay, St. Thomas, U.S.V.I. 00802. www.pavilionsandpools.com. ℭ **800/524-2001** or 340/775-6110. Fax 340/776-5694. 25 units. Winter $325–$360 double; off season $250–$275 double. Rates include continental breakfast. AE, MC, V. **Amenities:** Restaurant; private pools; watersports equipment/rentals; Wi-Fi (free in lobby). *In room:* A/C, ceiling fan, TV, hair dryer, kitchen.

Camping Out on Water Island

If you dream of sleeping in a rustic cabin on an isolated tropical island, head for the **Virgin Islands Campground on Water Island** (© 340/776-5488; www.virginislandscampground.com), on Water Island, just off of St. Thomas. This is the most eco-sensitive accommodation in the vicinity of St. Thomas. Nestled among lush foliage, the cabins have electricity, comfortable beds, and clean linens, and open onto private terraces. There is no restaurant, but you can grill your own meals in the Pavilion; you can also store your food in a refrigerator or freezer.

Water Island is very small; to get around, simply hike along the island's pristine trails. From the campgrounds, it is only a 5-minute walk to the idyllic Honeymoon Beach, where you can swim, snorkel, or just bask in the sun. Regular ferry service takes visitors between Water Island and St. Thomas (trip time: 7 minutes).

A 3-night minimum stay is required; cabins cost $170 per night in winter and $129 per night in the off season. Cabins accommodate up to 3 adults and 2 children. MasterCard and Visa are accepted.

Point Pleasant Resort ★　This is a very private, unique resort on Water Bay, on the northeastern tip of St. Thomas. Beachcombers who stay here in one of the spacious Caribbean-villa suites can go to Pineapple Beach, adjacent to the resort's shoreline, or wander over to secluded Sugar Beach at the end of a nature trail on Point Pleasant's 15-acre island preserve. Or they can stay on the grounds, basking in one of the hotel's three intimate pools nestled against the backdrop of a lush hillside. Condo units, which are rented when their owners are not in residence, are set on a 15-acre bluff with flowering shrubbery, century plants, frangipani trees, secluded nature trails, old rock formations, and lookout points. The villa-style accommodations have light and airy furnishings, with very comfortable beds and fine linens. From your living room, you'll have a gorgeous view over Tortola, St. John, and Jost Van Dyke. The restaurant, **Agavé Terrace** (p. 77), is one of the finest on St. Thomas, serving a blend of nouvelle American dishes and Caribbean specialties. Local entertainment performs Tuesday and Thursday nights. **Fungi's on the Beach** (p. 80) is a great option for those interested in Caribbean cuisine and lots of reggae music.

6600 Estate Smith Bay, St. Thomas, U.S.V.I. 00802. www.pointpleasantresort.com. © **800/524-2300** or 340/775-7200. Fax 340/776-5694. 128 units. Winter $300 junior suite, $320–$395 deluxe suite, $550 2-bedroom suite; off season $180 junior suite, $195–$255 deluxe suite, $355 2-bedroom suite. Ask about package deals. Children 11 and under stay free in parent's room. AE, DC, DISC, MC, V. **Amenities:** 2 restaurants; 2 bars; 3 pools (outdoor); watersports (snorkeling); Wi-Fi (free in lobby). *In room:* A/C, ceiling fan, TV, kitchen.

Secret Harbour Beach Resort ★ ☺　This small and intimate all-suites condo resort is on the stunning white-sand beach at Nazareth Bay, just outside Red Hook Marina. All four low-rise buildings have southwestern exposure (great for sunsets), and each unit has a private deck or patio. You'll be just steps from the sand, and good snorkeling is right offshore. There are three types of accommodations: studio apartments, one-bedroom suites, and two-bedroom suites. Each studio apartment has a bedroom/sitting room area, patio, and dressing room area; each one-bedroom suite has a living/dining area, a separate bedroom, and a sun deck; and each luxurious two-bedroom suite has two bedrooms, two bathrooms, a private living room, and a patio.

Each unit has a kitchen. Not only are all the space and the location great for families, but children 12 and under stay free in their parent's room. Honeymooners are likely to show up in the winter months. Secret Harbour is also home to one of the most celebrated restaurants on the island, the **Blue Moon Cafe** (p. 78).

6280 Estate Nazareth, Charlotte Amalie, St. Thomas, U.S.V.I. 00802-1104. www.secretharbourvi.com. ℂ **800/524-2250** or 340/775-6550. Fax 340/775-1501. 60 units. Winter $365–$395 double, $390–$475 1-bedroom suite; off season $195–$265 double, $245–$335 1-bedroom suite. Children 12 and under stay free in parent's room. AE, MC, V. **Amenities:** Restaurant; bar; exercise room; pool (outdoor); 3 tennis courts (lit); watersports equipment/rentals; Wi-Fi on beach (free). *In room:* A/C, hair dryer, Internet (in some rooms; free).

WHERE TO EAT

The dining scene in St. Thomas these days is among the best in the West Indies, but it has its drawbacks: Fine dining (and even not-so-fine dining) tends to be expensive, and the best spots (with a few exceptions) are actually not right in Charlotte Amalie and can be reached only by taxi or car.

You'll find an eclectic mix of cuisines on St. Thomas, including American, Italian, Mexican, Asian, and other options. We recommend exploring some of the local Caribbean dishes at least once or twice, especially the seafood specialties like "ole wife" and yellowtail, which are usually prepared with a spicy Creole mixture of peppers, onions, and tomatoes. The winner among native side dishes is *fungi* (pronounced *foon*-gee), made with okra and cornmeal. Most local restaurants serve johnnycake, a popular fried, unleavened bread.

In Charlotte Amalie
EXPENSIVE

Amalia Café ★ SPANISH   Even though the owners, Randolph and Helga Maynard, are not from Spain (he's from Antigua and she's from Germany), they offer the most savory Spanish cuisine in town, including a varied selection of tasty tapas. The restaurant is romantically located in a Spanish inn in the cobblestone Palm Passage in the center of Charlotte Amalie. The razor-sharp Spanish cooking techniques are generated by a team of chefs from the Dominican Republic, who have been extensively trained in the preparation of Spanish culinary traditions. We like to make a full meal just out of the tapas, especially garlic shrimp, clams in green sauce, and delightful mussels in a brandy sauce. That Castilian classic, garlic soup, is also offered as a starter. These DR chefs make the best *paella Valenciana* in town (the secret is in the fish stock). Their *zarzuela de mariscos,* or seafood casserole, is as good as you might get along Spain's Costa Brava. Not only do they serve the best pitchers of sangria on the island, but the cooks also make the best caramel flan for dessert.

24 Palm Passage. ℂ **340/714-7373.** www.amaliacafe.com. Reservations recommended. Main courses lunch $15–$23, dinner $28–$49. AE, MC, V. Mon–Sat 11am–10pm; Sun 11am–3pm (winter only).

Banana Tree Grille INTERNATIONAL   This place offers candlelit dinners, sweeping views over the busy harbor, and a decor that includes genuine banana plants artfully scattered through the two dining rooms. The cuisine is creative and changes frequently; the patrons are often hip and laid-back. Start off with grilled bacon-wrapped horseradish shrimp over a mango glaze. Main dishes are filled with flavors influenced by Asian, Caribbean, and Italian cuisines. Especially noted are the house specialties of sugar-cane-and-cocoa-lacquered tuna, lobster tail tempura with an orange-pepper sauce, and the divine mango-and-mustard-glazed salmon. Try the aïoli shank, a house specialty, if it's offered: A shank of lamb is slowly braised in Chianti and served with an aïoli sauce over white beans and garlic mashed potatoes. The desserts are truly decadent.

In Bluebeard's Castle, Bluebeard's Hill. ✆ **340/776-4050.** www.bananatreegrille.com. Reservations recommended. Main courses $20–$56. AE, MC, V. Tues–Sun 5:30–9:30pm.

Grande Cru/Wikked/Fat Turtle ★ INTERNATIONAL   This trio of genuinely intriguing restaurants lies side by side beside the WICO docks, immediately adjacent to where some of the world's biggest cruise ships moor. Each of the three is part of a fast-evolving marina/hotel/condo development, Yacht Haven Grande. The most expensive, formal, and elegant of the three restaurants is Grande Cru, whose meticulously crafted dining room manages to be both romantic and jazzy at the same time. Tables spill outdoors onto a covered veranda that's open to a view of privately owned yachts. Look for stylish menu items like braised short ribs on horseradish and lemon risotto, pistachio-and-basil-crusted goat cheese on greens with a truffle-flavored vinaigrette, and roasted chicken with preserved lemon and sun-dried tomatoes.

The charming middle-bracket contender within the group is Wikked, a breezy, amiable, and likable restaurant that some of the local boat and condo owners have transformed into their favorite. And the most raucous and animated is Fat Turtle, a booze-and-burger joint that's a favorite with the college crowd looking for flavorful grub, very stiff drinks, and large-screen TVs broadcasting sporting events.

In the Yacht Haven Marina. Grande Cru ✆ **340/775-8CRU** (775-8278); Wikked ✆ **340/775-8WKD** (775-8953); Fat Turtle **340/775-8FAT** (775-8328). Reservations recommended at Grande Cru, not necessary at Wikked or Fat Turtle. Main courses at Grande Cru $24–$38; platters and main courses at Wikked and Fat Turtle $11–$42. AE, MC, V. Grande Cru Mon–Fri noon–3pm; Mon–Sat 5:30–10pm. Wikked Mon–Sat 11am–10pm; Sun 9am–10pm. Fat Turtle daily 11am–10pm.

Hervé Restaurant & Wine Bar ★ AMERICAN/CARIBBEAN/FRENCH   A panoramic view of Charlotte Amalie and a historic setting are side benefits—it's the cuisine that matters. Hervé Paul Chassin is a restaurateur with a vast classical background. In an unpretentious setting, he offers high-quality food at reasonable prices. There are two dining areas: a large open-air terrace and a more intimate wine room. Start with the pistachio-encrusted brie, shrimp in a stuffed crab shell, or conch fritters with mango chutney. For a main course, try the house special bouillabaisse, or a delectable black-sesame-crusted tuna with a ginger/raspberry sauce. There are also nightly specials of game, fish, and pasta. Desserts are divine—you'll rarely taste a creamier crème caramel or a lighter, fluffier mango or raspberry cheesecake.

Next to Hotel 1829, Government Hill. ✆ **340/777-9703.** www.herverestaurant.com. Reservations required. Main courses lunch $9–$48, dinner $21–$49. AE, MC, V. Mon–Fri 11am–3pm; daily 6–10pm.

Petite Pump Room ★ WEST INDIAN/INTERNATIONAL   This restaurant is housed on the second floor of the industrial-looking ferryboat terminal at the edge of the harborfront in Charlotte Amalie, departure point for boats headed off to the British Virgin Islands and St. Croix. Established in 1963 by the then-owner of the famous Pump Room restaurant in Chicago, it does a thriving breakfast and lunch business among local boat owners and downtown office workers. The draw is some of the best West Indian cooking on the island, a cuisine that takes the preparation of callaloo greens very seriously (they're fabulous), and the nuances of pounded conch steak and grouper with fries with devotion. If you want something "international" (meaning American), the menu lists club sandwiches, steaks, chicken dishes, and burgers, but

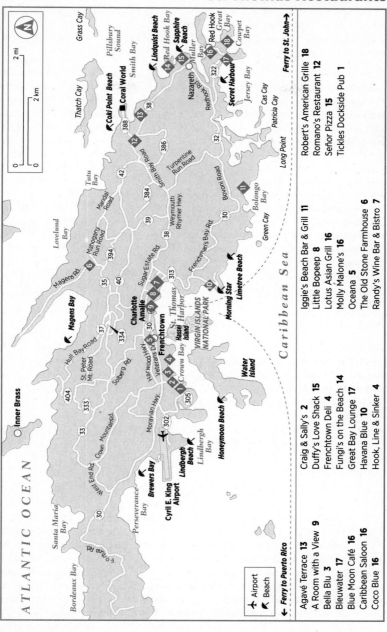

St. Thomas Restaurants

Agavé Terrace 13
A Room with a View 9
Bella Blu 3
Bleuwater 17
Blue Moon Café 16
Caribbean Saloon 16
Coco Blue 16

Craig & Sally's 2
Duffy's Love Shack 15
Frenchtown Deli 4
Fungi's on the Beach 14
Great Bay Lounge 17
Havana Blue 10
Hook, Line & Sinker 4

Iggie's Beach Bar & Grill 11
Little Bopeep 8
Lotus Asian Grill 16
Molly Malone's 16
Oceana 5
The Old Stone Farmhouse 6
Randy's Wine Bar & Bistro 7

Robert's American Grille 18
Romano's Restaurant 12
Señor Pizza 15
Tickles Dockside Pub 1

Ferry to St. John→

Caribbean Sea

ATLANTIC OCEAN

✈ Airport
➤ Beach

← Ferry to Puerto Rico

virtually everyone who comes here orders the West Indian food. Examples? Stewed oxtail or chicken, or fried potfish with Creole sauce, always served with your choice of pigeon peas and rice, mashed potatoes, dumplings, macaroni and cheese, *fungi* with vegetables, fried plantains, or two kinds of potatoes.

In the Edward Wilmoth Blyden Building, Veterans Dr. ℂ **340/776-2976.** www.petitepumproom.com. Breakfast $7–$13; sandwiches and salads $8–$18; platters $14–$20. AE, MC, V. Daily 7am–4:30pm.

Tavern on the Waterfront ★ 🍴 CARIBBEAN/FRENCH   This is often the place of choice for celebrities visiting the island. The menu changes often and is composed with Caribbean and French flair; the chefs are inventive but draw from a solid technique. All the dishes have a distinctive flavor, beginning with such appetizers as conch fritters or coconut shrimp with mango chutney. Main dishes include the award-winning barbecue pork ribs that take 120 hours—from the marinade to the cooking—to prepare. We've also enjoyed their exotic pork platter, with espresso-and-cinnamon-encrusted pork medallions covered with a passion fruit demi-glace. The blackened seafood linguine, another winner, comes with mahimahi, jumbo sea scallops, New Zealand mussels, and shrimp, bathed in a Cajun cream sauce.

Live entertainment is often featured, which you can enjoy while taking in harbor views. The setting is relatively simple but still elegant, with tables resting under African mahogany vaulted ceilings. Original artwork hangs on the white walls.

Waterfront at Royal Dane Mall. ℂ **340/776-4328.** www.tavernonthewaterfront.com. Reservations required. Main courses $14–$37. AE, DISC, MC, V. Mon–Sat 11am–3pm; Mon–Thurs 5–9pm; Fri–Sat 5–10pm.

Virgilio's ★ NORTHERN ITALIAN   Virgilio's is the best northern Italian restaurant in the Virgin Islands. Its neobaroque interior is sheltered under heavy ceiling beams and brick vaulting. A well-trained staff serves meals against a backdrop of stained-glass windows, crystal chandeliers, and soft Italian music. The *cinco peche* (clams, mussels, scallops, oysters, and crayfish simmered in a saffron broth) is delicious, and the fettuccine Alfredo is one of the best we've tasted. Classic dishes are served with a distinctive flair—the lamb shank, for example, is filled with a porcinimushroom stuffing and glazed with a roasted garlic aïoli. The marinated grilled duck is served chilled. You can also order individual pizzas. The place does a thriving takeaway business as well.

18 Dronningens Gade (entrance on a narrow alley running btw. Main and Back sts.). ℂ **340/776-4920.** Reservations recommended. Main courses lunch $13–$29, dinner $23–$50. AE, MC, V. Mon–Sat 11:30am–10:30pm.

MODERATE

Cuzzin's Caribbean Restaurant & Bar ★ 🍴 CARIBBEAN   For some real, old-fashioned Virgin Islands cooking, head to this offbeat place installed in an 18th-century stable on Back Street. The dining room is comfortable, with stone-and-brick walls. The restaurant boasts island dishes, with a focus on seafood, especially conch, lobster, and freshly caught fish that arrives the day it's served. Native dishes include stews and curries, such as island-style mutton, curried chicken, and conch stewed in a rich onion-butter sauce. The signature dish is Cuzzin' Nemo, a mélange of lobster, conch, scallops, and shrimp served over pasta. Fried green bananas or fried plantains accompany most dishes, and desserts are rich and luscious. The drinks of choice include local beverages such as ginger beer, *mauby,* and sea moss.

7 Wimmelskafts Gade (Back St.). ℂ **340/777-4711.** Reservations recommended. Main courses $12–$45. AE, DISC, MC, V. Mon–Sat 11am–4:30pm.

The Greenhouse AMERICAN/CARIBBEAN Fronted by big windows, this sunny Waterfront restaurant attracts cruise-ship passengers who need a place to drop. The food here is not the island's best, but it's satisfying if you're not too demanding. The house specializes in chicken, often with exotic fruit flavors, such as mango-banana chicken or coconut chicken. The excellent appetizers range from conch fritters to stuffed jalapeño peppers. A kettle of soup is always on the stove, and you can make a meal of the freshly made salads. The most popular item on the menu is the big, juicy burger, the island's finest, made with certified Angus beef. There's a wide selection of seafood, like the baked stuffed swordfish with garlic-cream sauce, plus chef's specialties such as baby back ribs.

The Greenhouse is also a prime nightlife spot. A daily happy hour from 4:30 to 7pm seduces party animals early. On Tuesday nights, after 9:30pm, the Greenhouse turns into a hip nightclub attracting a 21-and-over crowd with two-for-one drinks. This is the biggest event on Tuesday night in St. Thomas. On Friday nights, there's live reggae music; on other nights, the sounds are selected by a DJ.

Veterans Dr. ℂ **340/774-7998.** www.thegreenhouserestaurant.com. Main courses $8.95–$28. AE, DISC, MC, V. Daily 11am–10pm. Bar daily 11am until the last customer leaves.

INEXPENSIVE

Bumpa's AMERICAN This deli-style, open-air joint isn't that special, but it's an ideal choice for a good, filling, inexpensive breakfast or lunch. It's on the second level of a little old West Indian house with a canvas-roof porch offering a panoramic view of the harbor. Hordes of shoppers find this a favorite refueling stop. The cook prepares good sandwiches and freshly made salads. Many patrons stop in just to order some ice cream, one of the homemade pastries, or a refreshing lemonade on a hot day.

38-A Waterfront Hwy. ℂ **340/776-5674.** Main courses $8.50–$14. DC, MC, V. Mon–Sat 7:30am–5pm; Sun 8am–3pm.

Café Amici ITALIAN/CARIBBEAN Located in an old stone alley cascading with tropical plants, this is a good lunch spot in Charlotte Amalie. Select a seat at this open-air cafe and dig into the day's offerings. There's always a delightful variety of antipasti, salads, and a soup du jour. Pastas are also menu standards, including the famous Rasta Pasta, with grilled vegetables, olive oil, garlic, and the chef's "secret" spices. The pizzas and sandwiches are the best in the center of town. We always gravitate to the Clams Casino pizza, which has added flavorings of bacon, mozzarella, and garlic. A rarer pizza is called Tropical, and it's served with a hot, spicy tamarind sauce, grilled cheese, and both feta and mozzarella cheese. Vegetarians will be glad to see the grilled portobello mushroom served with roasted red pepper and smothered in melted provolone cheese and offered on homemade bread with pesto mayonnaise.

Riise's Alley. ℂ **340/714-7704.** www.cafeamicivi.com. Lunch specials $9.95–$13; pizza $14–$18. MC, V. Mon–Sat 10:30am–4pm.

Gladys's Café ★ 🍴 CARIBBEAN/AMERICAN Antigua-born Gladys Isles is a warm, gracious woman who makes a visit here all the more special. Gladys's Café is housed in a 1700 pump house with a stonework courtyard that has a well (one of only three on the island) in the middle. The good, standard breakfast here is the best value in town. Lunch offerings feature various sandwiches, salads, and fresh seafood, including an excellent swordfish and dumplings. Along with local lobster, shrimp, and fish dishes, the house specialty is the hot chicken salad, made with pieces of sautéed breast with red-wine vinegar, pine nuts, and dill, all nestled on a bed of lettuce.

Royal Dane Mall. ☎ **340/774-6604.** Reservations required for groups of 6 or more. Breakfast $3.75–$19; lunch main courses $10–$25. AE, MC, V. Mon–Sat 7am–5pm; Sun 8am–3pm.

Jen's Island Café & Deli AMERICAN/DELI   Homesick New Yorkers especially head for this small eatery for breakfast or lunch while touring or shopping in Charlotte Amalie. Breakfast offerings include yogurt with granola and a three-cheese omelet with sausage, bacon, or ham. Want more? Order the buttermilk pancakes and to hell with the waistline. The smoked salmon platter is a morning favorite with lovers of deli food. At lunch you can enjoy fresh salad platters, including a grilled chicken salad or a chef's salad—or opt for one of the well-stuffed sandwiches, including slow-roasted beef, pastrami, or albacore tuna. Desserts are homemade daily.

Grand Hotel, 43–46 Norre Gade. ☎ **340/777-4611** or 514-5345. www.jensdeli.com. Breakfast $4–$7.75; main courses $6.75–$9. MC, V. Mon–Fri 7am–5pm; Sat 10:30am–4pm.

East of Charlotte Amalie

EXPENSIVE

A Room with a View ★ INTERNATIONAL   The finest restaurant within Bluebeard's Castle attracts diners from Charlotte Amalie, who come here for the succulent food and a wide-angle hillside view that some patrons, especially after a few drinks, have described as mystical. The intimate (40-seat) restaurant is outfitted in tones of burgundy and green, with floor-to-ceiling windows that sweep westward over the sunset, the harborfront of Charlotte Amalie, and as far away as the airport. There's a small-scale bar on the premises (the kind of five-stool bar that's appropriate for an aperitif, but not as an all-night hangout).

Your meal might begin with steamed littleneck clams in either white- or red-wine-based Provençal sauce; spanakopita, or spinach pie, as you might remember it tasting in Greece; grilled portobello mushrooms with goat cheese; or *dolmades,* stuffed grape leaves with dill and sun-dried tomatoes. Main courses feature lots of fresh fish, including an excellent version of yellowfin tuna, with teriyaki and ginger sauce; and locally caught lobster prepared Thermidor-style. Carnivores will enjoy the tender, succulent filet steak with peppercorn sauce. The chef is especially proud of the pork Marsala, simmered in butter with mushrooms, Marsala wine, and cream.

In Bluebeard's Castle, Bluebeard's Hill. ☎ **340/774-2377.** Reservations recommended. Main courses $20–$50. AE, DISC, MC, V. Mon–Sat 5–11pm.

MODERATE

Randy's Wine Bar & Bistro 🏠 CONTINENTAL   This is a local oddity, catering to deli devotees (usually from New York), cigar aficionados, and bistro fans. The on-site store sells a good selection of wines, along with the standard liquors and cigars. The deli serves the usual sandwiches and salads, and the bistro dishes up delectable cuisine. Look for one of the daily specials, such as pork tenderloin in a Dijon mustard sauce. At lunch, you might want to try the portobello mushroom sandwich marinated in balsamic vinegar with a basil mayonnaise, or the Carnegie Reuben, with half a pound of sliced meat enclosed within. For dinner, shrimp scampi is always a local favorite, and understandably so.

In Al Cohen's Plaza, 4002 Raphune Hill. ☎ **340/775-5001.** Main courses $15–$33. AE, DC, DISC, MC, V. Daily 11am–9pm.

INEXPENSIVE

Little Bopeep 🍴 CARIBBEAN   This plain little brick tavern serves up some of the best West Indian food on the island. No one puts on any airs at this place, and

Locals will direct you to one of three locations for **Texas Pit BBQ:** the Charlotte Amalie Waterfront, Red Hook, or Seabay. The owners brought their secret barbecue recipe from Texas, where they learned how to make a fiery sauce to wake up your palate—"and everything else," a habitué confided. These takeout stands are favored by yachties, St. Thomas cowboys, and frugal families. Chicken, tender ribs, and Texas-style beef are dished up in hearty portions, along with rice, coleslaw, and potato salad. One local pronounced these ribs the island's best. We tend to agree. The Waterfront joint, across from the Windward Passage Hotel on Veterans Drive, is open Monday to Saturday from 5:30 to 11pm; Red Hook, at the Red Hook Plaza, Monday to Saturday from 3 to 10pm; and Seabay, at the Nisky Center, Monday to Saturday from noon to 5:30pm. For information, call ℂ **340/776-9579.**

breakfast here is the least expensive in town. You can order (to go) meat patties and sandwiches, such as egg, bacon, and cheese. Lunch gets more interesting and a lot spicier, with curried chicken and curried conch. Fried plantains accompany most dishes.

Barber Plaza. ℂ **340/774-1959.** Breakfast $3–$6; main courses $7–$11. No credit cards. Mon–Fri 7am–5pm; Sat 7am–3pm.

West of Charlotte Amalie
EXPENSIVE

Oceana SEAFOOD/TAPAS   Upscale, hip, and stylish, this local favorite occupies what functioned as the Russian consulate during the Danish occupation of the island. Outfitted with slabs of carefully oiled paneling, and painted in bright blues and greens inspired by the colors of the ocean, the restaurant offers two distinctly different venues. The street level has a wine bar–cum–singles bar, where small platters of food (blini, *crostinis,* and cheese platters) are specifically designed to go with the changing array of wine. This area buzzes with convivial after-work chitchat. Upstairs, within a relaxed but relatively formal dining room, candles and oil lamps flicker amid bouquets of flowers. Menu items focus mainly on fish, with a healthy roster of beef and lamb as well. Expect a menu that includes spicy shrimp served with a cup of Andalusian-style gazpacho; house-marinated salmon; mussels in white-wine sauce; pan-fried freshwater trout from Idaho; oven-roasted sea bass with a white-wine, thyme, and olive oil sauce; grilled sirloin of lamb; several different preparations of Caribbean lobster; and New York strip, porterhouse, and filet mignon steaks. If the ambience and conviviality of the wine bar appeal to you more than the relative formality of the upstairs dining room, the staff will set up a dining table for you downstairs.

In the Villa Olga, 8 Honduras. ℂ **340/774-4262.** www.oceana.vi. Reservations required. Tapas $12–$20; main courses $25–$48. AE, DC, MC, V. Thurs–Tues 5:30–10pm.

MODERATE

Bella Blu ★ MEDITERRANEAN   West of Charlotte Amalie, this restaurant's 14 tables overlook the harbor. The fare here is light and focuses on the sunny flavors of the Mediterranean. You might start with the tuna tartare, and move on to a Moroccan-inspired chicken or lamb dish. Schnitzels are still on the menu, if you're so inclined. The menu changes with the season and what's fresh at the marketplace.

French Town Mall. ✆ **340/774-4349.** Reservations recommended. Main courses lunch $7–$28, dinner $11–$28. AE, MC, V. Mon–Sat 11:30am–10pm.

Craig & Sally's ★ SEAFOOD   This Caribbean cafe is set in an airy, open-sided pavilion in Frenchtown. Its eclectic cuisine is, according to the owner, "not for the faint of heart, but for the adventurous soul." Views of the sky and sea are complemented by a cuisine that ranges from pasta to seafood, with influences from Europe and Asia. Roast pork with clams, filet mignon with macadamia-nut sauce, and grilled swordfish with a sauce of fresh herbs and tomatoes are examples from a menu that changes every day. The lobster-stuffed twice-baked potatoes are inspired. The wine list is the most extensive and sophisticated on St. Thomas.

3525 Honduras, Frenchtown. ✆ **340/777-9949.** www.craigandsallys.com. Reservations recommended. Main courses $13–$22. MC, V. Wed–Fri 11:30am–3pm; Wed–Sun 5:30–10pm.

Hook, Line & Sinker AMERICAN   Locals and visitors alike flock here for the friendly service, good food at reasonable prices, and a panoramic view of the harbor. The setting evokes a New England seaport village; the building has a pitched roof and skylights, along with wraparound French doors and windows. A *Cheers*-like crowd frequents the bar. Breakfast, except for Sunday brunch, is standard. Lunch choices range from a Caesar salad to various grilled chicken dishes. The dinner menu is usually a delight, featuring delicious dishes such as mango-rum tuna, jerk swordfish, and snapper stuffed with mushrooms and red peppers and covered in a garlic sauce. Locals call the hearty soups "outrageous."

62 Honduras, Frenchtown. ✆ **340/776-9708.** www.hooklineandsinkervi.com. Main courses lunch $9–$15, dinner $14–$28; Sun brunch $8.50–$15. AE, MC, V. Mon–Sat 11:30am–4pm and 6–10pm; Sun 10am–2:30pm.

INEXPENSIVE

Frenchtown Deli DELI   Some of the island's best and thickest sandwiches are served here, along with Frenchtown's best coffee, house-baked breads, fresh salads, and beer, soda, and wine. Most dinners cost about $15 for two people, making this the bargain of St. Thomas. You can eat your dinner on the premises or take it out.

24-A Honduras, Frenchtown Mall, Frenchtown. ✆ **340/776-7211.** Sandwiches $6.50–$12; salads $4–$15. AE, MC, V. Mon–Fri 7am–8pm; Sat–Sun 7am–5pm.

Tickles Dockside Pub AMERICAN   This joint is dedicated to the concept of fun, comfort, and reasonably priced food in a friendly atmosphere. Diners at this open-air restaurant can sit back and relax while watching the sailboats and cruise ships on the water. The menu features a simple American-pub fare of burgers, including a veggie burger; sandwiches; fish; and pasta. Start off with a plate of Gator Eggs (lightly breaded jalapeño peppers stuffed with cheese) or Sweet Lips (strips of sweet, fried chicken served with a honey-mustard sauce), or a local version of conch chowder. Choose from ham, turkey, or corned beef for your Reuben, grilled with Tickles' own special Russian dressing, Swiss cheese, and sauerkraut. The cooks also turn out an array of classic dishes, like chicken Alfredo, prime rib, baby back ribs, fried catfish, and a fisherman's platter served over pasta.

Crown Bay Marina. ✆ **340/777-8792.** www.ticklesdocksidepub.com. Main courses lunch $8–$11, dinner $11–$25. AE, MC, V. Daily 7am–midnight.

The South Coast

Iggies Beach Bar & Grill ☺ AMERICAN/CONTINENTAL   Sports fans and others patronize this action-packed seaside spot. It's the island's best sports bar and grill, with giant TVs broadcasting the latest games. To make things even livelier, there's karaoke. The place has "indestructible" furniture, and an aggressively informal crowd. Bring the kids along; no one will mind if they make a ruckus, and they can order from the basic kids' menu. The regular menu changes nightly, and every night there's a theme, such as Lobster Night or Italian Night. Most popular is carnival night, when a West Indian all-you-can-eat buffet is presented along with a limbo show. Adults can order such tropical drinks as the Green Iguana (melon piña colada) or the Ultimate Kamikaze, the ingredients of which are a secret. There's a fine-dining restaurant in the back that has good fare at shockingly low prices.

At the Bolongo Bay Beach Resort (p. 65), 7150 Bolongo (Rte. 30). © **340/693-2600.** www.iggies beachbar.com. Burgers and sandwiches $6.50–$15; lunch and dinner main courses $14–$30. AE, MC, V. Daily 11am–midnight.

The East End
VERY EXPENSIVE

Bleuwater ★★ SEAFOOD/INTERNATIONAL One of the grandest dining spots on the island lies in the Ritz-Carlton hotel. It is decorated in a West Indian style, taking its decor from its name—candles, plates, cushions, and wall accents are all in blue. The executive chef, Jasper Schneider, is one of the finest on the island, carefully shopping for only the finest in top-quality ingredients to construct his divine meals. Guests can dine in air-conditioned comfort or select an umbrella-shaded table on the patio.

Breakfast dishes are about the best on the island, including both a hot and a cold buffet. The bananas foster French toast with whipped butter and aged rum is almost irresistible, as are the buttermilk pancakes with blueberries, strawberries, bananas, toasted coconut whipped butter, and maple syrup. Of course, if you order the Bleu-water Bloody Mary mimosa, the day is yours.

At dinner, start with duck wontons with pickled cucumber salad or scallop Carpaccio. You can follow with main-dish selections "from the sea" or "from the farm." Our oven-roasted grouper came with leeks and a chorizo-clam broth. Another specialty is a duo of beef—pan-seared *côte de boeuf* and red-wine-braised Kobe short ribs. A "tasting plate" is the way to go in desserts, though you may opt for the warm chocolate tart with a white chocolate–and-ginger ice cream.

In the Ritz-Carlton (p. 65), 6900 Great Bay. © **340/775-3333.** Reservations required. Main courses breakfast $10–$30, dinner $40–$65. AE, MC, V. Wed–Mon 7–10am and 6–10pm.

EXPENSIVE

Agavé Terrace ★★ CARIBBEAN Perched high above a steep and heavily forested hillside on the eastern tip of St. Thomas, this is one of the island's best restaurants. Order the house drink, Desmond Delight, a combination of Midori, rum, pineapple juice, and a secret ingredient, and enjoy your lovely view and unparalleled romantic atmosphere. After a few Delights, try the house appetizer, which includes portions of crabmeat, conch fritters, and a shrimp cocktail. The catch of the day features three different fish, which can be prepared in seven different ways, with a choice of nine sauces. Some of our favorite meals here include the chef's jerk chicken, and Coral Bay crab cakes served with island rémoulade. There is also an extensive wine list. A live steel-drum band draws listeners on Tuesday and Thursday nights.

In the Point Pleasant Resort (p. 68), 6600 Estate Smith Bay. © **340/775-4142.** www.point pleasantresort.com. Reservations recommended. Main courses $22–$50. AE, DC, MC, V. Daily 6–10pm.

Havana Blue ★★ CUBAN FUSION   This chic venue at the Marriott enjoys a beachfront ambience and a sophisticated menu that is the island's most inspired. An inventive crew is in the kitchen, running wild in their culinary imagination. Cool cigars, hip drinks (mango mojitos), and an ultrachic decor draw serious foodies to this cutting-edge restaurant, where Chef Jose Rodriguez intoxicates with his tantalizing aromas and flavors. Even the side dishes are called "sexy sides." Start with the black-bean hummus or the tuna tartare with soy-lime vinaigrette. For a main, try star anise duck confit, miso-crusted sea bass, or ancho chili–rubbed beef filet with espresso sauce. It's worth crossing the island just for dessert alone—the Cuban chocolate cake with coconut ice cream or warm banana and macadamia spring rolls with a strawberry balsamic purée are scrumptious.

In Frenchman's Reef & Morning Star Marriott Beach Resort (p. 64), 5 Estate Bakkeroe. © **340/715-2583.** www.havanabluerestaurant.com. Reservations required. Main courses $28–$42. AE, DC, MC, V. Daily 5:30-10:30pm.

MODERATE

Blue Moon Cafe ★ AMERICAN   This open-air restaurant is truly an idyllic dining spot. The beachfront restaurant claims, with some degree of accuracy, one of the most memorable settings for panoramic sunset views; *Wine Spectator* honored the restaurant twice for having the most romantic setting in St. Thomas. The menu, based on market-fresh ingredients, is changed twice seasonally. Tropical starters may include coconut-honey shrimp with a guava dipping sauce or a portobello mushroom–and–goat cheese tart with field onions. Mains are imaginative; look for the mahimahi with pecans, bananas, and a coconut-rum sauce, or grilled scallops with a tomato-basil risotto and fresh asparagus. For lunch, you'll have to confine yourself to burgers, wraps, salads, and sandwiches.

In the Secret Harbour Beach Resort (p. 68), 6280 Estate Nazareth Bay. © **340/779-2262.** www.blue mooncafevi.com. Reservations required. Main courses $17–$36. AE, DC, DISC, MC, V. Daily 8am–3pm and 6-10pm.

Caribbean Saloon AMERICAN/SEAFOOD   Yachties from the American Yacht Harbor come here to drink, eat, watch sports on the widescreen TVs, or listen to live music on the weekends. It's arguably the most active joint in Red Hook. The nearby fishing fleet always brings in the catch of the day, which is often grilled to your specifications. Lunch fare is mostly appetizers, sandwiches, and burgers. Dinner gets more elaborate, with appetizers such as crab cakes with shrimp sauce or conch fritters. Soups and fresh salads are followed by an array of ribs, chicken, pasta dishes, steaks, chops, and seafood. The baby back ribs are the perennial favorite, as are the filet mignon in a burgundy-wine sauce and a very juicy rib-eye steak. Mahimahi, swordfish, and lobster tail invariably appear on the menu in a variety of cooking methods, often served blackened. There's a late night menu which is served from 10pm to 4am.

American Yacht Harbor, Building B, Red Hook. © **340/775-7060.** www.caribbeansaloon.com. Main courses $17–$37. MC, V. Daily 11am-10:30pm.

Coco Blue ★★ CARIBBEAN/SUSHI   This Red Hook eatery, a sister restaurant of Havana Blue (see above), serves creative Caribbean cuisine. Chef James "Black Magic" Crowther features an inventive menu of such delights as calamari with a coconut–and–lime aïoli; spring rolls with jalapeño, grilled pineapple, and tamarind chutney; and blackened fish tacos with a sweet chili-glazed bacon and a citrus crème fraîche—and those are just the appetizers. The island's best sushi rolls include everything from local Caribbean wahoo to spicy tuna. Main courses include white wine–marinated sea bass with sautéed shiitake mushrooms; lemon grass–glazed salmon with a cilantro essence; and mahimahi wrapped in banana leaves and served with coconut black rice and a banana-pepper buerre blanc.

American Yacht Harbor, Red Hook. © **340/774-7253.** Reservations recommended. Main courses $16–$28; 6-course menu $85. AE, MC, V. Lunch Mon–Sat 11:30am–2:30pm and dinner daily 5:30–10:30pm.

Great Bay Lounge ★ TAPAS/SUSHI   This chic, clublike dining spot on the ground level of the Ritz-Carlton is the most sophisticated spot on the island for dining on light fare while dressed to impress. The lounge seating area here features a small library, four flatscreen TVs, and pool tables. The lounge is ideal for those who like to graze on the small plates—tapas, really—including crispy calamari with spicy mayonnaise, Jamaican-style jerk chicken, chicken tandoori, and the tempura of the day in dipping sauce. Of course, there are the standards such as macaroni with five cheeses (only black truffles are added here), and even New York–style steak fries or burger and fries with grilled onion. Sushi is delectable here, especially the soft-shell crab roll or the spicy tuna roll. There is a selection of house-made ice creams and sorbets, specialty coffees, and roasted banana crème brûlée.

In the Ritz-Carlton (p. 65), 6900 Great Bay. © **340/775-3333.** Small dishes and sushi $10–$20. AE, DC, MC, V. Daily 5:30–11:30pm.

Molly Malone's IRISH/CARIBBEAN   At the Red Hook American Yacht Harbor, join the good ol' boys and dig into some baby back ribs. You can dine outdoors under a canopy, right on the dock at the eastern end of Red Hook, where the ferry from St. John pulls in. If you're finding yourself nostalgic for the Emerald Isle, go for the shepherd's pie. The conch fritters are the best in the East End, or opt for the savory conch chowder. In one of the wildest culinary offerings we've seen lately, an Irish/Caribbean stew is a nightly feature. If the day's catch netted a big wahoo, game-fish steaks will be on the menu. No one can drink more brew than the boisterous crowd that assembles here every night to let the good times roll.

6100 Red Hook Quarters. © **340/775-1270.** Main courses $10–$28. AE, MC, V. Sun–Thurs 7am–11pm; Fri–Sat 7am–midnight.

Robert's American Grille ★ 🍴AMERICAN   When the shopping bazaars and the glut of cruise-ship passengers flooding Charlotte Amalie have got you down, head to this peaceful retreat in the Elysian Beach Resort. The restaurant opens onto the beach at Cowpet Bay, providing a great open-air setting for Chef/owner Kevin Kuepper's cuisine. He takes regional American dishes and applies his own creative and imaginative interpretations. You might start with his salad of mesclun, walnuts, and Gruyère, all topped with a house-made poppy-seed dressing. His Cherry Chicken is a delight, with dried cherries and tarragon, on top of buttermilk mashed potatoes. His pan-fried pork loin medallions are also excellent; the boneless center cut is sautéed and then glazed with a honey-lime wasabi glaze. Another treat for the palate is the tandoori-marinated mahimahi with purple sticky rice.

In the Elysian Beach Resort (p. 66), 6800 Estate Nazareth, Cowpet Bay. © **340/714-3663.** www.robertsamericangrille.com. Reservations recommended. Main courses lunch $9–$22, dinner $16–$34. AE, MC, V. Tues–Sat 11:30am–2:30pm and 5:30–10:30pm; Sun 5:30–9pm; Mon 6–9pm.

INEXPENSIVE

Duffy's Love Shack ★ 🏝 CARIBBEAN   This is a fun and happening place where you can mingle with the locals. As the evening wears on, the customers become the entertainment, often dancing on tables or forming conga lines. Yes, Duffy's also serves food. The restaurant is open air, with lots of bamboo and a thatched roof over the bar. Even the menu appears on a bamboo stick, like an old-fashioned fan. A standard American cuisine is spiced up with Caribbean flair. Start with the honey-barbecued ribs and conch fritters, then move on to jerk chicken or macadamia-nut mahimahi. After midnight, a late-night menu appears, mostly featuring sandwiches. The bar business is huge, and the bartender is known for his lethal rum drinks.

6500 Red Hook Plaza, Rte. 38. ℂ **340/779-2080.** www.duffysloveshack.com. Main courses $9–$20. No credit cards. Daily 11:30am–2am.

Fungi's on the Beach CARIBBEAN   Opening onto Pineapple Beach, this funky local bar with an outdoorsy atmosphere is a lot of fun, and the food is good, too. Come here for some of the juiciest burgers on the island, plus Caribbean specialties such as conch in butter sauce, roast suckling pig, johnnycakes, plantains, rice and beans, and callaloo soup. Stewed chicken is a local favorite. Nightly entertainment—reggae, reggae, and more reggae—is another draw.

In the Point Pleasant Resort (p. 68), 6600 Estate Smith Bay. ℂ **340/775-4142.** Main courses $7–$24. AE, MC, V. Daily 11:30am–10pm.

Señor Pizza PIZZA   Red Hook's best pizza is served here, and each generous slice is practically a lunch by itself. If you're staying nearby, the staff will deliver. If you're not, you can settle into one of the on-site picnic tables. Not in the mood for pizza? Try its close cousin, the tasty calzone.

Red Hook (across from the ferry dock). ℂ **340/775-3030.** Slice $3; whole pizza $16–$18. No credit cards. Daily 11am–9pm.

North Coast

EXPENSIVE

Romano's Restaurant ITALIAN   Located near Coral World, this hideaway is owned by New Jersey chef Tony Romano, who specializes in a flavor-filled and herb-laden cuisine that some diners yearn for after overdosing on Caribbean cooking. House favorites include linguine with pesto, four-cheese lasagna, a tender and well-flavored *osso buco,* scaloppini Marsala, and broiled salmon. All desserts are gratefully made on the premises. The restaurant, marked by exposed brick and well-stocked wine racks, always seems full of happy, lively diners.

66-97 Smith Bay Rd. ℂ **340/775-0045.** www.romanosrestaurant.com. Reservations recommended. Main courses $24–$42; pastas $24–$27. MC, V. Mon–Sat 6-10:30pm. Closed New Year's Day, 4 days in Apr for Carnival, Sept, and 4 days in Dec.

MODERATE

The Old Stone Farmhouse AMERICAN/INTERNATIONAL   Set in a wooded valley close to the 11th hole of the Mahogany Run Golf Course, this restaurant dates from the 1750s. It was created as a stable for a nearby Danish sugar plantation, and the walls are more than 2 feet thick. Ceiling fans and breezes blowing through the valley keep the place cool. For more than a quarter of a century, this restaurant has been feeding golfers and those who love them from an eclectic menu that takes advantage of the best seasonal produce. Begin, perhaps, with grilled portobello mushrooms with Asian duck. Many regulars come here for the well-prepared steak, and fresh fish dishes are always some of the best options.

Mahogany Run. (℠) **340/777-6277.** www.oldstonefarmhouse.com. Reservations recommended. Main courses $19–$32. AE, MC, V. Tues–Sun 5:30–9:30pm.

BEACHES

St. Thomas's beaches are renowned for their white sand and calm, turquoise waters, including the very best of them all, Magens Bay. Chances are that your hotel will be right on the beach, or very close to one. All the beaches in the Virgin Islands are public, and most St. Thomas beaches lie anywhere from 2 to 5 miles from Charlotte Amalie.

The North Coast

The gorgeous white sands of **Magens Bay ★★**—the family favorite of St. Thomas—lie between two mountains 3 miles north of the capital. The turquoise waters here are calm and ideal for swimming, though the snorkeling isn't as good. The beach is no secret, and it's usually terribly overcrowded, though it gets better in the midafternoon. Changing facilities, snorkeling gear, lounge chairs, paddle boats, and kayaks are available. There is no public transportation to get here (though some hotels provide shuttle buses). A taxi from Charlotte Amalie will cost about $8.50 per person. If you've rented a car, from Charlotte Amalie take Route 35 north all the way. The gates to the beach are open daily from 6am to 6pm. After 4pm, you'll need insect repellent. Admission is $1 per person and $1 per car. Don't bring valuables, and certainly don't leave anything of value in your parked car. Break-ins of cars and a few muggings are reported monthly.

A marked trail leads to **Little Magens Bay,** a separate, clothing-optional beach that's especially popular with gay and lesbian visitors. This is former U.S. President Clinton's preferred beach on St. Thomas (no, he doesn't go nude).

 HIDDEN BEACH discoveries

At this point, you'd think all the beaches on St. Thomas would be destroyed. But there are still a few hidden stretches of sand.

A sparkling beach of white sand, **Vessup Bay** is found at the end of Bluebeard's Road (Rte. 322) as it branches off Route 30 near the hamlet of Red Hook. Against a rocky backdrop, the beach curves around a pristine bay studded with vegetation, including cactuses, agave plants, and sea grape. The beach is popular with locals, singles, and couples; the east end of the beach is less populated than the west end. A watersports concessionaire operates here.

Another find is **Hull Bay,** on the north shore, just west of Magens Bay. Surfers are attracted to the waves along the western tip of Hull Bay, and local St. Thomas fishermen anchor in the more tranquil areas. Part of the beach is in the shade. Don't expect much in the way of watersports outfitters. There is a combined restaurant and open-air bar.

If you're relying on taxis, it will cost about $15 per person to reach either bay.

Coki Point Beach, in the northeast near Coral World, is good but often very crowded with both singles and families. It's noted for its warm, crystal-clear water, ideal for swimming and snorkeling; you'll see thousands of rainbow-hued fish swimming among the beautiful corals. Vendors even sell small bags of fish food, so you can feed the sea creatures while you're snorkeling. From the beach, there's a panoramic view of offshore Thatch Cay. Concessions can arrange everything from water-skiing to parasailing. A Vitrans East End bus runs to Smith Bay and lets you off at the gate to Coral World and Coki. Watch out for pickpockets.

Also on the north side of the island is luscious **Grand Beach,** one of St. Thomas's most beautiful, attracting families and couples. It opens onto Smith Bay and is near Coral World. Many watersports are available here. The beach is right off Route 38.

The East End

Small and special, **Secret Harbour** is near a collection of condos and has long been favored by singles of either sex and by those of all sexual persuasions. With its white sand and coconut palms, it's the epitome of Caribbean charm. The snorkeling near the rocks is some of the best on the island. No public transportation stops here, but it's an easy taxi ride east of Charlotte Amalie heading toward Red Hook.

Sapphire Beach ★ is set against the backdrop of the Sapphire Beach Resort and Marina, where you can have lunch or order drinks. Like Magens Bay Beach, this good, wide, safe beach is one of the most frequented by families. There are good views of offshore cays and St. John, and a large reef is close to the shore. Windsurfers like this beach a lot. Snorkeling gear and lounge chairs can be rented. Take the Vitrans East End bus from Charlotte Amalie, via Red Hook. Ask to be let off at the entrance to Sapphire Bay; it's not too far a walk from here to the water.

White-sand **Lindquist Beach** isn't a long strip, but it's one of the island's prettiest beaches. It's between Wyndham Sugar Bay Resort & Spa and the Sapphire Beach Resort. Many films and TV commercials have used this photogenic beach as a backdrop. It's not likely to be crowded, as it's not very well known. Couples in the know retreat here for sun and romance.

The South Coast

Morning Star ★—also known as Frenchman's Bay Beach—is near the Frenchman's Reef & Morning Star Marriott Beach Resort, about 2 miles east of Charlotte Amalie. Here, among the hip, savvy, often young crowds (many of whom are gay singles and couples), you can don your skimpiest bikini. Sailboats, snorkeling equipment, and lounge chairs are available for rent. The beach is easily reached by a cliff-front elevator at Frenchman's Reef. **Limetree Beach,** set against a backdrop of sea-grape trees and shady palms, also lures the hip folk. On this serene spread, you can bask in the sun and even feed hibiscus blossoms to the friendly iguanas. Snorkeling gear, lounge and beach chairs, towels, and drinks are available. There's no public transportation, but the beach can easily be reached by taxi from Charlotte Amalie.

West of Charlotte Amalie

Near the University of the Virgin Islands, in the southwest, **Brewers Bay** is one of the island's most popular beaches for families. The strip of white coral sand is almost as long as the beach at Magens Bay. Unfortunately, this isn't a good place for snorkeling. Vendors here sell light meals and drinks. From Charlotte Amalie, take the Fortuna bus heading west; get off at the edge of Brewers Bay, across from the Reichhold Center.

TAKING TO THE seas

On St. Thomas, most of the boat business is centered on the marina in Red Hook and Yacht Haven Marina in Charlotte Amalie.

The 50-foot *Yacht Nightwind,* Sapphire Marina (© **340/775-7017;** www.stjohndaysail.com), offers full-day sails to St. John and the outer islands. The $125 price includes continental breakfast, a champagne buffet lunch, and an open bar aboard. You're also given free snorkeling equipment and instruction.

New Horizons, 6501 Red Hook Plaza, Suite 16, Red Hook (© **800/808-7604** or 340/775-1171; www.newhorizonsvi.com), offers windborne excursions amid the cays and reefs of the Virgin Islands. The two-masted, 65-foot sloop has circumnavigated the globe, and has even been used as a design prototype for other boats. Owned and operated by Canadian Tim Krygsveld, it contains a hot-water shower, serves a specialty drink called a New Horizons Nooner, and carries a complete line of snorkeling equipment for adults and children. A full-day excursion with a continental breakfast, an Italian buffet lunch, and an open bar costs $120 per person ($80 for children ages 2–12). Excursions depart daily, weather permitting, from the Sapphire Beach Resort and Marina. Call ahead for reservations.

New Horizons also offers *New Horizons II* (© **340/775-1171;** www.newhorizonscharters.com), a 44-foot custom-made speedboat that takes you on a full-day trip, from 7am to 5pm, to some of the most scenic highlights of the British Virgin Islands. Trips cost $145 for adults or $95 for children ages 2 to 12. You will need your passport and will have to pay an additional $30-per-person Customs fee. *New Horizons II* leaves from the Sapphire Beach Resort at 7:15am and from the People Ferries' Dock in St. John at 7:45am.

You can avoid the crowds by sailing aboard the *Fantasy,* 6100 Leeward Way, no. 28 (© **340/775-5652;** fax 340/775-6256; www.daysailfantasy.com), which departs daily from the American Yacht Harbor at Red Hook at 9:30am and returns at 3pm. The boat takes a maximum of six passengers to St. John and nearby islands for swimming, snorkeling, and beachcombing. Snorkel gear and expert instruction are provided, as is a champagne lunch. The full-day trip costs $140 per person for adults and children. A half-day sail, usually offered only during the low season, lasts 3 hours and costs $100 for adults and children.

American Yacht Harbor Marina, Red Hook (© **340/775-6454;** www.igy-americanyachtharbor.com), offers both bareboat and fully crewed charters. Boats leave from a colorful yacht-filled harbor set against the backdrop of Heritage Gade, a reproduction of a Caribbean village. The harbor is home to numerous boat companies, including day-trippers, fishing boats, and sailing charters like **Nauti Nymph Powerboat Rentals** (© **340/775-5066**). There are also five restaurants on the property, serving everything from Continental to Caribbean cuisine. Another reliable charter-boat outfitter is **Charteryacht League,** at Flagship (© **800/524-2061** or 340/774-3944; www.vicl.org).

Sailors may want to check out the *Yachtsman's Guide to the Virgin Islands,* available at major marine outlets, at bookstores, through catalog merchandisers, or direct from **Tropic Isle Publishers,** P.O. Box 12, Adelphia, NJ 07710 (© **877/923-9653;** www.yachtsmansguide.com). This annual guide, which costs $17, is supplemented by photographs; landfall sketches and charts showing harbors and harbor entrances, anchorages, channels, and landmarks; and information on preparations necessary for cruising the islands.

Lindbergh Beach, with a lifeguard, restrooms, and a bathhouse, is at the Island Beachcomber Hotel (p. 63) and is used extensively by locals, who stage events from political rallies to Carnival parties here. Beach-loving couples are also attracted to this beach. It's not good for snorkeling. Drinks are served on the beach. Take the Fortuna bus route west from Charlotte Amalie.

FUN IN THE SURF & SUN

FISHING The U.S. Virgins have excellent deep-sea fishing—some 19 world records (eight for blue marlin) have been set in these waters. Outfitters abound at the major marinas like Red Hook. **Peanut Gallery Fishing Charters,** 8168 Crown Bay Marina, Suite 310 (© **340/642-7423;** www.fishingstthomas.com), offers both light-tackle inshore sportsfishing and deep-sea sportsfishing. Your captain will be Captain Steve Malpere, who has been fishing in Caribbean waters for more than 30 years, or Captain David Pearsall. The vessels provide inshore fishing year-round for the likes of barracuda, bonefish, kingfish, mackerel, and tarpon. The cost for 4 hours is $500; 6 hours, $600 to $650; and 8 hours, $800 to $880.

You can also line-fish from the rocky shore along Mandahl Beach on the north coast. The tourist office in Charlotte Amalie should have a listing of legal spots for line fishing around the island.

GOLF **Mahogany Run,** on the north shore at Mahogany Run Road (© **800/253-7103;** www.mahoganyrungolf.com), is an 18-hole, par-70 course. This beautiful course rises and drops like a roller coaster on its journey to the sea; cliffs and crashing sea waves are the ultimate hazards at the 13th and 14th holes. Greens fees are $125 to $165 for 18 holes. Carts are included. Club rental costs $45.

KAYAK TOURS **Virgin Islands Ecotours/Mangrove Adventures** (© **340/779-2155;** www.viecotours.com) offers half-day kayak trips through the mangrove lagoon on the southern coastline. The cost is $69 per person. The tour is led by professional naturalists who allow for 30 to 40 minutes of snorkeling.

SAILING ★ **Yacht Haven Grande St. Thomas,** 9100 Port of Sale, Charlotte Amalie (© **340/774-9500**), is the premier marine facilities for mega-yachts in the Caribbean. Located alongside Charlotte Amalie harbor, it encompasses a 48-slip

 A Thrilling Dive for Nondivers

Virgin Islands Snuba Excursions (© **340/693-8063;** www.visnuba.com) are ideal for beginning swimmers. These special excursions are offered both at Coral World on St. Thomas and at Trunk Bay on St. John. With Snuba's equipment—an air line that attaches to an air tank floating on the surface—even novices can breathe easily underwater without the use of heavy restrictive dive gear. The Snuba operations begin in waist-deep water and make a gradual descent to a depth of 20 feet. This is great fun for the whole family, as kids ages 8 and up can participate, and no snorkeling or scuba experience is needed. Most orientation and guided underwater tours take 1½ hours, costing $65 per person on St. John. On St. Thomas, a pass to Coral World (p. 92) is included, and the rate is $68 for adults and $65 for children 8 to 12. Reservations are required.

Bringing Out the Sir Francis Drake in You

Tired of escorted tours? **Nauti Nymph Magic Moments,** American Yacht Harbor, Red Hook (© **800/734-7345** in the U.S., or 340/775-5066; www.yachtmagicmoments.com), reaches out to the independent traveler and adventurer. The knowing staff assists in designing a personal itinerary for a bareboat rental, or can hook you up with a captained day trip. A choice of Coast Guard–approved and fully equipped vessels ranging in size from 25 to 31 feet are available. Boats are kept in top condition. On your own, you can explore the British Virgin Islands, including such little-known islands as Jost Van Dyke and Norman Island, in the tradition of Sir Francis Drake. Norman Island, incidentally, was the inspiration for Robert Louis Stevenson's *Treasure Island.* The fare for such sailing adventures begins at $425 per passenger, or half price for children 9 and under.

facility, with dining, entertainment, and recreational options. **American Yacht Harbor ★★**, Red Hook (© **340/775-6454;** www.igy-americanyachtharbor.com), can refer both bareboat and fully crewed charters. It leaves from the east end of St. Thomas in Vessup Bay. The harbor is home to numerous boat companies, including day-trippers, fishing boats, and sailing charters. There are also five restaurants on the property, serving everything from Continental to Caribbean cuisine. Another reliable outfitter is **Charteryacht League ★★**, at Gregory East (© **800/524-2061** in the U.S., or 340/774-3944; www.vicl.org).

Sailors may want to check out the *Yachtsman's Guide to the Virgin Islands,* available at major marine outlets, at bookstores, through catalog merchandisers, or directly from **Tropical Publishers,** P.O. Box 12, Adelphia, NJ 07710 (© **877/923-9653;** www.yachtsmansguide.com).

SCUBA DIVING & SNORKELING The best scuba-diving site off St. Thomas, especially for novices, has to be **Cow and Calf Rocks,** off the southeast end (45 min. from Charlotte Amalie by boat); here, you'll discover a network of coral tunnels filled with caves, reefs, and ancient boulders encrusted with coral. The *Cartanser Sr.,* a sunken World War II cargo ship that lies in about 35 feet of water, is beautifully encrusted with coral and is home to myriad colorful resident fish. Another popular wreck dive is the *Maj. General Rogers,* the stripped-down hull of a former Coast Guard cutter.

Experienced divers may want to dive at exposed sheer rock pinnacles like **Sail Rock** and **French Cap Pinnacle,** which are encrusted with hard and soft corals, and are frequented by lobsters and green and hawksbill turtles. Both spots are exposed to open-ocean currents, making these very challenging dives.

Coki Beach Dive Club, Coki Beach (© **800/474-COKI** [474-2654] or 340/775-4220; www.cokidive.com), a PADI center, offers scuba-diving courses and guided dive tours for beginners and certified divers alike. You can also rent diving and snorkeling gear here. A one-tank dive costs $65, while a two-tank dive is $85, if you use the club's equipment.

St. Thomas Diving Club, 7147 Bolongo Bay (© **877/538-8734** in the U.S., or 340/776-2381; www.stthomasdivingclub.com), is a full-service, PADI five-star IDC center, and the best on the island. An open-water certification course, including four

Racing with the Pros

ONDECK Ocean Racing, a company based in Portsmouth, England, maintains an armada of high-tech racing ships—Farr 65s and Farr 40s—which some experts say are the most technologically advanced wind-operated racing vessels anywhere. With Kevlar hulls and either aluminum or carbon-fiber masts, they set out between three and four times a day, weather conditions permitting, with groups of between 6 and 12 participants in each boatload. They then race against one another in circumstances that simulate Olympic racing conditions for experiences that are wild, foamy, and even scary. ONDECK recommends that passengers allocate 3 hours for an experience that invariably includes about 2 hours sailing. Expect blustery winds and the possibility of getting drenched as part of the process. Adults pay $99 per jaunt. The **headquarters** is at 9100 Havensight, Ste. 1 (✆ **843/971-0700**; www. ondeckgroup.com).

scuba dives, costs $429. An advanced open-water certification course, including five dives that can be accomplished in 2 days, goes for $425. You can also enjoy local snorkeling for $55.

DIVE IN!, in the Sapphire Beach Resort and Marina, Smith Bay Road, Route 36 (✆ **866/434-8346,** ext. 2144, in the U.S., or 340/777-5255; www.diveinusvi.com), is a well-recommended, complete diving center that offers some of the finest services in the U.S. Virgin Islands, including professional instruction (beginner to advanced), daily beach and boat dives, custom dive packages, snorkeling trips, and a full-service PADI dive center. An introductory resort course costs $105, with a one-tank dive going for $80 and two-tank dives costing $110. A six-dive pass costs $300.

With **Homer's Scuba and Snorkel Tours** (✆ **866/719-1856** or 340/774-7606; www.nightsnorkel.com), you're provided with a submersible flashlight, glow stick, and wet suit, and taken on an eerie underwater experience at night to meet the denizens of the deep. Various sea creatures such as an octopus will glide before you. The cost is $50 per person, and tours are conducted Tuesday to Saturday with reservations required.

Impressions

Men who settle at St. Thomas have most probably roughed it elsewhere unsuccessfully.
—Anthony Trollope, *The West Indies and the Spanish Main,* 1859

TENNIS The best tennis on the island is at the **Wyndham Sugar Bay Beach Club,** 6500 Estate Smith Bay (✆ **340/777-7100**), which has three Laykold courts lit at night and a pro shop. Nonguests pay $8 per hour.

Another good resort for tennis is the **Bolongo Bay Beach Resort,** Bolongo Bay (✆ **340/775-1800**), which has two courts that are lit until 8pm. They're free to members and hotel guests, but cost $10 per hour for nonguests.

Marriott Frenchman's Reef Tennis Courts, Flamboyant Point (✆ **340/776-8500**), has two courts. Again, nonguests are charged $15 per hour per court. Lights stay on until 10pm.

SEEING THE SIGHTS

In 1733, the Danish government acquired the Virgin Islands from the Danish West India Company. The Danes did not find land suitable for agriculture, and St. Thomas became a bustling port instead through which the products from the rest of the West Indies were traded. It also became a center for transporting slaves.

The Virgin Islands remained under Danish rule until 1917, when the U.S., fearing German infiltration in the Caribbean during World War I, purchased the islands from Denmark. Today the U.S. Virgin Islands claims the highest per-capita income in the Caribbean, with some 50,000 settlers of varying ethnicity making their home in St. Thomas alone. The port is also the busiest cruise-ship harbor in the West Indies, outranking Puerto Rico.

Today you can see many vestiges of the island's history. The capital, **Charlotte Amalie,** with its white houses and bright red roofs glistening in the sun, is one of the most beautiful towns in the Caribbean. It's most famous for shopping, but the town is also filled with historic sights, like Fort Christian, an intriguing 17th-century building constructed by the Danes. The town's architecture reflects the island's culturally diverse past: You'll pass Dutch doors, Danish red-tile roofs, French iron grillwork, and Spanish-style patios.

WALKING TOUR: CHARLOTTE AMALIE

START:	**King's Wharf.**
FINISH:	**Waterfront.**
TIME:	**2½ hours.**
BEST TIME:	**Before 10am to avoid cruise-ship passengers.**
WORST TIME:	**Around midday to 4pm, when traffic and pedestrians are at their most plentiful.**

Even with the crowds and shops, it is easy to see how the natural colors and charm of the Caribbean come to life in the waterfront town of Charlotte Amalie. The capital of St. Thomas once attracted seafarers from all over the globe, and pirates and sailors of the Confederacy used the port during the American Civil War. At one time, St. Thomas was the biggest slave market in the world. Today, the old warehouses, once used for storing stolen pirate goods, have been converted to shops. In fact, the main streets, called "gade" (a reflection of their Danish heritage), now coalesce into a virtual shopping mall, and are often packed. Sandwiched among these shops are a few historic buildings, most of which can be seen on foot in about 2 hours. Start your walking tour along the eastern harborfront at King's Wharf.

1 King's Wharf

This is the site of the Virgin Islands Legislature, which is housed in apple-green military barracks dating from 1874.

From here, walk away from the harbor up Fort Pladsen to:

2 Fort Christian

Dating from 1672 and named after the Danish King Christian V, this structure was a governor's residence, police station, court, and jail until it became a national historic landmark in 1977. A museum here illuminates the island's history and culture. Inside you'll see cultural workshops and an exhibit of late-Victorian furnishings. A museum shop features local crafts, maps, and prints. Fort Christian (© **340/776-8605**) is open Monday through Friday from 9am to 4pm; admission is $4.

Continue walking up Fort Pladsen to:

3 Emancipation Park

This is where a proclamation freeing African slaves and indentured European servants was read on July 3, 1848. The park is now mostly a picnic area for local workers and visitors. Near the park is the:

4 Grand Hotel

From here, a visitor center dispenses valuable travel information about the island. When this hotel was launched in 1837, it was a grand address, but it later fell into decay, and finally closed in 1975. The former guest rooms upstairs have been turned into offices and a restaurant.

Northwest of the park, at Main Street and Tolbod Gade, stands the:

5 Central Post Office

On display here are murals by Stephen Dohanos, who became famous as an artist for the *Saturday Evening Post*.

From the post office, walk east along Norre Gade to the:

6 Frederik Lutheran Church

This church was built between 1780 and 1793. The original Georgian-style building, financed by a free black parishioner, Jean Reeneaus, was reconstructed in 1825 and again in 1870, after it was damaged in a hurricane.

Exiting the church, walk east along Norre Gade to Lille Taarne Gade. Turn left (north) and climb to Kongens Gade (King St.), passing through a neighborhood of law firms, to:

7 Government House

This is the administrative headquarters for the U.S. Virgin Islands. It's been the center of political life in the islands since it was built, around the time of the American Civil War. Visitors can take a tour on the first two floors for free Monday through Saturday from 8am to noon and from 1 to 5pm.

After leaving Government House, turn immediately to your left and look for the sign for:

8 Seven Arches Museum

Browsers and gapers love checking out this museum at Government Hill (© **340/774-9295**), the private home of longtime residents Philibert Fluck and Barbara Demaras. This 2-centuries-old Danish house has been completely restored and furnished with antiques. Walk through the yellow ballast arches into the Great Room, which has a wonderful view of the Caribbean's busiest harbor. The $7 admission fee includes a cold tropical drink served in a beautiful, walled flower garden. It's open by appointment.

Walking Tour: Charlotte Amalie

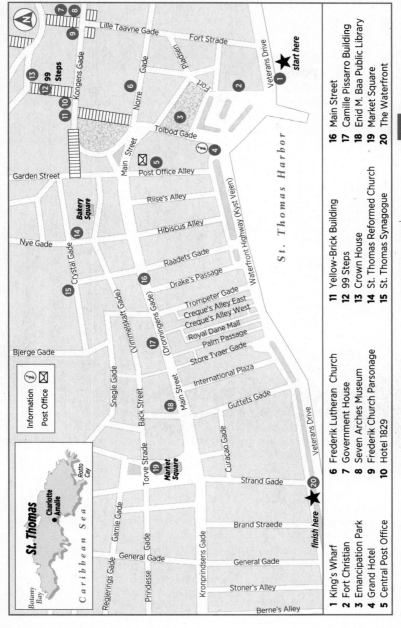

1 King's Wharf
2 Fort Christian
3 Emancipation Park
4 Grand Hotel
5 Central Post Office
6 Frederik Lutheran Church
7 Government House
8 Seven Arches Museum
9 Frederik Church Parsonage
10 Hotel 1829
11 Yellow-Brick Building
12 99 Steps
13 Crown House
14 St. Thomas Reformed Church
15 St. Thomas Synagogue
16 Main Street
17 Camille Pissarro Building
18 Enid M. Baa Public Library
19 Market Square
20 The Waterfront

After visiting the museum, return to Government House. Next to the building is:

9 Frederik Church Parsonage

This building dates from 1725. It's one of the oldest houses on the island, and the only structure in the Government Hill district to retain its simple 18th-century lines.

Continue west along Kongens Gade until you reach:

10 Hotel 1829

Formerly known as the Lavalette House, this place was designed in 1829 by one of the leading merchants of Charlotte Amalie. This is a landmark building and a charming hotel that has attracted many of the island's most famous visitors.

This is also a great place to take a break. Hotel 1829 provides the perfect veranda, with a spectacular view, for a midday drink or a sundowner. You may just fall in love with the place, abandon this tour, and stick around for dinner. The bar is open Monday to Saturday 4 to 11pm. For more information on the hotel, see p. 62.

Next door (still on the same side of the street), observe the:

11 Yellow-Brick Building

This structure was built in 1854 in what local architects called "the style of Copenhagen." You can go inside and browse the many shops within.

At this point, you might want to double back slightly on Kongens Gade to climb the famous:

12 99 Steps

These steps (actually 103 in total) were erected in the early 1700s, and take you to the summit of Government Hill, from where you'll see the 18th-century:

13 Crown House

This stately private house is immediately to your right, on the south side of the street. This was the home of von Scholten, the Danish ruler who issued the famous proclamation of emancipation in 1848 (see Emancipation Park, above).

Walk back down the steps and continue right (west) along Kongens Gade, then down a pair of old brick steps until you reach Garden Street. Go right (north) on Garden Street and take a left onto Crystal Gade. On your left, at the corner of Nye Gade and Crystal Gade, you'll see:

14 St. Thomas Reformed Church

This building is from 1844. Much of its original structure, designed like a Greek temple, has been preserved intact.

Continue up Crystal Gade. On your right (north side), you'll come to:

15 St. Thomas Synagogue

This is the oldest synagogue in continuous use under the American flag, and the second oldest in the Western Hemisphere. It was erected in 1833 by Sephardic Jews, and it still maintains the tradition of having sand on the floor, commemorating the exodus from Egypt. The structure was built of local stone, ballast brick from Denmark, and mortar made of molasses and sand. It's open to visitors

Monday to Friday 9am to 4pm. Next door, the **Weibel Museum** showcases 300 years of Jewish history. It keeps the same hours.

Retrace your steps (east) to Raadets Gade and turn south toward the water, crossing the famous Vimmelskaft Gade or "Back Street" (it can get a bit seedy at night, so be aware if you are walking after dark). Continue along Raadets Gade until you reach:

16 Main Street

This is Charlotte Amalie's major artery and most famous shopping street. Turn right (west) and walk along Main Street until you come to the mid-19th-century:

17 Camille Pissarro Building

This structure will be on your right, at the Amsterdam Sauer Jewelry Store. Pissarro, a Spanish Jew who became one of the founders of French Impressionism, was born in this building as Jacob Pizarro in 1830. Before moving to Paris, he worked for his father in a store on Main Street. Also housed in the building is **Gallery Camille Pissarro,** with a few Pissarro paintings on display and prints by local artists for sale.

Continuing west along Main Street, you will pass on your right the:

18 Enid M. Baa Public Library

This building, formerly the von Bretton House, dates from 1818. Keep heading west until you reach:

19 Market Square

This was the center of a large slave-trading market before the 1848 emancipation and is officially called Rothschild Francis Square. Today it's an open-air fruit and vegetable market, selling, among other items, *genips* (grape-type fruit; to eat one, break open the skin and suck the pulp off the pit). The wrought-iron roof covered a railway station at the turn of the 20th century. The market is open Monday to Saturday, its busiest day; hours vary, but it's busiest from 9am to 3pm.

If the *genip* doesn't satisfy you, take Strand Gade down (south) to:

20 The Waterfront

Also known as Kyst Vejen, this is where you can purchase a fresh coconut. One of the vendors here will whack off the top with a machete so that you can drink the sweet milk from its hull. You'll have an up-close view of one of the most scenic harbors in the West Indies, though it's usually filled with cruise ships.

In His Footsteps: Camille Pissarro (1830–1903)

The dean of the French Impressionist painters was the most famous resident ever born on the island of St. Thomas. Attracted by the work of Camille Corot and, later, Gustave Courbet, Pissarro moved in a lofty artistic circle of friends that included Monet, Cézanne, and Renoir. He painted landscapes and scenes of rural life, and also some portraits.

- **Birthplace:** Danish St. Thomas, July 10, 1830, son of Jewish parents of French/Spanish extraction.
- **Residences:** The Pissarro Building, off Main Street in Charlotte Amalie; Paris.
- **Resting Place:** Paris.

THE best VIEWS IN ST. THOMAS

The **Paradise Point St. Thomas Skyride** (© **340/774-9809;** www.stthomassky ride.com) affords visitors a dramatic view of Charlotte Amalie's harbor, with a ride to a 700-foot peak. The tramway, similar to those used at ski resorts, operates six cars, each with an eight-person capacity, for the 15-minute round-trip ride. It transports customers from the Havensight area to Paradise Point, where you can disembark to visit shops and the popular restaurant and bar. The tramway runs daily 9am to 5pm. Reservations are required; the cost is $21 per adult round-trip, $11 round-trip for children 6 to 12, and free for children 5 and under.

For those who can afford it or who simply aren't satisfied with the view from Paradise Point, there's **Air Center Helicopters,** Waterfront, Charlotte Amalie (© **340/775-7335;** www.aircenter helicopters.com). The short but dramatic rides go over the U.S. Virgins. A four- to six-seater helicopter flies at a cost of $750 per half-hour. Day trips to St. John and St. Croix can also be arranged, as well as trips to San Juan and the B.V.I.

Attractions in the West

Route 30 (Veterans Dr.) will take you west of Charlotte Amalie to **Frenchtown** (turn left at the sign to the Admiral's Inn). Early French-speaking settlers arrived on St. Thomas from St. Bart's after they were uprooted by the Swedes. Many of today's island residents are the direct descendants of those long-ago immigrants, who were known for speaking a distinctive French patois. This colorful village contains a bevy of restaurants and taverns. Because Charlotte Amalie has become somewhat dangerous at night, Frenchtown has picked up its after-dark business and is the best spot for dancing, drinking, and other local entertainment.

Farther west, Harwood Highway (Rte. 308) will lead you to **Crown Mountain Road,** a scenic drive opening onto the best views of the hills, beaches, and crystal-clear waters around St. Thomas.

Attractions Around the Island

A driving tour is the best way to see the island; see the itinerary below for our suggestions. **Tropic Tours,** 14AB the Guardian Building (© **800/524-4334** or 340/774-1855; www.tropictoursusvi.com), offers practically the same tour of St. Thomas, including Drake's Seat, the Estate St. Peter Greathouse, and Charlotte Amalie shopping. The cost is $45 per person, $36 for children 12 and under.

Coral World Ocean Park ★ ☺ This marine complex, which is St. Thomas's number-one tourist attraction, features a three-story underwater observation tower 100 feet offshore. Inside, you'll spy sea sponges, fish, coral, and other aquatic creatures in their natural state. An 80,000-gallon reef tank features exotic marine life of the Caribbean; another tank is devoted to sea predators, with circling sharks and giant moray eels. Activities include daily fish and shark feedings. The latest addition to the park is a semisubmarine that lets you enjoy the panoramic view and the "down under" feeling of a submarine without truly submerging.

Nondivers can get some of the thrill long known to scuba aficionados by participating in **Sea Trek,** which is slightly different from Snuba (p. 84). For $68, or $59 for

especially FOR KIDS

Coral World (p. 92) This is *the* place on St. Thomas to take your children. It's a hands-on experience—kids can even shake hands with a starfish at the Touch Pond. Later, they can discover exotic Marine Gardens, where 20 aquariums showcase the Caribbean's incredible natural marine treasures.

Magens Bay Beach (p. 81) This beach is one of the finest in the world, with calm waters, white sand, and lots of facilities, including picnic tables.

children, you can get a full immersion undersea with no experience necessary. Participants are given a helmet and a tube to breathe through. The tube is attached to an air source at the observatory tower. You then enjoy a 20-minute stroll in water that's 18 feet deep, observing rainbow-hued tropical fish and the coral reefs as you move along the seafloor. It's a marvelous way to experience the world through the eyes of a fish. *Note:* Reservations are required, so call ahead or log on to the park's website.

Coral World's guests can take advantage of adjacent **Coki Beach** for snorkel rentals, scuba lessons, or simply swimming and relaxing. Lockers and showers are available. Also included in the marine park are the Tropical Terrace Restaurant, duty-free shops, and a nature trail.

6450 Estates Smith Bay, a 20-min. drive from Charlotte Amalie off Rte. 38. (2) **340/775-1555.** www. coralworldvi.com. Admission $19 adults, $10 children ages 3–12. Daily 9am–4pm.

Estate St. Peter Greathouse & Botanical Gardens This estate consists of 11 acres set at the foot of volcanic peaks on the northern rim of the island. The grounds are laced with self-guided nature walks that will acquaint you with some 200 varieties of West Indian plants and trees, including an umbrella plant from Madagascar. From a panoramic deck in the gardens, you can see some 20 of the Virgin Islands, including Hans Lollick, an uninhabited island between Thatched Cay and Madahl Point. The house itself, filled with local art, is worth a visit.

At the corner of Rte. 40 (6A St. Peter Mountain Rd.) and Barrett Hill Rd. (2) **340/774-4999.** www. greathouse-mountaintop.com. Admission $5 adults, $2.50 children 11 and under. Daily 8am–4pm.

DRIVING TOUR: **ST. THOMAS**

START:	**Fort Christian.**
FINISH:	**Magens Bay Beach.**
TIME:	**2½ hours.**
BEST TIME:	**Sunday, when traffic is lightest.**
WORST TIMES:	**Wednesday and Saturday, when traffic is heaviest.**

Begin at Fort Christian, in the eastern part of Charlotte Amalie, and head west along the Waterfront. To your left, you'll see cruise ships anchored offshore, and to your right, you'll find several shops. Continue west on Route 30 and pass the Cyril E. King Airport on your left. As the road forks toward the airport, keep right along Route 30, which runs parallel to the airport.

The most famous woman pirate of the Caribbean teamed up with Calico Jack, and together they became the scourge of the Caribbean Basin until their arrest in 1720 off the coast of Jamaica. Calico Jack was hanged, but Anne, pregnant, approached the bench and said, "Milord, I plead with my belly." The judge ordered a stay of execution.

- **Birthplace:** Cork, Ireland, daughter of a prominent attorney and his wife's maid.
- **Residences:** Various pirate ships throughout the Caribbean; Charlotte Amalie. (She went there originally to slit the throat of her runaway first husband, a ne'er-do-well sailor whom she murdered in a brothel.)
- **Resting Place:** South Carolina.

At about 2½ miles from Fort Christian, on your right, will be:

1 University of the Virgin Islands

Established in 1961, this is the major university in the Virgin Islands. It's a modern complex with landscaped campus grounds; its primary attraction is the Reichhold Center for the Arts (p. 106).

Continue west on Route 30 until you reach:

2 Brewers Bay

The bay will be on your left. You may want to park and go for a swim, as this is one of the better beaches on the island.

Continue 4 miles west, climbing uphill through scrub country along a hilly drive past the junction with Route 301. This far-west stretch of Route 30 is called:

3 Fortuna Road

This is one of the most scenic areas in St. Thomas, with sweeping views of the water and offshore islands on your left. Along the way, you'll come across parking areas where you can pull off and enjoy the view (the **Bethesda Hill** vista is particularly panoramic). The districts you pass through—Bonne Esperance and Perseverance—are named after the old plantations that once stood here. The area is now primarily residential. At Bordeaux Hill, you descend sharply and the road narrows until you come to a dead end.

At this point, turn around and head back east along Route 30. Be careful: The road is poorly marked at this point. At the junction with Route 301, turn left and head northeast. You will come to another junction at:

4 Crown Mountain Road

This is the most scenic road in the Virgin Islands. Turn left here onto Route 33. The road will sweep northward before it makes an abrupt switch to the east. You will be traversing the mountainous heartland of St. Thomas. Expect hairpin turns during your descent. You'll often have to reduce your speed to 10 mph, especially in the Mafolie district. The road will eventually lead to the junction with Route 37, where you should go left, but only for a short distance, until you reach the junction with Route 40. At one point, routes 37 and 40 become the same highway. When they separate, turn right and stay on Route 40 to:

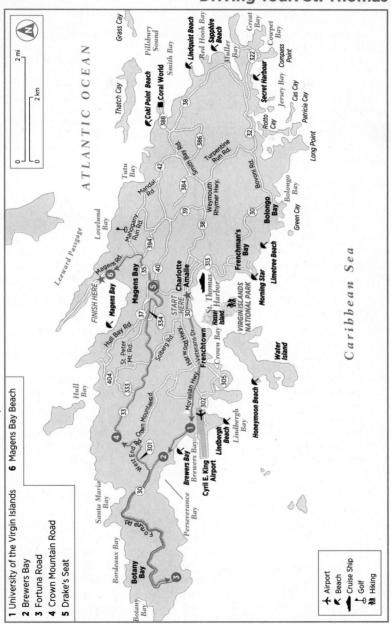

1 University of the Virgin Islands
2 Brewers Bay
3 Fortuna Road
4 Crown Mountain Road
5 Drake's Seat
6 Magens Bay Beach

Airport
Beach
Cruise Ship
Golf
Hiking

ATLANTIC OCEAN

Caribbean Sea

2 mi
2 km

5 Drake's Seat

This is where Sir Francis Drake is said to have looked out over the sea and charted the best routes through the Virgin Islands.

Continue left onto Route 35. The road will veer northwest. Follow it all the way to:

6 Magens Bay Beach

Magens Bay is hailed as one of the most beautiful beaches in the world. Here you can rent Sunfish sailboats, glass-bottom paddle boats, and sailboards. Lounge chairs, changing facilities, showers, lockers, and picnic tables are also available.

Finish up your tour at **Magens Bay Bar & Grill,** Magens Bay Beach (☎ **340/777-6270**), an ideal place for light meals on this heart-shaped beach. You can order sandwiches, salads, pizza by the slice, soft drinks, and beer and other alcoholic beverages. It's open daily 9:30am to 5pm.

WATER ISLAND lore & history

To the native residents of St. Thomas, Water Island remains a land of legend and lore, having been settled by the Arawak Indians in the early 15th century. In the days of Caribbean piracy, as evoked by Disney's *Pirates of the Caribbean* movies, the island was used for both anchorage and fresh water, as pirates found numerous freshwater ponds here. Islanders on St. Thomas claim that millions of dollars in pirate treasure remain buried on Water Island, but so far no one has dug it up. An old leather trunk was once discovered, but it was empty except for one gold doubloon.

When European colonization arrived in the late 17th century, many Danes tried to use the island for raising cows and goats. White plantation owners and colonists shunned the island because of its arid land, so unlike the rest of the Caribbean, Water Island was farmed by nonwhite plantation owners. These were freed men of color who operated the plantations, like Jean Renaud, a free mulatto who owned the entire island in 1769, working it with 18 slaves.

In 1944, the United States bought the island for $10,000. The military began planning Fort Segarra here but the war ended before it could be built. Traces of

"the fort that never was" can still be seen today.

In 1950, the Department of the Interior leased the island to Water Phillips, a developer, for $3,000 annually. He built homes and a 100-room hotel. Popular in the 1950s, the hotel then became the setting for Herman Wouk's 1965 novel, *Don't Stop the Carnival.* That novel remains even today one of the best-selling novels ever written with a Caribbean setting. Incidentally, native residents of St. Croix claim that the novel was based on a hotel being built in the harbor of Christiansted. The novel was turned into a short-lived musical by Jimmy Buffet in 1997. In 1989, Hurricane Hugo severely damaged the hotel, and it was shut down. It lies dormant today. The lease Phillips signed ran out 3 years later, and in 1996, Water Island was transferred to the federal government, in whose hands it remains today.

At present (and likely to remain so for a long time to come), no foundations have been poured on Water Island. Nothing has been inaugurated. The cost of developing roads, irrigation, and sewage lines in this eco-sensitive environment is a daunting challenge and a dream that, for the immediate future, remains too expensive an undertaking.

A historical adventure ON HASSEL ISLAND

You can have an offbeat adventure by exploring Hassel Island. Taking in some 136 acres, most of this island is protected as a Virgin Islands National Park.

This island, which was connected to the mainland of St. Thomas until 1865 (end of the Civil War) when a channel was dug for easier passages of ships, has a rich history. During the early 19th century's Napoleonic Wars, the British occupied the island, and the ruins of two forts that the troops constructed here, Willoughby and Shipley, can be seen today. You can explore these ruins.

Hassel Island was once used by the Danes to defend the port of Charlotte Amalie. In 1840, the Danes built a marine railway operation for boat and sail repairs. As late as the 1960s, the marine railway was still in operation. It was one of the earliest steam-powered marine railways in the Western Hemisphere, as well as the oldest surviving example of a steam-powered marine railway in the world.

In 1978, some 95% of Hassel Island was sold to the U. S. National Park Service by its owners, the Paiewonski family. For almost 30 years, the island sat untouched and deteriorating. Today some efforts are being made to restore the island as a living testimony to the historical heritage of St. Thomas.

Excursions from St. Thomas

WATER ISLAND

Water Island, ¾ mile off the coast from the harbor at Charlotte Amalie, is the fourth-largest island in the U.S. Virgins, with nearly 500 acres of land. Irregular in shape, 2½-mile-long Water Island is filled with many bays and peninsulas, and studded with several good, sandy beaches along with secluded coves and rocky headlands. Established as the fourth U.S. Virgin Island in 1996, Water Island was once a part of a peninsula jutting out from St. Thomas, but a channel was cut through, allowing U.S. submarines to reach their base in a bay to the west.

At palm-shaded **Honeymoon Beach,** you can swim, snorkel, sail, water-ski, or sunbathe. The beach has been significantly improved in the past few years, as loads of rocks and gravel were hauled off and trees and brush removed. The sand was sifted to get rid of debris, and a dredge removed the seaweed and deposited white sand on the shore. Today it looks quite beautiful.

There is no commerce on the island—no taxis, gas stations, hotels, shops, or even a main town. Residents are totally dependent on Charlotte Amalie, lying half a mile away. It you're planning on a visit, bring water and your own food supplies and other needs. Don't count on it, but there is often a food cart on Honeymoon Beach, serving surprisingly good meals, including an all-steak lunch.

A ferry (© **340/774-2255;** www.viferries.com) runs between Crown Bay Marina and Water Island several times a day for $5 one-way; $10 round-trip (Crown Bay Marina is part of the St. Thomas submarine base). If you prefer a guided tour, check in with **Water Island Adventures** (© **340/714-2186;** www.waterisland adventures.com). For $65 (cash only) per person, including transportation and equipment, a trip to Water Island includes a cycling tour. In the 3½ hours of the tour, beach time is allowed. Departures are from the dock at Havensight Mall or Crown Bay Marina.

HASSEL ISLAND

In the same bay, and even closer to shore, is **Hassel Island** (www.hasselisland.org). This island is almost completely deserted, and is protected as part of a U.S. National Park, which prohibits most forms of development. There are no hotels or services of any kind here, and swimming is limited to narrow, rocky beaches. Even so, many visitors hire a boat to drop them off for an hour or two.

A hike along the shoreline is a welcome relief from the cruise-ship congestion of Charlotte Amalie. The island is riddled with some trails which can be traversed, taking you across gentle hills with dry woods, lots of plants, and plenty of cacti— you'll think you're in the Arizona desert. Beach lovers head for the western shore, where they'll find white sands shaded by sea grapes. You can also explore the ruins of early-19th-century English fortifications and mid-19th-century shopping and coal stations. Bring water and food if you plan to spend more than 3 hours. The rather barren island has little shade, so dress accordingly and make sure you carry plenty of drinking water.

A small ferry runs from the Crown Bay Marina on St. Thomas to Hassel, costing $5 to $10 round-trip.

ST. JOHN

An even better option is a day trip to **St. John** (www.stjohnusvi.com/ferry.html), home of the world-famous Trunk Bay Beach. To get there, you can take one of many ferry services. Boats depart from Charlotte Amalie at Vendors Plaza or, more frequently, from Red Hook, and arrive in St. John's Cruz Bay. The one-way fare is $7 for adults from Red Hook and $11 for adults from Charlotte Amalie. The fare for children 11 and under is $1. Near the access ramp of the pier in Cruz Bay, St. John, you'll find rows of independently operated taxis and their drivers, who will take you on a tour of the island. Independent-minded visitors can usually get a 4-hour guided tour for $60 (often shared with another passenger or two). Cruise-ship passengers are generally charged $50 for a 2-hour tour. A full day (7 hr.) is $75 (children 12 and under, $65). If you want to skip the tour of St. John and head right to the beach at Trunk Bay for the day, simply negotiate a fare with one of the taxi drivers at the pier. Be sure to arrange a time to be picked up at the end of the day, too. The cost of a one-way trip is usually $5 to $10 per person, depending on how much the cabby thinks he can get out of you (note that $10 is the most expensive charge). See chapter 4 for more on St. John.

SHOPPING

The discounted, duty-free shopping in the Virgin Islands makes St. Thomas a shopping mecca. It's possible to find well-known brand names here at savings of up to 60% off mainland prices. But be warned—savings are not always good, so make sure you know the price of the item back home to determine if you are truly getting a good deal. Having sounded that warning, we'll mention some St. Thomas shops where we have indeed found really good buys. For more help, the local publications *This Week in St. Thomas* and *Best Buys* have updates on sales and shop openings.

Most shops are open Monday to Saturday 9am to 5pm. Some stores are open Sunday and holidays if a cruise ship is in port.

Shopping in Charlotte Amalie

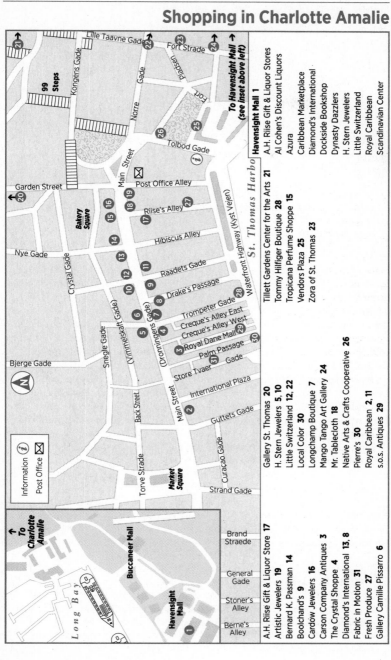

Havensight Mall 1

A.H. Riise Gift & Liquor Stores
Al Cohen's Discount Liquors
Azura
Caribbean Marketplace
Diamond's International
Dockside Bookshop
Dynasty Dazzlers
H. Stern Jewelers
Little Switzerland
Royal Caribbean
Scandinavian Center

Tillett Gardens Center for the Arts **21**
Tommy Hilfiger Boutique **28**
Tropicana Perfume Shoppe **15**
Vendors Plaza **25**
Zora of St. Thomas **23**

Gallery St. Thomas **20**
H. Stern Jewelers **5, 10**
Little Switzerland **12, 22**
Local Color **30**
Longchamp Boutique **7**
Mango Tango Art Gallery **24**
Mr. Tablecloth **18**
Native Arts & Crafts Cooperative **26**
Pierre's **30**
Royal Caribbean **2, 11**
s.o.s. Antiques **29**

A.H. Riise Gift & Liquor Store **17**
Artistic Jewelers **19**
Bernard K. Passman **14**
Boolchand's **9**
Cardow Jewelers **16**
Carson Company Antiques **3**
The Crystal Shoppe **4**
Diamond's International **13, 8**
Fabric in Motion **31**
Fresh Produce **27**
Gallery Camille Pissarro **6**

The Best Buys & Where to Find Them

The best buys on St. Thomas include china, crystal, perfumes, jewelry (especially emeralds), Haitian art, clothing, watches, and items made of wood. St. Thomas is also the best place in the Caribbean for discounts in porcelain, but remember that U.S. brands may often be purchased for 25% off the retail price on the mainland. Look for imported patterns for the biggest savings. Cameras and electronic items, based on our experience, are not the good buys they're reputed to be.

Nearly all the major shopping in St. Thomas is along the harbor of Charlotte Amalie. Cruise-ship passengers mainly shop at the **Havensight Mall,** at the eastern edge of Charlotte Amalie, where they disembark. The principal shopping street is **Main Street** or Dronningens Gade (the old Danish name). Some of the shops occupy former pirate warehouses. To the north is another merchandise-loaded street called **Back Street** or Vimmelskaft. Many shops are also spread along the **Waterfront Highway** (also called Kyst Vejen). Between these major streets is a series of side streets, walkways, and alleys—each one filled with shops. Other shopping streets are Tolbod Gade, Raadets Gade, Royal Dane Mall, Palm Passage, Storetvaer Gade, and Strand Gade.

Shopping Tip

Friday is the biggest cruise-ship visiting day at Charlotte Amalie (one time we counted eight ships at once), so try to avoid shopping then.

It is illegal for most street vendors (food vendors are about the only exception) to ply their trades outside of the designated area called **Vendors Plaza,** at the corner of Veterans Drive and Tolbod Gade. Hundreds of vendors converge here Monday through Saturday at 7:30am; they usually pack up around 5:30pm. (Very few hawk their wares on Sun, unless a cruise ship is scheduled to arrive.)

When you tire of French perfumes and Swiss watches, head for **Market Square,** as it's called locally, or more formally, Rothschild Francis Square. Here, on the site of a former slave market and under a Victorian tin roof, locals with machetes slice open fresh coconuts so you can drink the milk, and women sell ackee, cassava, and breadfruit.

Other noteworthy shopping districts include **Tillett Gardens,** a virtual oasis of arts and crafts—pottery, silk-screened fabrics, candles, watercolors, jewelry, and more—located on the highway across from Four Winds Shopping Center. The Jim Tillett Gallery here is a major island attraction in itself.

All the major stores in St. Thomas are located by number on an excellent map in the center of the publication *St. Thomas This Week,* distributed free to all arriving plane and boat passengers, and available at the visitor center. A lot of the stores on the island don't have street numbers or don't display them, so look for their signs instead.

Don't Be Shy About Bargaining

Theoretically, bargaining is not the rule on the islands, but over the years we have found merchant after merchant willing to do so, particularly on expensive items such as jewelry and perfume. The slow late spring, summer, and fall seasons are the best times to try to make deals with local vendors.

Shopping A to Z
ANTIQUES

s.o.s. Antiques ★★   This is a maritime gallery full of collectibles dating from the early 16th century, including antique maps and charts, prints, instruments, sextants, and barometers. The outlet also carries one of the Caribbean's largest collections of antique and reproduction cannons, swords, flintlock pistols, and daggers, enough for a fifth installment of *Pirates of the Caribbean*. In all, it's got the island's best shipwreck salvage, including treasure coins found locally and from shipwrecks around the world; they are mounted in 14-karat and 18-karat gold. Pieces of eight are sold both set and unset. 5132 Dronningens Gade 1. ✆ **340/774-2074.**

ART

Bernard K. Passman ★★   Bernard K. Passman is the world's leading sculptor of black coral art and jewelry. He's famous for his *Can Can Girl* and his four statues of Charlie Chaplin. On Grand Cayman, he learned to fashion exquisite treasures from black coral found 200 feet under the sea. After being polished and embellished with gold and diamonds, some of Passman's work has been' treasured by royalty. For us laymen with an eye for good sculpture, there are simpler and more affordable pieces for sale. There is also a sister location in the Havensight Mall. 5195 Dronningens Gade, Ste. No. 2. ✆ **340/777-4580.** www.passman.com.

The Color of Joy   This is a showcase for the vivid watercolors of Corinne Van Rensselaer, who also does custom framing (the best on the island). This little gallery also sells original prints by local artists, crafts, and gifts, including batiks, etchings, cards, and prints, along with glass and larimar (a type of volcanic stone) jewelry. There is also a selection of ceramics, coral sculptures (much of it done locally), and Haitian artwork. American Yacht Harbor, 6100 Red Hook Quarters. ✆ **340/775-4020.** http://thecolorofjoyvi.com.

Gallery Camille Pissarro ★   Located in the building where Pissarro was born in 1830 and where he lived until he was 26, this gallery displays many prints and originals by local artists in three high-ceilinged and airy brick-lined rooms. Paintings and artworks sell for between $50 and $15,000. The gallery also sells original batiks, alive in vibrant colors. You'll find this funky, charmingly bohemian place at the top of a flight of uneven steps—a welcome change from the endless rows of jewelry stores on the street outside. 14 Main St. ✆ **340/774-4621.** www.pissarro.vi.

Gallery St. Thomas ★   This is a showcase for the works of Virgin Islands painters, notably Lucinda Schutt, who is best known for her Caribbean land- and seascapes. At this second-floor gallery, to the west of Hotel 1829, Schutt not only sells artwork, beginning at $18, but also teaches watercolor painting. First building on Garden St., Government Hill. ✆ **877/797-6363** or 340/777-6363. www.gallerystthomas.com.

Mango Tango Art Gallery   This is one of the largest art galleries in St. Thomas, closely connected with half a dozen internationally recognized artists. Original artwork begins at $500; prints and posters are cheaper. Represented are internationally known artists who spend at least part of their year in the Virgin Islands, many of them sailing during breaks from their studio time. Examples include Don Dahlke, Max Johnson, Anne Miller, David Millard, Dana Wylder, and Shari Erickson. Al Cohen's Plaza, Raphune Hill, Rte. 38. ✆ **340/777-3060.** www.mangotango-art.com.

Native Arts & Crafts Cooperative ★   This is the largest arts and crafts emporium in the U.S.V.I., combining the output of 90 different artisans into one sprawling shop. Contained within the former headquarters of the U.S. District Court, a 19th-century brick building adjacent to Charlotte Amalie's tourist information office, it specializes in items small enough to be packed into a suitcase or trunk. Examples include spice racks, paper towel racks, lamps crafted from conch shells, salad utensils and bowls, crocheted goods, and straw goods. Tarbor Gade 1. ✆ **340/777-1153.**

Tillett Gardens Center for the Arts ★★   Since 1959, Tillett Gardens, once an old Danish farm, has been the island's arts-and-crafts center. This tropical compound is a series of buildings housing studios, galleries, and an outdoor garden restaurant and bar. Prints in the galleries start as low as $20. The best work of local artists is displayed here—originals in oils, watercolors, and acrylics. The Tillett prints on fine canvas are all one of a kind. The famous Tillett maps on fine canvas are priced from $45. Tillett Gardens, 4126 Anna's Retreat, Tutu. ✆ **340/775-1405.** www.tillettgardens.com. Take Rte. 38 east from Charlotte Amalie.

BOOKS

Dockside Bookshop   If you need a beach read, head for this well-stocked store near the cruise-ship dock. It has the best selection of books on island lore, as well as a variety of general reading selections. Havensight Mall. ✆ **340/774-4937.**

BRIC-A-BRAC

Carson Company Antiques   This shop's small space is loaded with merchandise, tasteless and otherwise, from virtually everywhere. Its clutter and eclectic nature just might be part of the attraction. Bakelite jewelry is cheap and cheerful, and the African artifacts are often interesting. Royal Dane Mall, off Main St. ✆ **340/774-6175.**

CAMERAS & ELECTRONICS

Boolchand's   This is the place to go when you're in the market for a camera. Famous throughout the Caribbean, this is the major retailer of not only cameras, but also electronics and digital products throughout the West Indies. Now into its 8th decade, it sells all the big names, from Kodak to Leica, and from Nikon to Fuji. In the electronics division are the latest in DVDs, minidiscs, and other items. There is also a jewelry department and a wide selection of watches. 31 Main St. ✆ **340/776-0794.** www.boolchand.com.

New Age Photo   Don't expect a traditional array of camera and film at this place—it's a lot more evolved than that. For sale is a medley of ornaments—made from black onyx, granite, cut crystal, or clear plastic polymers—which accept lasered-on replicas of any photo you'd present to a staff member. Photos come out looking like fine art when laser-engraved on their new surface. Here, you can create some high-tech, unique souvenirs of your trip. In the Crown Bay Center. ✆ **340/777-9324.**

Royal Caribbean ★ 🖊   This is the largest camera and electronics store in the Caribbean. It carries Nikon, Minolta, Pentax, Canon, and Panasonic products. It's a good source for watches, too, featuring such brand names as Seiko, Movado, Corum, Fendi, and Zodiac. There's also a complete collection of Philippe Charriol watches, jewelry, and leather bags, and a wide selection of Mikimoto pearls, 14- and 18-karat jewelry, and Lladró figurines. Another branch is located at Havensight Mall (✆ **340/776-8890**). 33 and 35 Main St. ✆ **340/776-4110.** www.royalcaribbean.vi.

CLOTHING

Fresh Produce   This California chain, with its tropical apparel for women, has now invaded St. Thomas with its colorful wares. Much of the clothing is dyed like native fruits: banana yellow, pink guava, lime-green mangoes, and zesty orange. A wide array of summer dresses, slacks, shirts, and skirts, along with accessories and handbags, are for sale in this sunny place. Riise's Alley. © **340/774-0807.**

Local Color   Located at the Waterfront, this retail outlet has a wide selection of affordable clothing for men, women, and children, as well as island furnishings and accessories such as handbags, hats, and jewelry. Royal Dane Mall at the Waterfront. © **340/774-2280.** www.usviweb.com/localcolor.

Tommy Hilfiger Boutique   The world knows this merchandise, of course, but prices here might be cheaper than stateside. There is a good selection of men's and women's sportswear, as well as shoes, jeans, children's clothing, home furnishings, and fragrances. Waterfront Hwy. at Trompeter Gade 30. © **340/777-1189.**

CRYSTAL & CHINA

The Crystal Shoppe ★ 📷   This family-run store offers a dazzling array of crystal from around the world. All the big names in glass—Hummel, Waterford, Swarovski, and Mats Jonasson—are on parade, along with some particularly good pieces from the Swedish firm of Kosta Boda. The porcelain Lladró figurines from Spain are also fast-moving items. 14 Main St. © **800/323-7232.** www.crystalshoppe.net.

Little Switzerland ★★   For half a century, this duty-free retailer has been familiar to visitors to various islands in the Caribbean. On St. Thomas, its fine jewelry, watches, china, crystal, and accessories are showcased at three different locations, and the company also does a lively mail-order business. At any outlet, you can pick up a catalog. The finest crystal sold on the island is featured here, including Orrefors from Sweden as well as Waterford and Baccarat. 5 Dronningens Gade (© **340/776-2010**); Havensight Mall (© **340/776-2198**); and 48 AB Norre Gade (© **340/776-4595**).

Scandinavian Center   This family-owned and -operated shop specializes in some of the most famous products of Scandinavia, including glassware, silver, and crystal. You'll recognize such names as Bing & Grøndahl, Georg Jensen, Kosta Boda, Orrefors, and Royal Copenhagen. The jewelry department is especially enticing, with its 14-karat and 18-karat designs in white and yellow gold. Havensight Mall, Building III. © **877/454-8377** or 340/777-8620. www.scandinaviancenter.com.

FABRICS

Fabric in Motion   The owners of this store searched the globe for fabrics, and delight shoppers with a selection of silklike cottons from the fabled Liberty's of London, the best of linens from Italy, and flamboyant batiks from Indonesia. Many tempting items are for sale, including leather handbags from Colombia and useful beach bags. Storetvaer Gade. © **340/774-2006.**

FRAGRANCES

Tropicana Perfume Shoppe ★ 🕯   This outlet is billed as the largest perfumery in the world. It offers all the famous names in perfumes, skin care, and cosmetics, including Lancôme. Men will find Europe's best colognes and áftershave lotions here. A very friendly and attentive staff will enhance your shopping experience. 2 Main St. © **800/233-7948.** www.usvi.net/tropicana.

GIFTS & LIQUORS

A. H. Riise Gift & Liquor Stores   This is St. Thomas's oldest outlet for luxury items, such as jewelry, crystal, china, and perfumes. It also offers the widest sampling of liquors on the island. Everything is displayed in a 19th-century Danish warehouse that extends from Main Street to the Waterfront. The store boasts a collection of fine jewelry and watches from Europe's leading craftspeople, including Vacheron Constantin, Bulgari, Omega, and Gucci, as well as a wide selection of Greek gold, platinum, and precious gemstone jewelry. Imported cigars are stored in a climate-controlled walk-in humidor. There's also a vast selection of fragrances for both men and women, along with the world's best-known names in cosmetics and treatment products. Waterford, Lalique, Baccarat, and Rosenthal, among others, are featured in the china and crystal department. Specialty shops in the complex sell Caribbean gifts, books, clothing, food, art prints, note cards, and designer sunglasses. Delivery to cruise ships and the airport is free. 37 Main St., at A. H. Riise Gift & Liquor Mall (perfume and liquor branch stores at the Havensight Mall). ✆ **800/524-2037** or 340/776-2303.

Al Cohen's Discount Liquors   One of St. Thomas's most famous outlets occupies a big warehouse at Havensight, across from the West Indian Company docks, where cruise-ship passengers disembark. Inside is a huge storehouse of liquor and wine. The quarters have been expanded and remodeled, and there are now more brands and items on sale than before. The wine department is especially impressive. You can also purchase fragrances, T-shirts, and souvenirs. Long Bay Rd. ✆ **340/774-3690.**

Caribbean Marketplace   The best selection of Caribbean spices is found here, including Sunny Caribbee products, a vast array of condiments (ranging from spicy peppercorns to nutmeg mustard), and botanical products. Do not expect very attentive service. Havensight Mall, Building III. ✆ **340/776-5400.**

JEWELRY

Artistic Jewelers   This outlet is a leading merchant of designer jewelry, gems, and classic watches. 32 Main St. ✆ **800/653-3113.** www.artistic-jewelers.com.

Azura   This shop is known throughout the Caribbean for its collection of Columbia emeralds, both set and unset. Here you can buy direct from the source, which can mean significant savings. The store also stocks fine watches. Havensight Mall. ✆ **340/774-2442.**

Cardow Jewelers   Often called the Tiffany's of the Caribbean, Cardow Jewelers boasts the largest selection of fine jewelry in the world. This fabulous shop, where more than 20,000 rings are displayed, offers savings because of its worldwide direct buying, large turnover, and duty-free prices. Unusual and traditional designs are offered in diamonds, emeralds, rubies, sapphires, and Brazilian stones, as well as pearls. Cardow also has a whole wall of Italian gold chains, and features antique-coin jewelry as well. 39 Main St. ✆ **340/776-1140.** www.cardow.com.

Diamonds International ★★   If you believe that diamonds are a girl's best friend, you've come to the right place. These outlets have the largest selection of diamonds on the island. You can purchase tanzanite gems and emeralds as well.

Diamonds Are Forever

Jewelry is the most common item for sale in St. Thomas. Look carefully over the selections of gold and gemstones (emeralds are traditionally considered the finest savings). Gold that is marked 24-karat in the United States and Canada is marked 999 (or 99.9% pure gold) on European items. Gold marked 18-karat in the United States and Canada has a European marking of 750 (or 75% pure), and 14-karat gold is marked 585 (or 58.5% pure).

Patrons select the stone of their dreams and can have it mounted within an hour in the ring of their choice. With certain large purchases, women (or men) are rewarded with free diamond earrings. There are several on-island locations. 3 Drakes Passage in Charlotte Amalie (✆ **340/775-2010**); Havensight Mall, Rte. 30 (✆ **340/776-0040**); 31 Main St. in Charlotte Amalie (✆ **340/774-3707**); and Wyndham Sugar Bay Resort & Spa, Rte. 38, Estate Smith Bay (✆ 340/714-3248). www.shopdi.com.

Dynasty Dazzlers This shop offers diamond, tanzanite, ruby, emerald, sapphire, and blue diamond jewelry in one half, and liquor in the other. There's no better combination if you're in a luxurious mood. There are three other branch locations at the **Havensight Mall** (✆ **800/225-7052**). 1 Main St. ✆ **340/774-2222.** www. dynastydutyfree.com.

H. Stern Jewelers This international jeweler is one of the most respected in the world, with some 175 outlets. It's Cardow's leading competitor (see above). Besides this branch, there are two more on Main Street. Stern gives worldwide guaranteed service, including a 60-day exchange privilege. Havensight Mall. ✆ **340/776-1223.** www. hstern.net.

Pierre's ★ Connoisseurs of colored gemstones consider this store one of the most impressive repositories of collector's items in the Caribbean. It's a branch of a store based in Naples, Florida. In its inventory are glittering and mystical-looking gemstones you might never have heard of before. Look for alexandrites (garnets in three shades of green); spinels (pink and red); sphenes, yellow-green sparklers from Madagascar (as reflective as high-quality diamonds); and tsavorites, a green stone from Tanzania. 24 Palm Passage. ✆ **800/300-0634** or 340/776-5130. www.pierresdiamonds.com.

LEATHER
Longchamp Boutique ★ This store sells the best leather items around, each a French handcrafted product including handbags, wallets, briefcases, belts, and luggage. Their line of canvas and leather travel bags moves quickly. The well-known nylon-and-leather Pliage Shopping Bag is also sold here, as well as exquisite accessories, including a full line of signature scarves. 25 Main St. ✆ **800/233-7948.**

LINENS
Mr. Tablecloth This shop constantly receives new shipments of top-quality linens from China, including Hong Kong. It has the best selection of tablecloths and accessories, plus doilies, in Charlotte Amalie. Also check out the display of place mats, aprons, and runners. 6 Main St. ✆ **340/774-4343.** www.mrtablecloth-vi.com.

POTTERY
The Kilnworks Pottery and Art Gallery, Inc. A 12-foot green iguana sits at the entrance, and owner Peggy Seiwert turns out a series of lizard-ware pottery of remarkable beauty. If you're not into reptiles, you'll find a limited edition of Birds of Paradise vases. Some of the best Caribbean pottery is for sale here along with art and crafts created by local artists. 6029 Estate Smith Bay 4H (Rte. 38). ✆ **340/775-3979.** www.kilnworks potteryvi.com.

SANDALS
Zora of St. Thomas For custom-made sandals, they don't get any better in St. Thomas than the handmade ones sold here. Since 1962, Zora's sandals have been known for their quality and simplicity. Each pair is handmade from full-grain leather, with a durable rubber sole. Casual or more formal sandals come in a wide variety of

styles, sizes, and colors, great for an evening out in Frenchtown. In addition to the custom-made sandals, there is also a line of what islanders call "limin' shoes." The store carries canvas backpacks or canvas luggage, canvas "fish bags," and even purses and briefcases made of canvas. 34 Norre Gade. ℭ **340/774-2559.** www.zoraofstthomas.com.

ST. THOMAS AFTER DARK

St. Thomas has more nightlife than any other island in the U.S. or British Virgin Islands, but it's not as extensive as you might think. Charlotte Amalie is no longer the swinging town it used to be. Many of the streets are dangerous after dark, so visitors have stopped visiting the area for nightlife, with the exception of a few places, such as the Greenhouse. Much of the action has shifted to **Frenchtown ★★**, which has some great restaurants and bars. However, just as in Charlotte Amalie, some of these little hot spots are along dark, badly lit roads. The primary problem here is mugging, although some of the criminal activity appears to be drug-related. Sexual assault is known to occur, but happens rather infrequently.

The big hotels, such as Frenchman's Reef & Morning Star Marriott Beach Resort, Bolongo Bay, or the Ritz, have the most lively after-dark scenes. After a day of sight-seeing and shopping in the hot West Indies sun, sometimes your best bet is just to stay at your hotel in the evening, perhaps listening to a local fungi band playing traditional music on homemade instruments.

The Performing Arts

Pistarckle Theater On the grounds of **Tillett Gardens Center for the Arts** (p. 102), this professional theater presents four full-length plays as part of its subscription season. Occupying a vacant print shop, the 100-seat theater is air-conditioned. There is also a summer drama camp for children. Tillett Gardens, 4126 Anna's Retreat, Tutu. ℭ **340/775-7877.** www.pistarckletheater.vi. Tickets $19–$30.

Reichhold Center for the Arts ★ This artistic center, the premier performing arts venue in the Caribbean, lies west of Charlotte Amalie. Past performances have included the Alvin Ailey American Dance Theater and the likes of Al Jarreau. Call the theater or check with the tourist office to see what's on at the time of your visit. The lobby displays a frequently changing free exhibit of paintings and sculptures by Caribbean artists. A Japanese-inspired amphitheater, permeated by the scent of gardenias, is set into a natural valley, with seating space for 1,196. Performances usually begin at 8pm. University of the Virgin Islands, 2 John Brewers Bay. ℭ **340/693-1559.** www.reichholdcenter. com. Tickets $18–$45.

Bars & Clubs

The Bar at Paradise Point Any savvy insider will tell you to head to this bar to watch the sunset. It's located 740 feet above sea level, across from the cruise-ship dock, and provides excellent photo ops and panoramic sunset views. Cruise-ship passengers, usually a middle-aged crowd, flock to this bar. A tram takes you up the hill. Get the bartender to serve you a Bushwacker (his specialty). You can also order inexpensive food here during the day, such as pizza, hot dogs, and hamburgers, beginning at $8. Happy hour, with discounted drinks, begins at 5pm. Don't take the tram up if you plan on staying until closing. The last tram down is at 5pm. Otherwise, drive yourself or call a cab. It's open 7 days a week from 9am to 8pm, with hours extended to 9pm Wednesday. Paradise Point. ℭ **340/777-4540.** www.paradisepointtramway.com.

Sexual harassment can be a problem in certain bars in Charlotte Amalie. Any of the major resort hotels are generally safer, and any place we've recommended can be viewed as hospitable (though, of course, creeps can be found in any bar).

Cabana Bar   There's piano bar entertainment Thursday, Saturday, and Sunday at this scenic spot overlooking the yacht harbor. It's a popular gathering ground for residents and visitors alike, who are mainly in their 30s and 40s. You can dance from 7 to 10pm on Thursday and Saturday. Entertainment varies from month to month, but many nights are devoted to jazz. It's open daily from 5 to 10pm. Bluebeard's Castle. © **340/774-1600.**

Epernay   This stylish watering hole, with a view of the ocean, adds a touch of Europe to the neighborhood. You can order glasses of at least six different brands of champagne, or vintage wines also come by the glass. Appetizers include sushi and caviar, but there are also main courses, plus tempting desserts such as chocolate-dipped strawberries. A mature, sophisticated crowd seeks out this spot. It's open Monday to Thursday 11:30am to 11pm, Friday 11:30am to midnight, and Saturday 5pm to midnight. Rue de St. Barthélemy, Frenchtown. © **340/774-5348.**

Great Bay Lounge   If you're way out on the island's easternmost tip, you can visit this elegant but cozy lounge, an airy bar-cum-clubhouse on the grounds of the Ritz-Carlton. One of four restaurants on the grounds of the hotel, it's the most appropriate for late-night down-winding, and as such welcomes a large percentage of managers from other island resorts. Cocktails and glasses of wine cost from $9 to $21 each, platters of food from $10 to $42. Although it's open daily 10am to around 11pm, we find it's at its most appealing from 8pm on. The Ritz-Carlton, 6900 Great Bay. © **340/775-3333.** www.ritzcarlton.com.

The Greenhouse   Set directly on the Waterfront, this bar and restaurant is one of the few nightspots we recommend in the heart of Charlotte Amalie. You can park nearby and walk to the entrance. If you want to start early, come for dinner (p. 73). Each night, a different type of entertainment is featured, ranging from reggae to disco; there's also a daily happy hour from 4:30 to 7pm. Tuesday nights are the biggest draw with two-for-one drinks; there's a live reggae band on Friday nights. Almost all of the 30-something patrons are visitors. The Greenhouse is open daily 11am until the last customer leaves. Veterans Dr. © **340/774-7998.** www.thegreenhouserestaurant.com.

Hull Bay Hideaway   A 25-year-plus mainstay on the island scene, this funky surfer bar has a laid-back, casual atmosphere, attracting, in the words of a bartender, "people from all walks of life, from boaters to condo renters." Many locals and regulars like to spend lazy Sunday afternoons here. It's a cheap place to eat—hot dogs and hamburgers are served until 3:30pm. After 4pm, you can order affordable main courses in the restaurant, costing $5 to $18, including the catch of the day and the chef's pork stew. There is live music on Saturday nights beginning at 7pm and on Sunday afternoon from 4pm. There are also some gambling machines and a volleyball court, if that's your thing. Daily hours are 10am to 10pm. 10 Hull Bay. © **340/777-1898.**

Iggies Bolongo   This place functions during the day as an informal, open-air restaurant serving hamburgers, sandwiches, and salads. After dark, it presents karaoke and occasional live entertainment. This establishment attracts the broadest spectrum of age groups and professions in all of Charlotte Amalie. The hours and schedule changes daily, so call to find out what's happening. Bolongo Bay Beach Resort, 7150 Bolongo. © **340/693-2600.** www.iggiesbeachbar.com.

Latitude 18   This is the hot spot of the east coast, located where the ferryboats depart for St. John. The casual restaurant and bar, featuring a ceiling adorned with boat sails, offers live entertainment regularly, especially on Thursday through Sunday nights. It's open daily from 11:30am to 10:30pm. Red Hook Marina. © **340/777-4552.**

Turtle Rock Bar   This popular bar presents live music and karaoke to a young crowd. There's space to dance, but most patrons just sway and listen. The steel-pan bands that play from 2pm to closing on Sundays are excellent. Burgers, salads, steaks, and grilled fish are available at the Iguana Grill, a few steps away. Open daily noon to 6pm. In the Iguana Grill at the Wyndham Sugar Bay Resort & Spa, 6500 Estate Smith Bay (a few minutes' drive west of Red Hook). © **340/777-7100.**

Gay & Lesbian Nightlife

St. Thomas might be the most cosmopolitan of the Virgin Islands, but it is no longer the "gay paradise" it was in the 1960s and 1970s. The major gay scene in the U.S. Virgins is now on St. Croix (see chapter 5). That doesn't mean that gay men and lesbians aren't drawn to St. Thomas. They are, but many attend predominantly straight establishments, such as **the Greenhouse** (see "Bars & Clubs," above).

ST. JOHN

St. John, the smallest and least densely populated of the U.S. Virgin Islands, is a wonder of untouched rocky coastline, beautiful crescent-shaped bays, and white-sand beaches. Inland, miles of hiking trails lead past the ruins of 18th-century Danish plantations to panoramic views. A smattering of pastel-painted houses, Mongoose Junction shops, and restaurants and bars populate sleepy Cruz Bay. St. John is definitely sleepy, and that's why people love it.

4

Things to Do   Explore island history at the **Annaberg Sugar Plantation Ruins,** a once-thriving 18th-century mill and plantation. Hike the 22 trails of the **Virgin Islands National Park** to see archaeological sites dating back to the time of the Taíno people, while enjoying the forest and birdlife. Reefs and wreck dive spots ring the park's deserted beaches. Surrounded by hills, the golden sands of **Hawksnest Beach** seduce visitors as the perfect escape. Follow the underwater **snorkeling** trail at **Trunk Bay** to see grouper, parrot fish, and snappers.

Shopping   Shopping on St. John means a visit to the arts and crafts boutiques and shops of **Cruz Bay,** most of which are clustered at **Mongoose Junction.** Nearby **Wharfside Village** is a complex of courtyards, alleys, and shady patios with a mishmash of boutiques, restaurants, and bars. The most shopping fun takes place on **St. John Saturday,** a spicy, drum-beating feast for the senses, held on the last Saturday of every month. Vendors hawk handmade items, from jewelry and handicrafts to food and clothing.

Nightlife & Entertainment   The expatriate hippie crowd has created a mellow scene at **Cruz Bay,** where a few cafes and dive bars invite those who want to drink and gossip with the locals or listen to the occasional live band. Sip trademark **Plantation Punch** (lime and orange juice with three different kinds of rum, bitters, and nutmeg) at a resort bar in **Caneel Bay** or go celeb-spotting at **Morgan's Mango.** Most people, however, are simply content to have a long, leisurely dinner.

Restaurants & Dining   St. John's quiet, easygoing pace means that it's not unusual—indeed, it is perfectly acceptable—for dinner to comprise the whole of your evening. As a result, there are some posh options, particularly at the luxury resorts in **Caneel Bay,** where you can eat well on Caribbean, Creole, and Italian. In **Cruz Bay,** seaside bistros serve spicy blackened snapper and flying fish, while **West Indian** huts serve top-notch meals with plenty of local color and flavor.

ESSENTIALS

Getting There

BY BOAT

The easiest and most common way to get to St. John is by **ferry** (© **340/776-6282**), which leaves from the Red Hook landing pier on St. Thomas's eastern tip; the trip takes about 20 minutes each way. Beginning at 6:30am, boats depart more or less every hour. The last ferry back to Red Hook departs from St. John's Cruz Bay at 11pm. The service is frequent and efficient enough that even cruise-ship passengers temporarily anchored in Charlotte Amalie can visit St. John for a quick island tour. The one-way fare is $6 for adults, $1 for children 11 and under. Schedules change without notice, so call in advance.

To reach the ferry, take the **Vitran** bus from the ferry dock near Market Square (in Charlotte Amalie) directly to Red Hook. The cost is $1 per person each way. In addition, privately owned taxis will negotiate a price to carry you from virtually anywhere on the island to the docks at Red Hook.

If you've just landed on St. Thomas and want to go straight to your chosen ferry dock, your best bet is to take a cab from the airport (Vitran buses run from Charlotte Amalie but don't serve the airport area). Depending on the traffic, the cab ride on St. Thomas could take 30 to 45 minutes, at a fare between $20 and $22. After disembarking from the ferry on St. John, you'll have to get another cab to your hotel.

It's also possible to board a **boat** for St. John directly at the Charlotte Amalie waterfront, from Vendors Plaza at the corner of Veterans Drive and Tolbod Gade, for a cost of $10 each way for adults and $1 for children 11 and under. The ride takes 45 minutes. The boats depart from Charlotte Amalie at 7:15am and continue at intervals of 2 hours, until the last boat departs around 5:30pm. (The last boat to leave St. John's Cruz Bay for Charlotte Amalie departs at 3:45pm.) Call © **340/776-6282,** or visit www.vinow.com for more information.

Visitor Information

The **tourist office** (© **340/776-6450**) is located near the Battery, a 1735 fort that's a short walk from the St. Thomas ferry dock in Cruz Bay. It's open Monday to Friday from 8am to 5pm. A **National Park visitor center** (© **340/776-6201**) is also found at Cruz Bay, offering two floors of information and wall-mounted wildlife displays, plus a video presentation about the culture of the Virgin Islands; it's open daily 8am to 4pm.

You can pick up a map of the island from the tourist office and also a copy of *St. John This Week,* which is distributed free.

Island Layout

Most visitors will arrive on St. John at **Cruz Bay,** on a ferry from St. Thomas. This tiny town, with its few restaurants and shops, is quite the departure from the bustle of Charlotte Amalie. Cruz Bay is also the first stop on any trip to **Virgin Islands National Park,** which sprawls through the interior and encompasses almost all the coastline. The park service runs an information center in town. Route 20 leads north out of Cruz Bay, and passes the beaches at Caneel, Hawksnest, Trunk, Cinnamon, and Maho bays. At the far north, Route 20 leads to the start of the **Annaberg Trail,** a historic hike through the ruins of 18th-century sugar plantations. Route 10 cuts through the center of the island. Dozens of foot trails lead off this road, making for

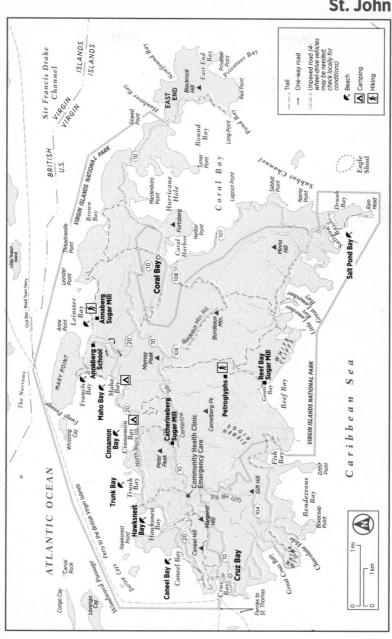

easy exploration of the peaks and mountains. On the east end of the island is **Coral Bay,** a favorite among yachties and home to a smattering of small restaurants and bars. Crumbling ruins of forts and plantations also dot the coastline here. The far east end is undeveloped and pales in comparison to the lush greenery of the park. The south coast is a favorite hideaway for locals, but little known by visitors. The coast here is sweeping and tranquil, yet rocky in parts and punctuated with a handful of small protected bays.

Getting Around

The 20-minute ferry ride from St. Thomas will take you to **Cruz Bay,** the capital of St. John, which seems a century removed from the life you left behind. Cruz Bay is so small that its streets have no names, but it does have the **Mongoose Junction** shopping center (definitely worth a visit), a scattering of restaurants, and a small park. Cruise ships are nonexistent here, so you won't find hordes of milling shoppers. After a stroll around town, seek out the natural attractions of the island.

BY BUS

The most popular way to get around is by the local **Vitran** (✆ **340/774-0165**) service, the same company that runs the buses on St. Thomas. Buses run between Cruz Bay and Coral Bay, costing $1 for adults and 75¢ for children.

BY TAXI

An open-air **surrey-style taxi** is more fun than taking a bus. Typical fares are $9 to Trunk Bay, $11 to Cinnamon Bay, and $14 to Maho Bay. Between midnight and 6am, fares are increased by 50%. Taxis meet the ferries as they arrive in Cruz Bay, or you can hail one if you see one. More than likely, you or your hotel will have to call one. Call ✆ **340/693-7530** for more information or **Paradise Taxi** at ✆ **340/714-7913.**

BY CAR OR JEEP

One of the most exciting ways to see St. John is by a four-wheel-drive vehicle, which you can rent in town (in winter, it's best to reserve in advance). The steep roadside panoramas are richly tinted with tones of forest green and turquoise and liberally accented with flashes of silver and gold from the strong Caribbean sun. Most visitors need a car for only a day or 2. *Remember:* Drive on the left and follow posted speed limits, which are generally very low.

Unless you need to carry luggage, which should probably be locked away in a trunk, you might consider one of the sturdy, open-sided, jeeplike vehicles that offer the best view of the surroundings and are the most fun way to tour St. John. Note that most of these vehicles have manual transmission, which can be especially tricky in a car built to drive on the left side of the road. They cost around $76 to $84 a day.

The largest car-rental agency on St. John is **Paris Car Rental** (✆ **340/693-7580;** www.rentalcarstjohn.com). If you want a local firm, try **St. John Car Rental,** across from the Catholic church in Cruz Bay (✆ **340/776-6103;** www.stjohncarrental.com).

[FastFACTS] ST. JOHN

Banks FirstBank Virgin Islands is at 90C Cruz Bay (✆ **340/776-6881**).

Business Hours Stores are generally open Monday to Friday 9am to 5pm, Saturday 9am to 1pm.

Dentists The **Virgin Islands Dental Association** (📞 **340/775-9110**) is a member of the American Dental Association and is also linked with various specialists.

Doctors Call 📞 **911** for a medical emergency. Otherwise, go to **St. John Myrah Keating Smith Community Health Center,** 3B Sussanaberg (📞 **340/693-8900**).

Drugstores Chelsea Drug Store, Marketplace Shopping Center, Route 104, Cruz Bay (📞 **340/776-4888**) is open Monday to Saturday 8:30am to 6:30pm and Sunday 9:30am to 4:30pm.

Emergencies For the police, an ambulance, or in case of fire, call 📞 **911.**

Internet Access At **Connections,** Parcel Street, Suite 6D (📞 **340/776-6922;** www.connectionsst john.com), expect to pay $5 for 30 minutes of Internet access. You can also use the computers at the **Elaine Lone Sprauve Public Library,** Enighted Street (📞 **340/776-6359**), for a charge of $2 for 1 hour.

Laundry Try **Santo's Laundromat,** 1321 Cruz Bay Valley (📞 **340/693-7733**), or **Super Clean,** Enighted Street (📞 **340/693-7333**).

Maps See "Visitor Information," p. 110.

Newspapers & Magazines Copies of U.S. mainland newspapers, such as the *New York Times* and the *Miami Herald,* arrive daily and are for sale at **Mongoose Junction, Caneel Bay,** and the **Westin St. John Resort & Villas.** The latest copies of *Time* and *Newsweek* are also for sale. *What to Do: St. Thomas/St. John,* the official guidebook of the St. Thomas and St. John Hotel Association, is available at the tourist office (see "Visitor Information," p. 110) and at hotels.

Post Office The **Cruz Bay Post Office** is at Cruz Bay (📞 **340/779-4227**).

Safety There is some crime here, but it's relatively minor compared to St. Thomas. Most crime against tourists consists of muggings or petty theft, but rarely violent attacks. Precautions, of course, are always advised. You are most likely to be the victim of a crime if you leave valuables unguarded on Trunk Bay, as hundreds of people seem to do every year.

Taxes The only local tax is an 8% surcharge added to all hotel rates.

Telephone All island phone numbers have seven digits. It is not necessary to use the 340 area code when dialing within St. John. Make long-distance, international, and collect calls as you would on the U.S. mainland by dialing 0 or your long-distance provider.

WHERE TO STAY

The number of accommodations on St. John is limited, and that's how most die-hard fans would like to keep it. There are four basic types of choices here: luxury resorts, condominiums and villas, guesthouses, and campgrounds. Prices are often slashed in summer by 30% to 60%.

Chances are that your location will be determined by your choice of resort. However, if you're dependent on public transportation and want to make one or two trips to St. Thomas by ferry, Cruz Bay is the most convenient place to stay. It also offers easy access to shopping, bars, and restaurants if you want to walk.

Luxury Resorts

Caneel Bay ★★ ☺ Still faithful to the vision of megamillionaire Laurance S. Rockefeller in 1956, this is the Caribbean's first eco-resort. Though it's long been one of the premier resorts of the Caribbean, Caneel Bay is definitely not one of the most luxurious and deliberately shuns modern glitz and digital distractions, making it the perfect getaway. A devoted fan once told us, "It's like living at summer camp." That means no phones or TVs in the rooms. Nevertheless, the movers and shakers of the world continue to descend on this place, though younger people tend to head elsewhere.

The resort lies on a 170-acre portion of the national park, offering a choice of seven beaches. Surrounded by lush greenery, the main buildings are strung along the bays, with a Caribbean lounge and dining room at the core. Other buildings housing guest rooms stand along the beaches. Most rooms are set back on low cliffs or headlands. The decor within is understated, with Indonesian wicker furniture, hand-woven fabrics, sisal mats, and plantation fans.

Caneel Bay: From Revolt to Resort

Caneel Bay, the chic Rockresort, was once the Pieter Duerloo plantation, where white settlers defended themselves against a slave revolt.

The resort has consistently maintained a high level of cuisine, often quite formal for the laid-back Caribbean. In recent years the food has been considerably improved and modernized, with more variety and more healthy choices on the menu. In fact, **Caneel Beach Terrace** (p. 122) and **Equator** (p. 122) are two of our favorites on St. John.

Virgin Islands National Park, St. John, U.S.V.I. 00831. www.caneelbay.com. ☏ **888/767-3966** or 340/776-6111. Fax 340/693-8280. 166 units. Winter $470–$1,060 double; off season $350–$730 double. MAP (breakfast and dinner) $90 per person per day extra. 1 child 15 and under stays free in parent's room. AE, MC, V. **Amenities:** 5 restaurants; 2 bars; babysitting; children's center; concierge; health center and spa; pool (outdoor); room service; 11 tennis courts. *In room:* A/C, TV, hair dryer, minibar, Wi-Fi (free).

Westin St. John Resort & Villas ★★★ ☺   This is the only resort on St. John that actually pampers its guests, from the best spa treatments in the U.S.V.I. to such deals as special "romance packages." Come here if you like megaresort flash and glitter as opposed to the "old-school ties" of Caneel Bay (see above). This is the most architecturally dramatic and visually appealing hotel on St. John. The complex is set on 34 acres of landscaped grounds on the southwest side of the island. It consists of 21 cedar-roofed postmodern buildings, each with ziggurat-shaped angles and soaring ceilings. Herringbone-patterned brick walkways connect the gardens (with 400 palms imported from Puerto Rico) to the 1,181-foot mediocre beach and one of the largest pools in the Virgin Islands. Some of the stylish accommodations contain fan-shaped windows and curved ceilings. Most units open onto private balconies, and some have their own whirlpools. Villas, of course, offer more space and come with a full kitchenette. Cuisine options here are more varied than those at Caneel, featuring a contemporary cuisine, buffets, and even New York deli sandwiches.

Great Cruz Bay, St. John, U.S.V.I. 00831. www.westinresortstjohn.com. ☏ **866/716-8108** in the U.S., or 340/693-8000. Fax 340/714-6038. 367 units. Winter $490–$640 double, from $1,000 villa; off season $400–$550 double, from $900 villa. AE, DC, DISC, MC, V. Round-trip shuttle and private ferryboat transfers from St. Thomas airport $95 per adult, $80 ages 4–12. **Amenities:** 4 restaurants; 2 bars; airport transfers ($95 per adult, $80 ages 4–12); children's programs; concierge; golf nearby; pool (outdoor); room service; 6 lit tennis courts; extensive watersports equipment/rentals. *In room:* A/C, TV, hair dryer, Jacuzzi (in some), kitchenette (in some), minibar, Wi-Fi (free).

Condos & Villas

Villa vacations are on the rise in St. John for travelers who want a home away from home. There are actually more villa and condo beds available on St. John than there are hotel beds. These units offer spaciousness and comfort, as well as privacy and

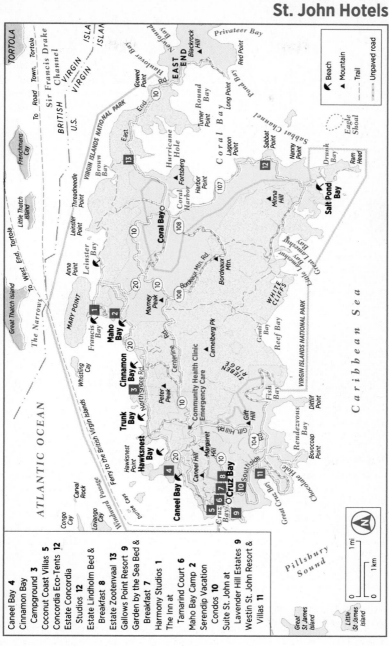

St. John Hotels at a Glance

	Wheelchair access	A/C in bedrooms	Child-care facilities	Children are welcome	Convention facilities	Credit cards accepted	Directly beside beach	Health club
Caneel Bay		✓		✓		✓	✓	✓
Coconut Coast Villas	✓			✓		✓	✓	
Estate Concordia Studios				✓		✓		
Estate Lindholm Bed & Breakfast	✓					✓		✓
Estate Zootenvaal				✓			✓	
Gallows Point Resort	✓			✓		✓		
Garden by the Sea Bed & Breakfast	✓							
Harmony Studios				✓		✓		
The Inn at Tamarind Court	✓			✓		✓		
Serendip Vacation Condos	✓			✓				
Suite St. John at Lavender Hill Estates	✓			✓		✓		
Westin St. John Resort & Villas	✓	✓	✓	✓		✓	✓	✓

freedom, and they often come with fully equipped kitchens, dining areas, bedrooms, and such amenities as VCRs and patio grills. Rentals range from large multiroom resort homes to simply decorated one-bedroom condos.

Caribbean Villas & Resorts, P.O. Box 458, St. John, U.S.V.I. 00831 (© **800/ 338-0987** or 340/776-6152; fax 207/510-6308 in the U.S.; www.caribbeanvilla. com), the island's biggest real estate agency, is an excellent choice if you're seeking a villa, condo, or private home. Most condos go for between $125 and $295 per night, though private homes are more expensive. Villa rentals begin at $1,750 per week.

EXPENSIVE

Coconut Coast Villas ★ ☺   This is a good choice for families seeking a vacation condo, although there are no special facilities for children. Some units are studios, suitable for couples, but other, more spacious accommodations contain two or three bedrooms. The location is a 10-minute walk from Cruz Bay in a quiet suburban neighborhood. There's a small beach but it's pebbly, and there are some steep steps so it's not ideal for the mobility impaired. All units are oceanfront with private porches and kitchens. Extra features include a hot tub, grill, laundry facilities, beach chairs, coolers, and beach towels. A minimum stay of 4 nights is imposed.

Turner Bay, Cruz Bay, St. John, U.S.V.I. 00831. www.coconutcoast.com. © **2340/693-9100.** 9 units. Winter $289 studio, $389 2-bedroom condo, $559 3-bedroom condo; off season $189–$229 studio, $289–$329 2-bedroom condo, $349–$439 3-bedroom condo. MC, V. **Amenities:** Internet (free); outdoor pool. In room: A/C, TV, kitchenette.

Golf course nearby	Live entertainment	Marina facilities	Restaurant and/or bar	Spa facilities	Swimming pool	Tennis courts	TV in bedroom	Watersports
		✓	✓		✓		✓	
					✓		✓	
				✓			✓	
		✓		✓		✓		
							✓	
		✓		✓	✓			
		✓					✓	
	✓	✓				✓		
							✓	
				✓		✓		
		✓	✓	✓	✓	✓	✓	

Estate Lindholm Bed & Breakfast ★ 🛎 Located within the national park on St. John's north shore, this guesthouse is just a 10-minute drive from the world-famous beach at Trunk Bay. The island's best B&B grew out of an estate originally settled by Dutch planters in the 1720s. Set among the Danish ruins, Estate Lindholm is a charming guesthouse on a hill overlooking Cruz Bay, each of its nonsmoking bedrooms opening onto a view. The spacious bedrooms are attractively and comfortably furnished, many resting under ceiling beams. Guests can enjoy private balconies as well. On the property is the **Asolare** restaurant, one of the island's best (p. 121). The staff is helpful in hooking you up with any number of outdoor activities, including everything from sea kayaking to windsurfing. The estate has been owned as a residence by the Morrisette family since the 1950s.

P.O. Box 1360, Cruz Bay, St. John, U.S.V.I. 00831. www.estatelindholm.com. © **800/322-6335** in the U.S., or 340/776-6121. Fax 340/776-6141. 10 units. Winter $340–$390 double; off season $170–$210. Rates include continental breakfast. AE, DISC, MC, V. **Amenities:** Restaurant; exercise room; pool (outdoor). *In room:* A/C, TV, fridge, Wi-Fi (free).

Estate Zootenvaal ★ This is a good bet for escapees from urban life who want privacy and tranquillity and who have the use of a secluded beach ideal for snorkeling. This property is located on 30 acres within the boundaries of the national park at the edge of a horseshoe-shaped bay. The accommodations sport designer fabrics in muted tones. Each has its own color scheme and comes with a fully equipped kitchen. Rooms have ceiling fans, but most have no telephones or televisions. Maid service can be arranged at an extra cost.

FAMILY-FRIENDLY ACCOMMODATIONS

Caneel Bay (p. 113)   The resort's children's center, which caters to children ages 3 to 12, features arts and crafts, themed days, family vacation packages, activity-filled programs, and special kids menus.

Coconut Coast Villas (p. 116)   This is one of the best places for families with up to six guests, because units have two to three bedrooms, with fully equipped kitchens for preparing your own meals to cut down on food costs.

Cinnamon Bay Campground (p. 120) Tents or cottages come with cooking gear at this National Park Service site.

Maho Bay Camp (p. 121)   The tents in this laid-back hideaway are really more like small canvas houses with kitchen areas and sun decks.

Suite St. John at Lavender Hill Estates (p. 118)   Families often save money by staying at one of these condos. There's a swimming pool, and units have fully equipped kitchens. Children age 11 and under stay free in their parent's room; older kids are charged $35 extra per night.

Westin St. John Resort & Villas (p. 114)   Kids will love the giant pool, expansive beach, and varied dining choices at this luxury resort.

Hurricane Hole, St. John, U.S.V.I. 00830. www.estatezootenvaal.com. ✆ **340/776-6321** or 216/861-5337. 4 units. Winter $275 1-bedroom unit, $360–$550 2-bedroom unit; off season $180 1-bedroom unit, $240–$360 2-bedroom unit. Extra person $50–$175. No credit cards. *In room:* Ceiling fans, kitchen, no phone (in some).

Gallows Point Resort ★   This little resort has been a favorite with vacationers for 30 years. The first complex of buildings you see as you arrive at Cruz Bay is this colony of condos just outside the town. Lying on 5 acres of lush landscaping, the complex blends into its setting, a tropical landscape with island-style architecture. You're within walking distance of the restaurants and shops of Cruz Bay. In all, there are 15 well-furnished buildings, each structure with four one-bedroom suites, coming with a full kitchen and spacious living area. The best views, of course, are in the apartments on the upper level. Harborside villas tend to get more noise. The beach nearby is small and rocky, so you may want to go farther afield for the sands. The garden suites are one story with sunken living rooms. The property also includes multilevel sunbathing decks. On-site is **ZoZo's Ristorante** (p. 125).

Gallows Point, St. John, U.S.V.I. 00831. www.gallowspointresort.com. ✆ **800/323-7229** or 340/776-6434. Fax 340/776-6520. 60 units. Winter $465–$655 suite; off season $265–$495 suite. AE, MC, V. **Amenities:** Restaurant; bar; pool (outdoor). *In room:* A/C, TV, hair dryer, kitchen, Wi-Fi (free).

Suite St. John at Lavender Hill Estates ★ ☺   This outfit offers some of the best condo values on this tiny island. It's a short walk away from the shops, markets, restaurants, and safari buses of Cruz Bay. The two units overlook Cruz Bay Harbor, and both have a spacious central living/dining area opening onto a tiled deck, along with a fully equipped kitchen and one or two bedrooms.

P.O. Box 8306, Lavender Hill, Cruz Bay, St. John, U.S.V.I. 00831-8306. www.lavenderhillestates.com. ✆ **340/690-4692.** Fax 301/977-4252. 2 units. Winter $350 1-bedroom apt; off season $195–$250 1-bedroom apt. Extra person $35 per night. MC, V. **Amenities:** Pool (outdoor). *In room:* A/C, TV/DVD, CD player, kitchen, Wi-Fi (free).

MODERATE

Estate Concordia Studios Vacationing families, even honeymooners, flock to this environmentally sensitive 50-acre development, which has been widely praised for its integration with the local ecosystem. Its elevated structures were designed to coexist with the stunning southern edge of St. John. The secluded property is nestled on a low cliff above a salt pond, surrounded by hundreds of pristine National Park acres. It's best for those with rental vehicles. Each building was designed to protect mature trees and is connected to its neighbors with boardwalks. The nine studios are contained in five postmodern cottages. Each unit has a kitchen, a shower-only bathroom, a balcony, and a ceiling fan; some have an extra bedroom. For information on the on-site **Concordia Eco-Tents,** see "Campgrounds," below.

20-27 Estate Concordia, Coral Bay, St. John, U.S.V.I. 00830. www.maho.org. © **800/392-9004** or 212/472-9453 in the U.S. and Canada, or 340/715-0501. Fax 340/776-6504. 9 units. Winter $160–$250 double; off season $115–$160 double. MC, V. **Amenities:** Internet cafe ($10 per hr.); pool (outdoor). *In room:* Ceiling fan, kitchen, no phone.

Garden by the Sea Bed & Breakfast ★ 📶 This cozy little choice is like the quintessential Caribbean home, in a setting of coconut and banana trees, with nesting birds, iguanas, and peacocks. Overlooking the ocean, near a bird-filled salt pond, this B&B lies a 10-minute walk south of the little port of Cruz Bay. It has easy access to the north-shore beaches and lies between Frank and Turner bays. From the gardens of the house, a short path along Audubon Pond leads to Frank Bay Beach. Be sure to reserve a room ahead, as it offers only three bedrooms. Artifacts from around the world have been used to furnish the units. Each bedroom features elephant bamboo canopy beds, Japanese fountains, hardwood floors, and well-kept bathrooms. Don't expect phones or TVs, as this is a getaway, not a communications center. The 1970s house is designed in a Caribbean gingerbread style with cathedral beamed ceilings.

P.O. Box 37, Cruz Bay, St. John, U.S.V.I. 00831 www.gardenbythesea.com. © **340/779-4731.** 3 units. Winter $250–$275 double; off season $160–$200 double. No credit cards. Closed Sept. *In room:* A/C, ceiling fan, hair dryer, no phone, Wi-Fi (free).

Harmony Studios ★ Tree frogs and hummingbirds greet you as you arrive here, as this complex was designed to combine both ecological technology and comfort; it's one of the few resorts in the Caribbean to operate exclusively on sun and wind power. Built on a hillside above the Maho Bay Camp, this is a small-scale cluster of 12 luxury studios in six two-story houses with views sweeping down to the sea. Most of the building materials are derived from recycled materials, including reconstituted plastic and glass containers, newsprint, old tires, and scrap lumber. The studios contain ceiling fans, tiled shower-only bathrooms, kitchenettes, dining areas, and outdoor terraces. The managers and staff are committed to offering educational experiences, as well as the services of a small-scale resort. Guests can walk a short distance downhill to use the restaurant, grocery store, and watersports facilities at the Maho Bay Camp.

P.O. Box 310, Cruz Bay, St. John, U.S.V.I. 00831. www.maho.org. © **800/392-9004** in the U.S. and Canada, or 340/776-6240. Fax 340/776-6504. 12 units. Winter $225–$250 studio for 2; off season $130–$155 studio for 2. Extra person $25. MC, V. **Amenities:** Extensive watersports equipment/rentals. *In room:* Ceiling fan, kitchenette, no phone.

Serendip Vacation Condos   This coveted island hideaway attracts a loyal clientele, many of whom return every year. Its drawback is that it is not on the beach, and most visitors need a car to get around. This property is set on sloping land on a hillside above Cruz Bay. Its angular lines and concrete verandas are shielded by masses of shrubbery. Serendip is a no-frills place, attracting independent types when compared to the other recommended, more luxurious properties in this price category. The units have simple Caribbean-style furniture and contain concrete latticework, a ceiling fan, and a terrace or balcony. A gas-heated barbecue grill on the grounds is available for use. Prices here are especially attractive for vacationers in small groups, plus the studio apartments have sleeper couches.

P.O. Box 273, Cruz Bay, St. John, U.S.V.I. 00831. www.serendipstjohn.com. © **888/800-6445** in the U.S. and Canada, or 340/776-6646. 10 apts. Winter $225 studio, $295 1-bedroom apt; off season $135 studio, $170 1-bedroom apt. Extra person $25; $15 children ages 3–10; children 2 and under stay free in parent's apt. MC, V. **Amenities:** Pool (outdoor). *In room:* A/C, TV, kitchen, Wi-Fi (free).

INEXPENSIVE
The Inn at Tamarind Court   This is a laid-back, homey sort of place, with a very casual atmosphere and a friendly staff. Right outside Cruz Bay but still within walking distance of the ferryboat dock, this modest place consists of a small hotel and an even simpler West Indian inn. The inn is pretty basic and won't please you if you're too demanding, but it's one of the few low-cost options on St. John. Bedrooms are small, evoking those in a little country motel. Most have twin beds. Shower-only bathrooms in the inn are shared among the single rooms; units in the hotel have small private bathrooms. The social life here revolves around its courtyard bar and the in-house restaurant under the same name. From the hotel, you can walk to shuttles that take you to the beaches.

South Shore Rd. (P.O. Box 350), Cruz Bay, St. John, U.S.V.I. 00831. www.tamarindcourt.com. © **800/221-1637** in the U.S., or 340/776-6378. Fax 340/776-6722. 20 units, 14 with bathroom. Winter $75 single without bathroom, $148 double with bathroom, $240 apt for 4 with bathroom; off season $60–$65 single without bathroom, $110–$120 double with bathroom, $170–$190 apt for 4 with bathroom. Rates include continental breakfast. AE, DISC, MC, V. **Amenities:** Restaurant; bar. *In room:* A/C, ceiling fan, TV, fridge, no phone.

CAMPGROUNDS
Cinnamon Bay Campground ★★ ☺   This National Park Service campground is the most complete in the Caribbean. The site is directly on the beach, surrounded by thousands of acres of tropical vegetation. Life is simple here: You have a choice of a tent, a cottage, or a bare site. At the bare campsites, you get just the site, with no fancy extras. Each canvas tent is 10×14 feet and has a floor as well as a number of extras, including all cooking equipment; your linens are even changed weekly. Each cottage is 15×15 feet, consisting of a room with two concrete walls and two screen walls. Each cottage contains cooking facilities and four twin beds with thin mattresses; one cot can be added. Lavatories and cool-water showers are in separate buildings nearby. In winter, guests can camp for a maximum of 2 weeks; the rest of the year camping is limited to 30 days.

P.O. Box 720, Cruz Bay, St. John, U.S.V.I. 00831. www.cinnamonbay.com. © **340/776-6330.** Fax 340/776-6458. 126 units, none with bathroom. Winter $120–$155 cottage for 2, $88 tent site, $30 bare site; off season $77–$100 cottage for 2, $64 tent site, $30 bare site. Extra person $19. AE, MC, V. Closed Sept. **Amenities:** Restaurant; extensive watersports equipment/rentals. *In room:* No phone.

Concordia Eco-Tents   On the southern tip of St. John, overlooking Salt Pond Bay and Ram Head Point, these solar- and wind-powered tent-cottages combine sustainable technology with some of the most spectacular views on the island. The light framing, fabric walls, and large screened-in windows lend a tree-house atmosphere to guests' experiences. Set on the windward side of the island, the tent-cottages enjoy natural ventilation from the cooling trade winds. Inside, each has two twin beds with rather thin mattresses in each bedroom, one or two twin mattresses on a loft platform, and a queen-size futon in the living room area. (Each unit can sleep up to six people comfortably.) In addition, each Eco-Tent has a small solar-powered private shower, rather meager towels, and a composting toilet. The secluded hillside location, surrounded by hundreds of acres of pristine national park land, requires guests to arrange for a rental vehicle.

20–27 Estate Concordia, Coral Bay, St. John, U.S.V.I. 00830. www.maho.org. © **800/392-9004** in the U.S., or 212/472-9453. Fax 212/861-6210. 18 units (4 are wheelchair accessible). Winter $155–$185 tent for 2; off season $105 tent for 2. Extra person $15. MC, V. **Amenities:** Pool (outdoor). *In room:* No phone.

Maho Bay Camps ★ ☺   Right on Maho Bay, this is an intriguing concept in ecology vacationing, where you camp close to nature, but with considerable comfort. It's set on a hillside above the beach surrounded by the Virgin Islands National Park. To preserve the existing ground cover, all 114 tent-cottages are on platforms, above a thickly wooded slope. Utility lines and pipes are hidden under wooden boardwalks and stairs. Each tent-cottage, covered with canvas and screens, has two twin beds with thin mattresses, a couch, electric lamps and outlets, a dining table, chairs, a propane stove, an ice chest (cooler), linens, thin towels, and cooking and eating utensils. Guests share communal bathhouses. Maho Bay Camps is more intimate and slightly more luxurious than its nearest competitor, Cinnamon Bay.

P.O. Box 310, Cruz Bay, St. John, U.S.V.I. 00830. www.maho.org. © **800/392-9004** in the U.S., or 340/715-0501. Fax 340/776-6504 or 212/861-6210. 114 units, none with bathroom. Winter $135 tent-cottage for 2 (minimum stay of 7 nights); off season $80 tent-cottage for 2. Extra person winter $15, off season $12. MC, V. **Amenities:** Restaurant; extensive watersports equipment/rentals.

WHERE TO EAT

St. John has some posh dining, particularly at the luxury resorts like Caneel Bay, but it also has West Indian restaurants with plenty of local color and flavor. Many of the restaurants command high prices, but you can lunch almost anywhere at reasonable rates. Dinner is often quite an event on St. John, as it's about the only form of nightlife the island has.

Expensive

Asolare ★ FRENCH/ASIAN   This is the most beautiful and elegant restaurant on St. John, with the hippest and best-looking staff. Asolare is in the Estate Lindholm Bed & Breakfast (p. 117) and sits on top of a hill overlooking Cruz Bay and some of the British Virgin Islands. *Asolare* translates to "the leisurely passing of time without purpose" in Greek, and that's what many diners prefer to do here. The chef roams the world for inspiration and cooks with flavor and flair, using some of the best and freshest ingredients available on the island. To begin, you might try the grilled Asian barbecued shrimp, or the squid-and-shrimp medley. For a main course, you will be tempted by the ginger lamb or the peppercorn-dusted filet of beef. Two truly excellent dishes are the chicken Kiev and the sashimi tuna with plum–passion fruit sake vinaigrette. For dessert, try the fresh berry dishes or the chocolate pyramid cake.

In the Estate Lindholm Bed & Breakfast, Cruz Bay. ✆ **340/779-4747.** www.asolarestjohn.com. Reservations required. Main courses $29–$38. AE, MC, V. Tues–Sun 6–9pm.

Caneel Beach Terrace ★ INTERNATIONAL/SEAFOOD Right below the Equator (see below) is an elegant, open-air dining room on the beach catering to elite palates. Although the cuisine here has varied over the years, the professional standards remain high. Start with an appetizer of papaya with prosciutto, and move on to one of the wonderful fresh salads. The menus change nightly, but main dishes are likely to include baked filet of red snapper or roast prime rib of blue-ribbon beef. For dessert, try strawberry cheesecake or Boston cream pie. The self-service buffet luncheon is one of the best and most popular in the Virgin Islands.

At Caneel Bay (p. 113), Caneel Bay. ✆ **340/776-6111.** www.caneelbay.com/dine4.cfm. Reservations required for dinner. Breakfast buffet $31; main courses $20–$45; grand seafood buffet Mon night $69; lunch buffet $32; grand buffet $69. AE, DC, MC, V. Daily 7–10:30am, 11:30am–2pm, and 6:30–9pm.

Cruz Bay Prime ★★ AMERICAN At the Westin, this luxurious restaurant features one of the island's best dining experiences, especially if you like steak and seafood. To enter the restaurant, head for the upper level of the Westin's open-air lobby. The talented chefs turn out savory dishes redolent of Caribbean sunshine and full of flavor. Specialties of the chef include mahimahi and yellowfin tuna, as well as delectable crab cakes and a 2-pound lobster special.

In the Westin St. John Resort & Villas (p. 114), Great Cruz Bay. ✆ **340/693-8000.** Reservations recommended. Main courses $28–$38. AE, MC, V. Daily 6–9:30pm.

Equator ★ CARIBBEAN This restaurant lies behind the tower of an 18th-century sugar mill, where ponds with water lilies fill former crystallization pits for hot molasses. A flight of stairs leads to a monumental circular dining room, with a wraparound veranda and sweeping views of the water and St. Thomas. In the center rises the stone column that horses and mules once circled to crush sugar-cane stalks. A giant Poinciana-like Asian tree of the *Albizia lebbeck* species—islanders call it "woman's tongue tree"—grows in the middle of the restaurant.

The cuisine is the most daring on the island, and for the most part, the chefs pull off their transcultural dishes. A spicy and tantalizing opener is lemon grass–and–ginger-cured salmon salad. Daily Caribbean selections are offered, such as a classic Caribbean callaloo soup, or you can opt for such fine dishes as seared Caribbean tuna, or penne pasta with shiitake mushrooms and roasted tomatoes in an herb-garlic cream sauce. There's always a dry, aged Angus steak or a grilled veal chop for the more traditional palate.

At Caneel Bay (p. 113), Caneel Bay. ✆ **340/776-6111.** www.caneelbay.com/dine3.cfm. Reservations required. Main courses $24–$44. AE, MC, V. Tues–Sun 6–9pm.

La Plancha Del Mar ★★ MEDITERRANEAN This restaurant is a little bit off the beaten path, but it's worth searching out. It serves hearty food with an exotic twist, and is named *plancha* for its piping hot iron grill, likely to be sizzling with steak. The house specialty is a churrasco steak with garlic-herb fries and a citrus aioli, a tasty treat. Other specialties include seared mahimahi with a spicy tomato-and-basil purée, or a paella à la *plancha* studded with tiger prawns, mussels, bits of chicken, and chorizo. Appetizers are some of the best on the island, featuring a toasted pine nut hummus or a crusted brie with a strawberry coulis. At lunch you get a selection of

St. John Restaurants

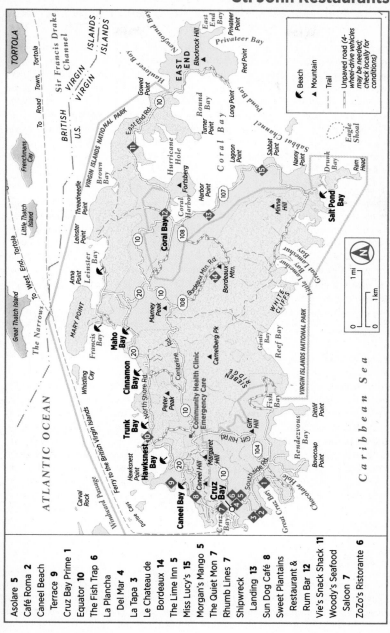

Asolare **5**
Café Roma **2**
Caneel Beach Terrace **9**
Cruz Bay Prime **1**
Equator **10**
The Fish Trap **6**
La Plancha
Del Mar **4**
La Tapa **3**
Le Chateau de Bordeaux **14**
The Lime Inn **5**
Miss Lucy's **15**
Morgan's Mango **5**
The Quiet Mon **7**
Rhumb Lines **7**
Shipwreck Landing **13**
Sun Dog Café **8**
Sweet Plantains Restaurant & Rum Bar **12**
Vie's Snack Shack **11**
Woody's Seafood Saloon **7**
ZoZo's Ristorante **6**

4

ST. JOHN | Where to Eat

123

pizzas, sandwiches, and wraps. Nothing is overpriced or oversauced, as the owners believe in preserving the natural flavor of their ingredients.

Route 104, Marketplace Shopping Center, outside Cruz Bay. © **340/777-7333.** www.laplanchadelmar. com. Reservations recommended for dinner. Main courses $24–$40. MC, V. Mon–Fri 11:30am–2pm; Mon–Sat 5–9pm.

La Tapa INTERNATIONAL/MEDITERRANEAN   There's a tiny bar with no more than five stools, a two-tiered dining room, and lots of original paintings. (The establishment doubles as an art gallery.) Menu items are thoughtful and well conceived, and include fast-seared tuna with a Basque-inspired relish of onions, peppers, garlic, and herbs; filet poivre, a steak soaked with rum and served with a cracked-pepper sauce and mashed potatoes; and linguine with shrimp, red peppers, and leeks in peanut sauce. Live jazz is offered on Mondays.

Centerline Rd. (across from FirstBank), Cruz Bay. © **340/693-7755.** Reservations recommended. Main courses $30–$41. AE, MC, V. Wed–Mon 6–10pm (daily in winter).

Le Château de Bordeaux ★ CONTINENTAL/CARIBBEAN   This restaurant is 5 miles east of Cruz Bay, near the center of the island and close to one of its highest points. It's known for having some of the best views on St. John. A lunch grill on the patio serves burgers and drinks Monday through Saturday. In the evening, amid a Victorian decor with lace tablecloths, you can begin with a house-smoked chicken spring roll or a velvety carrot soup. After that, move on to one of the saffron-flavored pastas or a savory West Indian seafood chowder, the island's best. Smoked salmon and filet mignon are a bow to the international crowd, although the wild-game specials are more unusual. The well-flavored Dijon mustard–and-pecan-crusted roast rack of lamb with a shallot port reduction is also a good choice. For dessert, there's a changing array of cheesecakes, among other options. The specialty drink is a passion fruit daiquiri.

Junction 10, Bordeaux Mountain. © **340/776-6611.** Reservations required. Main courses $28–$38. AE, MC, V. Tues–Sat 5:30–9:30pm.

Rhumb Lines ★ ☺ CARIBBEAN/PACIFIC RIM   In the heart of Cruz Bay, this restaurant with its West Indian courtyard has a South Seas ambience. The chefs take you on a culinary tour that travels from the Caribbean to the Pacific Ocean, seeking recipes to inspire them. Appetizers are among the island's best, ranging from hot-and-sour grilled duck breast glazed with rum punch to cracked pepper–crusted tuna over a seaweed salad. Ever had gazpacho made with mango? The main dishes are full of flavor and are delectable, especially the fresh mahimahi in banana leaf with a gingered banana beurre blanc, or the tenderloin of Cuban pork marinated in garlic and citrus juices. For the adventurous palate, there is a special menu of Pupu (tapas), with everything from lemon grass–and-tofu cakes to spicy Szechuan noodles. There is also a kids' menu. The drink menu has some of the most imaginative drinks on the island.

Meada's Plaza, Cruz Bay. © **340/776-0303.** www.rhumblinesstjohn.com. Reservations recommended. Main dishes $14–$29. MC, V. Wed–Mon 5:30–10pm; Sun brunch 10am–2:30pm.

Sweet Plantains Restaurant & Rum Bar ★ CARIBBEAN/CREOLE   Cool drinks, a tropical ambience, and authentic flavors lure locals and visitors alike to this eatery, where comfort and good food go hand in hand. You can dine alfresco in the sea-bordering courtyard or in a lush tropical garden surrounded by West Indian art. A helpful staff will guide you through the menu, beginning with such appetizers as saltfish cakes with a sweet-mango purée or a spicy crab spread with green-plantain chips. A freshly made soup is also featured daily. For a main you can order tender short ribs of beef or pork tenderloin in a guava barbecue sauce. Choice top-quality beef cuts and game are also featured. Nightly specialties are offered, ranging from curries with a choice of seafood or chicken, or else French Caribbean dishes.

16118 Little Plantation, Coral Bay. ⓒ **340/777-4653.** www.sweetplantains-stjohn.com. Reservations recommended. Main courses $21–$34. MC, V. Wed–Mon 5:30–9pm.

ZoZo's Ristorante ITALIAN   An in-the-know crowd of locals and visitors flocks to this charming Italian trattoria, with an open-air terrace and a sweeping panoramic view over the sea. First-rate ingredients, style, and fresh seasonings contribute to such winning dishes as the Eggplant Tower (layers of eggplant, fontina, ricotta, and red peppers); littleneck clams in white wine, garlic, and plum tomatoes; and lump crab cakes with a roasted-pepper aïoli. The pastas are the island's best, especially the lobster ravioli with wild mushrooms and toasted pine nuts, and the basil-infused linguine. Tuck into such fish dishes as a grilled sea bass with an eggplant tapenade in a roasted garlic–shrimp sauce or pan-seared black grouper with a sauce flavored with orange and fresh basil. Their *osso buco* is slowly simmered in red wine, tomato, and veal stock and is a tasty main course.

Gallows Point. ⓒ **340/693-9200.** www.zozos.net. Reservations recommended. Main courses $33–$40. AE, MC, V. Daily 5:30–9pm.

Moderate

Café Roma ☺ ITALIAN   This restaurant in the center of Cruz Bay is not a place for great finesse in the kitchen, but it's a longtime favorite and has pleased a lot of families who just want a casual meal. To enter, you have to climb a flight of stairs. You might arrive early and have a strawberry colada, then enjoy a standard pasta, veal, seafood, or chicken dish. There are usually 30 to 40 vegetarian items on the menu. The owner claims, with justification, that his pizzas are the best on the island. Italian wines are sold by the glass or bottle, and you can end the evening with an espresso.

Cruz Bay. ⓒ **340/776-6524.** www.stjohn-caferoma.com. Main courses $13–$29. MC, V. Daily 5–10pm.

The Fish Trap ★ SEAFOOD   This aptly named place serves St. John's best seafood. It's a casual, laid-back atmosphere, with tables placed on a covered patio open to the trade winds, an easy walk up from the ferry dock. Chef Aaron Willis is the island's favorite, bringing his New York culinary training with him but showing a total familiarity with West Indian seasonings and flavors. Nobody on St. John does conch fritters better, and he's been praised by such national magazines as *Vogue* and *Gourmet*. Depending on the catch of the day, there will be a fresh fish special, most likely wahoo, shark, mahimahi, or snapper. The grilled tuna, for example, comes in a wasabi sauce, and the swordfish is made more appetizing by the use of lemon grass. An array of steaks, tasty pastas, chicken cutlets, and burgers are always served.

Cruz Bay, next to Our Lady of Mount Carmel Church. ⓒ **340/693-9994.** www.thefishtrap.com. Reservations required for groups of 6 or more. Main courses $13–$42. MC, V. Tues–Sun 4:30–10pm.

The Lime Inn SEAFOOD   This lively open-air restaurant is located at the Lemon Tree Mall in the heart of Cruz Bay. It's known for its fresh grilled Caribbean-style lobster. Other grilled seafood choices range from shrimp to the fresh catch of the day. The seared whole snapper, when served, is a delight. If you're not in the mood for seafood, try one of the daily chicken and pasta specials or one of the grilled steaks.

FAMILY-FRIENDLY RESTAURANTS

Café Roma (p. 125)   This informal place is a family favorite with the best pizza on the island.

Miss Lucy's (below)   There is no better place in St. John to introduce your child to West Indian cookery than this restaurant. It's fun, it's local, and families enjoy it, often ordering a big paella that all members can feast on. The fish is among the best on the island.

Rhumb Lines (p. 125)   Children will love the South Seas ambience and the Caribbean/Pacific Rim cuisine at this restaurant with a designated kids' menu. The appetizers are among the island's best.

There's also a tender grilled filet mignon stuffed with crabmeat. A beautifully prepared chicken Wellington is one of the chef's specialties. The most popular night of the week here is Wednesday with the all-you-can-eat peel-and-eat shrimp feast for $19.

In the Lemon Tree Mall, Konges Gade, Cruz Bay. ✆ **340/776-6425.** www.limeinn.com. Reservations recommended. Main courses lunch $7.95–$13, dinner $19–$28. AE, MC, V. Mon–Fri 11:30am–3pm and 5:30–10pm; Sat 5:30–10pm. Closed Sept.

Miss Lucy's ★ ☺ CARIBBEAN   For the broadest array of island cuisine, nobody does it better than Miss Lucy. Her food is the way it used to taste in the Caribbean long before anyone ever heard of upscale resorts. Before becoming the island's most famous female chef, Miss Lucy was a big hit with tourists as St. John's first female taxi driver. Her paella is scrumptious: a kettle brimming with hot Italian sausage, deep-fried chicken, shrimp, and mussels over perfectly cooked saffron rice. Traditional conch fritters appear with a picante sauce, and you can gobble them down with Miss Lucy's callaloo soup. She has a magic touch with this soup. Her fish is pulled from Caribbean waters, and does she ever know how to cook it! When a local fisherman catches a wahoo, he is often likely to bring it here for Miss Lucy to cook. Main dishes come with *fungi*, a cornmeal-and-okra side dish. At one of her "full moon parties," she'll cook a roast suckling pig. For dessert, try her banana pancakes.

Salt Pond Rd., near Estate Concordia, Coral Bay. ✆ **340/693-5244.** Reservations recommended. Main courses $13–$30. AE, MC, V. Tues–Sat 11am–2pm and 6–9pm; Sun 10am–2pm.

Morgan's Mango CARIBBEAN   The chefs here roam the Caribbean for tantalizing flavors, which they adapt for their ever-changing menu. The restaurant is easy to spot, with its big canopy, the only protection from the elements. The bar wraps around the main dining room and offers some 30 frozen drinks. Some think the kitchen tries to do too much with the nightly menu, but it does produce some zesty fare—everything from Anegada lobster cakes to spicy Jamaican pickapeppa steak. Try flying fish served as an appetizer, followed by Haitian voodoo snapper pressed in Cajun spices, then grilled and served with fresh-fruit salsa. Equally delectable is mahimahi in Cruzan rum–and-mango sauce. The knockout dessert is the mango-banana pie.

Cruz Bay (across from the National Park dock). ✆ **340/693-8141.** Reservations recommended. Main courses $16–$34. AE, MC, V. Daily 5:30–10pm.

Shipwreck Landing SEAFOOD/CONTINENTAL   Eight miles east of Cruz Bay on the road to Salt Pond Beach, Shipwreck Landing has palms and tropical plants on a veranda overlooking the sea. The intimate bar specializes in tropical frozen drinks. Lunch features a lot more than just sandwiches, salads, and burgers—try pan-seared blackened snapper in Cajun spices, or the conch fritters. The chef shines at night, offering a pasta of the day along with such specialties as tantalizing Caribbean blackened shrimp. A lot of the fare is routine, including New York strip steak and fish and chips, but the grilled mahimahi in lime butter is worth the trip. Entertainment, mainly jazz, is featured Thursday and Sunday nights, with no cover.

34 Freeman's Ground, Rte. 107, Coral Bay. (ℓ) **340/693-5640.** Reservations requested. Lunch $9–$17; main courses $16–$26. AE, DISC, MC, V. Daily 11am–9pm. Bar daily until 11pm. Closed Sept–Oct.

Inexpensive

The Quiet Mon 🛏 AMERICAN   Many of us have heard the country singer Kenny Chesney sing of his life on Cinnamon Bay and his travels to Jost Van Dyke in the B.V.I. He even sings of this pub, the Quiet Mon. Chesney remains a frequent visitor, but count yourself lucky if he gets up late one night and sings such hits as "She Thinks My Tractor's Sexy." The pub lies upstairs. Tom Selleck and Alan Alda are just some of the celebrities who have visited here, ordering from a limited menu that consists mostly of hot dogs and french fries. You can also enjoy homemade chili and sloppy Joes. Look for lunch specials, including a homemade soup of the day. There are about six beers on tap.

Cruz Bay. (ℓ) **340/779-4799.** www.quietmon.com. Lunch plates $4–$7. No credit cards. Lunch specials Mon–Fri 12:30–6pm. Bar daily 10am–4am.

Sun Dog Café INTERNATIONAL   This little eatery is hidden away on the upper floors of the Mongoose Shopping Center. It's known to locals and the occasional visitor who stumbles upon it. The white artichoke pizza is our favorite, while the black-bean quesadilla is a local favorite. You can order sandwiches throughout the day—including a great marinated mahimahi concoction. If you're not too hungry, you can enjoy drinks at the Gecko Gazebo Bar instead.

Mongoose Junction, N. Shore Rd. (ℓ) **340/693-8340.** Main courses $14–$19. AE, MC, V. Daily 11am–9pm. Bar daily 11am–10pm.

Vie's Snack Shack ★ 🛏 WEST INDIAN   Vie's looks like little more than a plywood-sided hut, but its charming and gregarious owner is known as one of the best local chefs on St. John. Her garlic chicken is famous. She also serves conch fritters, johnnycakes, island-style beans and rice with meat sauce, and coconut and pineapple tarts. Don't leave without a glass of homemade limeade. The place is open most days, but, as Vie says, "Some days, we might not be here at all"—so you'd better call before you head out.

East End Rd., Rte. 10 (13 miles east of Cruz Bay). (ℓ) **340/693-5033.** Main courses $7–$12. No credit cards. Tues–Sat 10am–5pm (but call first). Closed Oct.

Woody's Seafood Saloon SEAFOOD/AMERICAN   This local dive and hangout at Cruz Bay is more famous for its beers on tap than for its cuisine. A mix of local fishermen, taxi drivers, tour guides, aimless island drifters, and an occasional husband and wife show up here to sample the spicy conch fritters. Shrimp appears in various styles, and you can usually order fresh fish and other dishes, including burgers, blackened shark, drunken shellfish, and mussels and clams steamed in beer.

Cruz Bay (150 ft. from the ferry dock). ℃ **340/779-4625.** www.woodysseafood.com. Main courses $7–$18. AE, DISC, MC, V. Sun–Thurs 11am–1am; Fri–Sat 11am–2am.

BEACHES

The best beach, hands down, is **Trunk Bay ★★★**, the biggest attraction on St. John. To miss its picture-perfect shoreline of white sand would be like touring Paris and skipping the Eiffel Tower. One of the loveliest beaches in the Caribbean, it offers ideal conditions for diving, snorkeling, swimming, and sailing. There are even lifeguards on duty. The only drawback is the crowds (watch for pickpockets). Beginning snorkelers in particular are attracted to the underwater trail near the shore (see "Watersports," under "Fun in the Surf & Sun," below); you can rent snorkeling gear here. Admission is $4 for adults 17 and over. If you're coming from St. Thomas, both taxis and safari buses to Trunk Bay meet the ferries from St. Thomas when they dock at Cruz Bay.

Caneel Bay, the stomping ground of the rich and famous, has seven beautiful beaches on its 170 acres, and all are open to the public. **Caneel Bay Beach** is easy to reach from the main entrance of the Caneel Bay resort. A staff member at the gatehouse will provide directions. **Hawksnest Beach** is one of the most beautiful beaches near Caneel Bay, but because it's near Cruz Bay, where the ferry docks, it is the most crowded, especially when cruise-ship passengers come over from St. Thomas. Safari buses and taxis from Cruz Bay will take you along Northshore Road.

The campgrounds of **Cinnamon Bay** have their own beach, where forest rangers sometimes have to remind visitors to put their swim trunks back on. This is our particular favorite, a beautiful strip of white sand with hiking trails, great windsurfing, ruins, and wild donkeys (don't feed or pet them!). Changing rooms and showers are available, and you can rent watersports equipment. Snorkeling is especially popular; you'll often see big schools of purple triggerfish. This beach is best in the morning and at midday, as afternoons are likely to be windy. A marked **nature trail,** with signs identifying the flora, loops through a tropical forest on even turf before leading up to Centerline Road.

Maho Bay Beach is immediately to the east of Cinnamon Bay, and it also borders campgrounds. As you lie on the sand, you can see a whole hillside of pitched tents. This is also a popular beach, often with the campers themselves.

Francis Bay Beach and **Watermelon Cay Beach** are just a few more of the beaches you'll encounter when traveling eastward along St. John's gently curving coastline. The beach at **Leinster Bay** is another haven for those seeking the solace of a private sunny retreat. You can swim in the bay's shallow water or snorkel over the spectacular and colorful coral reef, perhaps in the company of an occasional turtle or stingray.

The remote **Salt Pond Bay** is known to locals but often missed by visitors. It's on the beautiful coast in the southeast, adjacent to **Coral Bay.** The bay is tranquil, but the beach is somewhat rocky. It's a short walk down the hill from a parking lot. (*Beware:* A few cars have recently been broken into.) The snorkeling is good, and the bay has some fascinating tidal pools. The Ram Head Trail begins here and, winding for a mile, leads to a belvedere overlooking the bay. Facilities are meager but include an outhouse and a few tattered picnic tables.

SUSTAINABLE ST. JOHN: A ROCKEFELLER DREAM

St. John is the most tranquil, unspoiled island in the Virgins. All of this came about in 1956 when multimillionaire Laurance Rockefeller sailed around the island with friends on his yacht. Rockefeller was so enchanted with the island that he established his own resort here and donated 9,500 acres of rolling green hills and an underwater preserve to the federal government to be set aside as a national park that would be here for future generations to enjoy.

Sustainable tourism programs and eco-friendly practices keep the island clean and pristine. St. John, more than any other island in the Caribbean, works to ensure the preservation of its natural resources and ecosystems.

You can live here instead of in overcrowded St. Thomas. For those who seek luxury, there is **Caneel Bay resort** (p. 113) or **Westin St. John Resort & Villas** (p. 114). But for those who want to get back to nature, St. John boasts several eco-tourism resorts and campgrounds. Chief among these are **Estate Concordia Studios** (p. 119); **Cinnamon**

Bay Campground (p. 120); **Concordia Eco-tents** (p. 121) and **Maho Bay Camp** (p. 121).

Two-thirds of St. John's 19 square miles is protected national parkland today. The island also has some of the most beautiful beaches in the Caribbean, including Trunk Bay and Hawksnest Bay.

Snorkelers and scuba divers come here to explore underwater St. John, with its rainbow-hued fish and coral. Many divers are attracted to Pillsbury Sound, where the Caribbean Sea meets the Atlantic Ocean.

To protect this underwater paradise, in 1962 the boundaries of the National Park were expanded to include 5,650 acres of submerged lands and waters around St. John, with their coral reefs and marine life.

You can explore the park by boat or foot, especially by hiking and nature walks. Camping, fishing, kayaking, scuba diving, snorkeling, and bird-watching are also possible.

If you want to escape the crowds, head for **Lameshur Bay Beach,** along the rugged south coast, west of Salt Pond Bay and accessible only via a bumpy dirt road. The sands are beautiful and the snorkeling is excellent. You can also take a 5-minute stroll down the road past the beach to explore the nearby ruins of an old plantation estate that was destroyed in a slave revolt.

Does St. John have a nude beach? Not officially, but lovely **Solomon Bay Beach** is a contender, although park rangers of late have sometimes asked people to give up their quest for the perfect tan. Leave Cruz Bay on Route 20 and turn left at the park service sign, about one-quarter mile past the visitor center. Park at the end of a cul-de-sac, then walk along the trail for about 15 minutes. Go early, and you'll practically have the beach to yourself. As we mentioned earlier, people also sometimes shed their swimwear at **Cinnamon Bay** (see above). Again, rangers frequently ask beachgoers to put their (only slightly more modest) bathing suits back on.

FUN IN THE SURF & SUN

St. John offers some of the best snorkeling, scuba diving, swimming, fishing, hiking, sailing, and underwater photography in the Caribbean. The island is known for the

Virgin Islands National Park, as well as for its coral-sand beaches, winding mountain roads, hidden coves, and trails that lead past old, bush-covered sugar-cane plantations. Just don't visit St. John expecting to play golf.

Watersports

The most complete line of watersports equipment available, including rentals for windsurfing, snorkeling, kayaking, and sailing, is offered at the **Cinnamon Bay Watersports Center,** on Cinnamon Bay Beach (✆ **340/776-6330**). One- and two-person sit-on-top kayaks rent for $15 to $30 per hour. You can also sail away in a 14- or 16-foot Hobie monohull **sailboat** for $30 to $50 per hour.

BOAT EXCURSIONS   You can take half- and full-day boat trips, including a full-day excursion to the Baths at Virgin Gorda. **Cruz Bay Watersports** (✆ **340/776-6234**) offers trips to the British Virgin Islands for $150, including food and beverages. *Note:* Be sure to bring your passport for any excursions to the British Virgin Islands.

Sail Safaris (✆ **866/820-6906;** www.sailsafaris.net) offers guided tours with a captain, sailing lessons, and rentals of their fleet of Hobie catamarans. Right on the beach in Cruz Bay, just down from the ferry dock, this outfitter answers the often-asked question, "Where can we rent a small sailboat?" These catamarans, capable of sailing to the remote and wilder spots of the Virgin Islands, carry four passengers and feature a range of destinations not available by charter boat or kayak, including trips to uninhabited islands. On guided tours, passengers can go island-hopping in the B.V.I. Sail Safaris also has sailing lessons for those with an interest in sailing as a hobby. Half-day tours cost $70 per person; full-day jaunts, including lunch, go for $110; a 1-hour sailing lesson is $95.

FISHING   Outfitters located on St. Thomas offer sportfishing trips here—they'll come over and pick you up. Call the **Charter Boat Center** (✆ **340/775-7990**) at Red Hook. Count on spending from $550 to $750 per party for a half-day of fishing. Fisherman can use hand-held rods to fish the waters in Virgin Islands National Park. Stop in at the tourist office at the St. Thomas ferry dock for a listing of fishing spots around the island.

SCUBA DIVING & SNORKELING ★★   **Cruz Bay Watersports,** P.O. Box 252, Cruz Bay, St. John (✆ **340/776-6234;** www.divestjohn.com), is a PADI and NAUI five-star diving center. Certifications can be arranged through a dive master, for $385. Beginner scuba lessons start at $120. Two-tank reef dives with all dive gear cost $100, and wreck dives, night dives, and dive packages are available. In addition, snorkel tours are offered daily for $60.

Divers can ask about scuba packages at **Low Key Watersports,** Wharfside Village (✆ **800/835-7718** in the U.S., or 340/693-8999; www.divelowkey.com). All wreck dives offered are two-tank/two-location dives and cost $90, with night dives also going for $90. Snorkel tours are also available at $75 per person. The center also rents watersports gear, including masks, fins, snorkels, and dive skins, and arranges day sailing trips, kayaking tours, and deep-sea fishing.

The best place for snorkeling is **Trunk Bay** (see "Beaches," above). Snorkeling gear can be rented from the Cinnamon Bay Watersports Center (see above) for $5, plus a $25 deposit. Two other choice **snorkeling spots** around St. John are **Leinster Bay** ★★ and **Haulover Bay** ★★. Usually uncrowded Leinster Bay offers some of the best snorkeling in the U.S. Virgins. The water is calm, clear, and filled with brilliantly

A Water Wonderland

At Trunk Bay, divers and snorkelers can follow the **National Park Underwater Trail** (© 340/776-6201), which stretches for 650 feet and helps you identify what you see—everything from false coral to colonial anemones. You'll pass lavender sea fans and schools of silversides. Rangers are on hand to provide information. There is a $4 admission fee to access the beach.

hued tropical fish. Haulover Bay is a favorite among locals. It's often deserted, and the waters are often clearer than in other spots around St. John. The ledges, walls, and nooks here are set very close together, making the bay a lot of fun for anyone with a little bit of experience.

Beginning swimmers can experience a snorkel-like adventure with **Virgin Islands Snuba Excursions** (© 340/693-8063; www.visnuba.com) at Trunk Bay. Divers use special equipment that allows them to breathe easily through a tube attached to an air tank above water. You'll see and experience everything as any other snorkeler would. Children ages 8 and up can participate; the fee is $65 per person.

SEA KAYAKING   Arawak Expeditions, based in Cruz Bay (© 800/238-8687 in the U.S., or 340/693-8312; www.arawakexp.com), provides kayaking gear, healthful meals, and experienced guides for full- and half-day outings. Trips cost $100 and $75, respectively. Multiday excursions with camping are also available; call their toll-free number if you'd like to arrange an entire vacation with them. These 5-day trips range in price from $1,250 to $1,450.

WINDSURFING   The windsurfing at Cinnamon Bay is some of the best anywhere, for either the beginner or the expert. The **Cinnamon Bay Watersports Center** (see above) rents high-quality equipment for all levels, even for kids. Boards cost $25 to $65 an hour; a 2-hour introductory lesson costs $80.

More Outdoor Adventure

Along St. John's rocky coastline are beautiful crescent-shaped bays and white-sand beaches—the interior is no less impressive. The variety of wildlife is the envy of naturalists around the world. And there are miles of **hiking trails,** leading past the ruins of 18th-century Danish plantations to panoramic views. At scattered spots along the trails, you can find mysteriously geometric petroglyphs of unknown age and origin incised into boulders and cliffs. The terrain ranges from arid and dry (in the east) to moist and semitropical (in the northwest). The island boasts more than 800 species of plants, 160 species of birds, and more than 20 trails maintained in fine form by the island's crew of park rangers.

Thanks to the efforts of Laurance Rockefeller, who purchased many acres of land and donated them to the United States in 1956, the island's shoreline waters, as well as more than half of its surface area, make up the **Virgin Islands National Park.** The hundreds of coral gardens that surround St. John are protected rigorously—any attempt to damage or remove coral is punishable with large and strictly enforced fines. Visitors must stop by the **Cruz Bay Visitor Center,** where you can pick up the park brochure, which includes a map of the park, and the *Virgin Islands National Park News,* which has the latest information on park activities. It's important to carry a lot of water and wear sunscreen and insect repellent when you hike.

4

ST. JOHN | Fun in the Surf & Sun

St. John is laced with clearly marked walking paths. At least 20 of these originate from Northshore Road (Rte. 20) or from the island's main east-west artery, Centerline Road (Rte. 10). Each is marked at its starting point with a preplanned itinerary; the walks can last anywhere from 10 minutes to 2 hours. Maps are available from the national park headquarters at Cruz Bay.

One of our favorite hikes, the **Annaberg Historic Trail** (identified by the U.S. National Park Service as trail no. 10), requires only about a .5-mile stroll. It departs from a clearly marked point along the island's north coast, near the junction of routes 10 and 20. This self-guided tour passes the partially restored ruins of a manor house built during the 1700s, and signs along the way give historical and botanical data. Visiting the ruins is free. If you want to prolong your hiking experience, take the **Leinster Bay Trail** (trail no. 11), which begins near the point where trail no. 10 ends. It leads past mangrove swamps and coral inlets rich with plant and marine life; markers identify some of the plants and animals. Scattered throughout the park, and sometimes hidden by plants, are mysterious petroglyphs incised into boulders and cliffs. Their ages and origins are unknown.

Near the beach at **Cinnamon Bay,** there's a marked nature trail, with signs identifying the flora. It's a relatively flat walk through a tropical forest, eventually leading straight up to Centerline Road.

The **National Park Service** (✆ **340/776-6201;** www.nps.gov/viis) provides a number of ranger-led activities. One of the most popular is the guided 2.5-mile **Reef Bay Hike.** Included is a stop at the only known petroglyphs on the island and a tour of the sugar-mill ruins. A park ranger discusses the area's natural and cultural history along the way. The hike starts at 9:30am on Monday, Tuesday, Thursday, and Friday and costs $21 per person. Reservations are required and can be made by phone (at least 2–3 weeks in advance).

Another series of hikes traversing the more arid eastern section of St. John originates at clearly marked points along the island's **southeastern tip,** off Route 107. Many of the trails wind through the grounds of 18th-century plantations, past ruined schoolhouses, rum distilleries, molasses factories, and great houses, many of which are covered with lush, encroaching vines and trees.

EXPLORING ST. JOHN

The best way to see St. John quickly, especially if you're on a cruise-ship layover, is to take a 2-hour **taxi tour.** The cost is $25 per person. Almost any taxi at Cruz Bay will take you on these tours, or you can call the **St. John Taxi Association** (✆ **340/ 693-7530**).

Many visitors spend time at **Cruz Bay,** where the ferry docks. This village has interesting bars, restaurants, boutiques, and pastel-painted houses. It's a bit sleepy, but relaxing after the fast pace of St. Thomas.

Much of the island is taken up with the **Virgin Islands National Park** ★★ (✆ **340/776-6201**), with the lushest concentration of flora and fauna in the U.S. Virgin Islands. The park totals 12,624 acres, including submerged lands and water adjacent to St. John, and has more than 20 miles of hiking trails to explore. From pelicans to sandpipers, from mahogany to bay trees, the park abounds in beauty, including a burst of tropical flowers such as the tamarind and the flamboyant. The mongoose also calls it home. Park guides lead nature walks through this park that often take you past ruins of former plantations. See "More Outdoor Adventure," above, for information on trails and organized park activities.

St. John's Mascot

The mongoose (plural *mongooses*) was brought to St. John to kill rats. It has practically been adopted as the island mascot—watch for mongooses darting across roads.

Other major sights on the island include **Trunk Bay** (see "Beaches," earlier in this chapter), one of the world's most beautiful beaches, and **Fort Berg** (also called Fortsberg), at Coral Bay, which served as the base for the soldiers who brutally crushed the 1733 slave revolt. Finally, try to make time for the **Annaberg Sugar Plantation Ruins** on Leinster Bay Road, where the Danes maintained a thriving plantation and sugar mill after 1718. It's located off Northshore Road, east of Trunk Bay. Admission is free. On certain days of the week (dates vary), guided walks of the area are given by park rangers. For information on the **Annaberg Historic Trail,** see "More Outdoor Adventure," above.

DRIVING TOUR: ST. JOHN

START & FINISH:	**Ferry docks in Cruz Bay.**
TIME:	**3 to 7 hours, depending on beach time, bar stops, and pedestrian detours.**
BEST TIME:	**Any warm, sunny day.**
WORST TIME:	**Any rainy day, when you are likely to get stuck in the mud on bad roads.**

Important note: Before you begin this tour, make sure you have at least three-quarters of a tank of gas, because there are only two gas stations on St. John, one of which is often closed. The more reliable of the two stations is in the upper regions of Cruz Bay, beside Route 104. Ask for directions when you pick up your rented vehicle. And *remember to drive on the left.*

Head out of Cruz Bay, going east on Route 20. Within about a minute, you'll pass the catwalks and verandas of:

1 Mongoose Junction

This shopping emporium, a major island attraction, contains some unusual art galleries and jewelry shops. (See "Shopping," below.)

Continuing east on Route 20, you'll pass:

2 Caneel Bay

Past the security guard, near the resort's parking lots, are a gift shop and a handful of bars and restaurants. Continuing on, you'll see within a mile the first of many stunning vistas. Note the complete absence of billboards and electrical cables, a prohibition rigidly enforced by the National Park Service.

In less than 3 miles, you'll come to:

3 Hawksnest Beach

Hawksnest is one of the island's best beaches. Continuing your drive, you'll pass, in this order, Trunk Bay, Peter Bay (private), and Cinnamon Bay, all of which have sand, palm trees, and clear water. For more information about these beaches, see p. 128.

A few steps from the entrance to the Cinnamon Bay Campground is a redwood sign marking the beginning of the:

4 Cinnamon Bay Trail

Laid out for hikers by the National Park Service, this 1-mile walk takes about an hour. Its clearly marked paths lead through shaded forest trails along the rutted cobblestones of a former Danish road, past ruins of abandoned plantations.

A short drive beyond Cinnamon Bay is the sandy sweep of **Maho Bay,** site of one of the most upscale and eco-friendly campgrounds in the Caribbean. Shortly after Maho Bay, the road splits. Take the left fork, which merges in a few moments with an extension of Centerline Road. Off this road will appear another NPS signpost marked DANISH ROAD; this detour takes you on a 5-minute trek along a potholed road to the ruins of an 18th-century school.

At the next fork, bear right toward Annaberg. (Make sure you don't go toward Francis Bay.) You'll pass the beginning of a 1-mile walking trail to the Leinster Bay Estate, which leads to a beach good for snorkeling. In less than a minute, you'll reach the parking lot of the:

5 Annaberg Historic Trail

The highlight of this driving tour, the Annaberg Historic Trail leads pedestrians within and around the ruined buildings of the best-preserved plantation on St. John. During the 18th and 19th centuries, the smell of boiling molasses permeated the air here. About a dozen NPS plaques identify and describe each building within the compound. The walk takes about 30 minutes. From a terrace near the ruined windmill, a map identifies the British Virgin Islands to the north, including Little Thatch, Tortola, Watermelon Cay, and Jost Van Dyke.

Back in the car, retrace your route to the first major division, and take the left fork. Soon a sign will identify your road as ROUTE 20 EAST. Stay on this road, forking left wherever possible, until you come, after many bends in the way, to:

6 Emmaus Moravian Church

At the sandy bottomlands you'll see an elementary school, a baseball field, and, on a hilltop, a simple barnlike building known as the Emmaus Moravian Church. This church, with its yellow clapboards and red roof, is often closed to visitors. Near its base yet another NPS walking trail begins: the 1.5-mile Johnny Horn Trail, known for its scenic views and steep hills. You will now be about 13 miles east of Cruz Bay.

The roads at this point are not very clearly marked. Avoid the road beyond the elementary school below the church; it's pretty, but leads only to the barren and rather dull expanses of the island's East End. Instead, backtrack a very short distance to a cluster of signs that point to the restaurant Shipwreck Landing. Follow these signs heading south about a mile to:

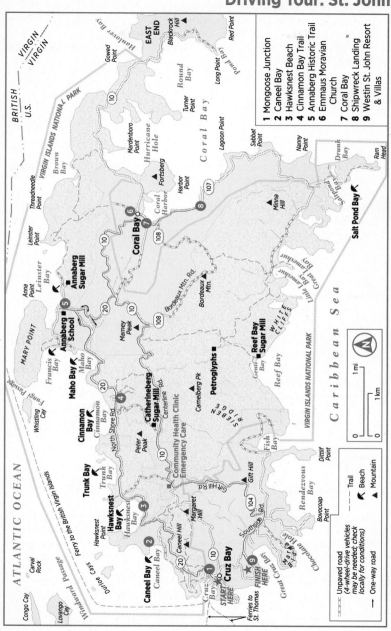

1 Mongoose Junction
2 Caneel Bay
3 Hawksnest Beach
4 Cinnamon Bay Trail
5 Annaberg Historic Trail
6 Emmaus Moravian Church
7 Coral Bay
8 Shipwreck Landing
9 Westin St. John Resort & Villas

Unpaved road (4-wheel-drive vehicles may be needed; check locally for conditions)
→ One-way road
--- Trail
⚓ Beach
▲ Mountain

7 Coral Bay

Claimed by the Danes in the 1600s and used to unload Danish ships, the bay still contains a crumbling stone pier. This was also the site of the first plantation on St. John, which was established in 1717 and abandoned long ago; it predates the far-better-developed facilities of Cruz Bay. You can also follow the posted signs to see the remains of Fort Berg, which stationed the soldiers that suppressed the 1733 slave revolt. Today, Coral Bay shelters a closely knit community of yachting enthusiasts, who moor and live on their yachts between excursions to other parts of the Caribbean.

Ringing the bay's perimeter is a widely spaced handful of restaurants and bars. One of these is called:

8 Shipwreck Landing

This is an ideal place to drop in for a meal or a tropical drink (p. 127). You can sit amid palms and tropical plants on a veranda overlooking the sea.

After your break, continue driving south along Coral Bay, perhaps stopping in at another of the two or three shops and bars beside the road.

Backtrack north along Coral Bay to a point near the Emmaus Moravian Church, which you'll see in the distance. At the cluster of restaurant signs, turn left onto Route 10 West (Centerline Rd.), which has high-altitude views in all directions as you follow it back toward Cruz Bay. (An alternate, but much steeper, way is King Hill Rd., which merges later with Rte. 10 W.)

Within 7 or 8 miles, Route 10 merges with Route 104 (Gift Hill Rd.) just after the island's only hospital, the St. John Myrah Keating Smith Community Health Clinic. Take Route 104 and begin one of the steepest descents of your driving tour. (Use *low gear* whenever possible, and honk around the many blind curves.) When the land levels off, you'll see, on your left, the entrance to the most imaginative pieces of modern architecture on the island, the postmodern:

9 Westin St. John Resort & Villas

If you're a gardening or architecture enthusiast, stop in for a look at a hotel whose inspirations include ancient Mesopotamia, colonial Denmark, and the coast of California. What makes all of this even more impressive is that it was built only a few years ago on what, at the time, was unusable swampland.

From here, your return to Cruz Bay entails only a short drive along Route 104, through a slightly urbanized periphery of private homes.

SHOPPING

Compared to St. Thomas, St. John's shopping isn't much, but what's here is interesting. The boutiques and shops of Cruz Bay are individualized and quite special. Most of the shops are clustered at **Mongoose Junction** (North Shore Rd., Cruz Bay), in a woodsy area beside the roadway, about a 5-minute walk from the ferry dock.

Before you leave the island, you'll want to visit the recently expanded **Wharfside Village** (✆ **340/693-8210;** www.wharfsidevillage.com), just a few steps from the ferry departure point. This complex of courtyards, alleys, and shady patios is a mishmash of boutiques, along with some restaurants, fast-food joints, and bars.

The Best Shopping Day

The most fun shopping on the island takes place on **St. John Saturday ★**, a colorful, drum-beating, spicy feast for the senses, held on the last Saturday of every month. This daylong event begins early in the morning in the center of town and spills across the park. Vendors hawk handmade items, ranging from jewelry to handicrafts and clothing, and food made from local ingredients. One vendor concocts soothing salves from recipes passed on by her ancestors; another designs and makes porcelain earrings; another flavors chicken and burgers with her own wonderful secret hickory barbecue sauce; yet another hollows out and carves gourds from local calabash trees.

Bajo El Sol, Mongoose Junction (✆ **340/693-7070;** www.bajoelsolgallery.com), is a cooperative and award-winning gallery displaying the work of many island artists. For sale are paintings, sculpture, ceramics, and jewelry.

Bamboula, Mongoose Junction (✆ **340/693-8699;** www.bamboulastjohn.com), has an exotic and very appealing collection of gifts from St. John, the Caribbean, India, Indonesia, and Central Africa. The store also has men's and women's clothing under its own label—hand-batiked soft cottons and rayons made for comfort in a hot climate.

Here's your chance to pick up a unique item. A total of 100 artists, artisans, and designers have their work showcased at the **Best of Both Worlds** (✆ **340/639-8520;** www.thebestofstjohn.com), in Mongoose Junction. The shop is a great place for one-of-a-kind gifts and local art. Many award-winning designers display their work, ranging from jewelry to art glass, lamps, dishware, and clocks. You will find especially good buys in artistic glasswork.

If you're planning to hike the trails of lush St. John, and you've arrived unprepared, **Big Planet Adventure Outfitters,** Mongoose Junction (✆ **340/776-6638**), is the best place to go to stock up on outdoor clothing. Reef footwear and Naot sandals are sold, along with a selection of other durable items, including backpacks, luggage, sunglasses, and the like.

Coconut Coast Studios, Frank Bay (✆ **800/887-3798** or 340/776-6944; www. coconutcoaststudios.com), is the studio of Elaine Estern, best known for her Caribbean landscapes. It's 5 minutes from Cruz Bay; walk along the waterfront, bypassing Gallows Point. The outlet also sells calendars, gifts, limited edition prints, and lithographs. From November to April, the studio hosts a free sunset cocktail party Wednesday 5:30 to 7pm.

Donald Schnell Studio ★, next to the Texaco gas station, Cruz Bay (✆ **340/776-6420;** www.donaldschnell.com), is a working studio and gallery where Mr. Schnell and his assistants have created one of the finest collections of handmade pottery, sculpture, and blown glass in the Caribbean. The staff can be seen working daily. They're known for their rough-textured coral work. Water fountains are a specialty item, as are house signs and coral-pottery dinnerware. The studio will ship all over the world, so no need to worry about carrying it all back on the plane. Go in and discuss any particular design you may have in mind.

Every Ting, Bay Street, Cruz Bay (✆ **340/693-7730**), is the best of the all-purpose stores, and it's also a gathering point for locals and visitors alike. It's like a

4

ST. JOHN | Shopping

nerve center where you can drop in for a "cuppa" or to use the Internet. You can find reading material here for the beach along with music CDs, cotton resort wear, and, of course, campy picture frames decorated with pinkish shells gathered on the beach.

Fabric Mill, Mongoose Junction (✆ **340/776-6194**), features silk-screened and batik fabrics from around the world and around the corner. Vibrant rugs and bed, bathroom, and table linens can add a Caribbean flair to your home. Whimsical soft sculpture, sarongs, scarves, and handbags are also made here.

The **Marketplace,** Cruz Bay (✆ **340/776-6455**), with its dramatic architecture and native stone, is a cool place to shop on a hot day, thanks to its verandas and courtyards. It's ideal if you're renting a condo on St. John, as many visitors do, as the market here includes everything from a hardware shop to a video store, plus health-care needs and a lot more.

R&I PATTON Goldsmithing, Mongoose Junction (✆ **340/776-6548;** www. pattongold.com), is one of the oldest businesses on the island. Three-quarters of the merchandise here is made on St. John, with a large selection of jewelry in sterling silver, gold, and precious stones. Also featured are the works of goldsmiths from outstanding American studios, as well as Spanish coins.

The location of the **Shop at Caneel Bay,** in the Caneel Bay resort (✆ **340/776-6111**), guarantees both an upscale clientele and an upscale assortment of merchandise. Scattered over two simple, elegant floors are drugstore items, books, sundries, and handicrafts, as well as some unusual artwork and pieces of expensive jewelry. There are also racks of resort wear and sportswear for men and women. The shop carries handbags and watches by top designers.

ST. JOHN AFTER DARK

Bring a good book. When it comes to nightlife, St. John is no St. Thomas, and everybody here seems to want to keep it that way. Most people are content to have a leisurely dinner and then head to bed.

The **Caneel Bay Bar,** at the Caneel Bay resort (✆ **340/776-6111**), has live music Tuesday to Sunday 11am to 11pm. The most popular drinks are the Cool Caneel (local rum with sugar, lime, and anisette) and the trademark **Plantation Punch** (lime and orange juice with three kinds of rum, bitters, and nutmeg).

If you'd like to drink and gossip with the locals, try **JJ's Texas Coast Café,** Cruz Bay (✆ **340/776-6908**), a real dive, across the park from the ferry dock, open 8am to 9pm. The margaritas here are lethal. Also at Cruz Bay, check out the action at **Fred's** (✆ **340/776-6363**), across from the Lime Inn. Fred's brings in bands and has dancing on Friday nights. It's just a little hole in the wall and can get crowded fast. It's open 10am to 5pm, but stays open until Saturday morning.

St. John's best sports bar is **Skinny Legs,** Emmaus, Coral Bay, beyond the fire station (✆ **340/779-4982**). This shack made of tin and wood also happens to have the best burgers in St. John. (The chili dogs aren't bad, either.) The yachting crowd likes to hang out here, though you wouldn't know it at first glance—it often seems that the richer they are, the poorer they dress. The bar has a satellite dish, a dartboard, and horseshoe pits. There is live music on Friday and Saturday nights during high season when it stays open until midnight; regular hours are 11am to 9pm.

Morgan's Mango (p. 126; ✆ **340/693-8141**), a restaurant, is also one of the hottest watering holes on the island. It's in Cruz Bay, across from the national park dock. Count yourself lucky if you get in on a crowded night in winter. The place became famous locally when it turned away Harrison Ford, who was vacationing at Caneel Bay. Thursday night is Margarita Night, and Tuesday night is Lobster Night.

Woody's Seafood Saloon, Cruz Bay (p. 127; © **340/779-4625**), is the local dive and hangout at Cruz Bay, 150 feet from the ferry dock. It draws both visitors and a cross section of island life from expats to villa owners. Michigan-born Woody Mann, the bartender, is often compared to the character of the same name on the sitcom *Cheers.* The place is particularly popular during happy hour from 3 to 6pm, and it's about the only place on the island you can order food as late as 1am. The joint jumps Sunday to Thursday 11am to 1am, Friday and Saturday 11:50am to 2am.

Of course, there is also the **Quiet Mon** (p. 127), which is adjacent to Woody's. This is St. John's very own Irish pub and one of the hottest spots on the island.

ST. CROIX

S t. Croix is the largest of the U.S. Virgin Islands, but its easygoing vibe seems unchanged from when the Danish settled here in the late 18th century. Its history is enshrined in the colorful buildings of picturesque Christiansted, while smaller and earthier Frederiksted, on the island's rocky east end, comes alive when cruise ships dock and keep the local Cruzan Rum Factory busy. Inland, the island is a lush feast of mango and mahogany trees, tree ferns, and dangling lianas, ringed by beautiful beaches and rolling hills.

Things to Do   Discover St. Croix's Danish colonial history on a walking tour amid brightly painted Georgian buildings in **Christiansted,** then climb to the top of **Fort Christiansvaern** for a view of the harbor. In **Frederiksted,** sample the delights of the **Cruzan Rum Factory,** or take a **boat trip** to **Buck Island,** in the middle of a marine sanctuary. Sunbathe on the white sands under swaying palms at **Davis Bay,** follow the footpaths through the private **"Rain Forest,"** or see fine black coral while snorkeling in **Salt River Bay.**

Shopping   **Christiansted** is the shopping hub of St. Croix, where hole-in-the-wall and chic boutiques sell an array of handmade goods, beachwear, and decorative carvings. Along the boardwalk try the **King's Alley Complex,** a pink-sided compound filled with the densest concentration of shops, for china and leather goods. In **Frederiksted,** look for framed engravings and West Indies antiques in the urban mall at **Frederiksted Pier.**

Nightlife & Entertainment   The waterfront bars and clubs at **Christiansted** hum to a lighter groove than they do on St. Thomas, but you can still have a nice night out listening to live reggae and soca, linger over a beer at a hip dive, or listen to DJs spin island sound. Try to catch an exciting performance of the flamboyant **Quadrille Dancers**—watch and learn their steps, and then join them on the dance floor.

Restaurants & Dining   **Christiansted** is filled with a variety of restaurants, so it's not hard to settle into a bistro serving spicy Creole seafood, steaks, or homemade soups. **Frederiksted** features simpler, more laid-back dining rooms where you can sample the local *fungi* (fish with cornmeal and gravy), *daube* (meat roasted in a pot with spicy seasoning), or *souse* (a lime-flavored stock of pig's feet, head, and tail).

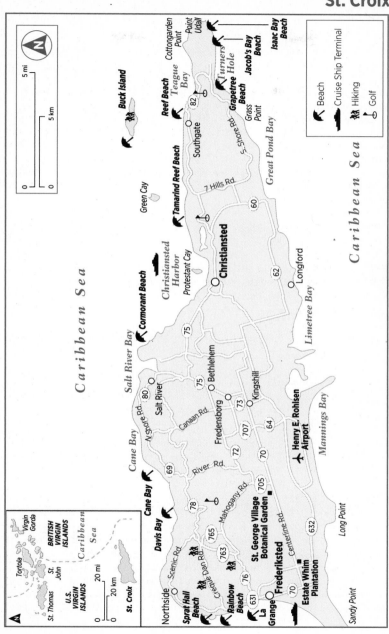

St. Croix

Point Udall

Isaac Bay Beach

Jacob's Bay Beach

Turners Hole

Grapetree Beach

Cottongarden Point

Teague Bay

Reef Beach

82

S. Shore Rd.

Grass Point

Great Pond Bay

Southgate

Tamarind Reef Beach

7 Hills Rd.

60

Buck Island

Green Cay

Christiansted Harbor

Protestant Cay

Cormorant Beach

Christiansted

62

Longford

Limetree Bay

Caribbean Sea

75

Salt River Bay

Bethlehem

75

Salt River

N. Shore Rd.

80

Kingshill

Canaan Rd.

Fredensborg

73

707

64

Mannings Bay

Cane Bay

72

River Rd.

Henry E. Rohlsen Airport

70

705

Davis Bay

69

78

Mahogany Rd.

St. George Village Botanical Garden

Long Point

Northside

Scenic Rd.

765

Creque Dan Rd.

763

Frederiksted

Centerline Rd.

632

Caribbean Sea

Sprat Hall Beach

Rainbow Beach

76

631

La Grange

70

Estate Whim Plantation

Sandy Point

Beach

Cruise Ship Terminal

Hiking

Golf

Caribbean Sea

Virgin Gorda

Tortola

St. John

St. Thomas

BRITISH VIRGIN ISLANDS

U.S. VIRGIN ISLANDS

Caribbean Sea

St. Croix

0   20 mi

0   20 km

0   5 mi

0   5 km

N

5

ST. CROIX | Introduction

ESSENTIALS

Getting There

BY PLANE

All flights to St. Croix land at the **Henry E. Rohlsen Airport,** Estate Mannings Bay (© **340/778-1012;** www.viport.com/airports.html; airport code STT), on the southern coast of the island. There are no ATMs at the airport, so come prepared with cash. Take a taxi to your hotel or rent a car. The major car-rental firms maintain kiosks here, but make reservations before you arrive.

American Airlines (© **800/433-7300;** www.aa.com) offers the most frequent and most reliable service to St. Croix. Passengers flying to the island connect through San Juan from either New York City's JFK airport or Newark, New Jersey. From San Juan, **American Eagle** (© **800/433-7300;** www.aa.com) offers several daily nonstop flights to St. Croix. There's also one flight daily from Miami, with one stop (but no change of plane) in St. Thomas. The flight originates in Dallas–Fort Worth, American's biggest hub.

Travel time to St. Croix from New York is 4 hours, from Chicago 5½ hours, from Miami 3½ hours, and from Puerto Rico 20 minutes. There are no direct flights to St. Croix from Canada or the United Kingdom; connections are made via Miami.

There are also easy air links between St. Thomas and St. Croix. **American Eagle** (see American Airlines, above, for contact info) has three daily flights; in addition, **Seaborne Airlines** (© **888/359-8687** or 340/773-6442; www.seaborneairlines. com) offers 17 flights daily. Flight time is only 25 minutes.

Visitor Information

You can begin your explorations at the **St. Croix Visitor Bureau,** 53A Company St., in Christiansted (© **340/773-0495**), a yellow building across from the open-air market. It's open Monday to Friday 8am to 5pm.

The U.S. Virgin Islands Division of Tourism also has an office at the Customs House Building, Strand Street (© **340/772-0357;** www.stcroixtourism.com), in Frederiksted.

Tourist offices provide free maps to the island. *St. Croix This Week,* distributed free to cruise-ship and air passengers, has detailed maps of Christiansted, Frederiksted, and the entire island, pinpointing individual attractions, hotels, shops, and restaurants. If you plan to do extensive touring of the island, purchase *The Official Road Map of the U.S. Virgin Islands,* available at island bookstores.

Island Layout

St. Croix has only two sizable towns: Christiansted on the northcentral shore and Frederiksted in the southwest. The Henry E. Rohlsen Airport is on the south coast, directly west of the Hess Oil Refinery, the major industry on the island. No roads circle St. Croix's coast.

To continue east from Christiansted, take Route 82 (also called the East End Rd.). Route 75 will take you west from Christiansted through the central heartland, then south to the Hess Oil Refinery. Melvin H. Evans Highway, Route 66, runs along the southern part of the island. You can connect with this route in Christiansted and head west all the way to Frederiksted.

Did You Know . . . ?

- Columbus, the first tourist to St. Croix, was driven away by a rain of arrows from the Carib Indians.
- Under FDR's New Deal, the federal government produced a rum here

- called "Government House." FDR designed the label himself.
- Alexander Hamilton once worked in a hardware store on St. Croix.

CHRISTIANSTED

The historic district of Christiansted has four main streets leading toward the water: Strand Street, King Street, Company Street, and Queen Street. Because the city is compact, it can easily be explored on foot. All streets start at the harbor and go up slightly sloped hillsides, and each street heads back down the hill to the port so you can't get lost. The **visitor information center** is located at 53A Company St. The center of Christiansted can get very congested, and driving around is difficult because of the one-way streets. It's usually more practical to park your car and cover the small district on foot. You will find open-air parking on both sides of Fort Christiansvaern. See the "Walking Tour: Christiansted" map, on p. 171, to orient yourself.

THE NORTH SHORE

This coastal strip that stretches from Cottongarden Point, the eastern tip of the island, all the way west past Christiansted and up and around Salt River Bay, comes to an end as it reaches the settlement of Northside in the far west. It is the most touristy region of St. Croix, site of the best beaches, the most hotels, and the finest resorts and shopping. It is also the takeoff point (at Christiansted Harbor) for excursions to Buck Island, St. Croix's most popular attraction. Many visitors confine their stay in St. Croix entirely to the north coast. The northern coastline is not only long but also diverse, going from a lush tropical forest that envelops most of the northwest to the eastern sector, which is dry with palm-lined beaches.

THE EAST END

The East End begins immediately east of Christiansted, the capital, taking in Tamarind Reef Beach and Reef Beach before it reaches Teague Bay, coming to an end at Cottongarden Point, the far eastern tip of St. Croix. This section of St. Croix is linked by Route 82 (also called East End Rd.). The Buccaneer, the major resort of St. Croix, is found here, along with the Tamarind Reef Hotel. The area is far less congested than the section immediately to the west of Christiansted, and many visitors prefer the relative isolation and tranquillity of the East End. This section of St. Croix is relatively dry, the landscape a bit arid, but its compensating factor is a number of palm-lined beaches. The best place for a beach picnic is Cramer Park at the far eastern tip, a U.S.V.I. territorial beach popular with islanders.

FREDERIKSTED

It's hard to get lost in tiny Frederiksted, but it is a port of call for cruises, so sometimes you can find yourself lost in a crowd. Most visitors head for the central historic district, where the Frederiksted Pier juts out into the sea. The two major streets, both of which run parallel to the water, are Strand Street and King Street. See the "Frederiksted" map on p. 175 to help get your bearings.

In both Christiansted and Frederiksted, in St. Croix, buildings are numbered consecutively on one side, stretching all the way across town; then the numbers "cross the street" and begin consecutively on the opposite side. That means that even and odd numbers appear on the same side of the street. The numbering system begins in Christiansted at the waterfront. In Frederiksted, the first number appears at the north end of town for streets running north-south and at the waterfront for streets running east-west.

Getting Around

If you plan to do some serious sightseeing on the island, you'll need to rent a car, as getting around by public transportation is a slow, uneven process. There is bus service, but you might end up stranded somewhere and unable to reach your destination without a taxi.

BY CAR

Remember to *drive on the left.* In most rural areas, the speed limit is 35 mph; certain parts of the major artery, Route 66, are 55 mph. In towns and urban areas, the speed limit is 20 mph. Keep in mind that if you're going into the "bush country," you'll find the roads very difficult. Sometimes the government smoothes the roads out before the rainy season begins (often in Oct or Nov), but they rapidly deteriorate.

St. Croix offers moderately priced car rentals, even on cars with automatic transmissions and air-conditioning. However, because of the island's higher-than-normal accident rate (which is partly the result of visitors who forget about driving on the left-hand side of the road), insurance costs are a bit higher than elsewhere. **Avis** (© **800/331-1212** or 340/778-9355; www.avis.com), **Budget** (© **800/472-3325** or 340/778-9636; www.budget.com), and **Hertz** (© **800/654-3131** or 340/778-1402; www.hertz.com) all maintain headquarters at the airport; look for their kiosks near the baggage-claim areas. Collision-damage insurance costs $14 per day, depending on the company and size of car, and we feel that it's a wise investment. Some credit card companies grant you collision-damage protection, if you pay for the rental with their card. Verify coverage before you go.

BY TAXI

At Henry E. Rohlsen International Airport, official taxi rates are posted. From the airport, expect to pay about $16 to $36 to Christiansted and about $12 to $24 to Frederiksted. Cabs are unmetered, so agree on the rate before you get in. Taxis line up at the docks in Christiansted and Frederiksted; otherwise, call the **St. Croix Taxicab Association** (© **340/778-1088**).

BY BUS

Air-conditioned **buses** run between Christiansted and Frederiksted about every 45 minutes daily between 5:30am and 8pm. They start at Tide Village, to the east of Christiansted, and go along Route 75 to the Golden Rock Shopping Center. They transfer along Route 70, with stopovers at the Sunny Isle Shopping Center, La Reine Shopping Center, St. George Village Botanical Garden, and Whim Plantation Museum before reaching Frederiksted. The fare is $1, or 55¢ for seniors. For more information, call © **340/773-1664.**

[FastFACTS] ST. CROIX

Banks Several major banks are represented in St. Croix. Most are open Monday to Thursday 9am to 3pm and Friday 9am to 4pm. **Virgin Islands Community Bank** has a branch at 6 King's St. (℃ **340/773-0440**) in Christiansted and another branch on Strand Street in Frederiksted.

Business Hours Typical business hours are Monday to Friday 9am to 5pm, Saturday 9am to 1pm.

Doctors For a referral, call **Sunny Isle Medical Center** (℃ **340/778-0069**).

Drugstores Try the **Golden Rock Pharmacy,** Golden Rock Shopping Center (℃ **340/773-7666**), open Monday to Saturday 8am to 7pm and Sunday 8am to 3pm.

Emergencies To reach the police, fire department, or an ambulance, call ℃ **911.**

Hospitals The main facility is **Governor Juan F. Luis Hospital & Medical Center,** 4007 Estate Diamond Ruby (℃ **340/778-6311**).

Internet Access A Better Copy, 52 Company St., Christiansted (℃ **340/692-5303**), charges $10 for every hour of Internet service.

Laundry Try **Tropical Cleaners & Launderers,** 16–17 King Cross St. (℃ **340/773-3635**), in Christiansted. Hours are Monday to Saturday 8am to 5:30pm.

Maps See "Visitor Information," in "Orientation," above.

Newspapers & Magazines Newspapers, such as the *Miami Herald,* are flown into St. Croix daily. St. Croix also has its own newspaper, *St. Croix Avis. Time* and *Newsweek* are widely sold as well. Your best source of local information is *St. Croix This Week,* which is distributed free by the tourist offices.

Police Police headquarters is on Market Street in Christiansted. In case of emergency, dial ℃ **911;** for nonemergency assistance, call ℃ **340/778-2211.**

Post Office The post office is on Company Street (℃ **340/773-3586**), in Christiansted. The hours of operation are Monday to Friday 8:30am to 5:30pm.

Safety St. Croix is safer than St. Thomas. Although there have been random acts of violence against tourists in the past, even murder, most crime on the island is petty theft, usually of possessions left unguarded at the beach

while vacationers go into the water for a swim, or muggings (rarely violent) of visitors wandering the dark streets and back alleys of Frederiksted and Christiansted at night. Exercise caution at night by sticking to the heart of Christiansted and not wandering around in Frederiksted. Avoid night strolls along beaches. Night driving in remote parts of the island can also be risky; you might be carjacked and robbed at knifepoint.

Taxes The only local tax is an 8% surcharge added to all hotel rates.

Taxis For an airport taxi, call ℃ **340/778-1088;** in Christiansted call ℃ **340/773-5020.**

Telephone You can dial direct to St. Croix from the mainland by using the 340 area code. Omit the 340 for local calls. Make long-distance, international, and collect calls as you would on the U.S. mainland by dialing 0 or your long-distance provider.

Toilets There are few public restrooms, except at the major beaches and the airport. In Christiansted, the National Park Service maintains some restrooms within the public park beside Fort Christiansvaern.

Tourist Offices See "Visitor Information," above.

WHERE TO STAY

St. Croix's deluxe resorts lie along the North Shore; its charming old waterfront inns are mostly in Christiansted. You may also choose to stay at a former plantation or in a condo complex, which offers privacy and the chance to save money by preparing your own meals. The choice is yours: a location in Christiansted or Frederiksted close to shops and nightlife, but away from the beach; or an isolated resort where, chances are, your accommodations will be either on the beach or a short walk from it. From such resorts, you'll have to drive into town for a shopping binge or for restaurants and clubs.

In general, rates are steep, but in summer, hotels slash prices by about 25% to 50%. All rooms are subject to an 8% hotel tax, not included in the rates given below.

Note: If you need a hair dryer, pack your own. Apparently, a lot of visitors have packed up hotel hair dryers upon departure, and some innkeepers are reluctant to provide them.

North Shore
VERY EXPENSIVE

The Buccaneer ★★★ ☺   Family run for generations, this gracious, elegant, legendary resort is St. Croix's pocket of posh. Both historic and modern, it is the longest-running resort in the U.S. Virgin Islands. In the Caribbean, it would certainly rank among the top 20 platinum resorts. This large, luxurious resort has three of the island's best beaches, and the best sports program on St. Croix. The property was once a cattle ranch and a sugar plantation; its first estate house, which dates from the mid–17th century, stands near a freshwater pool. Accommodations are either in the main building or in one of the beachside properties. The baronial-arched main building has a lobby opening onto landscaped terraces, with a sea vista on two sides and Christiansted to the west. The rooms are fresh and comfortable, though some of the standard units are a bit small. All have wicker or mahogany furnishings and full bathrooms. The best bathrooms are in the Beachside Doubloons, and come complete with whirlpool tubs. The free Kid's Camp is available year-round.

P.O. Box 25200, Gallows Bay (2 miles east of Christiansted on Rte. 82), Christiansted, St. Croix, U.S.V.I. 00824. www.thebuccaneer.com. ✆ **800/255-3881** in the U.S., or 340/712-2100. Fax 340/712-2105. 138 units. Winter $288–$560 double, $430–$990 suite; off season $260–$360 double, $370–$730 suite. Children 17 and under stay free in parent's room. Rates include American breakfast. AE, DISC, MC, V. **Amenities:** 4 restaurants, including The Terrace (p. 160); bar; babysitting; children's program; health club and spa; 2 pools (outdoor); room service; 8 tennis courts (2 lit); watersports equipment/rentals. *In room:* A/C, TV, fridge, hair dryer, Wi-Fi (free).

Carambola Beach Resort   This hotel clustered within 26 buildings is set on 28 acres above Davis Bay, about a 30-minute drive from Christiansted. It's one of the largest hotels on St. Croix, and it lies adjacent to an outstanding golf course, in a lovely, lush setting on a white-sand beach whose turquoise waters provide fine snorkeling. The property is surrounded by rolling hills, palm trees, and rocky cliffs. Despite its spectacular physical location, this resort doesn't match the Buccaneer's class and style. Guests are housed in red-roofed, two-story buildings, each of which contains six units. The accommodations, each a suite, are furnished in mahogany, with Danish design; each has a balcony partially concealed from outside view, overlooking either the garden or the sea. Rooms have an upscale flair, with louvered doors, tile floors, mahogany trim, and sometimes extras like screened-in porches with rocking chairs.

Estate Davis Bay (P.O. Box 3031), Kingshill, St. Croix, U.S.V.I. 00851. www.carambolabeach.com. ✆ **888/503-8760** in the U.S., or 340/778-3800. Fax 340/778-1682. 150 units. Winter $350–$530 suite;

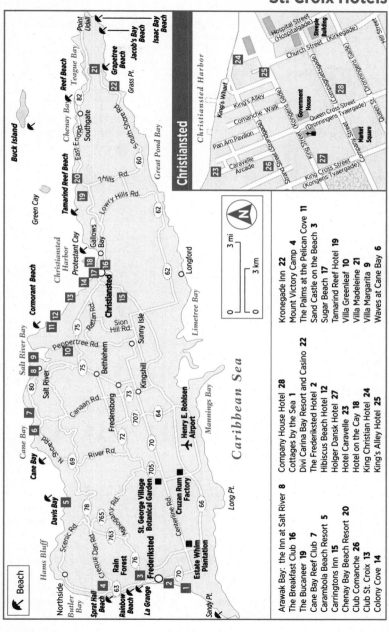

St. Croix Hotels at a Glance

	Wheelchair access	A/C in bedrooms	Child-care facilities	Children are welcome	Convention facilities	Credit cards accepted	Directly beside beach	Health club
Arawak Bay: the Inn at Salt River		✓				✓		
The Breakfast Club		✓						
The Buccaneer	✓	✓	✓	✓	✓	✓	✓	✓
Cane Bay Reef Club		✓		✓		✓	✓	
Carambola Beach Resort		✓	✓	✓	✓	✓	✓	✓
Carringtons Inn		✓				✓		
Chenay Bay Beach Resort		✓	✓	✓		✓	✓	
Club Comanche		✓						
Club St. Croix		✓	✓	✓		✓	✓	
Colony Cove		✓	✓	✓		✓	✓	
Company House Hotel		✓		✓		✓		
Cottages by the Sea	✓	✓	✓	✓		✓	✓	
Divi Carina Bay Resort and Casino	✓	✓	✓	✓	✓	✓	✓	✓
The Frederiksted Hotel		✓		✓		✓		
Hibiscus Beach Hotel		✓	✓	✓		✓	✓	
Holger Danske Hotel	✓	✓		✓		✓		
Hotel Caravelle	✓	✓		✓	✓	✓		
Hotel on the Cay		✓		✓	✓	✓	✓	
King Christian Hotel		✓		✓		✓		✓
King's Alley Hotel		✓				✓		
Kronegade Inn		✓				✓		
The Palms at Pelican Cove	✓	✓				✓	✓	✓
Sand Castle on the Beach		✓	✓	✓		✓	✓	
Sugar Beach		✓		✓		✓	✓	
Tamarind Reef Hotel		✓		✓		✓	✓	
Villa Greenleaf		✓		✓		✓		
Villa Madeleine		✓		✓		✓		
Villa Margarita		✓				✓		
Waves at Cane Bay	✓	✓		✓		✓	✓	

off season $250–$380 suite. AE, DISC, MC, V. **Amenities:** 2 restaurants, including Saman Dining Room (p. 160); bar; exercise room; golf course; spa; pool (outdoor); 2 tennis courts (lit); Wi-Fi (free). *In room:* A/C, TV, fridge, hair dryer, kitchenette (in some).

Divi Carina Bay Resort and Casino ★　It's Las Vegas in the Tropics. Opening onto 1,000 feet of sugar-white beach, this all-inclusive resort brought gambling to the U.S. Virgin Islands. That fact seems to obscure its success as a place of barefoot

Golf course nearby	Live entertainment	Marina facilities	Restaurant and/or bar	Spa facilities	Swimming pool	Tennis courts	TV in bedroom	Watersports
			✓		✓		✓	
							✓	
✓		✓	✓	✓	✓	✓	✓	
		✓		✓		✓		
✓		✓	✓	✓	✓	✓	✓	
				✓				
✓		✓		✓	✓		✓	
		✓		✓		✓		
		✓		✓	✓	✓	✓	
				✓	✓	✓	✓	
		✓		✓		✓		
						✓	✓	
✓		✓	✓	✓	✓	✓	✓	
		✓		✓		✓		
✓		✓		✓		✓		
	✓	✓		✓		✓		
		✓	✓		✓		✓	
✓		✓		✓	✓		✓	
	✓	✓		✓		✓	✓	
						✓		
						✓		
		✓		✓		✓		✓
		✓		✓		✓		
				✓	✓	✓		
	✓	✓		✓	✓	✓	✓	
				✓				
				✓	✓	✓	✓	
	✓			✓	✓	✓	✓	
		✓		✓		✓	✓	

elegance and a top resort property. Accommodations feature oceanfront guest rooms and villa suites with views of the Caribbean. Rooms are good size and equipped with a small kitchen, full bathrooms, and balconies. We prefer the accommodations on the ground floor as they are closer to the water's edge. The 20 villas across the street are about a 3-minute walk from the sands. The most up-to-date building contains 50 oceanfront accommodations with balconies. You can simply go upstairs for a massage at the spa on the top floor.

5025 Estate Turner Hole, Christiansted, St. Croix, U.S.V.I. 00820. 📞 **800/823-9352** in the U.S., or 340/773-9700. Fax 340/773-6802. www.diviresorts.com. 180 units. Winter $365–$470 double, from $495 suite; off season $366–$406 double, from $476 suite. Rates are all inclusive, 7-night minimum. Children 15 and under stay free in parent's room. AE, MC, V. **Amenities:** 2 restaurants; 2 bars; babysitting; casino; health club and spa; 2 pools (outdoor); tennis court (lit); watersports equipment/rentals; Wi-Fi (free in lobby). *In room:* A/C, TV/VCR player, hair dryer, kitchen (in some).

EXPENSIVE

Chenay Bay Beach Resort ★ ☺   These West Indian–style cottages are nestled on a lushly landscaped hillside overlooking 1 mile of white, soft, sandy beach. Next to a natural preserve, it was once a sugar plantation. The resort can serve as a venue for a romantic getaway, a honeymoon, or even a family vacation. Home to one of the island's finest beaches for swimming, snorkeling, and windsurfing, Chenay Bay is just 3 miles east of Christiansted and is a terrific choice for families thanks to the spacious cottages and the children's programs. With a quiet and barefoot-casual ambience, each cottage contains a fully equipped kitchenette and bathroom. The 20 original cottages are smaller and more weathered than the modern duplexes numbered 21 to 50. Accommodations are medium in size, with firm mattresses resting on comfortable beds. Most bathrooms are compact but with adequate shelf space and tubs.

Rte. 82, East End Rd. (P.O. Box 24600), St. Croix, U.S.V.I. 00824. www.chenaybay.com. 📞 **866/226-8677** in the U.S., or 340/718-2918. Fax 340/718-6665. 50 cottages. Year-round $70–$300 cottage for 1 or 2. Extra person $25. Children 17 and under stay free in parent's room. $50 per person for all meals. AE, DISC, MC, V. **Amenities:** Restaurant; bar; babysitting; children's program; pool (outdoor); 2 tennis courts (lit); watersports equipment/rentals; Wi-Fi ($8 per day). *In room:* A/C, TV, fridge, kitchenette.

The Palms at Pelican Cove ★★   At ocean's edge, this family-oriented resort stands on 7 acres of beachfront property at a point 3 miles northwest of Christiansted. Its bedrooms are inviting in a Caribbean style with an upgraded decor. Designed in a boxy, modern-looking series of rectangles, it has outcroppings of exposed natural stone, striking a balance between seclusion and accessibility. Long Reef lies less than 100 feet offshore from the resort's sandy beachfront. The spacious guest rooms have a private balcony or patio with ocean views. Social life revolves around an open-air lounge, bar, and restaurant with sea views (see The Palms, p. 161). During the day, guests can be found limin' (chilling out) around the pool, which is one of the largest on St. Croix.

4126 La Grande Princesse, St. Croix, U.S.V.I. 00820. www.palmspelicancove.com. 📞 **800/548-4460** or 340/718-8920. Fax 340/718-0218. 35 units. Winter $230–$290 double, $290–$320 suite; off season $190–$220 double, $240–$280 suite. AE, MC, V. **Amenities:** Restaurant; bar; Internet (free); pool (outdoor); watersports (scuba).

Tamarind Reef Hotel   A sandy beach at the Tamarind Reef's doorstep and good snorkeling along the reef highlight this casual, low-rise property. The resort exudes a fresh, bright, new look. Each motel-style room features a garden patio or private balcony, affording guests a view of the blue Caribbean. In addition, 18 of the suites provide fully equipped kitchenettes and accommodate up to four people. Guests can relax by the pool and enjoy cocktails, light lunches, and snacks from the poolside bar and grill. For those who want to explore St. Croix underwater, the hotel offers complimentary watersports equipment. Adjoining the hotel is the Green Cay Marina, where guests can charter boats for deep-sea fishing or sailing expeditions.

5001 Tamarind Reef, St. Croix, U.S.V.I. 00820. www.tamarindreefhotel.com. 📞 **800/619-0014** in the U.S., or 340/773-4455. Fax 340/773-3989. 39 units. Winter $275–$325 double; off season $200–$300 double. Extra person $35–$50. Children 6 and under stay free in parent's room. Ask about dive, golf, and honeymoon packages. AE, DC, MC, V. **Amenities:** 2 restaurants; bar; pool (outdoor); 4 tennis courts (lit); watersports equipment/rentals. *In room:* A/C, ceiling fan, fridge, hair dryer, kitchenette (in some), Wi-Fi (free).

MODERATE

Villa Margarita ★ ▮▮ This is a cozy hideaway catering only to couples or adult singles. Lying about a 20-minute drive from Christiansted, it is located next to the Salt River Bay Park, where Columbus anchored in 1493 to get fresh water. It is one of the most private enclaves on the island—private transportation is needed because of the remote location. There is no restaurant on-site but the property adjoins the Salt River Marina with its Columbus Cove Restaurant. The condos are built around a West Indian plantation great house and each unit is its own functioning studio or suite, with a full kitchen and an oceanfront balcony. The grounds feature a banana garden and a small oceanside pool. Guests come to get away from the crowds, but don't expect much in terms of swimming and watersports, although you can snorkel right in front of the property. Regardless, a short walk will bring you to an adequate swimming beach. Kayak tours and scuba diving along Salt River Wall can also be arranged at the marina.

Salt River Bay, off Rte. 80, 9024 Salt River, Christiansted, St. Croix, U.S.V.I. 00820. www.villamargarita. com. Ⓒ **866/274-8811** or 340/713-1930. Fax 340/719-3389. 3 units. Winter $165-$280 double; off season $145-$195 double. AE, MC, V. **Amenities:** Pool; tennis court. *In room:* A/C, ceiling fans, TV/DVD, kitchenette, no phone, Wi-Fi (free).

Waves at Cane Bay Nestled in the midst of coconut palms at water's edge, this intimate and tasteful condo property is about 8 miles from the airport, midway between the island's two biggest towns. It's set on a well-landscaped plot of oceanfront property on Cane Bay, the heart of the best scuba and snorkeling at Cane Bay Beach. The renovated accommodations are within a pair of two-story cement-sided buildings, each directly on the beach. Each of the accommodations is high ceilinged and relatively large, with a well-equipped kitchenette, a selection of reading material, tiled floors, and a private veranda that's partially or fully concealed from the views of any of the other verandas. Attached to one of the buildings is an open-sided pavilion that functions as a bar and restaurant, open Monday to Saturday for dinner.

Cane Bay (P.O. Box 1749), Kingshill, St. Croix, U.S.V.I. 00851. www.canebaystcroix.com. Ⓒ **800/545-0603** in the U.S., or 340/718-1815. Fax 340/778-4945. 12 units. Winter $150-$175 double; off season $110-$130 double. Extra person $20. AE, MC, V. From the airport, go left on Rte. 64; after 1 mile, turn right on Rte. 70; after another 1 mile, go left at the junction with Rte. 75; after 2 miles, turn left at the junction with Rte. 80; follow for 5 miles. **Amenities:** Restaurant; bar; pool (outdoor); watersports equipment/rentals. *In room:* A/C, ceiling fan, TV, kitchen, Wi-Fi (free).

INEXPENSIVE

Arawak Bay: the Inn at Salt River ★ ▮▮ This modern B&B on the North Shore opens onto panoramic views of Salt River Bay and the Caribbean. Each accommodation comes with a balcony where you can relax and take in the view. There are even telescopes for ship- or stargazing. Bedrooms are furnished in a simple but comfortable Caribbean motif, with either one king or two full-size beds. A complimentary breakfast includes house specialties and local pastries. The location is convenient to beaches, including Cane Bay, Christiansted, and the airport.

Kingshill, St. Croix, U.S.V.I. www.arawakbaysaltriver.co.vi. Ⓒ **877/261-5385** or 340/772-1684. Fax 340/772-1686. 14 units. Winter $140 double; off season $120 double. AE, DC, MC, V. **Amenities:** Bar; outdoor pool. *In room:* A/C, TV, Wi-Fi (free).

Christiansted

Only one hotel in Christiansted is located on a good swimming beach: **Hotel on the Cay** (see below). As luck would have it, this beach is easily reached by a 4-minute, $3 ferry ride from the main harbor in town.

MODERATE

Hibiscus Beach Hotel ★ This casual boutique hotel, on one of the island's best beaches, attracts a lively clientele of the sandals-and-sunscreen type. The accommodations are in six two-story white-and-blue buildings. Each guest room is a retreat unto itself, with a private patio or balcony and a view of the Caribbean, plus tasteful Caribbean furnishings and floral prints. Shower-only bathrooms are small but well maintained. Guests who stay here are a bit isolated and will find a car useful.

4131 La Grande Princesse (about 3 miles northwest of Christiansted, beside Rte. 75, next to the Cormorant), St. Croix, U.S.V.I. 00820. www.1hibiscus.com. © **800/442-0121** in the U.S., or 340/718-4042. Fax 340/718-7668. 38 units. Winter $200–$295 double; off season $150–$245 double. Honeymoon, dive, and golf packages available. AE, DISC, MC, V. **Amenities:** Restaurant; babysitting; pool (outdoor); watersports (snorkeling). *In room:* A/C, ceiling fan, hair dryer, Wi-Fi (free).

Hotel Caravelle ★ 🍴 The biggest hotel in the historic core of Christiansted, Hotel Caravelle often caters to vacationers and international business travelers who prefer to be near the center of town. Many sports activities, such as sailing, deep-sea fishing, snorkeling, scuba, golf, and tennis, can be arranged at the reception desk. A swimming pool and sun deck face the water, and all the shopping and activities in town are close at hand. The Caribbean restaurant **RumRunners** (p. 162) sits right on the water. Accommodations, which are generally spacious and comfortably furnished, are priced according to their views. Bedrooms are a bit small but are still comfortable. We prefer the rooms on the third floor because they have high ceilings and the best views, although there are no elevators. The least expensive units open onto a parking lot. Be sure to ask when booking to avoid the view of your rental car.

44A Queen Cross St., Christiansted, St. Croix, U.S.V.I. 00820. www.hotelcaravelle.com. © **800/524-0410** or 340/773-0687. Fax 340/778-7004. 44 units. Winter $170–$190 double, $340 suite; off season $140–$160 double, $209 suite. AE, DC, DISC, MC, V. **Amenities:** Restaurant; bar; pool (outdoor); Wi-Fi (free). *In room:* A/C, TV, fridge.

Hotel on the Cay With its buff-colored stucco, terra-cotta tiles, and archways, this rather sterile-looking hotel evokes Puerto Rico or the Dominican Republic, but it's the most prominent building on a 5-acre island set in the middle of Christiansted's harbor. Reaching it requires a 4-minute boat ride from a well-marked quay in the town center (hotel guests ride free; nonguests pay $3 round-trip). Its position in the clear waters of the harbor is both its main plus and its main drawback: Its wide, sandy beaches provide the only pollution-free swimming in the town center, but it's the first hotel to be battered when a hurricane strikes.

The 50-year-old property is believed to have been the inspiration for Herman's Wouk's *Don't Stop the Carnival,* perhaps the most famous novel ever written about the Caribbean. It does provide adequate, simple, and clean accommodations near the beach. Units are fairly roomy, and open onto small metal-railed balconies with a view of the garden or Christiansted Harbor. There's a watersports center on-site, where you can rent windsurfing and snorkeling equipment, as well as jet skis. The restaurant, **Harbormaster** (p. 163), is the only choice on the cay, but really hits the spot after a long day at the beach.

FAMILY-FRIENDLY HOTELS

The Buccaneer (p. 146) Children get a big welcome at this family-owned resort, and those ages 11 and under stay free in their parent's room. During school holidays, the hotel has organized activities for kids.

Chenay Bay Beach Resort (p. 153) Guests have their own cottages here overlooking the Caribbean. The resort has a swimming pool and a fine beach nearby.

Colony Cove (p. 157) Families staying at Colony Cove have their own kitchens and laundry machines. The hotel is near a beach and has a swimming pool.

Villa Madeleine (p. 157) These two-story villas constructed around a West Indian plantation great house afford secluded comfort for families on Teague Bay. Units have full kitchens and living areas, and some have private pools.

Protestant Cay, Christiansted, St. Croix, U.S.V.I. 00820. www.hotelonthecay.com. © **800/524-2035** or 340/773-2035. Fax 340/773-7046. 53 units. Winter $150 double, $190 suite; off season $120 double, $150 suite. Extra person $25. AE, DISC, MC, V. **Amenities:** Restaurant; bar; pool (outdoor); watersports equipment/rentals; Wi-Fi (free). *In room:* A/C, ceiling fan, TV, fridge, kitchenette.

King's Alley Hotel ★ This inn stands on the waterfront near Christiansted Harbor's yacht basin. We like the atmosphere of the Alley much better than its neighbor, the King Christian Hotel (see below). Although short on amenities, this is one of our favorites in town. More charm. Better decor. More inviting ambience—a real St. Croix feeling. The King's Alley is furnished with a distinctly Mediterranean flair. Many of its rooms—which are small to medium in size—overlook its courtyard terrace surrounded by tropical plants. All units have twin or king-size beds with good mattresses, and the deluxe units have four-poster mahogany beds.

57 King St., Christiansted, St. Croix, U.S.V.I. 00820. © **800/843-3574** or 340/773-0103. Fax 340/773-4431. 21 units. Winter $180 double; off season $160 double. AE, DC, DISC, MC, V. **Amenities:** 3 restaurants; pool (outdoor); watersports equipment/rentals; Wi-Fi (free in lobby). *In room:* A/C, TV, fridge, hair dryer.

INEXPENSIVE

Club Comanche Opened in 1948, this famous old West Indian inn is right on the Christiansted waterfront. It's based around a 250-year-old Danish-inspired main house, once the home of Alexander Hamilton. Because accommodations come in such a wide range of styles and sizes, your opinion of this place is likely to be influenced almost entirely by your room assignment. Some of its small- to medium-size bedrooms have slanted ceilings (which can be either charming or cramping), old chests, and mahogany mirrors. A more modern addition is reached by a covered bridge that passes over a shopping street to the waterside. Most of the units face the pool instead of the ocean. Club Comanche also features **Comanche Club,** a popular restaurant in Christiansted.

1 Strand St., Christiansted, St. Croix, U.S.V.I. 00820. www.usvi.net/hotel/comanche. © **800/524-2066** or 340/773-0210. Fax 340/713-9145. 42 units. Winter $100–$200 double; off season $65–$150 double. MC, V. **Amenities:** Restaurant; bar; pool (outdoor); watersports equipment/rentals. *In room:* A/C, TV, hair dryer, Internet (free).

A condo OF ONE'S OWN

Aside from staying at the hotels and big resorts, you can also easily rent a condo on St. Croix. While initially it may seem pricey, a condo is an excellent option for small vacationing groups and families on longer trips.

The major companies renting villas include **Island Hideaways** (✆ 800/832-2302; www.islandhideaways.com), **Caribbean Days** (✆ 800/942-6725; www.caribbeandays.com), **Villa**
Madeleine Vacation Villas (✆ 800/533-6863 or 340/690-3465), **Caribbean Property Management** (✆ 800/496-7379 or 340/778-8782; www.enjoyst croix.com), and **Teague Bay Properties** (✆ 800/964-9755 or 340/773-4665; www.teaguebayproperties.com).

For more condo options, see "Self-Sufficient Units Around the Island," below.

Company House Hotel ★ Lying 1½ blocks from the waterfront, this inn operated for decades as the Danish Manor. The inn recently underwent a renovation which enlarged it and improved its decor and amenities. The hotel building was once a warehouse for the West Indies Company. Its bedrooms, most of which have no view of the sea, are decorated in a bright tropical decor. However, accommodations on the top (third) floor overlook the sands of Protestant Cay. Favorite haunts include the Victor Borge Piano Bar, the cobblestone courtyard, and the pool area.

2 Company St., Christiansted, St. Croix, U.S.V.I. www.companyhousehotel.com. ✆ **340/773-1377.** Fax 340/719-5161. 33 units. Winter $125 double, $160 suite; off season $85 double, $150 suite. Rates include continental breakfast. AE, MC, V. **Amenities:** Piano bar; pool (outdoor). *In room:* A/C, TV, fridge, Wi-Fi (free).

Holger Danske Hotel 🥄 This hotel is one of the best bets in the heart of town for the budget traveler. It's located right on the boardwalk, with the harbor and docks for boating excursions only a breath away. The rooms are pleasantly furnished but small; each has a private furnished balcony. If you're looking to save even more money, book one of the units with an efficiency kitchen, where you can cook your own small meals. The property has a pool patio and a garden path walkway, but only the superior rooms open onto the harbor and the cay.

1200 King Cross St., Christiansted, St. Croix, U.S.V.I. 00820. www.holgerhotel.com. ✆ **340/773-3600.** Fax 340/773-8828. 39 units. Winter $125–$165 double; off season $110–$155 double. Children 17 and under stay free in parent's room. AE, DC, DISC, MC, V. **Amenities:** Restaurant; bar; room service; Wi-Fi (free in lobby). *In room:* A/C, TV, fridge, hair dryer.

King Christian Hotel In business for 200 years, this historic property, originally a warehouse, is directly on the waterfront, right in the heart of everything. All of the front rooms have two double beds and a private balcony overlooking the harbor. The no-frills economy rooms have two single beds or one double and no view or balcony, although they have fresh mattresses and modern fixtures in the tiny bathrooms. While it's not on a beach, there is a sun deck, pool, and shaded patio. The watersports center in the lobby offers daily trips to Buck Island's famous snorkeling trail.

59 King St., P.O. Box 24467, Christiansted, St. Croix, U.S.V.I. 00824. www.kingchristian.com. ✆ **800/524-2012** in the U.S., or 340/773-6330. Fax 340/773-9411. 38 units. Winter $120–$155 double; off season $115–$140 double. Children 11 and under stay free in parent's room. AE, DC, DISC, MC, V. **Amenities:** 2 restaurants; exercise room; pool (outdoor); extensive watersports. *In room:* A/C, ceiling fan, TV, Wi-Fi (free).

Kronegade Inn ★ 🗡 This small inn offers a certain down-home comfort at reasonable rates. Some guests call it the "best-kept secret in Christiansted." The inn has suites and guest rooms, each with full kitchen. The decor is in a tropical motif, with white-rattan furnishings. The beds are comfortable, and the small bathrooms are tidily maintained. The inn doesn't offer food service, but a number of restaurants and cafes are nearby.

11–12 Western Suburb, Christiansted, St. Croix, U.S.V.I. 00820. 📞 **340/692-9590.** Fax 340/692-9591. www.kronegadeinn.com. 18 units. Winter $85 1-bedroom suite, $107 2-bedroom suite; off season $75 1-bedroom suite, $95 2-bedroom suite. AE, MC, V. *In room:* A/C, ceiling fan, TV, fridge, kitchen.

Frederiksted
MODERATE
Cottages by the Sea 🗡
On the western end of St. Croix, these isolated cottages are located on a wide and sandy beach right outside Frederiksted, about 6 miles from the airport, attracting honeymooners and families since the 1950s. Some cottages are made of cinder blocks, and others are wood. The paneled interiors are a bit worn and the whole look is a bit spartan, but reasonably comfortable. Most bedrooms have king-size or twin beds, with tight, compact bathrooms. All cottages have private patios. The hotel has kayaks and snorkel equipment free for guests to use at the beach. Because of the location, you'll have to depend on taxis or rent a car to get around the island. On the other hand, you can walk over to the center of Frederiksted for restaurants, bars, and shopping.

127A Smithfield, Frederiksted, St. Croix, U.S.V.I. 00840. www.caribbeancottages.com. 📞 **800/323-7252** or 340/772-0495. Fax 340/772-0495. 21 units. Winter $155–$215 cottage for 2, $175–$215 villa for 4; off season $115–$165 cottage for 2, $145–$175 villa for 4. Extra person $15. Up to 2 children 17 and under stay free in parent's cottage. AE, DISC, MC, V. **Amenities:** Watersports equipment/rentals. *In room:* A/C, ceiling fan, TV, fridge, hair dryer, kitchen, Wi-Fi (free).

Sand Castle on the Beach
This beachside boutique hotel has a gay and lesbian following, among others. It lies just half a mile from the town's shopping and dining facilities. Rooms are comfortably furnished but small; all have good mattresses, tiny private bathrooms, and extras such as kitchenettes and coolers. There are two fresh-water swimming pools (one is clothing optional), a hot tub, and a beachfront patio, where you'll often encounter men in G-strings. The resort's restaurant, Beach Side Café, has great atmosphere, right on the beach.

Frederiksted Beach, 127 Smith Field, Frederiksted, St. Croix, U.S.V.I. 00840. www.sandcastleonthebeach.com. 📞 **800/524-2018** or 340/772-1205. Fax 340/772-1757. 21 units. Winter $149–$199 double, $259–$349 suite, $319–$449 villa for up to 4 people; off season $109–$219 double, $235–$339 suite, $269–$399 villa for up to 4 people. Rates include continental breakfast. AE, DISC, MC, V. **Amenities:** Restaurant; exercise room; Internet (free in lobby); 2 pools (outdoor); watersports equipment/rentals. *In room:* A/C, ceiling fan, TV, TV/VCR, fridge, hair dryer, kitchenette.

INEXPENSIVE
The Breakfast Club ★ 🗡
Here you'll get the best value of any bed-and-breakfast on St. Croix. This comfortable place combines a 1950s compound of efficiency apartments with a traditional-looking stone house that was rebuilt from a ruin in the 1930s. Each of the units has a cypress-sheathed ceiling, off-white walls, a beige-tile floor, and summery furniture. An on-site chef specializes in banana pancakes and will prepare lunch or dinner on request. When there is a full house count, occasional "party nights" are staged, featuring recorded music.

18 Queen Cross St., Christiansted, St. Croix, U.S.V.I. 00820. © **340/773-7383.** Fax 340/773-8642. 10 units. Year-round $75 double. Rates include breakfast. AE, V. *In room:* A/C (in some), TV, fridge, no phone.

The Frederiksted Hotel   This waterfront four-story inn is a good choice for the heart of historic Frederiksted. It's in the center of town, about a 10-minute ride from the airport. Much of the activity takes place in the outdoor tiled courtyard, where guests enjoy drinks. The cheery rooms are like those of a motel on the U.S. mainland, perhaps showing a bit of wear, and with good ventilation but bad lighting. They're done in a tropical motif of pastels and are equipped with small fridges. The best (and most expensive) rooms are those with ocean views; they're subject to street noise but have the best light. The nearest beach is Fort Frederik, a 3-minute walk away.

442 Strand St., Frederiksted, St. Croix, U.S.V.I. 00840. © **800/595-9519** in the U.S., or 340/772-0500. Fax 340/719-1272. www.frederikstedhotel.dk. 36 units. Winter $80–$150 double; off season $80–$140 double. AE, DISC, MC, V. **Amenities:** Restaurant; bar; pool (outdoor). *In room:* A/C, TV, fridge, Wi-Fi (free).

Self-Sufficient Units Around the Island

If you're interested in a villa or condo rental, contact the places reviewed below or **Vacation St. Croix,** 4000 La Grande Princesse, Christiansted, St. Croix, U.S.V.I. 00820 (© **877/788-0361** or 340/718-0361; fax 340/718-5491; www.vacationstcroix. com), which offers some of the best accommodations on the island. Some are private residences with pools; many are on the beach. Rentals range from one-bedroom units to seven-bedroom villas. In winter, prices per week range from $1,050 to $15,000, reduced in summer to $750 to $12,500. A 7-night minimum is usually imposed.

Cane Bay Reef Club ★ 🏻   Directly on the Caribbean Sea, this is one of the little gems of the island, offering large suites, each with a living room, a full kitchen, and a balcony. It's on the north shore, about a 20-minute taxi ride from Christiansted, fronting the rocky Cane Bay Beach near the Waves at Cane Bay. Sunsets are beautiful, and the snorkeling's great. The decor is breezily tropical, with cathedral ceilings, overhead fans, and Chilean tiles. Bedrooms are spacious, cool, and airy, with comfortable beds; living rooms also contain futons. There's a golf course nearby, and there's a dive shop within walking distance. You can cook in your own kitchen, barbecue, or dine at the in-house restaurant, Bogey's.

P.O. Box 1407, Kingshill, St. Croix, U.S.V.I. 00851. www.canebay.com. © **800/253-8534** in the U.S., or 340/778-2966. Fax 340/778-2966. 9 units. Winter double $150–$250 daily, $970–$1,600 weekly; off season double $110–$160 daily, $700–$990 weekly. Extra person $20. AE, DC, DISC, MC, V. **Amenities:** Restaurant; bar; pool (outdoor). *In room:* A/C, ceiling fan, fridge, kitchen, minibar, no phone (in some), Wi-Fi (free).

Club St. Croix   Flowery gardens and a quarter-mile beach in front of the resort are the big attractions here. This is a well-managed, upscale apartment complex with a pool and three tennis courts. It's slightly better choice than its nearest competitor, Sugar Beach condominiums (see review below). Set in a three-story, cream-colored building, each private apartment has its own kitchen, one or two bedrooms, and good views from Buck Island to the glittering lights of Christiansted.

3280 Estate Golden Rock (about ¼ mile north of the town center on Rte. 70), Christiansted, St. Croix, U.S.V.I. 00820. www.clubstcroix.com. © **800/524-2025** or 340/718-4800. Fax 340/718-4009. 54 units. Winter efficiencies and junior suites $195 double, $225 1-bedroom suite for up to 4, $265 2-bedroom suite for up to 6; off season efficiencies and junior suites $170 double, $190 1-bedroom suite for up to 4, $195 2-bedroom suite for up to 6. Children 12 and under stay free in parent's room. AE, MC,

V. **Amenities:** Restaurant; bar; pool (outdoor); 3 tennis courts (lit); watersports equipment/rentals; Wi-Fi (free in lobby). *In room:* A/C, TV, kitchen.

Colony Cove ★ ☺   This all-suite beachfront resort lies west of Christiansted on the same beach as Club St. Croix (see above). Of all the condo complexes on St. Croix, Colony Cove is the most like a full-fledged hotel, with a relatively large staff on hand. There's even an on-site watersports desk that can arrange all manner of daily tours and activities. Each apartment has a washer and dryer (rare for St. Croix), an especially modern kitchen with microwave, an enclosed veranda or gallery, two air-conditioned bedrooms, and a pair of full bathrooms. All have a light, airy, tropical feel. The four three-story buildings ring a swimming pool next to a palm-shaded beach.

3221 Estate Golden Rock (about 1 mile west of Christiansted), St. Croix, U.S.V.I. 00820. www.colonycove. com. ℂ **800/524-2025** or 340/718-1965. Fax 340/718-5397. 60 units. Winter $235 2-bedroom suite; off season $175 2-bedroom suite. Extra person $20. Children 11 and under stay free in parent's unit. AE, DISC, MC, V. Go east on Rte. 75 heading toward Christiansted as far as Five Corners; turn left and pass Mill Harbor; Colony Cove is the next driveway to the left. **Amenities:** Restaurant; pool (outdoor); 2 tennis courts (lit); watersports equipment/rentals. *In room:* A/C, TV, kitchen, Wi-Fi (free).

Sugar Beach   Set on 7 acres of lush landscaping, this miniresort opens onto a 500-foot premier beachfront. Just 1.45 miles from Christiansted, it features a pool adjacent to a historic 18th-century Danish sugar mill. This row of modernized studios and one-, two-, and three-bedroom apartments is strung along 500 feet of sandy beach on the north coast off North Shore Road. The apartments, with enclosed balconies, are staggered to provide privacy. Of course, all open toward the sea. Each unit has a fully equipped kitchen, full bathrooms, and ample closet space. When you tire of the sand, you can float in the pool.

3245 Estate Golden Rock, St. Croix, U.S.V.I. 00820. www.sugarbeachstcroix.com. ℂ **800/524-2049** in the U.S., or 340/718-5345. Fax 340/718-1359. 43 units. Winter $200 studio, $245–$265 1-bedroom apt, $290 2-bedroom apt, $365 3-bedroom apt, $395 4-bedroom apt; off season $155 studio, $175–$195 1-bedroom apt, $225 2-bedroom apt, $275 3-bedroom apt, $295 4-bedroom apt. Maid service extra. AE, DISC, MC, V. **Amenities:** Pool (outdoor); 2 tennis courts (lit); watersports equipment/rentals; Wi-Fi (free in clubhouse and pool area). *In room:* A/C, ceiling fans, TV, TV/VCR.

Villa Madeleine ★ ☺   For the ultimate hideaway retreat, book one of the two-story villas at this condo complex, constructed around a West Indian plantation great house in a setting of lush tropical planting. This was once a posh hotel, but has been turned into a series of well-furnished condos by the property owners. These villas stand on 6½ acres of landscaped property opening onto Teague Bay, 8 miles east of Christiansted. The units in general contain free-standing villas with one or two bedrooms; most have pink marble showers, and many of the rentals are adorned with West Indian four-poster beds. Each of the accommodations contains a full kitchen with a living and dining area. Some of the villas have private pools, and most of the rentals are suitable for two couples or else a family with children.

Off Rte. 82, Teague Bay, P.O. Box 5014 Villa Madeleine, Christiansted, 00820 St. Croix. www.villamadeleine-stcroix.com. ℂ **800/533-6863** or 340/690-3465. 43 units. Winter $1,950 (weekly) 1-bedroom unit, $2,450 (weekly) 2-bedroom unit; off season $1,750 (weekly) 1-bedroom unit, $2,250 (weekly) 2-bedroom unit. AE, DISC, MC, V. **Amenities:** 2 pools (outdoor); tennis court (lit); watersports equipment/rentals; Wi-Fi (free). *In room:* A/C, TV, CD player, kitchen, MP3 docking station.

BED & BREAKFASTS

Carringtons Inn ★ 👬   This grandly elegant B&B was once the home of a wealthy family who spent winters here. Much evidence of their former lifestyle remains. This is an intimate B&B with personalized attention and five spacious and beautifully furnished guest rooms with first-class private bathrooms. Some rooms have a king-size canopy bed, and wicker furnishings are in tasteful abundance. When guests gather around the pool, a house-party atmosphere prevails. Even your breakfast of such delights as rum-flavored French toast can be served poolside.

4001 Estate Hermon Hill (1 mile west of Christiansted), St. Croix, U.S.V.I. 00820. www.carringtonsinn. com. ✆ **877/658-0508** in the U.S., or 340/713-0508. Fax 340/719-0841. 5 units. Winter $125–$165 double; off season $100–$125 double. Rates include breakfast. AE, MC, V. **Amenities:** Breakfast room; health club (nearby); outdoor pool; tennis courts (nearby). *In room:* A/C, ceiling fan, hair dryer, kitchenette (in some), Wi-Fi (free).

Villa Greenleaf ★★ 🎁   This is one of the best B&Bs on the island, owned and operated by the same staff that made the Greenleaf Inn at Boothbay Harbor one of the leading inns of New England. This snug family retreat still adheres to its New England innkeeping tradition, offering personal service and the elegant ambience of a private home. It's very small, so make reservations well in advance. The building dates from the 1950s when it was a private home, but it's been completely renovated postmillennium. Four-poster beds are just some of the elegant details associated with the roomy bedrooms of this house. Each of the suites is individually decorated and imbued with muted Caribbean charm and grace. The location is to the west of Christiansted, so you'll need a car for excursions down from the hill.

Island Center Rd., Montpelier, St. Croix, U.S.V.I. 00821. www.villagreenleaf.com. ✆ **888/282-1001** in the U.S., or 340/719-1958. Fax 340/772-5425. 5 units. Winter $275–$300 double; off season $220–$225 double. Rates include breakfast. AE, DC, MC, V. **Amenities:** Pool (outdoor). *In room:* A/C, ceiling fan, fridge, hair dryer, no phone, Wi-Fi (free).

Camping

Mount Victory Camp ★ 🐚   On 8 lush acres in St. Croix's forest, these well-landscaped and well-maintained campgrounds lie about a 10-minute drive north of Frederiksted. A beautiful beach of white sand lies only a 2-mile drive down the hill. The grounds are the creation of hosts Bruce and Mathilde Wilson, who are perhaps the most knowledgeable of all islanders about their area's flora and fauna. This is the ideal choice for an adventurous family or group looking to stay close to nature but still have countless organized activities available.

Each of the five open-to-the-breezes dwellings accommodate four to six adults, or you can indulge in tent camping—but bring your own gear. Handcrafted, eco-friendly dwellings are equipped with furnishings crafted from tropical hardwood. There are basic cooking and eating facilities in each unit, and all guests have use of the immaculately kept bathhouse with flush toilets and an open-air shower with solar-heated water. Communal events are staged, including campfires and a Sunday-afternoon pig roast. On the grounds is a vegetable and herb garden, a tropical fruit orchard, even a tortoise colony. Outdoor activities include hiking in the rainforest, horseback rides, kayaking, and fishing.

Creque Dam Rd., Frederiksted, St. Croix, U.S.V.I. 00841. www.mtvictorycamp.com. ✆ **866/772-1651** or 340/772-1651. 5 dwellings. Winter $85–$95 double; off season $75–$85 double. Extra person $10. No credit cards. **Amenities:** Public phone; picnic tables. *In room:* No phone.

WHERE TO EAT

Don't limit yourself to your hotel for dining. Most visitors sample diversity in their dining at lunch when, chances are, they are out indulging in beach life, shopping, or seeing the sights. Christiansted is filled with excellent restaurants offering lunch, but

St. Croix Restaurants

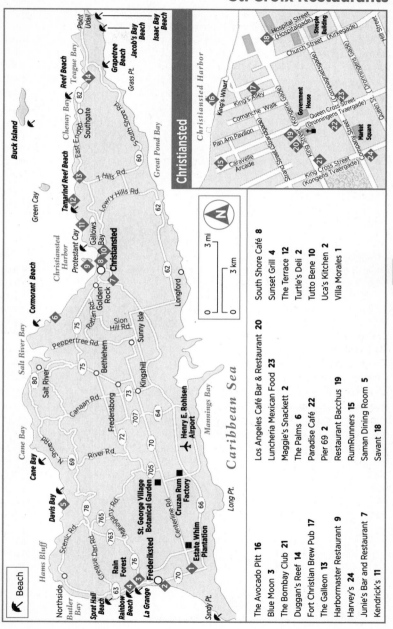

Beach

Northside
Butler Bay
Hams Bluff
Sprat Hall Beach
Rainbow Beach
La Grange
Frederiksted
Davis Bay
Rain Forest
Cane Bay
Cane Bay
Salt River Bay
Salt River
Cormorant Beach
Christiansted Harbor
Protestant Cay
Gallows Bay
Christiansted
Golden Rock
Sion Hill Rd.
Peppertree Rd.
Bethlehem
Kingshill
Sunny Isle
Fredensborg
Canaan Rd.
River Rd.
St. George Village Botanical Garden
Cruzan Rum Factory
Estate Whim Plantation
Henry E. Rohlsen Airport
Mannings Bay
Long Pt.
Sandy Pt.

Caribbean Sea

Green Cay
Tamarind Reef Beach
Chenay Bay
Reef Beach
Teague Bay
Southgate
East End
7 Hills Rd.
Lowry Hills Rd.
South Shore Rd.
Great Pond Bay
Longford
Buck Island
Point Udall
Isaac's Bay Beach
Jacob's Bay Beach
Grapetree Beach
Grass Pt.

Christiansted

Hospital Street (Hospitalgade)
Steeple Building
Church Street (Kirkegade)
Hill Street
King's Wharf
King's Alley
Government House
Comanche Walk
Pan Am Pavilion
Queen Cross Street (Dronningens Tvaergade)
Caravelle Arcade
King Street (Kongens Gade)
Queen Street
Market Square
King Cross Street (Kongens Tvaergade)
Company Street (Compagnietsgade)
Strand Street (Strandgade)
Christiansted Harbor

0   3 mi
0   3 km

The Avocado Pitt **16**
Blue Moon **3**
The Bombay Club **21**
Duggan's Reef **14**
Fort Christian Brew Pub **17**
The Galleon **13**
Harbormaster Restaurant **9**
Harvey's **24**
Junie's Bar and Restaurant **7**
Kendrick's **11**

Los Angeles Café Bar & Restaurant **20**
Luncheria Mexican Food **23**
Maggie's Snackett **2**
The Palms **6**
Paradise Café **22**
Pier 69 **2**
Restaurant Bacchus **19**
RumRunners **15**
Saman Dining Room **5**
Savant **18**

South Shore Café **8**
Sunset Grill **4**
The Terrace **12**
Turtle's Deli **2**
Tutto Bene **10**
Uca's Kitchen **2**
Villa Morales **1**

lunch in Frederiksted is a bit dicey if cruise ships have arrived. If so, the few restaurants here may be packed with your next-door neighbors (the ones you went to St. Croix to avoid).

At night, dining becomes more of a problem if you want to venture out. If you're not familiar with the badly lit roads and driving on the left, driving to the restaurant of your choice might present some difficulties. Of course, the easiest way to go is to have your hotel call a taxi and let the driver deliver you to a restaurant. Agree upon the hour you're to be picked up, and he'll even return for you, or the restaurant will summon a cab for you if you don't want to lock yourself into a time frame. Most of the resorts are along the north shore, and dining at a different resort every night (unless you're on a meal plan) is easily arranged by taxi.

If you're staying at one of the small hotels or guesthouses in and around Christiansted, you can even walk to your restaurant of choice. If you're at a hotel in Frederiksted, the night is yours, as the cruise-ship crowds have departed and there is a less expensive, earthier, and more laid-back feeling in the small dining rooms here.

North Shore
EXPENSIVE

The Galleon FRENCH/NORTHERN ITALIAN   This restaurant, which overlooks the ocean, is a local favorite, and deservedly so. It serves northern Italian and French cuisine, occasionally including *osso buco,* just as good as that dished up in Milan, although lunchtime offers include tacos and burgers. The dinner menu always offers at least one local fish, such as wahoo, tuna, swordfish, or mahimahi, or you might try the fresh Caribbean lobster. You can order a perfectly done rack of lamb, which will be carved right at your table. There's an extensive wine list, including many options sold by the glass. Music from a baby grand accompanies dinner several nights a week, and you can enjoy guitar music on Thursday and Saturday.

East End Rd., Green Cay Marina, 5000 Estate Southgate. © **340/773-9949.** www.galleonrestaurant. com. Reservations recommended. Main courses $22–$40. MC, V. Daily 11am–4pm and 6–10pm; happy hour 4–6pm. Go east on Rte. 82 from Christiansted for 5 min.; after going 1 mile past the Buccaneer, turn left into Green Cay Marina.

Saman Dining Room ★ AMERICAN   This informal enclave is located in the Carambola Beach Resort. The restaurant seats 100 under a vaulted cathedral ceiling. The chefs focus on chicken, beef, and the fresh catch of the day. Tangy appetizers include jumbo prawn cocktail, while the dinner specialties include rib-eye steak. For a touch of island flavor, opt for tuna, which is quickly seared and served with chutney. Steaks are handled with care and grilled to your preference; lamb and veal, although flown in frozen, still turn out tasty.

In Carambola Beach Resort (p. 146), Estate Davis Bay. © **340/778-3800.** Main courses $22–$35. AE, DC, DISC, MC, V. Tues–Sat 6–10pm.

The Terrace ★★ INTERNATIONAL   This is the island's finest dining room in a hotel. Menu items vary but are likely to include grilled local lobster cakes, served with lemon-caper beurre blanc and accented with fresh tarragon. You might also opt for the poached shrimp with a fresh lime cocktail sauce or a hand-cut New York strip steak in a tamarind dark-rum sauce. The delectable pecan-crusted roast pork tenderloin is served sliced over pesto mashed potatoes and red-eye gravy. The roast rack of lamb and the Thai barbecue salmon are classics.

At the Buccaneer (p. 146), Gallows Bay. ℂ **340/712-2100.** www.thebuccaneer.com/dine.htm. Reservations recommended. Main courses $25–$34. AE, DC, DISC, MC, V. Daily 7–10:30am and 6–9:30pm.

MODERATE

The Palms ★ INTERNATIONAL   Both the restaurant and its bar are meccas for gay or gay-friendly people who appreciate their relaxed atmospheres, well-prepared food, and gracefully arched premises overlooking the sea. The menu changes daily. Lunch specialties may include meal-size salads, club sandwiches, burgers, and fresh fish. In the evening expect such dishes as roast rack of lamb served with a pecan-and-Parmesan-herb crust or grilled local mahimahi, its flavor enhanced with fresh cilantro and lime-butter sauce. Desserts are sumptuous, especially the Cruzan rum cake with bananas, chocolate, or coconut and the chocolate rum torte with layers of mousse and rum cake sealed in chocolate.

In the Palms at Pelican Cove (p. 150), 4126 La Grande Princesse. ℂ **340/718-8920.** www.palmspelican cove.com. Reservations recommended. Main courses lunch $4–$15, dinner $9–$24. AE, MC, V. Daily 7:30–10:30am, 11:30am–2:30pm, and 6:30–9pm.

Christiansted

EXPENSIVE

Kendrick's ★★ FRENCH   Kendrick's, the island's toniest restaurant, lies in the historic Quin House complex at King Cross and Company streets. Some of its recipes have been featured in *Bon Appétit,* and deservedly so. You'll immediately warm to such specialties as grilled filet mignon with a port-wine demi-glace and red-onion confit. The signature appetizer is king crab cakes with lemon-pepper aïoli. Another great choice is the pecan-crusted roast pork loin with ginger mayonnaise.

2132 Company St. ℂ **340/773-9199.** Main courses $26–$39. AE, MC, V. Mon–Sat 6–9:30pm. Closed Mon Sept–Oct.

Restaurant Bacchus ★ STEAKHOUSE/CONTINENTAL   In a restaurant dedicated to the god of wine, it's no surprise that the wine menu receives as much attention as the food. Both *Wine Spectator* and *Food & Wine* have praised the cellar here. The decor, the fine service, and the presentation of the dishes make for a fine evening out. The kitchen uses first-class ingredients, many imported, to craft a number of dishes that combine flavor and finesse. To finish, it doesn't get any better than the rum-infused sourdough bread pudding. Most dishes, except lobster, are at the lower end of the price scale.

52 King St. ℂ **340/692-9922.** www.restaurantbacchus.com. Reservations requested. Main courses $27–$40. AE, DC, DISC, MC, V. Tues–Sun 6–10pm.

Tutto Bene ITALIAN   Lying directly east of Christiansted, this place seems more like a bistro-cantina than a full-fledged restaurant. The owners, Smokey Odom and Kelly Williams, believe in simple, hearty, and uncomplicated *paisano* dishes, the kind that Mamma fed her sons back in the old country. You'll dine in a warehouselike setting, amid warm colors and often lots of hubbub. The menu is written on a pair of oversize mirrors against one wall. The antipasti are some of the best on the island; an intriguing appetizer is the calamari stuffed with ground veal and served in a broth. Pizza lovers can start with pizza Sottile, with a thin crust and a choice of three toppings. A full range of delectable pastas and well-prepared seafood is offered nightly, along with steaks and chops. You can order a seafood pasta dish with mussels, clams, and shrimp in a white-wine pesto sauce over capellini. A fish of the day, based on the local catch, is served at market price (meaning the tab changes from day to day).

Boardwalk Building, Hospital St., Gallows Bay. ☎ **340/773-5229.** www.tuttobenerestaurant.com. Reservations recommended. Main courses $21–$42. AE, MC, V. Tues–Sun 6–10pm.

MODERATE

The Bombay Club INTERNATIONAL   This is one of the most enduring restaurants in Christiansted. It's concealed from the street by the brick foundations of an 18th-century planter's town house. You enter through a low stone tunnel and eventually end up near the bar and the courtyard that contains many of its tables. The food, though not overly fancy, is plentiful, full of flavor, and reasonably priced. The best items include the catch of the day and regional dishes such as conch, beef filet, and pasta. The island's best fresh-lobster pasta is served here. On a recent visit, we enjoyed the grilled fish with sun-dried tomatoes and roasted garlic butter, and fettuccine with sliced prime rib.

5A King St. ☎ **340/773-1838.** Reservations recommended. Main courses $14–$21. MC, V. Mon–Fri 11:30am–4pm and 5:30–10pm; Sat–Sun 6–10pm.

RumRunners ☺ CARIBBEAN   This open-air restaurant sits right on the boardwalk and offers some fabulous views to accompany the excellent dining. The ambience is purely Caribbean—the sound of waves in the background can put even the tensest of people at ease. Sunday brunch is even accompanied by a steel-pan band. Excellent choices here include the New York strip steak; the fresh, broiled whole lobster; the Caribbean pork tenderloin served with a grilled banana; and one of the house specials, baby back ribs slow-cooked in island spices and Guinness. The younger vacationers can pick from the children's menu.

In the Hotel Caravelle (p. 152), on the boardwalk at Queen Cross St. ☎ **340/773-6585.** www.rumrunnersstcroix.com. Reservations recommended. Main courses $15–$34. AE, MC, V. Mon–Sat 7–10:30am, 11:30am–3pm, and 5:30–9:30pm; Sun 8am–2pm and 5:30–9:30pm.

Savant ★ 🏫 CARIBBEAN/THAI/MEXICAN/FUSION   The spicy cuisines of one region and two nations are combined into a marvelous fusion to wake up your palate. The stylish bistro atmosphere is a delightful place to dine, but know that the chefs take the food seriously. We gravitate to the tantalizing Thai curries; most of them are mildly spiced for the average diner, but you can request the chef "to go nuclear" if that is your desire. The red-coconut-curry sauce is one of the best we've ever had on the island. Enchilada lovers will find much happiness here too, especially in the seafood enchiladas. The maple-teriyaki pork tenderloin is one of the chef's specialties and deserves the praise heaped upon it. There are only 20 candlelit tables, so call for a reservation as far in advance as you can.

4C Hospital St. ☎ **340/713-8666.** Reservations required. Main courses $14–$39. AE, MC, V. Mon–Sat 6–10pm.

INEXPENSIVE

The Avocado Pitt AMERICAN/VEGETARIAN   This is an all-around good choice for breakfast or lunch while you explore the shops and attractions of Christiansted. One of the town's best breakfasts is served here, as patronage by locals reveals. Their omelets and pancakes are rib-sticking fare and full of flavor. Lunch options include "Kahuna burgers" and tuna sandwiches, but you can also find more creative offerings, including tofu with sautéed vegetables or fresh yellowfin tuna. Vegetarians rejoice for the veggie or soy burgers along with freshly made salads and a variety of protein-enriched fruit smoothies. The staff will also pack you a boxed lunch for your tour of the island or all-day sailing adventure. The cafe also serves as something of a small art gallery, displaying paintings by Caribbean artists. Many of the works are for sale.

Kings Wharf. ✆ **340/773-9843.** Main courses breakfast $3–$13, lunch $7–$15. AE, MC, V. Daily 7am–4pm.

Fort Christian Brew Pub CAJUN   This fish house and brewery boasts one of the best harbor views in Christiansted. It's the only licensed microbrewery in the U.S.V.I. Rotating beer choices can include a pale ale (Hammerhead), a red ale (Blackbeard's), and a dark stout (West Indies Porter), all of which have earned a formidable reputation on the island. Many patrons come just to drink, staying until closing, which is around 1am. A roster of burgers and sandwiches is served at lunch and dinner. In the evening, the upstairs dining room offers a two-fisted menu that includes a 16-ounce rib-eye with caramelized onions. A favorite of ours is Bourbon Street Jambalaya. Maybe it's better in New Orleans, but this version tastes very much of Louisiana, as does the shrimp étouffée, slow-cooked in a blend of Creole spices and stock. The blackened or pan-seared catfish also takes you way down south. For something West Indian, order the red snapper with *fungi*. There is also a microbrewery storefront in Charlotte Amalie that gives out free samples (and sells beer).

55 King's Alley Walk. ✆ **340/713-9820.** www.fortchristianbrewpub.com. Platters in brew pub $8–$10; main courses in upstairs restaurant $17–$25. MC, V. Daily 11am–10pm.

Harbormaster Restaurant ☺ AMERICAN   This is where guests at the local town inns head for a day at the beach. It's a 4-minute, $3 ferry ride across the harbor from Christiansted, at Hotel on the Cay. While here, you don't want to go back into town for lunch, so the hotel has wisely decided to accommodate its many day visitors by offering this quite acceptable restaurant. It offers the usual array of salad platters, sandwiches, omelets, and burgers, but many main dishes are more elaborate and appealing, especially the grilled filet of mahimahi (or swordfish); the conch in a lemon, garlic, and butter sauce; and the barbecued ribs. The excellent Tuesday-evening West Indian barbecue costs $27 for all you can eat (kids eat at a 50% discount); steel-band music, limbo, fire-eating, broken-bottle dancing, and the Mocko Jumbie stilt dance accompany the feast.

At the Hotel on the Cay (p. 152), Protestant Cay. ✆ **340/719-5438.** Main courses $7–$40; breakfast $6–$11. AE, DISC, MC, V. Daily 7:30am–4:30pm; Tues 7–10pm.

Harvey's CARIBBEAN   Forget the plastic and the flowery tablecloths that give this place a 1950s feel and enjoy the thoroughly zesty cooking of island matriarch Sarah Harvey, who takes joy in her work and aims to fill your stomach with her basic but hearty fare. Try one of her homemade soups, especially the callaloo or chicken. She'll even serve you conch in butter sauce as an appetizer. For a main dish you might choose from barbecue chicken, barbecue spareribs, boiled filet of snapper, and sometimes even lobster. *Fungi* comes with just about everything. For dessert, try one of the delectable tarts made from guava, pineapple, or coconut.

11B Company St. ✆ **340/773-3433.** Main courses $6–$22. V. Mon–Sat 11:30am–3:30pm.

Junie's Bar and Restaurant ★ 🍴 CARIBBEAN   A local favorite, particularly among the corps of taxi drivers, this restaurant occupies a white-painted cement building about a half-mile south of Christiansted, adjacent to a church and a discount store. Inside, wooden tables, metal chairs, bowls of cut flowers, and a well-scrubbed kind of simplicity add to the appeal. Your hosts, Junie Allen and her daughter Denise, prepare a flavor-filled but basic medley of West Indian staples, including a roster of drinks that you might not have tasted before. Sea moss (a kind of eggnog flavored with pulverized seaweed), *mauby* (fermented from rainwater and tree bark), and ginger beer are only some of the options. The menu features boiled fish, conch, lobster in butter sauce, stewed goat, stewed Creole-style lobster, and pork chops with greens and yams. Desserts include carrot cake, cheesecake, and Key lime pie. Because the place has been here for 30 years, it's known by virtually everybody on the island.

132 Peter's Rest. ✆ **340/773-2801.** Main courses lunch $11–$24, dinner $10–$23. AE, MC, V. Daily 11:30am–10pm.

Luncheria Mexican Food 🍴 MEXICAN/CUBAN   This restaurant is a bargain. You get the usual tacos, tostadas, burritos, nachos, and enchiladas, as well as chicken fajitas, enchiladas verde, and *arroz con pollo* (spiced chicken with brown rice). Daily specials feature both low-calorie and vegetarian choices (the chef's refried beans are lard-free), and whole-wheat tortillas are offered. The complimentary salsa bar has mild to hot sauces, plus jalapeños. Some Cuban and Puerto Rican dishes appear on the menu; these include a zesty chicken curry, black-bean soup, and roast pork. The bartender makes the island's best margaritas.

In the historic Apothecary Hall Courtyard, 2111 Company St. ✆ **340/773-4247.** Main courses $5–$13. MC, V. Mon–Sat 11am–9pm.

Paradise Café 🍴 DELI/AMERICAN   This neighborhood favorite draws locals seeking good food and great value. Its brick walls and beamed ceiling were originally part of an 18th-century great house. New York–style deli fare is served during the day. The homemade soups are savory, and you can add grilled chicken or fish to the freshly made salads. At breakfast, you can select from an assortment of omelets, or try the steak and eggs. Dinners are more elaborate. The 12-ounce New York strip steak and the freshly made pasta specialties are good choices. Appetizers include mango chicken quesadillas and crab cakes.

53B Company St. (at Queen Cross St., across from Government House). ✆ **340/773-2985.** Breakfast $6–$11; lunch $7–$12; dinner $15–$27. MC, V. Mon–Sat 7:30am–9pm.

In & Around Frederiksted

MODERATE

Blue Moon INTERNATIONAL/CAJUN   The best little bistro in Frederiksted becomes a hot, hip spot during Sunday brunch and on Friday nights when it offers live entertainment. The 200-year-old stone house on the waterfront is a favorite of visiting jazz musicians, and tourists have discovered (but not spoiled) the fun. It's decorated with funky, homemade art from the States, including a trash-can-lid restaurant sign. The atmosphere is casual and cafelike, with a frequently changing menu. You might begin with the Lunar Pie, with feta cheese, cream cheese, onions, mushrooms, and celery in phyllo pastry, or the artichoke-and-spinach dip. Main courses include the catch of the day and, on occasion, Maine lobster. The clams served in garlic sauce are also from Maine. There's also the usual array of steak and chicken dishes. Save room for the brownie ice cream.

17 Strand St. ✆ **340/772-2222.** www.bluemoonstcroix.com. Reservations recommended. Main courses $23–$29. AE, MC, V. Tues–Fri 11:30am–2pm; Tues–Sat 6–9pm; Sun 11am–2pm.

Los Angeles Café Bar & Restaurant ☺ AMERICAN   Here's another great spot favored by locals. Jean Claude Michelle, known as Bert, was an executive chef in Los Angeles, where he grew up, until he left to start a career in St. Croix. Bert runs this cafe with a jovial attitude that is nothing short of contagious. The menu is widely varied, including everything from mozzarella sticks to mahimahi. The lobster with crabmeat is grilled to perfection and the fresh fish is always an excellent choice. The basics and more can be found on the children's menu.

King St. ℂ **340/772-0016.** Reservations recommended. Main courses $15–$35. AE, MC. Hours are irregular—call in advance to see if it's open.

Villa Morales PUERTO RICAN   This inland spot is the premier Puerto Rican restaurant on St. Croix. But then again, no one will mind if you come here just to drink; a cozy bar is lined with the memorabilia collected by several generations of the family who maintains the place. Look for a broad cross-section of Hispanic tastes here, including many that Puerto Ricans remember from childhood. Savory examples include fried snapper with white rice and beans, stewed conch, roasted or stewed goat, and stewed beef. Most of the dishes are at the lower end of the price scale. On special occasions, the owners transform the place into a dance hall, bringing in live salsa and merengue bands at no extra charge to patrons.

Plot 82C, Estate Whim (off Rte. 70 about 2 miles from Frederiksted). ℂ **340/772-0556.** Reservations recommended. Main courses $9–$35. MC, V. Thurs–Sat 10am–9pm.

INEXPENSIVE

Maggie's Snackett CARIBBEAN   If you're looking for a home-cooked meal in St. Croix, this is the place for you. White doors and yellow exterior make you feel as if you're going to Sunday dinner at Grandma's house. The menu changes every day and you should call ahead to see what's cooking. However, you can always expect Caribbean classics, like smoked mackerel, fish, goat, or chicken stew, and a wide variety of fresh-baked island breads are old-time favorites on Maggie's menu.

65 King St. ℂ **340/772-5070.** Breakfast $6–$7; main courses $12–$15. No credit cards. Daily 8am–midnight.

Pier 69 AMERICAN/CARIBBEAN   You can get a decent platter of food here, but this place is far more interesting for its funky, Greenwich Village–style atmosphere than for its cuisine. New York–born Unise Tranberg is the earth mother/matriarch of the place, which looks like a warm and somewhat battered combination of a 1950s living room and a nautical bar. Counterculture fans make this their preferred drinking hangout, sometimes opting for a mango colada or a lime lambada. Menu items include a predictable array of salads, and sandwiches. Expect the likes of fried shrimp and potatoes, broiled red snapper served with a butter sauce, and steak with baked potatoes.

69 King St. ℂ **340/772-0069.** Sandwiches and platters $5.75–$12; main courses $14–$24. DISC, MC, V. Mon–Wed 8am–3pm; Thurs–Sun 8am–1am.

Turtle's Deli DELI   This is the only seafront deli on St. Croix. Lots of folks take their overstuffed sandwiches to the handful of outdoor tables that sit atop the wharf around back. The selection includes salads, freshly baked bread, bagels, lox, and cold cuts, as well as pastries and munchies. The place is especially good at packing boxed picnics, great for a sailing or snorkeling expedition.

625 Strand St. ℂ **340/772-3676.** Sandwiches $5–$9. No credit cards. Mon–Fri 8:30am–5pm; Sat 9am–5:30pm.

Uca's Kitchen 🍴 VEGETARIAN   Don't come here looking for a glamorous setting—you won't find one. The joint doesn't look like much, but it's the best vegetarian option on island, and one of the most economical places to dine. Just straight off the cruise dock, the kitchen is a local hangout. Try such dishes as the cook's barbecued tofu kebab or his callaloo with a *fungi* polenta. The house specialty is a tasty mushroom lasagna. Everything is washed down with fresh tropical fruit juices.

King St.✆ **340/772-5063.** Reservations not required. Main courses $10–$15. No credit cards. Daily 12:30pm–midnight.

Out on the Island

Duggan's Reef CONTINENTAL/CARIBBEAN   This is one of the most popular restaurants on St. Croix. It's only a few feet from the still waters of Reef Beach and makes an ideal perch for watching windsurfers and Hobie Cats. At lunch, an array of salads, crepes, and sandwiches is offered. The more elaborate night menu features the popular house specialties: Duggan's Caribbean lobster pasta and Irish whiskey lobster. Begin with fried calamari or conch chowder. Main dishes include New York strip steak, fish, and pastas. The local catch of the day can be baked, grilled, blackened Cajun style, or served island style (with tomato, pepper, and onion sauce).

East End Rd. ✆ **340/773-9800.** Reservations required for dinner in winter. Main courses $23–$39; pastas $19–$30. MC, V. Mon–Sat 6–9pm; Sun brunch 11am–2:30pm. Closed for lunch in summer.

South Shore Café AMERICAN   Set in a simple, breezy building on an isolated inland region ("in the middle of nowhere"), this is a charming and intensely personal family-style restaurant. Decorating quirks (including a collection of umbrellas hanging from the ceiling of the lattice-trimmed dining room) add a funky, offbeat note to what are usually well-turned-out meals with a rural North American twist. Excellent choices include ravioli stuffed with sweet potatoes and spring onions, a tomato-based Sicilian clam chowder, baked brie with a rum sauce, local grilled fish with herb-flavored butter sauce, and homemade grilled chicken lasagna with sun-dried tomatoes and a sherry-flavored cream sauce.

6 Petrinelli Farm. ✆ **340/773-9311.** Reservations required. Main courses $25–$30. MC, V. Wed–Sun 5–9pm.

Sunset Grill ★ 🍴 CARIBBEAN/AMERICAN   This informal spot is on the west coast, near Sprat Hall Plantation. It's the best place on the island to combine lunch and a swim. The restaurant has been in business since 1948, feeding locals and visitors alike. Try such local dishes as seafood chowder and the fried fish of the day. These dishes have authentic island flavor, perhaps more so than any other place on St. Croix. You can also get salads and burgers. The bread is baked fresh daily. The owners allow free use of the showers and changing rooms.

Rte. 63 (1 mile north of Frederiksted). ✆ **340/772-5855.** Sandwiches $6–$13; main courses $17–$32. MC, V. Daily 11am–9pm; Sun brunch 10:30am.

BEACHES

Beaches are St. Croix's big attraction. The problem is that getting to them from Christiansted, home to most of the hotels, isn't always easy. It can also be expensive, especially if you want to go back and forth each day of your stay. From Christiansted a taxi will cost about $30 for two people to Davis Bay, $24 to Cane Bay, and $20 to Rainbow Beach. Of course, you can rent a condo or stay in a hotel right on the water.

The most celebrated beach is offshore **Buck Island,** part of the U.S. National Park Service network. Buck Island is actually a volcanic islet surrounded by some of the most stunning underwater coral gardens in the Caribbean. The white-sand beaches on the southwest and west coasts are beautiful, but the snorkeling is even better. The islet's interior is filled with cactus, wild frangipani, and pigeonwood. There are picnic areas for those who want to make a day of it. Boat departures are from Kings Wharf in Christiansted; the ride takes half an hour. For more information, see the section "A Side Trip to Buck Island," later in this chapter.

Your best choice for a beach in Christiansted is the one at the **Hotel on the Cay.** This white-sand strip is on a palm-shaded island. To get here, take the ferry from the fort at Christiansted; it runs daily from 7am to midnight. The 4-minute trip costs $3 round-trip, free for guests of the Hotel on the Cay. Five miles west of Christiansted is the **Palms at Pelican Cove,** where some 1,200 feet of white sand shaded by palm trees attracts a gay and mixed crowd. Because a reef lies just off the shore, snorkeling conditions are ideal.

Recommended highly are **Davis Bay** and **Cane Bay,** with swaying palms, white sand, and good swimming. Because they're on the north shore, these beaches are often windy, and as a result their waters are not always calm. The snorkeling at Cane Bay is truly spectacular; you'll see elkhorn and brain corals, all some 750 feet off the Cane Bay Wall. Cane Bay adjoins Route 80 on the north shore. Davis Beach doesn't have a reef; it's more popular among bodysurfers than snorkelers. There are no changing facilities. It's near Carambola Beach Resort.

On Route 63, a short ride north of Frederiksted, lies **Rainbow Beach,** with white sand and ideal snorkeling conditions. Nearby, also on Route 63, about 5 minutes north of Frederiksted, is another good beach, called **La Grange.** Lounge chairs can be rented here, and there's a bar nearby.

Sandy Point, directly south of Frederiksted, is the largest beach in all the U.S. Virgin Islands, but it's open to the public only on weekends from 10am to 4pm. Its waters are shallow and calm, perfect for swimming. Try to concentrate on the sands and not the unattractive zigzagging fences that line the beach. This beach is protected as a nesting spot for endangered sea turtles. Continue west from the western terminus of the Melvin Evans Highway (Rte. 66). For more on visiting the refuge, see p. 177.

There's an array of beaches at the east end of the island; they're somewhat difficult to get to, but much less crowded. The best choice here is **Isaac Bay Beach,** ideal for snorkeling, swimming, or sunbathing. Windsurfers like **Reef Beach,** which opens onto Teague Bay along Route 82, East End Road, a half-hour ride from Christiansted. You can get food at Duggan's Reef (p. 166). **Cramer Park** is a special public park operated by the Department of Agriculture. It's lined with sea-grape trees and has a delightful picnic area, a restaurant, and a bar. **Grapetree Beach** is off Route 60 (the South Shore Rd.), wide and sandy, with calm water. The beach is flanked only by a few private homes, although the beach at the Divi Carina is a short walk away.

FUN IN THE SURF & SUN

St. Croix can offer many outdoor adventures. In the east, the terrain is rocky and arid, getting little water. But the western part of the island is lush, including a small "rain forest" of mango, tree ferns, and dangling lianas. Between the two extremes are beautiful sandy beaches, rolling hills, and pastures—all of which can be explored. Watersports galore abound, including boating, sailing, diving, snorkeling, fishing, hiking, and windsurfing.

The **St. Croix Landmarks Society,** on Sundays between November and May, occasionally offers "rambles" into the countryside to see ruins, many of them plantations that flourished in the 18th century. The owners of the remains of these former sugar plantations open their gates to the tours, so you have a chance to see a bit of the hidden St. Croix that the average visitor misses.

Guides are often St. Croix historians who will fill you in on the land and its lore. Count yourself lucky if you get to visit Castle Nugent Farm, a cattle ranch on the southeastern coast and one of the oldest working ranches in the West Indies. You can still visit the slave quarters at this ranch and the great house dating from 1730. For information about these tours and other programs of the society, call ✆ 340/772-0598, or log on to www.stcroixlandmarks.com.

FISHING   The fishing grounds at **Lang Bank** are about 10 miles from St. Croix. Here you'll find kingfish, dolphin fish, and wahoo. Using light-tackle boats to glide along the reef, you'll probably turn up jack or bonefish. At **Clover Crest,** in Frederiksted, local anglers fish right from the rocks. For more information on legal shore-fishing spots around the island, contact the tourist office in Christiansted or Frederiksted.

Serious sport fishermen, and those who don't have their own dinghy, can board the *Island Girl II,* a 38-foot Bertram special. It's anchored at King's Alley Hotel at 59 Kings Wharf in Christiansted. Reservations can be made by calling ✆ 340/773-2628 during the day. The cost for up to six passengers is $550 for 4 hours, $750 for 6 hours, and $950 for 8 hours with bait and tackle and drinks included.

GOLF   St. Croix has the best golf in the Virgin Islands. Guests staying on St. John and St. Thomas often fly over for a round on one of the island's three courses.

Carambola Golf & Country Club, on the northeast side of St. Croix (✆ 340/778-5638; www.golfcarambola.com), adjacent to the Carambola Beach Resort (p. 146), was created by Robert Trent Jones, Sr., who called it "the loveliest course I ever designed." It's been likened to a botanical garden. The par-3 holes here are known to golfing authorities as the best in the Tropics. The greens fee of $95 in winter, or $65 in the off season, allows you to play as many holes as you like. Carts are included.

The **Buccaneer,** Gallows Bay (p. 146; ✆ 340/712-2144), 3 miles east of Christiansted, has a challenging 5,685-yard, 18-hole course with panoramic vistas. Non-guests pay $100 in winter or $60 off season, including use of a cart.

The **Reef,** on the east end of the island at Teague Bay (✆ 340/773-8844), is a 3,100-yard, 9-hole course, charging greens fees of $20 for 9 holes and $35 for 18 holes. Golf carts can also be rented at an additional $15 for 9 holes or $20 for 18 holes. The longest hole here is a 465-yard par 5.

HIKING   Scrub-covered hills make up much of St. Croix's landscape. The island's western district, however, includes a dense, 15-acre forest known as the **"Rain Forest"** (though it's not a real one). The network of footpaths here offers some fantastic nature walks. For more details on hiking in this area, see the section "Exploring the

'Rain Forest,'" later in this chapter. **Buck Island** (see the section "A Side Trip to Buck Island," later in this chapter), just off St. Croix, also has nature trails.

The **St. Croix Environmental Association,** Arawak Building, Suite 3, Gallows Bay (© **340/773-1989;** www.stxenvironmental.org), has regularly scheduled informative hikes to more remote sections of the island, costing $10 per person.

HORSEBACK RIDING   Paul and Jill's Equestrian Stables, 2 Sprat Hall Estate, Route 58 (© **340/772-2880;** www.paulandjills.com), the largest equestrian stable in the Virgin Islands, is known throughout the Caribbean for its horses. It's set on the sprawling grounds of the island's oldest plantation great house. The operators lead scenic trail rides through the forests, along the beach, and past ruins of abandoned 18th-century plantations and sugar mills, to the tops of the hills of St. Croix's western end. Beginners and experienced riders alike are welcome. A 1½-hour trail ride costs $90. Tours usually depart daily in winter at 10:30am and 3pm, and in the off season at 4pm, with slight variations according to demand. Reserve at least a day in advance.

KAYAKING   The beauty of St. Croix is best seen from a kayak. Try the tour offered by **Caribbean Adventure Tours** (© **800/532-3483** or 340/778-1522; www.stcroix kayak.com). You use stable, sit-on-top ocean kayaks, enabling you to traverse the tranquil waters of Salt River, of Columbus landfall fame, and enjoy the park's ecology and wildlife. You also explore secluded mangrove estuaries. The highlight of the excursion is a dip for snorkeling on a pristine beach and paddling to where Christopher Columbus and his crew came ashore some 500 years ago. The tour, lasting 3 hours, costs $45 per person and includes water and a light snack.

SAFARI TOURS   St. Croix Safari Tours (© **340/773-6700;** www.gotostcroix.com/safaritours) offers a tour in a 25-passenger open-air bus run by a hip tour guide who knows all about the botany, cuisine, and history of the island. Tours crisscross the island with stops at plantation houses, historic Frederiksted, and the Salt River landfall of Columbus, and a drive through the rainforest, with a stop for lunch. There are lots of photo ops. The cost of the tour is $55 per person, including admission fees to the botanical garden, rum factory, and museum.

SNORKELING & SCUBA DIVING ★★   Sponge life, black coral (the finest in the West Indies), and steep drop-offs near the shoreline make St. Croix a snorkeling and diving paradise. The island is home to the largest living reef in the Caribbean, including the fabled north-shore wall that begins in 25 to 30 feet of water and drops to 13,200 feet, sometimes straight down. See "Beaches," above, for information on good snorkeling beaches. The **St. Croix Water Sports Center** (© **340/773-7060;** www.caribbeandays.com) rents snorkeling equipment for $20 a day, if your hotel doesn't supply it.

Buck Island ★★ is a major scuba-diving site, with a visibility of some 100 feet. It also has an underwater snorkeling trail. Practically all outfitters on St. Croix offer scuba and snorkeling tours to Buck Island. For more information on the island, see the section "A Side Trip to Buck Island," later in this chapter.

Other favorite dive sites include the historic **Salt River Canyon** (northwest of Christiansted at Salt River Bay), for advanced divers. Submerged canyon walls are covered with purple tube sponges, deepwater gorgonians, and black coral saplings. You'll see schools of yellowtail snapper, turtles, and spotted eagle rays. We also like the gorgeous coral gardens of **Scotch Banks** (north of Christiansted) and **Eagle Ray**

Touching any coral—including soft corals such as sea fans—is forbidden in any marine protected area and should be avoided at all costs everywhere. Even the lightest contact is deadly to the coral and can scrape and cut you as well, leaving rashes and stings much like that of a jellyfish (coral's free-floating cousin). Divers and snorkelers are also not permitted to touch, pet, or otherwise harass any fish, including eels and rays, whose delicate skin is coated with antibacterial slime, which protects them from potentially deadly skin infections.

Feeding fish is similarly dangerous, however innocuous it seems. It can alter natural feeding behavior or, worse, cause the fish to sicken or die from ingesting unfamiliar food.

But wait, there's more: By applying sunscreen or insect repellent before entering the water, divers release harmful chemicals to the water that can mimic the coral's hormones, causing premature death and illness.

It seems the more scientists learn, the more delicate these systems appear. Want to make up for past infractions? Check out REEF (Reef Environmental Education Foundation; www.reef.org), a volunteer monitoring program that allows divers to log in and add their fish sightings to a global database used by scientists to monitor populations.

—Christina P. Colón

(also north of Christiansted), the latter so named because of the rays that cruise along the wall there. **Cane Bay ★★** is known for its coral canyons.

Frederiksted Pier, near the historic area of Frederiksted, is the jumping-off point (literally) for a scuba voyage into a world of sponges, banded shrimp, plume worms, sea horses, and other creatures.

Davis Bay is the site of the 12,000-foot-deep Puerto Rico Trench. **Northstar Reef,** at the east end of Davis Bay, is a spectacular wall dive, recommended for intermediate or experienced divers only. The wall here is covered with stunning brain corals and staghorn thickets. At some 50 feet down, a sandy shelf leads to a cave where giant green moray eels hang out.

At **Butler Bay,** to the north of Frederiksted on the west shore, there are the submerged ruins of three ships: the *Suffolk Maid,* the *Northwind,* and the *Rosaomaira,* the latter sitting in 100 feet of water. These wrecks form the major part of an artificial reef system that also contains abandoned trucks and cars. This site is recommended for intermediate or experienced divers.

Anchor Dive Center, Salt River National Park (© **800/532-3483** in the U.S., or 340/778-1522; www.anchordivestcroix.com), is located within the most popular dive destination in St. Croix: Salt River National Park. It operates three boats and dives mainly in and around the park. The staff offers complete instruction, from resort courses through full certification, as well as night dives. A resort course is $90, with a two-tank dive going for $90. Dive packages begin at $250 for six dives.

Another recommended outfitter is the **Cane Bay Dive Shop** (© **800/338-3843** or 340/773-9913; www.canebayscuba.com), with five locations all around the island. The numerous locations means there's a variety of dive sites to choose from, without having to take a long boat ride. A beginner's lesson goes for $60, and packages go all the way up the scale to a six-tank dive package for $199.

TENNIS Some authorities rate the tennis at the **Buccaneer ★★**, Gallows Bay (*©* **340/773-3036**), as the best in the Caribbean. This resort offers a choice of eight courts, two lit for night play, all open to the public. Nonguests pay $8 daytime, $10 nighttime per person per hour; you must call to reserve a court at least a day in advance. A tennis pro is available for lessons, and there's also a pro shop.

WINDSURFING Head for the **St. Croix Water Sports Center** (*©* **340/773-7060**), on the small offshore island in Christiansted Harbor and part of the Hotel on the Cay. It's open daily from 10am to 5pm. Windsurfing rentals are $35 per hour. Lessons are available.

SEEING THE SIGHTS

Although the 21st century has definitely invaded St. Croix, with subdivisions, condo complexes, shopping centers, and modern strip malls, evidence of the past is everywhere across its 84 square miles. St. Croix contains the nostalgic ruins of some 100 plantations where sugar cane was once grown. Except for a few windmills and ruined Great Houses, that's about what's left of the slave-driven plantations that once grew tobacco and sugar cane.

Christopher Columbus named the island Santa Cruz (Holy Cross) when he landed on November 14, 1493. He anchored his ship off the north shore but was quickly driven away by the spears, arrows, and axes of the Carib Indians. The French laid claim to the island in 1650; the Danes purchased it from them in 1733. Under their rule, the slave trade and sugar-cane fields flourished until the latter half of the 19th century. Danish architecture and influence can still be seen on the island today. In a shrewd purchase deal with the Danes, the U.S. acquired the islands in 1917.

Today, the past is visible everywhere you go in St. Croix, from Fort Christiansvaern to Fort Frederick. Take the time to explore Christiansted and Frederiksted, where you can see the island's Danish roots.

WALKING TOUR: **CHRISTIANSTED**

START:	**The Visitors Bureau.**
FINISH:	**Christiansted's harborfront.**
TIME:	**1½ hours.**
BEST TIMES:	**Any day from 10am to 4pm.**
WORST TIMES:	**Monday to Friday 4 to 6pm.**

The largest town on St. Croix, Christiansted still has many traces of its Danish roots. Constructed by the Danish West India Company, the heart of town is still filled with many imposing buildings, mostly former warehouses, from the 18th century. Today they are registered as a U.S. National Historic Site. Across a small park stands **Fort Christiansvaern,** which the Danes built on the fortifications of a 1645 French fort. From its precincts, some of the best views of the harbor can be seen. Christiansted is best seen by walking tour.

1 The Visitors Bureau

This yellow-sided building with a cedar-capped roof is located near the harborfront. It was originally built as the Old Scalehouse in 1856, to replace a similar structure that had burned down. In its heyday, all taxable goods leaving and entering Christiansted's harbor were weighed here. In front of the building lies one of the most charming squares in the Caribbean. Its old-fashioned asymmetrical allure is still evident despite the mass of cars.

With your back to the scalehouse, turn left and walk through the parking lot to the foot of the white-sided gazebolike band shell that sits in the center of a park named after Alexander Hamilton. The yellow-brick building with the ornately carved brick staircase is the:

2 Old Customs House

This is currently the headquarters of the National Park Service. The gracefully proportioned 16-step staircase was added in 1829 as an embellishment to an older building. (There are public toilets on the ground floor.)

Continue climbing the hill to the base of the yellow-painted structure, which is:

3 Fort Christiansvaern

This is the best-preserved colonial fortification in the Virgin Islands. It's maintained as a historic monument by the National Park Service. Its original four-sided, diamond-shaped design was in accordance with the most advanced military planning of its era. The fort is the site of the St. Croix military museum, which documents police work on the island from the late 1800s to the present. Photos, weapons, and artifacts help bring to life the police force's past here. The admission price of $3 also includes admission to the Steeple Building (see below). The fort is open daily from 8am to 5pm. For information, call © **340/ 773-1460.**

Exit from the fort, and head straight down the tree-lined path toward the most visible steeple in Christiansted. It caps the appropriately named:

4 Steeple Building

Completed in 1753, the Steeple Building was embellished with a steeple between 1794 and 1796. For a time it served as the headquarters of the Church of Lord God of Sabaoth. The original structure can still be visited (see below). Inside is a local history museum. Hours are daily from 8am to 4:45pm; admission is included in the $3 ticket for Fort Christiansvaern.

Across Company Street from the Steeple Building is a U.S. post office.

5 The Danish West India and Guinea Warehouse

The building that houses the post office was built in 1749 as the warehouse for the Danish West India and Guinea Company. The structure was once three times larger than it is today and included storerooms and lodging for staff. Go to the building's side entrance, on Church Street, and enter the rear courtyard. For many years, this was the site of some of the largest slave auctions in the Caribbean.

From the post office, retrace your steps to Company Street and head west for 1 block. On your left, you'll pass the entrance to Apothecary Hall, 2111 Company St., which contains a charming collection of shops and restaurants.

Walking Tour: Christiansted

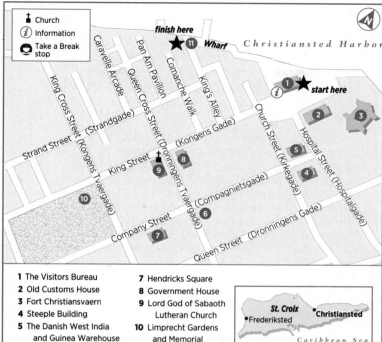

Key:
- 🕆 Church
- ⓘ Information
- ☕ Take a Break stop

Christiansted Harbor

finish here ★ ⑪ Wharf

start here ★ ① ⓘ

② ③

⑤

④

Caravelle Arcade

Pan Am Pavilion

Queen Cross Street

Comanche Walk

King's Alley

King Cross Street (Strandgade)

Strand Street (Kongens Tvaergade)

Queen Cross Street (Dronningens Tvergade)

(Kongens Gade)

King Street

Church Street (Kirkegade)

Hospital Street (Hospitalgade)

⑧

⑨

(Compagnietsgade)

⑥

⑩

⑦

Company Street

Queen Street (Dronningens Gade)

1 The Visitors Bureau
2 Old Customs House
3 Fort Christiansvaern
4 Steeple Building
5 The Danish West India and Guinea Warehouse (U.S. Post Office)
6 Luncheria ☕
7 Hendricks Square
8 Government House
9 Lord God of Sabaoth Lutheran Church
10 Limprecht Gardens and Memorial
11 Christiansted's harbor front

St. Croix
Frederiksted • • Christiansted
Caribbean Sea

6 Luncheria

If you need refreshment, try Luncheria, Apothecary Hall Courtyard, 2111 Company St. (ⓒ 340/773-4247). The bar's tables are grouped in a courtyard shaded by trees. The owners are margarita specialists, stocking more types of tequila (15-plus) than any other bar in the neighborhood. Luncheria serves burritos, tostadas, enchiladas, and tacos, as well as daily specials and vegetarian meals. See a full review on p. 164.

Exit Apothecary Hall and turn left onto Company Street. Walk across Queen Cross Street (Dronningens Tvergade). Half a block later, you'll arrive at the island's largest outdoor market:

7 Hendricks Square

The square was rebuilt in a timbered, 19th-century style after the 1989 hurricane. Fruits and vegetables are sold here Monday through Saturday from 7am to 6pm.

Retrace your steps half a block along Company Street, then turn left onto Queen Cross Street. Head downhill toward the harbor, walking on the right-hand side of the street. Within half a block, you'll reach an unmarked arched iron gateway, set beneath an arcade. Enter the charming gardens of:

8 Government House

The European-style garden here contains a scattering of trees, flower beds, and walkways. The antique building that surrounds the gardens was formed from the union of two much older town houses in the 1830s. The gardens are open Monday to Friday, 8am to 5pm.

Exit the same way you entered, turn right, and continue your descent of Queen Cross Street. At the first street corner (King St.), turn left and you'll see:

9 Lord God of Sabaoth Lutheran Church

This church was established in 1734. Take a moment to admire its neoclassical facade.

Continue walking southwest along King Street. Within 2 blocks is the:

10 Limprecht Gardens and Memorial

For 20 years (1888–1908), Peter Carl Limprecht served as governor of the Danish West Indies. Today, an occasional chicken pecks at seedlings planted near a Danish-language memorial to him.

At the end of the park, retrace your steps to Queen Cross Street, and go left. One very short block later, turn right onto Strand Street, which contains some interesting stores, including at least two different shopping arcades. The streets will narrow, and the pedestrian traffic will be more congested. Pass beneath the overpass belonging to a popular bar and restaurant, the Comanche Club.

Continue down the meandering curves of King's Alley. Within 1 block you'll be standing beside:

11 Christiansted's Harborfront

You can end your tour here by strolling on the boardwalk of the waterside piers.

Frederiksted ★

This former Danish settlement at the western end of the island, about 17 miles from Christiansted, is a sleepy port town that comes to life only when a cruise ship docks at its pier. Frederiksted was destroyed by a fire in 1879, and the citizens rebuilt it by putting wood frames and clapboards on top of the old Danish stone and yellow-brick foundations.

Most visitors begin their tour at russet-colored **Fort Frederik,** at the northern end of Frederiksted next to the cruise-ship pier (© **340/772-2021**). This fort, completed

---

In His Footsteps: Alexander Hamilton (1755–1804)

Alexander Hamilton was an American statesman from the West Indies who served brilliantly in the American Revolution. He wrote many of the articles contained in the Federalist Papers and became Secretary of the Treasury to George Washington. He was noted for both his literary and oratorical skills. Though he was born on the island of Nevis, Hamilton spent his adolescence in St. Croix.

- **Birthplace:** The British-held island of Nevis on January 11, 1755.
- **Residences:** Nevis, St. Croix, various cities in the United States.
- **Final Days:** In a duel fought with Aaron Burr, Hamilton was mortally wounded and died July 12, 1804.

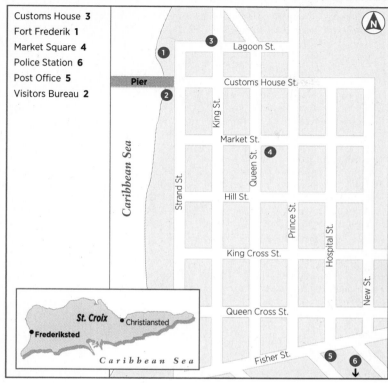

Customs House **3**
Fort Frederik **1**
Market Square **4**
Police Station **6**
Post Office **5**
Visitors Bureau **2**

Pier

Lagoon St.

Customs House St.

King St.

Market St.

Queen St.

Strand St.

Hill St.

Prince St.

Hospital St.

King Cross St.

New St.

Caribbean Sea

Queen Cross St.

St. Croix • Christiansted
• **Frederiksted**

Caribbean Sea

Fisher St.

in 1760, is said to have been the first fort in the Caribbean to salute the flag of the new United States. An American brigantine, anchored at port in Frederiksted, hoisted a crudely made Old Glory. To show its support for the emerging American colonies, the head of the fort fired a cannonball in the air to honor the Americans and their new independence. Such an act violated the rules of Danish neutrality. It was at this same fort, on July 3, 1848, that Governor-General Peter von Scholten emancipated the slaves in the Danish West Indies, in response to a slave uprising led by a young man named Moses "Buddhoe" Gottlieb. In 1998, a bust of Buddhoe was unveiled here. The fort has been restored to its 1840 appearance and today is a national historic landmark. You can explore the courtyard and stables. A local history museum has been installed in what was once the Garrison Room. Admission is $3, free for children 15 and under; it's open Monday through Friday from 8:30am to 4pm.

The **Customs House,** just east of the fort, is an 18th-century building with a 19th-century two-story gallery. To the south of the fort is the **visitor bureau** at Strand Street (© **340/772-0357**), where you can pick up a free map of the town.

THE ST. CROIX heritage trail

A trail that leads into the past, **St. Croix Heritage Trail** helps visitors relive the island's Danish colonial past. All you need are a brochure and map, available at the tourist office in Christiansted (p. 142). This 72-mile itinerary includes a combination of asphalt-covered roadway, suitable for driving, and narrow woodland trails which must be navigated on foot. Many aficionados opt to drive along the route whenever practical, descend onto the footpaths wherever indicated, and then return to their cars for the continuation of the tour. En route, you'll be exposed to one of the Caribbean's densest concentrations of historical and cultural sites.

The route connects Christiansted and Frederiksted, going past the sites of former sugar plantations, and traverses the entire 28-mile length of St. Croix. The route consists mainly of existing roadways. The brochure will identify everything you're seeing: You will pass cattle farms, suburban communities, even industrial complexes and resorts. It's not all manicured and pretty, but much is scenic and worth the drive. Allow at least a day for this trail, with stops along the way.

Nearly everyone gets out of the car at **Point Udall,** the easternmost point under the U.S. flag in the Caribbean. You'll pass an eclectic mix of churches and even a prison.

The highlight of the trail is the **Estate Mount Washington** (p. 179), a strikingly well-preserved sugar plantation. Another highlight is **Estate Whim Plantation Museum** (p. 179), one of the best of the restored great houses, with a museum and gift shop. Another stop is along **Salt River Bay,** which cuts into the northern shoreline. This is the site of Columbus's landfall in 1493.

Of course, you'll want to stop and get to know the locals. We recommend a refreshment break at **Smithens Market.** Vendors at this market, which lies off Queen Mary Highway, offer freshly squeezed sugar-cane juice and sell locally grown fruits and homemade chutneys.

Exploring the "Rain Forest" ★

The island's western district contains a dense, 15-acre forest, called the "Rain Forest" (though it's not technically a rainforest). The area is thick with mahogany trees, kapok (silk-cotton) trees, turpentine (red-birch) trees, *samaan* (rain) trees, and all kinds of ferns and vines. Sweet limes, mangoes, hog plums, and breadfruit trees, all of which have grown in the wild since the days of the plantations, are also interspersed among the larger trees. Crested hummingbirds, pearly eyed thrashers, green-throated caribs, yellow warblers, and perky but drably camouflaged banana quits nest here. The 150-foot-high Creque Dam is the major man-made sight in the area.

The "Rain Forest" is private property, but the owner lets visitors go inside to explore. To experience its charm, some people opt to drive along Route 76 (also known as Mahogany Rd.), stopping beside the footpaths that meander off on either side of the highway into dry riverbeds and glens. Stick to the most worn footpaths. You can also hike along some of the little-traveled four-wheel-drive roads in the area. Three of the best for hiking are the **Creque Dam Road** (Rte. 58/78), the **Scenic Road** (Rte. 78), and the **Western Scenic Road** (Rte. 63/78).

Our favorite trail in this area takes about 2½ hours one-way. From Frederiksted, drive north on Route 63 until you reach Creque Dam Road, where you turn right, park the car, and start walking. About a mile past the Creque Dam, you'll be deep within the forest's magnificent flora and fauna. Continue along the trail until you come to the Western Scenic Road. Eventually, you reach Mahogany Road (Rte. 76), near St. Croix LEAP Project. This trail is moderate in difficulty.

You could also begin near the junction of Creque Dam Road and Scenic Road. From here, your trek will cover a broad triangular swath, heading north and then west along Scenic Road. The road will first rise, and then descend toward the coastal lighthouse of the island's extreme northwestern tip, **Hams Bluff.** Most trekkers decide to retrace their steps after about 45 minutes of northwesterly hiking. Real die-hards, however, will continue all the way to the coastline, then head south along the coastal road (Butler Bay Rd.), and finally head east along Creque Dam Road to their starting point at the junction of Creque Dam Road and Scenic Road. Embark on this longer expedition only if you're really prepared for a hike lasting about 5 hours.

Sandy Point Wildlife Refuge ★

St. Croix's rarely visited southwestern tip is composed of salt marshes, tidal pools, and low vegetation inhabited by birds, turtles, and other wildlife. More than 3 miles of ecologically protected coastline lie between Sandy Point (the island's westernmost tip) and the shallow waters of the West End Salt Pond. This national wildlife refuge is one of only two nesting grounds of the leatherback turtle in the United States—the other is on Culebra, an offshore island of Puerto Rico. It's also home to colonies of green and hawksbill turtles, and thousands of birds, including herons, brown pelicans, Caribbean martins, black-necked stilts, and white-crowned pigeons. As for flora, Sandy Point gave its name to a rare form of orchid, a brown/purple variety. The area consists of 360 acres of subtropical vegetation, including the largest salt pond in the Virgin Islands.

Park rangers are determined to keep the area pristine, and in doing so they have to face such problems as the poaching of sea turtles and their eggs, drug smuggling,

 Sea Turtle Etiquette

These are some of the most highly endangered species in the oceans. Catching even a passing glimpse of one is a magical experience, but you'll blow the chance unless you heed some basic guidelines. When you first spot a sea turtle, resist the urge to move in and get a closer look; you will only scare it off and ruin the opportunity for others to see it. Instead, stay still and watch at a respectful distance as it goes about its business, searching for food or gliding along gracefully. Keep an eye out for identification tags on their flippers or shells—a sure sign these fellas are being closely studied and well protected. You should never approach a turtle or its nest, and never touch or try to touch one—for your safety and theirs. While it seems harmless to humans, it is in fact quite stressful for the turtles (how'd you like to be chased around the grocery store by strangers all day?). *Warning:* Do not swim above the turtles; it will prevent them from surfacing to breathe and subject them to undue respiratory stress. And, of course, if someone offers you sea turtle shell, egg, or meat products, just say no.

—Christina P. Colón

The rocky promontory of Point Udall, jutting into the Caribbean Sea, is the easternmost point of the United States. Die-hards go out to see the sun rise, but considering the climb via a rutted dirt road, you may want to wait until there's a bit more light before heading here. Once at the top, you'll be rewarded with one of the best scenic views in the U.S. Virgin Islands. On the way to the lookout point, you'll see "the Castle," or Mountaintop Eyrie, a villa that claims Transylvania as its architectural influence, owned by the island's most prominent socialite, the Contessa Nadia Farbo Navarro. Point Udall is reached along Route 82 (it's signposted).

dumping of trash, and the arrival of illegal aliens. Even the mongoose and feral dogs are a menace to the nesting female turtles.

Visitors are fascinated to see the leatherback sea turtle, the largest of its species, which can measure some six feet in length and weigh more than 1,000 pounds. Every 2, perhaps 3 years, the turtles come back to this refuge to nest from March to July. The average female will deposit anywhere from 60 to 100 eggs in her nest. The survival rate is only one in 1,000 hatchlings. The refuge is also home to the green sea turtle, which can grow to a maximum of four feet and weigh about 400 pounds. These turtles come here only from June to September, when the females come to lay from 75 to 100 eggs.

Birdies also flock to Sandy Point to see more than 100 species of birds, five of which are endangered. Endangered brown pelicans, royal terns, laughing gulls, Caribbean elaenias, bananaquits, and yellow warblers are just some of the birds that call Sandy Point home. Three species of geckos (yes, that annoying insurance salesman), along with several species of reptiles also live here. The reptiles usually stay out of your way.

The wildlife refuge is only open to the public on Saturday and Sunday from 10am to 4pm (admission is free). Activities include hiking, nature photography, and wildlife observation. To reach the refuge, drive to the end of the Route 66 (Melvin Evans Hwy.) and continue down a gravel road. For guided weekend visits, call © **340/773-4554** to make arrangements.

Around the Island

North of Frederiksted, you can drop in at **Sprat Hall,** the island's oldest plantation, or continue along to the "Rain Forest" (see above). Most visitors come to the area to see the jagged estuary of the northern coastline's **Salt River.** The Salt River was where Columbus landed on November 14, 1493. Marking the 500th anniversary of Columbus's arrival, former President George H. W. Bush signed a bill creating the 912-acre **Salt River Bay National Historical Park and Ecological Preserve.** The park contains the site of the original Carib village explored by Columbus and his men, including the only ceremonial ball court ever discovered in the Lesser Antilles. Also within the park is the largest mangrove forest in the Virgin Islands, sheltering many endangered animals and plants, plus an underwater canyon attracting divers from around the world. If you visit on your own, a taxi from Christiansted will cost $22. See "Fun in the Surf & Sun," earlier in the chapter, for suggestions on kayak and scuba tours to this very special park.

Carl and Marie Lawaetz Museum The home of one of the island's oldest and most prestigious families can be visited for a rare glimpse into plantation life. Set in a valley at La Grange, this 1750 farmstead has been owned by the Lawaetz family since 1899. Visitors can tour the estate with a member of the family. Originally a sugar plantation, the estate was later turned into a cattle ranch. On the grounds are the reminders of a bygone era, including a decaying sugar mill on a nearby hill. The 19 acres of land are filled with beautiful flowers and tropical trees and bushes.

Inside you can inspect the family heirlooms, many brought over from Denmark. Marie decorated the home with her paintings, still hanging in almost every room. You're even shown the mahogany four-poster bed in which all seven of the Lawaetz family were born.

Mahogany Rd., Rte. 76, Estate Little La Grange. © **340/772-0598.** www.stcroixlandmarks.com. Admission $10 adults, $5 students and seniors, $4 children 6–12, free for children 5 and under. May–Oct Thurs–Sat 10am–4pm; Nov–Apr Thurs–Sat 10am–4pm.

Cruzan Rum Factory This factory distills the famous Virgin Islands rum, which some consider the finest in the world. Guided tours depart from the visitor's pavilion and include a visit to the factory's old windmill. The whole affair is topped off with a complimentary mixed drink, of course. Call ahead for reservations.

Estate Diamond 3, W. Airport Rd., Rte. 64. © **340/692-2280.** www.cruzanrum.com. Admission $5 adults, $1 children 18 and under. Tours given Mon–Fri 9–11:30am and 1–4pm.

Estate Mount Washington Plantation This is the island's best-preserved sugar plantation and a highlight along the St. Croix Heritage Trail. It flourished from 1780 to 1820, when St. Croix was the second-largest producer of sugar in the West Indies. The on-site private residence is closed to the public, but you can go on a self-guided tour of the 13 acres at any time of the day you wish (there is no admission charge, although donations are accepted). You'll see what is the best antiques store on St. Croix, but you can only visit the little shop that houses them by calling © **340/772-1026** and asking for an appointment (see "Shopping," below).

At the very southwestern tip of the island, off Rte. 63, a mile inland from the highway that runs along the Frederiksted coast. Free admission.

Estate Whim Plantation Museum This restored great house is unique among those of the many ruined sugar plantations that dot the island. It's composed of only three rooms. With 3-foot-thick walls made of stone, coral, and molasses, the house resembles a luxurious European château. A division of Baker Furniture Company used the Whim Plantation's collection of models for one of its most successful reproductions, the "Whim Museum–West Indies Collection." Upscale reproductions of some of the furniture are on display within the Whim Plantation, and are for sale on-site. Slightly different inventories are available from an associated store in downtown Christiansted: the **St. Croix Landmarks Museum Store,** 58 Queen St. (© **340/713-8102**).

The ruins of the plantation's sugar-processing plant, complete with a restored windmill, also remain. The estate is also site of many events held by the St. Croix Landmarks Society, such as evening concerts and wine tastings. Check their website (www.stcroixlandmarks.com) to see what's happening during your visit.

Centerline Rd. (2 miles east of Frederiksted). © **340/772-0598.** Admission $10 adults, $5 children. Mon–Sat 10am–4pm.

St. George Village Botanical Garden This is a 16-acre Eden of tropical trees, shrubs, vines, and flowers. The garden is a feast for the eye and the camera, from the

Buck Island (p. 186)   The boat ride to Buck Island is great fun for kids. Equally appealing are the island's white-sand beaches and its profuse wildlife. Bring along a picnic.

Fort Christiansvaern (p. 183)   Children can explore dungeons and battlements and even see how soldiers of yesteryear fired a cannon.

entrance drive bordered by royal palms and bougainvillea to the towering kapok and tamarind trees. It was built around the ruins of a 19th-century sugar-cane workers' village. Self-guided walking-tour maps are available at the entrance to the garden's great hall. Facilities include restrooms and a gift shop.

127 Estate St., 1 St. George (just north of Centerline Rd.), 4 miles east of Frederiksted. (C) **340/692-2874.** www.sgvbg.org. Admission $8 adults, $6 seniors, $1 children 12 and under; donations welcome. Daily 9am–5pm.

Organized Tours

BUS TOURS   Organized tours operate according to demand. Many are conducted at least three times a week during the winter, with fewer departures in summer. A typical 4-hour tour costs $28 per person. Tours usually go through Christiansted and include visits to the botanical gardens, Whim Estate House, the rum distillery, the rainforest, the St. Croix LEAP mahogany workshop (see "Shopping," below), and the site of Columbus's landing at Salt River. Check with your hotel desk, or call **Travellers' Tours,** Henry E. Rohlsen Airport (C) **340/778-1636**), for more information.

TAXI TOURS   Many visitors explore St. Croix on a taxi tour (C) **340/778-1088**), which, for a party of two, costs about $120 for 3 hours. The fare should be negotiated in advance. Extra fees are charged for the following sights: $10 for the botanical gardens, $10 for the Whim Estate House, and $8 for the rum distillery. Taxi tours are far more personalized than bus tours; you can get on and off where you want and stay as long or as little as you wish at a destination.

WALKING TOURS   For a guided walking tour of either Christiansted or Frederiksted, contact **St. Croix House Tours** (C) **340/772-0598**). The tour of Christiansted is available upon request, leaves at 9:30am, and costs $30 per person. The Frederiksted tour leaves on Wednesday at 9:30am, and costs $30 per person. Call for details and to arrange meeting places. Tours are given only in February and March.

DRIVING TOUR: EAST ST. CROIX

START:	**The Buccaneer.**
FINISH:	**Fort Christiansvaern.**
TIME:	**1½ hours.**
BEST TIMES:	**Early morning or late afternoon.**
WORST TIMES:	**Any evening after 5pm.**

Head east from Christiansted on Route 75 (sometimes referred to as East End Rd.). Within a few miles, it will become Route 82, an area that residents consider the most

5

East St. Croix

ST. CROIX

Driving Tour: East St. Croix

Buck Island

Caribbean Sea

Green Cay

Tamarind Reef Beach

Chenay Bay

Reef Beach

Southgate

82

Teague Bay

Bay Knight Bay

4

Cramer Park

Point Udall

East End Bay

Grapetree Beach

60

Grass Pt.

3

East End Rd.

South Shore Rd.

Robin Bay

60

2

7 Hills Rd.

624

Great Pond Bay

5

75

Lowry Hills Rd.

62

1

Caribbean Sea

start here

75

Protestant Cay

Christiansted

6

finish here

62

Longford

area of detail

Christiansted

St. Croix

Frederiksted

Caribbean Sea

5

ST. CROIX | East St. Croix

1 The Buccaneer
2 Green Cay Marina
3 Mountaintop Eyrie
4 Duggan's Reef
5 Hartmann's Great Pond
6 Fort Christiansvaern

peaceful and dramatic on the island. It's especially memorable at sunset, when the vistas are highlighted and the sun is against your back. If you get confused at any time during this tour, remember that the ocean should always be on your left.

Landmarks you'll pass on your way out of town will include Gallows Point and:

1 The Buccaneer

You might want to return to this hotel for one of the nightly musical performances, which are among the island's best (see "St. Croix After Dark," below).

As you leave town, the landscape will open onto verdant countryside. Cows graze peacefully on a rolling landscape. Accompanying the cows are tickbirds, which feed on ticks buried in the cows' skin. An occasional small traffic jam might form as herds of goats cross the road.

Continue driving, and you'll pass:

2 Green Cay Marina

You might want to visit this marina to admire the yachts bobbing at anchor, or perhaps to have a swim at Chenay Bay. Nearby monuments include the Southgate Baptist Church and a handful of stone towers that once housed the gear mechanisms of windmills that crushed the juice from sugar cane.

As you drive on, you'll pass by scatterings of bougainvillea-covered private villas. About 7 miles along the route from Christiansted, you'll see the:

3 Mountaintop Eyrie

Mountaintop Eyrie is owned by the island's most prominent socialite, Contessa Nadia Farbo Navarro, a Romanian-born heiress to a great fortune. This opulent castle is the most outrageously unusual, most prominent, and most talked-about villa on St. Croix—an abode Count Dracula might enjoy. Understandably, its privacy is rigidly maintained.

A couple of miles farther along East End Road, you'll reach one of the most popular windsurfing beaches in St. Croix, Teague Bay. This is a good spot to take a break at:

4 Duggan's Reef

Duggan's Reef, East End Road, Teague Bay (© 340/773-9800), offers good lunches, more formal dinners, fruit daiquiris, and a bar only 10 feet from the waves. Many guests claim this is the best way to experience windsurfing without getting on a sailboard. See p. 166 for details.

After your stop, continue driving east along Route 82. At Knight Bay, near the eastern tip of the island, turn right onto Route 60 (South Shore Rd.) and head west. One of the several lakes you'll pass is:

5 Hartmann's Great Pond

Also known simply as Great Pond, this is a favorite of nesting seabirds, and a great photo opportunity of the sea and the rolling grasslands.

Route 60 merges with Route 624 a short distance north of Great Pond. Fork left onto Route 624, and, a short distance later, right onto Route 62 (Lowry Hill Rd.). You are now traveling the mountainous spine of the island through districts named after former farms, such as Sally's Fancy, Marienhøj, and Boetzberg.

Within 2 miles, Lowry Hill Road merges with Route 82 again. Fork left, and follow it as it turns into Hospital Gade and leads to the center of Christiansted. To your right will appear:

6 Fort Christiansvaern

You'll see it as you pull into the parking lot in front of Christiansted's tourist office (Old Scalehouse).

SHOPPING

Christiansted is the shopping hub of St. Croix, though it does not compare with Charlotte Amalie on St. Thomas. The emphasis here is on hole-in-the-wall boutiques selling handmade goods. Most of the shops are compressed into a half-mile or so. Between Company Street and the harbor are many courtyards, antique buildings, arcades, and walkways riddled with shops, many of which are smaller branches of parent stores on St. Thomas. Along the boardwalk is the **King's Alley Complex,** a pink-sided compound filled with the densest concentration of shops on St. Croix.

In recent years, **Frederiksted** has also become a popular shopping destination. Its urban mall appeals to cruise-ship passengers arriving at Frederiksted Pier.

Shopping A to Z in Christiansted

ANTIQUES

Estate Mount Washington Antiques ★★   The owners are always there and you'll be able to browse through the best treasure-trove of colonial West Indian furniture and "flotsam" in the Virgin Islands. But you'll have to call first for an appointment. Afterward, you can walk around the grounds of an 18th-century sugar plantation, **Estate Mount Washington** (p. 179). 4 Estate Mount Washington. ✆ **340/772-1026.**

CLOTHES

The Coconut Vine   This is one of the most colorful and popular little boutiques on the island. Hand-painted batiks for men and women alike are the specialty. Strand St. ✆ **340/773-1991.**

From the Gecko   At this hip and eclectic outlet, you can find anything from hand-painted local cottons and silks to the old West Indian staple, batiks. We found the Indonesian collection here among the most imaginative in the U.S. Virgin Islands—everything from glass jewelry to banana-leaf knapsacks. 1233 Queen Cross St. ✆ **340/778-9433.**

Gone Tropical   About 60% of the merchandise in this unique shop is made in Indonesia (usually Bali). Prices of new, semi-antique, or antique sofas, beds, chests, tables, mirrors, and decorative carvings are the same as (and sometimes less than) those of new furniture in conventional stores. Gone Tropical also sells art objects, jewelry, batiks, candles, and baskets. 5 Company St. ✆ **340/773-4696.** www.gonetropical.com.

Urban Threadz   This is the most comprehensive clothing store in Christiansted's historic core, with a two-story, big-city scale and appeal. It's the store where island residents prefer to shop because of the hip, urban styles. Men's items are on the street level, women's upstairs. The inventory includes everything from Bermuda shorts to lightweight summer blazers and men's suits. The store carries Calvin Klein, Polo, and Oakley, among others. 52C Company St. ✆ **340/773-2883.**

GIFTS

Many Hands   The merchandise here includes pottery and handmade jewelry. The collection of local paintings is also intriguing, as is the year-round Christmas tree. 110 Strand St. ✆ **340/773-1990.**

Purple Papaya   This is the best place to go for inexpensive island gifts. It has the biggest array of embroidered T-shirts and sweatshirts on the island. Although you're in the Caribbean and not Hawaii, there is a large selection of Hawaiian shirts and dresses, if you're into hibiscus flowers. There's also beachwear for the whole family, plus island souvenirs. 39 Strand St., Pan Am Pavilion. ✆ **340/713-9412.**

Royal Poinciana ★   This is the most interesting gift shop on St. Croix, looking like an antique apothecary. You'll find such local items as hot sauces, seasoning blends for gumbos, island herbal teas, Antillean coffees, and a scented array of soaps, toiletries, lotions, and shampoos. There's also a selection of museum-reproduction greeting cards and calendars. Also featured are educational but fun gifts for children. 1111 Strand St. ✆ **340/773-9892.**

JEWELRY

Crucian Gold ★ 👜   This small West Indian cottage holds the gold and silver creations of island-born Brian Bishop. His most popular item is the Crucian bracelet, which contains a "true lovers' knot" in its design. Unusual items are pendants framed in gold or silver. These encase shards of china dating from the 1600s or 1700s and found along the beaches of St. Croix. The shards were once collected by island kids who called them "China money" or "chiny." Bishop claims that each pendant is "a little piece of the island's romantic history." The chiny are also incorporated into bracelets. The outlet also sells hand-tied knots (bound in gold wire), rings, pendants, and earrings. Strand St. ✆ **877/773-5241.** www.cruciangold.com.

Sonya Ltd.   Sonya Hough is the matriarch of a cult of local residents who wouldn't leave home without wearing one of her bracelets. She's most famous for her sterling silver or gold (from 14- to 24-karat) versions of her original design, the C-clasp bracelet. Locals say that if the cup of the "C" is turned toward your heart, it means you're emotionally committed; if the cup is turned outward, it means you're available. Prices range from $30 to $2,000. She also sells rings, earrings, and necklaces. 1 Company St. ✆ **877/766-9284** or 340/773-8924. www.sonyaltd.com.

PERFUME

Violette Boutique   This is a small department store, with many boutique areas carrying famous lines. Here you can get famous and exclusive fragrances and hard-to-find toiletry items, as well as the latest in Cartier, Fendi, Pequignet, and Gucci. A selection of children's gifts, Montblanc pens, and other famous brand names are sold here and found nowhere else on St. Croix (but are certainly found elsewhere in the Caribbean). In the Caravelle Arcade, 38 Strand St. ✆ **800/544-5912** or 340/773-2148.

Around the Island

If you're touring western St. Croix in or around Frederiksted, you might want to stop off at the following offbeat shops.

St. Croix LEAP ★ 👜   If you're on western St. Croix, near Frederiksted, visit St. Croix LEAP for an offbeat adventure. In this open-air shop, you can see stacks of rare and beautiful wood being fashioned into tasteful objects. This is a St. Croix Life and

Environmental Arts Project, dedicated to manual work, environmental conservation, and self-development. The end result is a fine collection of local mahogany serving boards, tables, wall hangings, and clocks. Sections of unusual pieces are crafted into functional, artistic objects.

St. Croix LEAP is 15 miles from Christiansted, 2 miles up Mahogany Road from the beach north of Frederiksted. Large mahogany signs and sculptures flank the driveway. Visitors should bear to the right to reach the woodworking area and gift shop. The site is open Monday to Friday 9am to 5pm and Saturday 10am to 5pm. Mahogany Rd., Rte. 76. ℭ **340/772-0421.**

Whim Museum Store   This unique store offers a wide selection of gifts, both imported and local. They also carry historical books, local art, and West Indian furniture. And if you buy something, your money goes to a worthy cause: the upkeep of the museum and the grounds (p. 179). There is also an associated store in downtown Christiansted, with different inventory, at 58 Queen St. (ℭ **340/713-8102**). 52 Estate Whim Plantation Museum, east of Frederiksted on Centerline Rd. ℭ **340/772-0598.**

ST. CROIX AFTER DARK

St. Croix doesn't have the nightlife of St. Thomas. To keep abreast of the newest nightspots, you might consult the publication *St. Croix This Week,* which is distributed free to cruise-ship and air passengers and is available at the tourist office.

Try to catch a performance of the **Quadrille Dancers ★★★**, a real cultural treat. Their dances have changed little since plantation days. The women wear long dresses, white gloves, and turbans, and the men wear flamboyant shirts, sashes, and tight black trousers. When you've learned their steps, you're invited to join the dancers on the floor. Ask at your hotel if and where they're performing.

Note: Women entering bars alone at night in Christiansted or Frederiksted should expect some advances from men. It is generally assumed here that a woman alone at a bar is seeking companionship and not necessarily just looking to have a drink and survey the scene. Nonetheless, women are fairly safe in bars providing they know how to deal with some leering. It is not wise to leave the bar alone and walk the lonely streets to your hotel. Take a taxi back—it's worth the investment.

The Club & Music Scene

Blue Moon ★   This hip little dive, best known as a local stop for visiting jazz musicians, is not only a good bistro but also the hottest spot in Frederiksted on Friday, when a five-piece ensemble entertains until midnight. On Sunday, a jazz trio performs. Dinner is served Tuesday to Saturday 6 to 9pm. 7 Strand St. ℭ **340/772-2222.**

The Bar Scene

The Palms   This romantic bar lies within a resort about 3 miles northwest of Christiansted (p. 161). It caters to resort guests or visitors, gay or straight. You can sit at tables overlooking the ocean or around an open-centered mahogany bar, adjacent to a gazebo. The perfect accompaniment to the night out is one of their classic tropical drinks. It's open Monday to Saturday 9am to midnight, Sunday 9am to 11pm. 4126 La Grande Princesse. ℭ **340/718-8920.**

The Casino

Divi Carina Bay Casino After much protest and controversy, this casino introduced gambling to St. Croix in 2000. Many visitors who heretofore went to such islands as Aruba for gambling now come here. The 10,000-square-foot casino boasts 20 gaming tables and 300 slot machines. No passport is needed to enter, but you do need some form of ID. In lieu of a nightclub, the casino offers nightly live music on an open stage on the casino floor. There are two bars, plus a smaller cafe-style bar where you can order light meals. It's open Monday to Thursday noon to 4am and Friday to Sunday 24 hours a day. In the Divi Carina Bay Resort (p. 148). © **340/773-7529.** www.divicarina.com.

A SIDE TRIP TO BUCK ISLAND ★★★

The crystal-clear waters and white-coral sands of **Buck Island,** a satellite of St. Croix, are legendary. Some call it the single-most-important attraction of the Caribbean. Only about a half-mile wide and a mile long, Buck Island lies 1½ miles off the northeastern coast of St. Croix. A barrier reef here shelters many reef fish, including queen angelfish and smooth trunkfish. In years past, the island was frequented by the swashbuckling likes of Morgan, Lafitte, Blackbeard, and even Captain Kidd.

Buck Island's greatest attraction is its underwater **snorkeling trails,** which ring part of the island and are maintained by the National Park Service. This 850-acre National Monument features a snorkeling trail through a forest of elkhorn coral. Equipped with a face mask, swim fins, and a snorkel, you'll be treated to some of the most beautiful underwater views in the Caribbean. Plan on spending at least two-thirds of a day at this extremely famous ecological site. Labyrinths and grottoes await scuba divers. The sandy beach has picnic tables and barbecue pits, as well as restrooms and a small changing room. There are no concessions on the island.

You can hike the trails that twist around and over the island. Circumnavigating the island will take only about 2 hours. Trails meander from several points along the coastline to the sun-flooded summit, affording views over nearby St. Croix. **Warning:** The island's western edge has groves of poisonous manchineel trees, whose leaves, bark, and fruit cause extreme irritation when they come into contact with human skin. Always bring protection from the sun's merciless rays—including a hat and sun block.

Sometimes small-boat operators trying to make an extra buck will, for a negotiated fee, run people to Buck Island from Christiansted Harbor. These services are unscheduled and likely to be available in winter only. It's best to stick to the charter companies we recommend, as they are more reliable. Nearly all charters provide snorkeling equipment and allow for 1½ hours of snorkeling and swimming. See "Fun in the Surf & Sun," earlier in this chapter, for companies in addition to the two below.

Mile Mark Watersports, in the King Christian Hotel, 59 King's Wharf, Christiansted (© **340/773-2628**), conducts two types of tours. The first option is a half-day tour aboard a glass-bottom boat departing daily from the King Christian Hotel, from 9:30am to 1pm and 1:30 to 5pm; it costs $65 per person. The second is a daily full-day tour, from 10am to 4pm, on a 40-foot trimaran for $95. Included in this excursion is a box lunch.

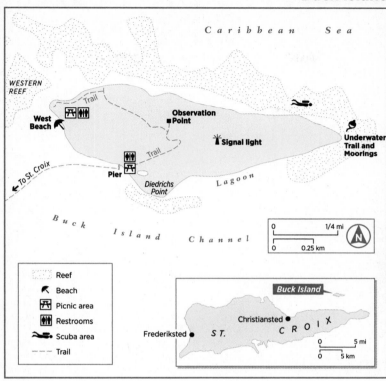

Captain Heinz (℡ **340/773-3161**) is an Austrian-born skipper with more than 25 years of sailing experience. His trimaran, *Teroro II,* leaves the Green Cay Marina "H" Dock at 9am and 2pm, never filled with more than 23 passengers. This snorkeling trip costs $65 for adults, $45 for children 11 and under. The captain is also a considerate host: He will even take you around the outer reef, which the other guides do not, for an unforgettable underwater experience.

6 THE BRITISH VIRGIN ISLANDS

The British Virgin Islands embrace 40-odd islands, some no more than just rocks or spits of land in the sea. Only three of the islands are of any significant size: Virgin Gorda (Fat Virgin), Tortola (Dove of Peace), and Jost Van Dyke. These craggy and remote volcanic islands are just 15 minutes by air or 45 minutes by ferry from St. Thomas.

With its small bays and hidden coves, once havens for pirates, the British Virgin Islands are among the world's loveliest cruising areas. The islands mainly attract those who like to sail, although landlubbers will delight in the beaches. Despite predictions that mass tourism will invade, the islands are still an escapist's paradise. The smaller islands have colorful names, such as Fallen Jerusalem and Ginger. Norman Island is said to have been the prototype for Robert Louis Stevenson's novel Treasure Island. On Deadman's Bay, Blackbeard reputedly marooned 15 pirates and a bottle of rum, giving rise to the well-known ditty.

Even though they are part of the same archipelago, the British Virgin Islands and the U.S. Virgin Islands are as different as Dame Judi Dench and Julia Roberts. U.S. islands like St. Thomas are deep into mega-resort tourism, but it's still a bit sleepy over in the B.V.I., where the pace is much slower and laid-back, and the people seem more welcoming. Even the capital, Tortola, seems to exist in a bit of a time capsule.

Most of the resorts on Virgin Gorda are so isolated from each other that you'll feel your hotel has the island to itself. For those who want to be truly remote, there is a scattering of minor hotels on a handful of the smaller islands. Peter Island has the poshest lodgings, and there are modest inns on Jost Van Dyke and Anegada. Some places are so small that you'll get to know all the locals after a week. With no casinos, no nightlife, no splashy entertainment, and often no TV, what does one do at night? Jost Van Dyke has only 150 souls but six bars. Question answered.

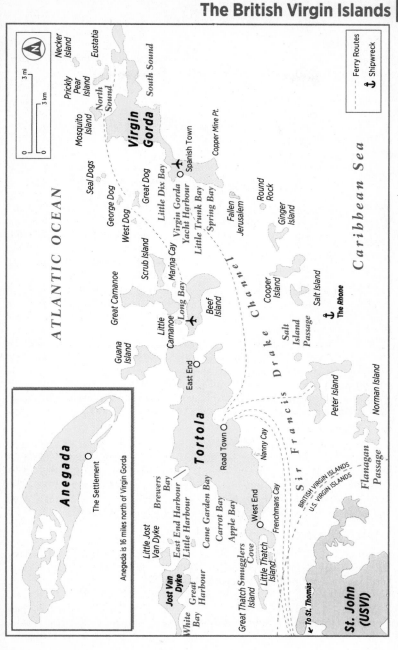

ATLANTIC OCEAN

Caribbean Sea

Ferry Routes
Shipwreck

Necker Island
Eustatia
Prickly Pear Island
Mosquito Island
North Sound
South Sound
Virgin Gorda
Seal Dogs
George Dog
West Dog
Great Dog
Little Dix Bay
Spanish Town
Copper Mine Pt.
Virgin Gorda Yacht Harbour
Little Trunk Bay
Spring Bay
Fallen Jerusalem
Round Rock
Ginger Island
Scrub Island
Marina Cay
Long Bay
Great Camanoe
Little Camanoe
Beef Island
Salt Island Passage
Cooper Island
Salt Island
The Rhone
Guana Island
East End
Drake Channel
Sir Francis
Tortola
Road Town
Nanny Cay
Peter Island
Norman Island
Flanagan Passage
Brewers Bay
Cane Garden Bay
Carrot Bay
Apple Bay
West End
Frenchmans Cay
BRITISH VIRGIN ISLANDS
U.S. VIRGIN ISLANDS
Little Jost Van Dyke
East End Harbour
Little Harbour
Jost Van Dyke
Great Harbour
White Bay
Great Thatch Island
Smugglers Cove
Little Thatch Island
To St. Thomas
St. John (USVI)

Anegada
The Settlement
Anegada is 16 miles north of Virgin Gorda

3 mi
3 km
0

ORIENTATION

Getting There

BY PLANE

Your gateway to the B.V.I. will most likely be either Tortola or Virgin Gorda. **Beef Island,** the site of the major airport serving the British Virgins, the Terrence B. Lettsome Terminal, is connected to Tortola by the one-lane **Queen Elizabeth Bridge.** Supplies and services on the other islands are extremely limited.

There are no direct flights from North America or Europe to Tortola or any of the British Virgin Islands, but you can make easy connections from St. Thomas, St. Croix, or San Juan in Puerto Rico. Beef Island, the site of the major airport serving the British Virgin Islands, is connected to Tortola by the one-lane Queen Elizabeth Bridge.

American Eagle (© 800/433-7300 in the U.S.; www.aa.com) has at least four daily flights from San Juan, Puerto Rico, to the airport at Beef Island. San Juan is serviced by dozens of daily nonstop flights from cities in North America, including Boston, Toronto, New York, Chicago, Miami, and Raleigh-Durham. You can also fly **American Airlines** (© 800/433-7300; www.aa.com) to St. Thomas, then hop on an American Eagle flight to Tortola. **Air Sunshine** (© 800/327-8900 or 284/495-8900; www.airsunshine.com) flies from San Juan or St. Thomas to Beef Island (connected to Tortola) and on to Virgin Gorda.

Currency Note

The British Virgin Islands use the U.S. dollar as their form of currency. British pounds are not accepted.

Another choice, if you're on one of Tortola's neighboring islands, is the much less reliable **LIAT** (© 888/844-5428 within the Caribbean, or 284/495-1187; www.liatairline.com). This Caribbean carrier makes short hops to Tortola from Antigua and St. Maarten in small planes not known for their careful scheduling.

Flying time to Tortola from San Juan is 30 minutes; from St. Thomas, 15 minutes; and from the most distant of the LIAT hubs (Antigua), 60 minutes.

BY BOAT

You can travel from Charlotte Amalie (St. Thomas) by public ferry to Road Town on Tortola, a 45-minute voyage. Boats making this run include **Native Son** (© 284/494-5674; www.nativesonferry.com), **Smith's Ferry Services** (© 284/495-4495; www.smithsferry.com), and **Inter-Island Boat Services** (© 284/495-4166). The latter specializes in a somewhat obscure routing—that is, from St. John to the West End on Tortola. One-way and round-trip fares range from $25 to $49.

Visitor Information

Before you go, contact the **British Virgin Islands Tourist Board,** 1270 Broadway, Ste. 705, New York, NY 10017 (© 800/835-8530 or 212/563-3117). Other branches of the **British Virgin Islands Information Office** are located at 3450 Wilshire Blvd., Ste. 1202, Los Angeles, CA 90010 (© 213/736-8931), and at 1275 Shiloh Rd., Ste. 2930, Kennesaw, GA 30144 (© 770/874-5951). In the United Kingdom, contact the **B.V.I. Information Office,** 15 Upper Grosvenor St., London W1K 7PJ (© 207/355-9585). The tourist board's official website is **www.bvitourism.com.**

SPECIAL moments IN THE BRITISH VIRGIN ISLANDS

Here are some of the best attractions the B.V.I. have to offer:

○ **Visit a Tropical Park:** If you'd like to explore mountainous landscapes that look the way they did when Christopher Columbus first landed, head to **Sage Mountain National Park** on Tortola (p. 216). Although it gets only 254 centimeters (100 in.) of rain a year, the park has the appearance of a primeval rainforest.

○ **Ponder the Mystery of the Baths:** The most celebrated site on the island of Virgin Gorda is the Baths (p. 233), on the island's southwest shore, where huge granite rocks are strewn along the beach. Granite is rarely found this far south, and according to ancient island mythology, the rocks were placed here by a race of giants. Or they were moved south by some ancient glacier. Most scientists favor the explanation that they were spewed up by volcanic activity. The important thing is not to solve the mystery but to explore the cavelike passages between the rocks and to seek out the hidden pools, which are just right for a quick dip.

○ **Explore Remote Anegada Island:** Anegada (p. 239) is easy to miss—it covers only 38 sq. km (15 sq. miles) and stands only 8.2m (26 ft.) above sea level at its highest point. Because of the treacherous coral shelf nearby, more than 300 ships have sunk just offshore. Here's the good news: The entire island is surrounded by white-sand beaches, and the population is only about 250 people, so you can often walk for miles without seeing anyone. You'll feel like a modern-day Robinson Crusoe.

○ **Exploring Deserted "Treasure Island":** Legend has it that tiny Norman Isle (p. 219), south of Tortola and east of St. John, was the inspiration for Robert Louis Stevenson's *Treasure Island*. The sea caves on this island are some of the best snorkeling spots in the British Virgin Islands. To cut costs, ask three or four other people to rent a sailboat with you to go over for a day's adventure.

Getting Around

BY BOAT

On Tortola, **Smith's Ferry** (✆ 284/495-4495; www.smithsferry.com) and **Speedy's Fantasy** (✆ 284/495-5240) operate ferry links to the Virgin Gorda Yacht Club (a 30-min. trip). The **North Sound Express** (✆ 284/495-2138), near the airport on Beef Island, has daily connections to the Bitter End Yacht Club on Virgin Gorda. **Peter Island Boat** (✆ 284/495-2000) also shuttles passengers between Road Town on Tortola and Peter Island at least seven times a day. The ferry cost for both round-trip and one-way is $20.

Did You Know . . . ?

- Richard Humphreys, a Tortola-born man, founded the first black university in the United States.
- William Thornton, a B.V.I. citizen, designed the U.S. Capitol Building.
- In 1752, the B.V.I. were the major Caribbean supplier of cotton to Britain.
- Tortola, in 1756, had 181 white men and 3,864 slaves—about 21 slaves to each planter.
- In 1831, free blacks living in the B.V.I. were accorded the full legal rights of British subjects.
- As late as 1869, the steamship *Telegrafo* was held in Tortola and officially charged with piracy.
- In 1969, the wreckage of the HMS *Nymph*, which sank off Road Town in 1783, was discovered.
- In the late 1960s, the British foreign secretary offered the B.V.I. for sale to the United States.

BY CAR, BUS, OR TAXI

There's no car-rental agencies on Virgin Gorda and Tortola; flat-fare taxis also operate on these islands, as well as on some of the smaller ones. Bus service is available on Tortola and Virgin Gorda only. See the "Orientation" section for each island for further details.

TORTOLA ★★

There's no better place to launch your own sailing adventure than in the bareboat capital of the world: Tortola, the largest (19km by 5km/12 miles by 3 miles) and most populous of the British Virgin Islands. But you don't have to be a sailor to appreciate the quiet, understated beauty of Tortola, no matter how many flocks of sails bob in the Road Town harbor. Unwind to the soft caress of trade winds, the gentle green hills that slope down to sparkling waters, and the secluded white-sand beaches and hidden coves.

Beaches Beaches are rarely crowded on Tortola. You'll have to navigate roller-coaster hills to get to the island's finest, **Cane Garden Bay,** but its fine white sand and sheltering palms are well worth the trip. **Smugglers Cove,** at the extreme western end of Tortola, is a crescent of white sand with calm turquoise waters. A favorite with locals, Smugglers Cove is also popular with snorkelers, who explore a world of sea fans, sponges, parrotfish, and elkhorn and brain corals.

Things to Do **Charter a sailboat,** if you haven't already arrived in your own boat—these are some of the world's best cruising waters—and explore the island's cays and coves by boat. Across **Drake Channel** lies **Norman Isle,** the inspiration for Robert Louis Stevenson's *Treasure Island,* for great snorkeling. No visit to Tortola is complete without a trip to **Sage Mountain National Park,** a primeval rainforest, where you can picnic while overlooking neighboring cays.

Eating & Drinking While many guests rarely dine outside their hotels, a venture out to one of the local restaurants is highly recommended. **Road Town** offers the largest concentration of cheap and authentic Caribbean eateries in the B.V.I. Be sure

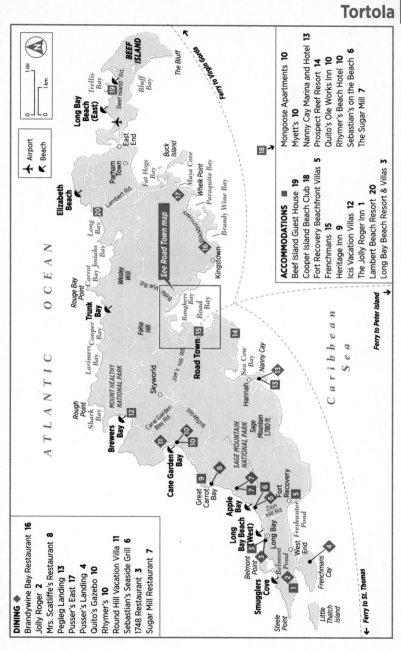

DINING ◆

Brandywine Bay Restaurant **16**
Jolly Roger **2**
Mrs. Scatliffe's Restaurant **8**
Pegleg Landing **13**
Pusser's East **17**
Pusser's Landing **4**
Quito's Gazebo **10**
Rhymer's **10**
Round Hill Vacation Villa **11**
Sebastian's Seaside Grill **6**
1748 Restaurant **3**
Sugar Mill Restaurant **7**

ACCOMMODATIONS ■

Beef Island Guest House **19**
Cooper Island Beach Club **18**
Fort Recovery Beachfront Villas **5**
Frenchmans **15**
Heritage Inn **9**
Icis Vacation Villas **12**
The Jolly Roger Inn **1**
Lambert Beach Resort **20**
Long Bay Beach Resort & Villas **3**
Mongoose Apartments **10**
Myett's **10**
Nanny Cay Marina and Hotel **13**
Prospect Reef Resort **14**
Quito's Ole Works Inn **10**
Rhymer's Beach Hotel **10**
Sebastian's on the Beach **6**
The Sugar Mill **7**

193

to sample the **roti**—Caribbean/Indian-style burritos or turnovers stuffed with curried chicken or goat, potatoes and peas, or carrots. **Rum punch** is the island cocktail of choice, but beware; it can be deceptively strong. **Conch** and **lobster** are top seafood selections.

Nightlife & Entertainment   Nightlife on Tortola is of the laid-back, **beach bar** variety; you'll have to go elsewhere for clanging casinos and big entertainment complexes. Head to a popular hangout like the **Bomba Shack** in Apple Bay—a surfside shack constructed of driftwood and broken surfboards—for rollicking full-moon parties. Steel bands and scratch bands appear regularly around **Road Town,** hammered oil drums or steel "pans" in tow. Pick up a copy of *Limin' Times,* an events listing guide, at your hotel.

Orientation

VISITOR INFORMATION

The **B.V.I. Tourist Board Office** (✆ **284/494-3134**) is in the center of Road Town near the ferry dock, south of Wickham's Cay I. Here you'll find information about hotels, restaurants, tours, and more. Pick up a copy of the *Welcome Tourist Guide,* which has a useful map of the island.

ISLAND LAYOUT

Tortola is the largest of the British Virgin Islands. Road Town is the capital, and Main Street in Road Town has many shops and restaurants. Wickham's Cay (sometimes called Wickham's Cay I) and Wickham's Cay II together form a small Inner Harbor in Road Town. This harbor takes in the Moorings complex area with Fort Burt and Prospect Reef standing near the port entrance. The cruise ship pier juts out at the far right of the cay, and passengers can stretch their "shopping legs" on land here at a number of gift shops.

GETTING THERE

Close to Tortola's eastern end is **Beef Island,** the site of the main airport for all of the British Virgin Islands. This tiny island is connected to Tortola by the one-lane Queen Elizabeth Bridge.

Taxis meet every arriving flight. Government regulations prohibit anyone from renting a car at the airport—visitors must take a taxi to their hotels. The fare from the Beef Island airport to Road Town is $15 for one to three passengers.

GETTING AROUND

The roads in Tortola are steep and twisting—not for the faint of heart. The island is fairly small, so driving distances aren't long.

BY TAXI   The best driver we've found on Tortola is O'Dean "Mr. Quick" Chalwell. What he doesn't know about his island isn't worth knowing. Call **Quick's Taxi Service** at ✆ **284/496-7127.** For other taxi options in Road Town, dial ✆ **284/494-2322;** on Beef Island, call ✆ **284/495-1982.** Your hotel can also call a taxi for you; there is a taxi stand in Road Town, near the ferry dock. A typical fare from Road Town to Cane Garden Bay is $25; from Road Town to Josiah's Bay on the north coast, it's $20.

BY BUS   It's better to use taxis, unless your budget is limited. If you wish to travel by bus, the **Scato's Bus Service** (✆ **284/494-2365**) operates from the north end of the island to the west end, picking up passengers who hail it down. The bus runs

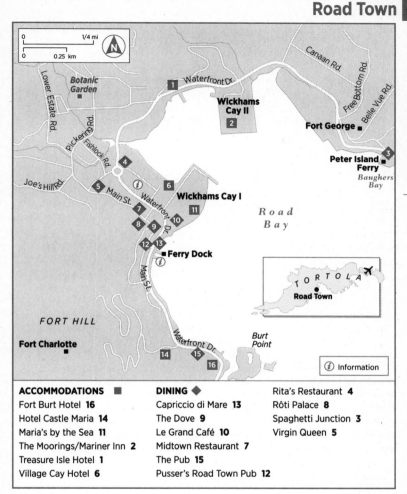

ACCOMMODATIONS ■	**DINING** ◆	Rita's Restaurant **4**
Fort Burt Hotel **16**	Capriccio di Mare **13**	Rôti Palace **8**
Hotel Castle Maria **14**	The Dove **9**	Spaghetti Junction **3**
Maria's by the Sea **11**	Le Grand Café **10**	Virgin Queen **5**
The Moorings/Mariner Inn **2**	Midtown Restaurant **7**	
Treasure Isle Hotel **1**	The Pub **15**	
Village Cay Hotel **6**	Pusser's Road Town Pub **12**	

Monday through Friday from 8am to dusk; it's most crowded in the morning when the school kids are picked up. Fares are $2 to $5.

BY CAR A handful of local companies and U.S.-based chains rent cars. **Itgo** (© **284/494-2639**) is located at 1 Wickham's Cay, Road Town; **Avis** (© **800/331-1212** in the U.S., or 284/494-2193 on Tortola; www.avis.com) maintains offices opposite police headquarters in Road Town; and **Hertz** (© **800/654-3131** in the U.S., or 284/495-4405 on Tortola; www.hertz.com) has offices outside Road Town, on the island's West End, near the ferryboat landing dock. Rental companies will usually deliver your car to your hotel. All three companies require a valid driver's license and a temporary B.V.I. driver's license, which the car-rental agency can sell to you for $10; it's valid for 3 months. Because of the volume of tourism to Tortola, you should reserve a car in advance, especially in winter.

Remember: Drive on the left. Roads are pretty well paved, but they're often narrow, winding, and poorly lit, and they have few, if any, lines. Driving at night can be tricky. It's a good idea to take a taxi to that difficult-to-find beach, restaurant, or bar.

[FastFACTS] TORTOLA

American Express The local representative is **Travel Plan, Ltd.,** located at Waterfront Drive (℡ 284/494-4000), in Road Town.

Banks Local bank branches include the **Bank of Nova Scotia** (Scotia Bank), Wickham's Cay I (℡ 284/494-2526), and **First Caribbean National Bank,** Wickham's Cay I (℡ 284/494-2171), both in Road Town. There's also a branch of **FirstBank** on Wickham's Cay I, in Road Town (℡ 284/494-2662). Each has its own ATM.

Bookstores The best bookstore is the **National Educational Services Bookstore,** Wickham's Cay I, in Road Town (℡ 284/494-3921).

Business Hours Most offices are open Monday to

Friday 9am to 5pm. Government offices are open Monday to Friday 8:30am to 4:30pm. Shops are generally open Monday to Friday 9am to 5pm and Saturday 9am to 1pm.

Dentists For dental emergencies, contact **Dental Surgery** (℡ 284/494-3274), which is in Road Town behind the police station, off Waterfront Drive.

Drugstores The best pharmacy is **Medicure Pharmacy,** Hodge Building, near Road Town Roundabout, Road Town (℡ 284/494-6189).

Emergencies Call ℡ 999. If you have a medical emergency, call **Peebles Hospital,** Porter Road, Road Town, Tortola (℡ 284/494-3497). Your hotel can also put you in

touch with the local medical staff.

Hospitals In Road Town, you can go to **Peebles Hospital,** Porter Road (℡ 284/494-3497), which has X-ray and laboratory facilities.

Internet Access If there's no Web access at your hotel, try **Data Pro,** Road Town (℡ 284/494-6633), and **Copyright Systems,** Palmgrove House, behind First Caribbean International Bank (℡ 284/494-5030).

Laundry One of the best places is **Freeman's Laundry & Dry Cleaning,** Purcell Estate, Road Town (℡ 284/494-2285).

Police The main police headquarters is on Waterfront Drive near the ferry dock on Sir Olva Georges Plaza (℡ 284/494-2945).

Where to Stay

Many of the island's hotels are small, informal, family-run guesthouses offering only the most basic amenities. Other lodgings are more elaborate, boasting a full range of resort-related facilities. None of them, however, is as big, splashy, and all-encompassing as the mega-resorts in the U.S. Virgin Islands, and many of the island's repeat visitors seem to like that just fine. Remember that all of Tortola's beaches are on the northern shore, so guests staying elsewhere (at Road Town, for example) will have to drive or take a taxi to reach them.

Note: All rates given within this chapter are subject to a 10% service charge and a 7% government tax. Rates are usually discounted significantly in summer. The term "MAP" stands for "Modified American Plan"; this means that the hotel provides breakfast and dinner (or lunch, if you prefer) for an extra charge.

IN ROAD TOWN

If you want to be near the center of all the activity (such as there is), opt for a hotel in or around Road Town. Some visitors might want to combine a night or 2 in Road Town with a few other nights in a more secluded part of the island.

Very Expensive

Frenchmans ★   This little boutique hotel has a certain chic. It is the latest reincarnation of the old Frenchman's Cay Hotel, which had become almost a landmark before it was shut down. In a dramatic renovation and under different owners, the emerging resort is far better than the older property. Standing on a 4.8-hectare (12-acre) peninsula, it is a cluster of luxurious cottages. You get some of the benefits of a larger resort, but with a lot more privacy. The hotel lies within walking distance of Soper's Hole, with its various marina services, markets, shops, and dining choices. Cottages open onto a private beach and a view of Sir Francis Drake Channel. All cottages contain full kitchens with modern appliances and accessories. The clubhouse restaurant on-site is open Monday, Wednesday and Friday, featuring set menus costing from $40 to $65.

West End, Road Town, Tortola, B.V.I. www.frenchmansbvi.com. ✆ **284/494-8811.** 9 units. Winter $380–$545 1-bedroom villa, $550–$985 2-bedroom villa; off season $305 1-bedroom villa, $470 2-bedroom villa. Rates include continental breakfast. MC, V. **Amenities:** Restaurant; bar; concierge; pool (outdoor); tennis court (lit). *In room:* A/C, ceiling fan, TV/DVD, MP3 docking station, Wi-Fi (free).

Expensive

The Moorings/Mariner Inn ★   The Moorings is a world leader in providing yacht charters, and it's been offering boating holidays for more than 40 years. You don't even have to be Bill Gates to stay here. Many visitors like the camaraderie of a bustling marina and the convivial atmosphere of its two bars where boaters meet and tell tall tales. Located right in Road Town, close to restaurants, shops, and bars, the Caribbean's most complete yachting resort is outfitted with at least 180 sailing yachts, some worth $2 million or more. This is an excellent place to stay if you want to rent your own yacht. Situated on a 3-hectare (7½-acre) property, the inn was obviously designed for yachties, offering not only support facilities and services but also shoreside accommodations. This lively spot is the place to go if you want to sample town life rather than tropical seclusion. The rooms are spacious; all the suites have kitchenettes, and most of them open onto the water. Obviously, the boaties get more attention here than the landlubbers do. The nearest beach is Cane Garden Bay, about 15 minutes away by car; you'll have to either drive there in a rental car or take a taxi.

Wickham's Cay II (P.O. Box 216), Road Town, Tortola, B.V.I. www.bvimarinerinnhotel.com. ✆ **800/535-7289** in the U.S., or 284/494-2333. Fax 284/494-1638. 38 units. Winter $220–$395 double, $340–$345 suite; off season $160–$320 double, $340–$380 suite. AE, MC, V. **Amenities:** Restaurant; 2 bars; pool (outdoor); room service; watersports equipment/rentals. *In room:* A/C, fridge, hair dryer, kitchenette (in suites), Wi-Fi (free).

Treasure Isle Hotel ★   One of Tortola's first hotels, this sprawling complex has lots of island flavor as evoked by its gingerbread-style houses around a freshwater swimming pool. It was built at the eastern edge of Road Town, 1.6km (1 mile) from the center, on 6 hectares (15 acres) of steeply inclined hillside overlooking the coastal

B.V.I. Hotels at a Glance

	Wheelchair access	A/C in bedrooms	Child-care facilities	Children are welcome	Convention facilities	Credit cards accepted	Directly beside beach	Health club
TORTOLA								
Beef Island Guest House			✓			✓		✓
Cooper Island Beach Club								✓
Fort Burt Hotel		✓	✓	✓		✓		
Fort Recovery Beachfront Villas	✓	✓	✓	✓	✓	✓	✓	✓
Frenchmans		✓				✓		
Heritage Inn		✓		✓		✓		
Hotel Castle Maria		✓	✓	✓		✓		
Icis Vacation Villas		✓		✓		✓		
The Jolly Roger Inn				✓		✓		
Lambert Beach Resort		✓	✓	✓		✓	✓	
Long Bay Beach Resort & Villas		✓	✓	✓	✓	✓	✓	✓
Maria's by the Sea		✓		✓		✓		
Mongoose Apartments			✓	✓		✓		
The Moorings/Mariner Inn	✓	✓		✓		✓		
Myett's		✓		✓		✓	✓	
Nanny Cay Marina and Hotel	✓	✓		✓			✓	
Prospect Reef Resort	✓	✓	✓	✓	✓	✓		
Quito's Ole Works Inn		✓		✓		✓	✓	
Rhymer's Beach Hotel		✓		✓		✓	✓	
Sebastian's on the Beach		✓	✓	✓		✓	✓	
The Sugar Mill Hotel	✓	✓				✓	✓	
Treasure Isle Hotel	✓	✓		✓	✓	✓		
Village Cay Hotel	✓	✓	✓	✓	✓	✓		
MARINA CAY								
Pusser's Marina Cay Resort			✓	✓		✓	✓	
VIRGIN GORDA								
Biras Creek Resort		✓				✓	✓	✓
Bitter End Yacht Club		✓	✓	✓	✓	✓	✓	✓
Fischer's Cove Beach Hotel		✓		✓		✓	✓	
Guavaberry Spring Bay Vacation Homes			✓	✓			✓	
Katitche Point Greathouse	✓	✓	✓	✓				
Leverick Bay Resort & Marina		✓	✓	✓	✓	✓	✓	
Mango Bay Resort	✓	✓		✓		✓	✓	
Nail Bay Resort		✓	✓	✓		✓	✓	✓

	Golf course nearby	Live entertainment	Marina facilities	Restaurant and/or bar	Spa facilities	Swimming pool	Tennis courts	TV in bedroom	Watersports
		✓							
								✓	
				✓		✓		✓	
				✓	✓	✓		✓	✓
				✓		✓	✓	✓	
			✓		✓				
				✓		✓		✓	
						✓		✓	
		✓	✓	✓					✓
			✓		✓	✓		✓	
		✓		✓	✓	✓	✓	✓	✓
				✓		✓		✓	✓
								✓	
			✓	✓		✓	✓	✓	✓
	✓		✓						
	✓		✓	✓		✓	✓	✓	
	✓			✓	✓	✓	✓	✓	✓
		✓		✓		✓		✓	
	✓		✓					✓	✓
		✓		✓				✓	✓
				✓		✓			✓
				✓		✓		✓	
		✓	✓	✓		✓		✓	
		✓	✓	✓					✓
	✓	✓	✓	✓	✓	✓		✓	
	✓	✓	✓		✓		✓		✓
		✓		✓					
									✓
				✓			✓		✓
		✓	✓	✓			✓	✓	✓
				✓					
				✓		✓	✓	✓	✓

B.V.I. Hotels at a Glance

	Wheelchair access	A/C in bedrooms	Child-care facilities	Children are welcome	Convention facilities	Credit cards accepted	Directly beside beach	Health club
Ocean View Hotel		✓	✓	✓		✓		
Rosewood Little Dix Bay		✓	✓	✓	✓	✓	✓	✓
Saba Rock Resort		✓				✓	✓	
Virgin Gorda Village	✓	✓	✓	✓		✓		
JOST VAN DYKE								
Sandcastle Hotel						✓	✓	
Sandy Ground Estates				✓		✓	✓	
White Bay Villas & Seaside Cottages						✓		
ANEGADA								
Anegada Beach Cottages				✓				
Anegada Reef Hotel		✓		✓		✓	✓	
PETER ISLAND								
Peter Island Resort	✓	✓	✓	✓		✓	✓	✓
GUANA ISLAND								
Guana Island Club						✓	✓	

road and a marina (not the beach). Accommodations are rented with either water or garden views. All rooms, with double or king-size beds, are designed with balconies or else private terraces on the hillside. The on-site Verandah Restaurant has been massively expanded to 250 seats and air-conditioned. The chefs serve Caribbean dishes but the menu has more of an international flair.

Pasea Estate (P.O. Box 68), Road Town, Tortola, B.V.I. www.pennhotels.com. © **284/494-2501.** Fax 284/494-2507. 65 units. Winter $249–$349 double, $399 suite; off season $199–$299 double, $349 suite. AE, DISC, MC, V. **Amenities:** Restaurant; bar; pool (outdoor); room service. In room: A/C, TV, hair dryer, Internet (free).

Moderate

Fort Burt Hotel   This is a small but special property, where guests get to know fellow guests. The staff at this inn devote much of their energy to the property's popular pub and restaurant, **The Pub** (p. 209), which is run by the New England Culinary Institute, but they also rent some very pleasant rooms. The hotel was built in 1960 on the ruins of a 17th-century Dutch fort, and is covered with flowering vines. Accommodations are set at a higher elevation than any others in Road Town, offering panoramic views from private terraces to the waterfront below. Simple, sun-flooded, and cozy, the rooms have a colonial charm and a feeling of relaxed warmth. The suite rentals are a bit expensive, but often have private pools. The regular doubles are spacious enough and have been refurbished. There's a pool on the grounds, and guests can walk to Garden Bay Beach or Smuggler's Cove Beach in just 3 minutes. The hotel's major competitor is **Fort Recovery Beachfront Villas** (p. 202), which is also built around the ruins of a sugar mill.

Golf course nearby	Live entertainment	Marina facilities	Restaurant and/or bar	Spa facilities	Swimming pool	Tennis courts	TV in bedroom	Watersports
			✓				✓	
✓		✓	✓		✓		✓	
		✓		✓	✓			
			✓	✓	✓	✓	✓	✓
			✓					✓
								✓
							✓	
							✓	
		✓						
	✓	✓	✓	✓	✓	✓		✓
			✓	✓		✓		✓

Fort Burt (P.O. Box 3380), Road Town, Tortola, B.V.I. ℂ **888/692-0993** or 284/494-2587. Fax 284/494-2002. 18 units. Winter $115–$160 double, $200–$385 suite; off season $95–$120 double, $200–$310 suite. AE, MC, V. **Amenities:** Restaurant; bar; pool (outdoor). *In room:* A/C, ceiling fans, TV, fridge, hair dryer, Wi-Fi (free).

Maria's by the Sea   This inn has long been a local favorite and attracts lots of repeat visitors attracted to its setting and its helpful, friendly staff. Right in the heart of Road Town, this hotel has a certain Caribbean charm, boasting little balconies that open right onto the harbor. At night, you can enjoy the harbor lights and the sound of the lapping waves from your balcony perch. During the day, you'll find it's a 10- to 20-minute drive to the nearest beach. The allure of the fairly minimalist bedrooms is the sea breeze that seems to blow here constantly. All units include a kitchenette, a balcony, and a small bathroom. Maria, the owner and manager, serves excellent local Caribbean cuisine at her on-site restaurant. From her famous conch chowder to her home-baked rolls fresh from the oven, dining here in the evening is a delight.

Road Town (P.O. Box 206), Tortola, B.V.I. www.mariasbythesea.com. ℂ **284/494-2595.** Fax 284/494-2420. 40 units. Winter $160–$200 double, $205 1-bedroom suite; $280 2-bedroom suite; off season $130–$170 double, $200 1-bedroom suite, $250 2-bedroom suite. AE, MC, V. **Amenities:** Restaurant; bar; pool (outdoor). *In room:* A/C, TV, fridge, Wi-Fi (free).

Village Cay Hotel ★   Yachties are often attracted to this small hotel right in the heart of Road Town, which overlooks a marina filled with boats from around the world. Set in the heart of Road Town, this is the most centrally located full-service lodging. The most expensive rooms (called "A" rooms) and the hotel restaurant open onto the marina. If you're seeking a beachfront location you'll have to look elsewhere. The "B" units are slightly smaller and don't have balconies, but are good values if you're on a budget. Anything you need is within a 5-minute walk of the premises, including ferry service to other islands, or taxi service to anywhere on Tortola. Sailing and motoring cruises can be booked directly through the hotel.

Wickham's Cay I, Road Town, Tortola, B.V.I. www.villagecayhotelandmarina.com. © **284/494-2771.** Fax 284/494-2773. 19 units. Year-round $150–$305 double, $225–$306 1- or 2-bedroom waterfront suite. Children 11 and under stay free in parent's room. AE, MC, V. **Amenities:** Restaurant; bar; pool (outdoor); room service; watersports equipment/rentals. *In room:* A/C, TV, fridge, hair dryer, Wi-Fi (free).

AROUND THE REST OF THE ISLAND
Very Expensive

Fort Recovery Beachfront Villas ★ A bit of Caribbean history is combined here with stylized accommodations opening onto a sandy beach. The complex is built around an original 17th-century Dutch fort, one of the oldest and most intact in the West Indies. Nestled in a small palm grove about 12km (7½ miles) from Road Town, this property faces the Sir Francis Drake Channel and fronts one of the best small beaches on this side of the island—it's perfect for swimming and snorkeling. Accommodations include villas and two houses, which are great for families. The large house has an art gallery hallway and a large wraparound porch. The resort has its own yoga instructor and classes are complimentary to guests, in case the sea breezes and the beach aren't relaxing enough. *Note:* If you book for 7 or more nights, dinner and a snorkeling trip are on the house.

The Towers, West End (P.O. Box 239), Road Town, Tortola, B.V.I. www.fortrecovery.com. © **800/367-8455** or 284/541-0955. Fax 284/495-4036. 30 units. Winter $310–$360 suite, $520 villa for 4, $750 villa for 6–8; off season $210–$250 suite, $360 villa for 4, from $560 villa for 6–8. Extra person $50 per night; children 11 and under $35 per night. AE, MC, V. MAP (breakfast and dinner) $45 per day. **Amenities:** Restaurant; babysitting; bikes; exercise room; pool (outdoor); watersports equipment/rentals. *In room:* A/C, TV, hair dryer, kitchenette, Wi-Fi (free).

Long Bay Beach Resort & Villas ★ For complete resort facilities, this is the premier choice. A favorite of travelers since the 1960s, this resort lies on a 2km-long (1¼-mile) sandy beach on the north shore, about 10 minutes from West End. It's a low-rise complex set in a 21-hectare (52-acre) estate. Complaints about overbuilding and problems with maintenance have marred the once-stellar reputation of this resort, but there is still much to enjoy. Accommodations include hillside rooms and studios, plus two- and three-bedroom villas complete with kitchens, living areas, and large decks with gas grills. The smallest and most basic units have simple furnishings, while the deluxe beachfront rooms and cabanas have either balconies or patios that overlook the ocean. Each unit does have an ocean view.

The two restaurants include **1748** (p. 209), built within the ruins of an old sugar mill, and the alfresco Palm Terrace, which serves a variety of local and international dishes in a more elegant and formal setting. The cuisine, especially the fresh fish, is among the finest at any hotel on the island, which is complemented by an extensive wine list.

Long Bay, Road Town, Tortola, B.V.I. www.longbay.com. © **866/237-3491** in the U.S. and Canada, or 284/495-4252. Fax 284/495-4677. 156 units. Winter $250–$395 double, $430 junior suite, $610–$900 villa; off season $195–$345 double, $375 junior suite, $570 villa. Extra person $35. Children 11 and under stay free in parent's room. MAP (breakfast and dinner) $48 per day. AE, DISC, MC, V. **Amenities:** 3 restaurants; 3 bars; babysitting; health club and spa; pool (outdoor); 2 tennis courts (lit); limited watersports; Wi-Fi (free in lobby). *In room:* A/C, TV, hair dryer, kitchen (in villas).

The Notorious Pirate: Sir Francis Drake

Sir Francis Drake (1543–96) was an English navigator and explorer famous for leading his country's defense against the Spanish Armada in 1588. He was also one of the most notorious pirates in the Caribbean. Arriving in the West Indies as the young captain of the *Judith*, this favorite of Queen Elizabeth I brought the swashbuckling attitudes of the Elizabethan Age to the Virgin Islands. Although a military hero to the English, he was a pirate to his main enemy, the Spaniards. Because of his attacks on Spanish ships, King Phillip II put a reward of 20,000 ducats on his head (or $6.5 million in today's U.S. currency). A channel through the Virgin Islands now bears his name. In 1580, Drake became the first Englishman to circumnavigate the globe. He died aboard his ship off Panama on January 27, 1596, and was buried at sea.

The Sugar Mill Hotel ★ On a 2-hecatare (5-acre) site opening onto Apple Bay, this inn combines a first-rate cuisine with intimate accommodations. Set in a lush tropical garden on the site of a 300-year-old sugar mill on the north side of Tortola, this secluded cottage colony sweeps down the hillside to its own little beach, with vibrant flowers and fruits brightening the grounds. The accommodations are contemporary and well designed, ranging from suites and cottages to studios, all with kitchenettes. The most modern addition, the Plantation House suites, relies on traditional Caribbean architectural tastes, complete with an airy porch and gingerbread detailing. Families might opt for a two-bedroom villa, or a pool suite, which has a sleeper couch.

Lunch is served down by the beach at Islands, which features standard Caribbean specialties such as jerk ribs and stuffed crab, plus burgers and salads. Dinner is offered at the acclaimed **Sugar Mill Restaurant** (p. 212).

Apple Bay (P.O. Box 425), Road Town, Tortola, B.V.I. www.sugarmillhotel.com. ℂ **800/462-8834** in the U.S., or 284/495-4355. Fax 284/495-4696. 23 units. Winter $340 double, $380 triple, $395 quad, $695 2-bedroom villa; off season $255–$275 double, $305 triple, $330–$350 quad, $275–$295 1-bedroom villa, $535–$585 2-bedroom villa. MAP (breakfast and dinner) $70 per person extra. Children 11 and under not accepted in winter, but stay free in parent's room mid-Apr to mid-Dec. AE, MC, V. Closed Aug–Sept. From Road Town, drive west 11km (6¾ miles), turn right (north) over Zion Hill, and turn right at the T-junction opposite Sebastian's; Sugar Mill is .8km (½ mile) down the road. **Amenities:** 2 restaurants; 2 bars; babysitting; concierge; pool (outdoor). *In room:* A/C, ceiling fan, TV (in some), hair dryer, Wi-Fi (free).

Expensive

Cooper Island Beach Club ★ 📖 In the northwest corner of Tortola, this mini-resort opens onto Manchioneel Bay in a setting of coconut palms. It's especially popular with certified divers, as many of the Caribbean's most celebrated dive sites are easily accessible, with all their coral gardens, canyons, and shipwrecks. This ultimate escapist's retreat is far from luxurious, but is the perfect place for those who want simplicity. This one-of-a-kind hotel lies on a hilly island on the southern tier of the Sir Francis Drake Channel, about 8km (5 miles) south of Tortola. A ferry connects the island to Road Town. Snorkelers come here for the waters at the southern end of Manchioneel Bay, and charter boaters often stop off to eat at the casual beach-front restaurant, which serves marvelous grilled fish and makes a mean conch Creole.

Outside of the occasional visits, the island slumbers in the past, with no roads and no electricity.

The midsize units come with a bedroom, living room, and kitchen, plus a balcony and bathroom with a shower that is practically outdoors. Everything in the rooms is run on rechargeable batteries. Lighting and ceiling fans are powered by 12-volt DC, and there is one 110-volt outlet in each room which can be used to recharge batteries for razors. A cistern under each room stores fresh rainwater, which is heated by solar power. All toilets are flushed with seawater. The on-site Sail Caribbean Divers offers snorkeling, kayaks, dinghy rentals, and full scuba services.

Manchioneel Bay, Road Town, Tortola, B.V.I. www.cooper-island.com. ⓒ **800/542-4624** or 284/495-9084. Fax 284/495-9180. 8 units. Winter $250 double; off season $200 double. Extra person $25. MC, V. **Amenities:** Restaurant; bar; watersports equipment/rentals. *In room:* Ceiling fan, kitchenette, no phone, Wi-Fi (free).

Heritage Inn ★ Balmy trade winds from the Caribbean blow across this .8 hectares (2 acres) of landscaped property where the owners "guarantee" 350 magnificent sunsets a year. On the northern coast nothing beats the views as witnessed from this tiny hotel, perched on top of Windy Hill. You can spot no fewer than three lovely bays, including Carrot, Apple, and Long bays, and about a dozen islands and cays, including Jost Van Dyke, Great Tobago, Green Cay, and even St. Thomas and St. John in the U.S. Virgin Islands. Bedrooms are attractively and comfortably furnished in a tropical motif, consisting of three two-bedroom suites and six one-bedroom suites, complete with a living room. Each one of the units also has a full kitchen, which helps take pressure off the fact that there is little within walking distance of the hotel and that the on-site restaurant is closed on Mondays. Beaches and swimming are only a few minutes by car down the hill. The Bananakeet Café serves a Caribbean fusion cuisine, each dish prepared to order.

> **Impressions**
>
> *Question: Where are the British Virgin Islands?*
> *Answer: I have no idea, but I should think that they are as far as possible from the Isle of Man.*
> —**Sir Winston Churchill**

Windy Hill, Tortola, B.V.I. www.heritageinnbvi.com. ⓒ **877/831-7230** or 284/494-5842. Fax 284/495-4100. 9 units. Winter $200 1-bedroom suite, $315 2-bedroom suite; off season $125 1-bedroom suite, $185 2-bedroom suite. MC, V. **Amenities:** Restaurant; bar; pool (outdoor); Wi-Fi (free). *In room:* A/C, ceiling fan, kitchen.

Lambert Beach Resort ★ ☺ Ask for a packed lunch and set out to explore the small bays and coves in the vicinity of this resort—and the day is yours. Surfing, boogie boarding, kayaking—it's all available to you. If you don't want something so active, you can always set out with a fishing rod. On the remote northeastern section of the island, this is the place for escapists who want isolation. In an amphitheater sloping to the water, the resort opens onto a .8km (½-mile) beach of white sand set against a backdrop of palm trees. To reach the resort, you'll need to rent a car or take a taxi; it's about a 15-minute car ride from Road Town. Once here, you'll find some of the B.V.I.'s best white-sand cove beaches, along with a large swimming pool. Playground facilities for children make this a family favorite.

The cottage cluster is designed in the Mediterranean style, with accommodations spread across eight one-floor structures. The preferred rooms open onto the beach, while the others front tropical gardens. The spacious bedrooms feature sand-hued walls, stained wood, ceramic-tile floors, and tropical motifs. Each comes with a private bathroom and a porch. The cottages are a combination of suites with a living room, veranda, and bedrooms.

The food here is Caribbean, but ventures into Italian, French, and international territory. The open-air restaurant is set on the beach, amid a cluster of palm trees.

Lambert Bay, East End, Tortola, B.V.I. www.lambertresort.com. *C* **284/495-2877.** Fax 284/495-2876. 38 units. Winter $169–$270 double, $400 suite; off season $120–$215 double, $300 suite. AE, DC, MC, V. **Amenities:** Restaurant; bar; pool (outdoor); watersports equipment/rentals; Wi-Fi (free in lobby). *In room:* A/C, ceiling fan, minibar.

Moderate

Mongoose Apartments An easy stroll of 3 minutes through a coconut palm grove will bring you to Cane Garden Bay, the island's best beach, where you can engage in watersports ranging from kayaking to windsurfing. Elroy and Sandra Henley, your hosts, are on hand to help you enjoy your vacation, arranging car rentals, deep-sea fishing excursions, island tours, or day sails to other islands. The reasonably priced accommodations are housed in a U-shaped, two-story building; some have an ocean view. Each of the one-bedroom apartments, although simply furnished, has a living room with a twin sleeper couch, kitchen, balcony, and ceiling fan. You'll have to rely on the office phone, as there are no phones in the rooms. Sandra grows medicinal teas, which guests are invited to try. There is a minimum stay of 3 nights.

Cane Garden Bay (P.O. Box 581), Tortola, B.V.I. www.mongooseapartments.com. *C* **284/495-4421.** Fax 284/495-9721. 6 units. Winter $198 apt for 2; off season $135 apt for 2. Extra person $68–$99. Children 16 and under $40. AE, MC, V. **Amenities:** Babysitting; Internet (free). *In room:* Ceiling fan, hair dryer, kitchen, no phone.

Myett's In lush tropical foliage, this very small Caribbean inn opens onto the island's most romantic beach. Unlike some of the remote, tranquil inns recommended, Myett's stands in a beachfront garden right near the nightlife of Cane Garden Bay, the most happening place on the island when the sun goes down (not to mention one of the best places for swimming). The spacious bedrooms have air-conditioning, tropical decor, and a king-size bed. Extras include a small fridge and wet bar. There's no need to chance the hazardous roads of Tortola at night; you can stay right on the grounds, enjoying dinner or happy hour at Myett's Garden & Grille, offering a tasty Caribbean cuisine in a lush tropical-garden setting. Try the fresh lobster or the catch of the day along with more routine offerings such as shrimp, steak, and vegetarian dishes. Good music and live entertainment are presented on weekends. Ask the bartender to make you a "Sex in the Jungle," but don't bother to ask what's in it.

Cane Garden Bay, Tortola, B.V.I. www.myettent.com. *C* **284/495-9649.** Fax 284/495-9579. 6 units. Winter $200 double; off season $130 double. AE, MC, V. **Amenities:** Restaurant; bar; Wi-Fi (free). *In room:* A/C, fridge.

Nanny Cay Marina and Hotel Don't expect the spit and polish of a resort catering to the conventional trade. The place is artfully raffish, which seems to be the way its boating clientele here want to keep it. The resort sprawls over 10 hectares (25 acres) of steamy flatlands, adjacent to a saltwater inlet that's favored because of the protection it offers boats during storms and hurricanes. Few other resorts cater as aggressively to yacht owners as Nanny Cay, a sprawling, somewhat disorganized complex where great wealth (in the form of hyperexpensive yachts) lies cheek by jowl with more modest fishing craft. This place competes with Village Cay for the boat owner or sailor; we think Village Cay is superior. Accommodations are within a two-story motel-style building, where windows overlook open-air hallways. Each unit contains a refrigerator and comfortable (albeit bland) furniture. The heart and soul of the resort is the 180-slip marina, headquarters to at least three yacht-chartering companies and permanent home to many fishing and pleasure boats. The restaurant, **Peg-leg Landing** (p. 212), is a reasonable choice for standards like steak and grilled fish.

Road Town (P.O. Box 281), Tortola, B.V.I. www.nannycay.com. © **284/494-2512.** Fax 284/494-0555. 40 units. Winter $180–$240 double, $260 suite, $200–$240 triple; off season $120–$160 double, $210 suite, $140–$180 triple. Children 11 and under stay free in parent's room. MC, V. **Amenities:** Restaurant; bar; babysitting; exercise room; pool (outdoor); tennis court (lit); watersports equipment/rentals. *In room:* A/C, TV, hair dryer, kitchenette (in some), Wi-Fi (free).

Prospect Reef Resort ★   This low-rise resort stands on 4.4 tropical hectares (11 acres) of an oceanfront estate, which boasts such features as a freshwater junior Olympic-size pool, plus all sorts of watersports, and the best selection of hotel restaurants on island, even a marina for visiting yachties. This is one of the largest resorts in the British Virgin Islands, rising above a private harbor in a compound of two-story concrete buildings scattered over a sloping, landscaped terrain. The panoramic view of Sir Francis Drake Channel from the bedrooms is one of the best anywhere, though there's no beach to speak of. All of the accommodations have private balconies or patios, and some of the larger units are suitable for families, complete with kitchenettes, living and dining areas, and separate sleeping areas. The food at the hotel's restaurant is a combination of Continental specialties and island favorites.

Drake's Hwy. (P.O. Box 104), Road Town, Tortola, B.V.I. © **800/356-8937** in the U.S., or 284/494-3311. Fax 284/494-7600. www.prospectreefbvi.com. 100 units. Winter $150–$190 double, $210–$310 suite; off season $115–$135 double, $150–$250 suite. AE, MC, V. **Amenities:** 4 restaurants; bar; babysitting; health club and spa; 2 pools (outdoor); 5 tennis courts (lit); watersports equipment/rentals; Wi-Fi (free in lobby). *In room:* A/C, ceiling fan, TV, Internet (in some; free).

Sebastian's on the Beach   On the north shore of Tortola, this casual, laid-back retreat opens right onto the sands. The water here is one of the best places in the B.V.I. for surfing action. The hotel really comes alive on weekends at the beach bar when you can dance under the stars, listening to the live music of some of Tortola's best fungi and steel bands. This hotel is located at Little Apple Bay, about a 15-minute drive from Road Town. The rooms are housed in three buildings, with only one on the beach. All come with rattan furniture and balconies or porches. You should be careful here about room selection, as accommodations vary considerably. Most sought after are the beachfront rooms, only steps from the surf; they have an airy tropical feeling, with tile floors, balconies, patios, and screened jalousies. The rear accommodations on the beach side are less desirable—not only do they lack views but they're also subject to traffic noise. Also, avoid the two noisy bedrooms above the commissary. The dozen less expensive, rather spartan rooms in the back of the main building lack views, but they're only a short walk from the beach. **Sebastian's Seaside Grill** (p. 214) overlooks the bay and has live entertainment on Saturday and Sunday.

Little Apple Bay (P.O. Box 441), West End, Tortola, B.V.I. www.sebastiansbvi.com. © **800/336-4870** in the U.S., or 284/495-4212. Fax 284/495-4466. 30 units. Winter $110–$235 double; off season $85–$135 double. MAP $50 per person extra. Children 12 and under stay free in parent's room. AE, DISC, MC, V. **Amenities:** Restaurant; bar; Wi-Fi (free in restaurant and courtyard). *In room:* A/C, TV, fridge, no phone (in some units).

Inexpensive

Beef Island Guest House 🏄 Staying at this little inn is like joining in a house party. You can sit out and chill out, enjoying the trade winds blowing in from Trellis Bay. This little B&B is on a small island reached by a bridge from Tortola. (This is the same island that the airport is on.) In a converted cottage, it offers only a handful of private rooms and a communal living room. In front is a swimming area, but a good beach lies a short walk away. The rooms are comfortable and cozy, with ceiling fans and private bathrooms with showers. All of the accommodations share a large veranda with a panoramic view of the bay. Next door is a casual beach bar and restaurant serving banana pancakes in the morning, homemade burgers at lunch, and nightly specials such as grilled fish, fried chicken, or spicy baby back ribs.

Trellis Bay, East End, Beef Island, Tortola, B.V.I. www.beefislandguesthouse.com. © **284/495-2303.** Fax 284/495-1611. 4 units. Winter $130 double; off season $100 double. Extra person $25. Rates include continental breakfast. AE, MC, V. **Amenities:** Restaurant; bar; limited watersports; Wi-Fi (free on patio). *In room:* Ceiling fan, no phone.

Hotel Castle Maria This inn sits on a hill overlooking Road Town Harbour, just a few minutes' walk from the center of Road Town. The lush, tropical garden out front is one of the most beautiful in the British Virgin Islands. An orchard produces avocados, mangos, and bananas, which guests can enjoy. Rooms are basic, but offer reasonable comfort, with balconies, patios, and kitchenettes. The hotel is a 10- to 15-minute taxi ride away from the nearest sands.

Road Town (P.O. Box 206), Tortola, B.V.I. www.castlemaria.com. © **284/494-2553.** Fax 284/494-2111. 34 units. Year-round $105–$110 double, $130 triple, $150 quad. MC, V. **Amenities:** Restaurant; bar; pool (outdoor); Wi-Fi (free). *In room:* A/C, ceiling fan, TV, fridge, kitchenette (in some).

Icis Vacation Villas In a setting planted with coconut palms, this vacation retreat stands in close proximity to Brewer's Bay Beach. The grounds are lushly landscaped. Accommodations are varied, but the best unit is a romantic honeymoon suite. A deluxe one-bedroom suite, however, has two double beds. All the units, except the villa, have both air conditioning and ceiling fans; each unit opens onto a patio or porch. These apartment units are located in a tranquil part of the island. There are no room phones, but an on-site pay phone is available.

Brewers Beach (P.O. Box 383), Tortola, B.V.I. www.icisvillas.com. © **284/494-6979.** Fax 284/494-6980. 15 units. Winter $145 efficiency, $180 1-bedroom apt, $290 3-bedroom apt, $185–$290 suite; off season $125 efficiency, $145 1-bedroom apt, $230 3-bedroom apt, $150–$230 suite. Extra person $25. Children 12 and under stay free in parent's unit. Rates include continental breakfast. AE, MC, V. **Amenities:** Restaurant; bar; babysitting; pool (outdoor); Wi-Fi (free). *In room:* A/C (in some), ceiling fans, TV, fridge, kitchenette.

The Jolly Roger Inn 🏄 In high-priced Tortola, this little inn is a haven for the frugal traveler. This small harborfront hotel is located at Soper's Hole, a breath away from the ferry dock to St. Thomas and St. John. The accommodations are clean and very simple. The small rooms are comfortably and pleasantly decorated, but only two have a private bathroom. There's no air-conditioning in some units, but all the rooms do enjoy the sea breeze. The atmosphere is fun, casual, and definitely laid-back; the restaurant is a good place for dinner (p. 214) or a night out (p. 222). The beach at Smuggler's Cove is a 20- to 30-minute walk over the hill.

West End, Tortola, B.V.I. www.jollyrogerbvi.com. © **284/495-4559.** Fax 284/495-4184. 5 units. Winter $85–$97 double without bathroom, $106 double with bathroom, $97–$109 triple without bathroom, $119 triple with bathroom; off season $67–$83 double without bathroom, $89 double with bathroom,

$79–$96 triple without bathroom, $90 triple with bathroom. AE, MC, V. Closed early Aug–Sept. **Amenities:** Restaurant; watersports equipment/rentals. *In room:* A/C (in some), no phone, Wi-Fi (free).

Quito's Ole Works Inn ★ 🎒 This hotel occupies the historic premises of a 300-year-old sugar refinery. It is a far less expensive alternative to the Sugar Mill Hotel, although it doesn't have the cuisine or the facilities of that more famed property. Still, it puts you right on the beach. It's set inland from Cane Garden Bay, and has the best musical venue on Tortola—a rustic indoor/outdoor bar called **Quito's Gazebo** (p. 213). The rooms are cramped but cozy; many rooms have water views, some with balconies. The bathrooms are all a bit too small. The most romantic unit is the large honeymoon suite in the tower. On the premises is a boutique-style art gallery showing watercolors by local artists and selling souvenirs.

The in-house bar is a magnet for fans of modern calypso music, largely because it's supervised by the hotel owner Quito (Enriquito) Rymer, who's the most famous recording star ever on Tortola. Quito himself performs Tuesday, Thursday, Saturday, and Sunday.

Cane Garden Bay (P.O. Box 560), Tortola, B.V.I. www.quitorymer.com. © **284/495-4837.** Fax 284/495-9618. 17 units. Winter $120–$165 double, $180–$235 suite; off season $100–$135 double, $155–$185 suite. Extra person $35. Children 11 and under stay free in parent's room. AE, MC, V. **Amenities:** Restaurant; bar; pool (outdoor); Wi-Fi (free in bar). *In room:* A/C, ceiling fan, TV, fridge, kitchenette (in some).

Rhymer's Beach Hotel This comfortable, unpretentious miniresort is composed of a low-slung pink building next to a white-sand beach on the island's north shore. The hotel's social center is a wide veranda where beach and bar life merge. The simple accommodations have ceiling fans, basic kitchenettes, and small bathrooms. The on-site restaurant (p. 213) is great for lobster or spareribs, and features weekly entertainment by a local steel-drum band. Music lovers can also head for the bar of the nearby Quito's Ole Works Inn (see above), where calypso star Quito Rymer performs. In winter, there's a 3-night minimum stay.

Cane Garden Bay (P.O. Box 570), Tortola, B.V.I. www.canegardenbaybeachhotel.com. © **284/495-4639.** Fax 284/495-4820. 21 units. Winter $117 double; off season $87 double. Extra person $20. AE, DC, DISC, MC, V. **Amenities:** Restaurant; Wi-Fi (free in restaurant). *In room:* A/C, ceiling fans, TV, kitchenette.

Where to Eat

Most guests dine at their hotels, but if you want to venture out, try one the suggestions below. ***Note:*** Many of the less expensive restaurants on the island serve rotis, Indian-style turnovers stuffed with such treats as potatoes and peas or curried chicken.

IN ROAD TOWN

Road Town offers the largest concentration of cheap and authentic Caribbean eateries in the B.V.I.

Expensive

The Dove ★★ FRENCH/ASIAN This is one of the best places for haute cuisine in town. You can begin by sipping a martini under the shade of the restaurant's mango tree, or else drink in a luxurious bar while listening to jazz. The small menu changes every week, but offers inventive dishes prepared from both locally grown and imported ingredients. Seafood is flown in fresh daily, and sushi and soft-shell crab appetizers appear frequently on the menu. Main-course specialties include prawns seasoned with vanilla and jalapeño peppers or a five-peppercorn steak. The chef makes his own ice cream and sorbets, and a homemade chocolate soufflé is his specialty. A champagne happy hour is staged from 5 to 7pm Tuesday to Saturday, featuring $3 champagne cocktails, and the restaurant boasts Tortola's largest wine *carte*.

67 Main St. ☎ **284/494-0313.** Reservations recommended. Main courses $19–$35. MC, V. Tues–Fri 6–11pm.

Le Grand Café FRENCH   How about a touch of Gaul in the Tropics? Islanders and visitors gather at this restaurant and bar to enjoy good French food on the outdoor patio. Delicious appetizers include Mediterranean fish soup with rouille, herring and potato salad, and Camembert flambé with Calvados. Much of the menu is classically inclined, including dishes such as snapper meunière. Especially tasty options include the almond-curried Madras chicken, the Chilean sea bass with wasabi sauce, and the yellowfin tuna in a soy-and-basil sauce. For dessert, finish off with a crème brûlée or the chocolate mousse accurately billed as "heavenly" on the menu.

Waterfront Dr. ☎ **284/494-8660.** Reservations recommended. Main courses $21–$34. MC, V. Mon–Fri noon–3pm and 7–10pm; Sat 7–10pm.

Moderate

The Pub INTERNATIONAL   This establishment attracts many of the island's yachties, as well as the local sports teams, who celebrate here after their games. More than 25 kinds of beer are available. You'll find the Pub housed in a low-slung timbered building on a narrow strip of land between the coastal road and the southern edge of Road Town's harbor. It has a barnlike interior and a rambling veranda built on piers over the water. If you're here for a meal, some of the best options include Bahamian fritters, Caesar or Greek salads, pastas, four kinds of steaks, and burgers. Locals and regulars are especially fond of the chef's jerk chicken and his combo platter of spareribs, chicken, and fried shrimp. The chef also prepares a catch of the day. Happy hour brings discounted drinks Saturday through Thursday from 5 to 7pm and on Friday, when hot wings and raw vegetable platters are offered.

In the Fort Burt Hotel (p. 200), Harbour Rd. ☎ **284/494-2608.** Reservations recommended. Main courses $19–$35. AE, MC, V. Mon–Sat 6am–10pm; Sun 5pm–midnight.

1748 Restaurant CONTINENTAL   This alfresco dining room is the beachfront restaurant of the Long Bay Beach Resort (p. 202). Invitingly casual, the much frequented deck restaurant was the site of an 18th-century sugar mill. Beginning with one of the island's most lavish breakfast buffets, it serves both lunch and dinner from a daily changing menu. On about 2 nights a week, special buffets are offered, featuring live entertainment from a local band. Try the Barbecue Cook-out or a Taste of Tortola lavish buffet of island specialties. One of the best-liked starters is a creamy seafood soup, though other diners opt for the chef's seafood salad. Baby back ribs is a specialty, prepared with the chef's secret sauce. A catch of the day, often lobster, is featured; if not, perhaps try the pan-seared red snapper. Vegetarians are also catered to, and every night the pastry chef bakes about a half-dozen luscious desserts—try his most delicious fluffy coconut lemon cake.

In the Long Bay Beach Resort, Long Bay, Road Town. ☎ **284/495-4252.** www.longbay.com. Reservations recommended. Main courses lunch $15–$30, dinner $15–$45. AE, DISC, MC, V. Daily 7:30–10am, noon–3pm, and 6:30–9pm.

Spaghetti Junction ★ ITALIAN   Boaters like this popular place. It's located just east of Road Town near several marinas, and the bar remains open long after the food service has stopped. The Italian dishes, although standard, are quite good. Chicken Parmigiana, beef Marsala, and several seafood items are featured. The *frutta di mare* (medley of seafood) is always a winner—it's served in a light cream sauce over angel-hair pasta. Other specialties include rack of lamb with garlic-laced mashed potatoes, grilled fresh snapper topped with a mango purée, and the best lobster Thermidor on the island. Look for the blackboard specials for other gems.

Baughers Bay, Road Town. ℂ **284/494-4880.** Main courses $18–$34. AE, MC, V. Mon–Sat 11am–3pm and 6–10pm. Closed Sept to mid-Oct.

Inexpensive

Capriccio di Mare ★ ITALIAN   Created in a moment of whimsy by the owners of the more upscale **Brandywine Bay Restaurant** (see below), this local favorite is small, casual, and laid-back. It's the most authentic-looking Italian cafe in the Virgin Islands. At breakfast time, many locals stop in for an Italian pastry along with a cappuccino, or even a full breakfast. If it's evening, you might try the mango Bellini, a variation of the famous champagne-based cocktail served at Harry's Bar in Venice. Begin with such appetizers as *piedini* (flour tortillas with various toppings), then move on to a selection of fresh pastas, the best pizzas on the island, or the well-stuffed sandwiches. We prefer the pizza topped with grilled eggplant. If you arrive on the right night, you might be treated to stuffed Cornish hen with scalloped potatoes.

Waterfront Dr. ℂ **284/494-5369.** Main courses $8–$18. MC, V. Mon–Sat 8am–9pm.

Midtown Restaurant CARIBBEAN   Set in the heart of Road Town, this hangout offers typical local fare. Options include curried chicken and mutton, conch soup, pea soup, boiled bull-foot soup, stewed beef ribs, jerk chicken, and chicken roti. A wide selection of fresh seafood is also on offer—specifics depend on the day's catch. Most dishes come with your choice of *fungi,* plantains, or Caribbean carrots. A good breakfast is also served here.

Main St. ℂ **284/494-2764.** Main courses $9–$14. No credit cards. Daily 7am–9pm.

Pusser's Road Town Pub CARIBBEAN/ENGLISH   Standing on the waterfront across from the ferry dock, the original Pusser's serves Caribbean fare, English pub grub, and good pizzas. This place is not as fancy as **Pusser's Landing,** in the West End (see below), nor is the food as good, but it's a lot more convenient and has faster service. The complete lunch and dinner menu includes savory English pies (*Gourmet* magazine once asked for the recipe for the chicken-and-asparagus pie) and deli-style sandwiches. John Courage ale is on draft, but the drink to order here is the famous Pusser's Rum, the same blend of five West Indian rums that the Royal Navy has served to its men for more than 300 years. Thursday is nickel-beer night.

Waterfront Dr. and Main St. ℂ **284/494-3897.** www.pussers.com. Reservations recommended. Main courses $7.95–$20. AE, DISC, MC, V. Daily 10am–11pm.

Rita's Restaurant CARIBBEAN   If you're looking for an inexpensive eatery serving local fare, stop at Rita's. The surroundings are simple, but the atmosphere is lively. Breakfast ranges from standard American fare to local favorites such as fried fish or saltfish, which is chopped up with a variety of spices and sautéed in butter. Both are served with johnnycakes. The lunch menu includes pea soup, curried chicken, and stewed mutton. Those who want a taste of the mainland can try the barbecued chicken and ribs, sandwiches, or that old standby, spaghetti and meatballs.

Round-A-Bout, Road Town. ☏ **284/494-6165.** Main courses breakfast $8–$12, lunch and dinner $10–$18. AE, MC, V. Daily 7am–10pm.

Rôti Palace CARIBBEAN   The best rotis in the British Virgin Islands are served here, right on the old main street of the island's capital—they're just as good as those in Port-of-Spain, Trinidad. This is primarily a lunch stop, although it's also a good choice for an affordable dinner or a standard breakfast. Choices (other than the famed rotis) include a wide selection of tasty vegetable, local conch, lobster, beef, and chicken dishes, many of which are spicy. Sea snails are a specialty; they're mixed with onions, garlic, and celery, spiced with curry, and served in a butter sauce. Ginger beer, juices, and wines serve as accompaniments to your meal.

Main St. ☏ **284/494-4196.** Main courses $8–$25. No credit cards. Mon–Sat 10am–6pm.

Virgin Queen CARIBBEAN/ENGLISH   This restaurant offers casual dining in a modest cinder-block building decorated with nautical pictures. The menu includes a wide spectrum of dishes ranging from local fare, such as curried chicken, to more international offerings of barbecued chicken, baby back ribs, and pastas. Included among the British specialties are shepherd's pie, bangers and mash, and a steak-and-ale pie. The portions are substantial, so wear your elastic-banded pants.

Fleming St. ☏ **284/494-2310.** Reservations recommended. Main courses lunch $7–$12, dinner $8–$23. MC, V. Mon–Fri 11am–10pm; Sat 6–10pm.

AROUND THE ISLAND
Expensive

Brandywine Bay Restaurant ★★ ITALIAN   Set on a cobblestone garden terrace along the south shore, overlooking Sir Francis Drake Channel, this is one of Tortola's most elegant and romantic restaurants. Davide Pugliese, the chef, and his wife, Cele, have earned a reputation for their outstanding Florentine fare. The skillful cooking produces dishes that range from classic to inspired. Davide changes his menu daily, based on the availability of fresh produce. The best dishes include beef carpaccio, roast duck, homemade pasta, his own special calf-liver dish (the recipe is a secret), and homemade mozzarella with fresh basil and tomatoes.

Brandywine Estate, Sir Francis Drake Hwy. ☏ **284/495-2301.** www.brandywinebay.com. Reservations and appropriate dress required. Main courses $25–$29. AE, MC, V. Mon–Sat 6:30–9:30pm. Closed Aug–Oct. Drive 5km (3 miles) east of Road Town (toward the airport) on South Shore Rd.

Mrs. Scatliffe's Restaurant ★ 🍴 WEST INDIAN   This Tortola mama offers home-cooked meals on the deck of her island home. Some of the vegetables come right from her garden, although others might be from a can. You'll enjoy excellent authentic West Indian dishes: perhaps spicy conch soup followed by curried goat, "old wife" fish (triggerfish, in this case filleted, boiled, and served with onion sauce), or chicken in a coconut shell. Service, usually from an inexperienced teenager, is not exactly efficient. Decide early in the evening if you want to enjoy dinner here, as there is only one seating and reservations must be made before 5pm. *Note:* You may be exposed to Mrs. Scatliffe's gentle preaching of her Christian faith. A Bible reading and a heartfelt rendition of a gospel song sometimes accompany a soft custard dessert.

Carrot Bay. ☏ **284/495-4556.** Fixed-price meal $35–$38. No credit cards. 1 seating daily begins 7–8pm.

Round Hill Vacation Villa ★ 🍴 CARIBBEAN   One of your most memorable meals in Tortola is likely to be eaten with Joycelyn and Allan Rhymer, who will dazzle you with a home-cooked five-course dinner. You'll get good food, made with fresh ingredients, and a warm welcome from the Rhymers. (Mr. Rhymer may even regale you with stories about Jimmy Carter and other luminaries that he's met during his hospitality career.) The villa opens onto a panoramic vista over Cane Garden Bay Beach. This is one of the best vantage points for enjoying the sinking sun, so you may want to arrive early to enjoy the view.

The menu changes every night based on market availability. Sample dishes include Cornish game hen in a fruit-flavored tropical sauce, poached mahimahi in a delectable garlic-laced lemon-butter sauce, and tender and perfectly roasted prime rib.

You must call for a reservation as early as possible, as this is a small and special place. If you're interested, there is a one-bedroom apartment here that goes for $800 a week in winter, reduced to $500 a week off season. The apartment offers a handsomely furnished bedroom with a queen-size bed, along with a sizeable eat-in kitchen and a living room with a TV.

West End, Tortola ℭ **284/495-9353.** Fax 284/495-9458. Reservations required. Fixed-price 5-course dinner $55 per person. No credit cards. Daily at 7pm.

Sugar Mill Restaurant ★ CALIFORNIA/CARIBBEAN   This transformed 3-century-old sugar mill is a romantic spot for dining. Colorful works by Haitian painters hang on the old stone walls, and big copper basins have been planted with tropical flowers. Before going to the dining room, once part of the old boiling house, visit the open-air bar on a deck that overlooks the sea. Your hosts, the Morgans, know a lot about food and wine. Some of their recipes have even been printed in *Gourmet*. One of their most popular creations, published in *Bon Appétit*, is curried banana soup. You might also begin with the roasted-pepper salad or the especially tasty wild-mushroom soup. For a main course, we recommend the pan-roasted duck breast served with Asian coleslaw and soba noodles, or the grilled fresh fish with a pineapple-pepper salsa.

In the Sugar Mill Hotel (p. 203), Apple Bay. ℭ **284/495-4355.** www.sugarmillhotel.com/restaurant. Reservations required. Main courses $26–$35. AE, MC, V. Daily 8–10am, noon–2pm, and 7–9pm. Closed Aug–Sept. From Road Town, drive west 11km (6¾ miles), turn right (north) over Zion Hill, and turn right at the T-junction opposite Sebastian's on the Beach; Sugar Mill is .8km (½ mile) down the road.

Moderate

Pegleg Landing INTERNATIONAL   This restaurant lies 2.4km (1½ miles) southwest of Road Town, overlooking the yachts of the Nanny Cay Marina. You'll find accents of stained glass, mastheads from old clipper ships, lots of rustic paneling, and a nautical theme brought to life by the views and breezes from the sea. Food is competent, but hardly exciting. Specialties include charbroiled New York strip steak with mushrooms, and fresh filets of fish, such as dolphin (again, not Flipper), swordfish, tuna, and wahoo.

At the Nanny Cay Marina and Hotel (p. 219). ℭ **284/494-0028.** Reservations required. Main courses $18–$35. AE, MC, V. Daily 11:30am–midnight.

Pusser's East CARIBBEAN/BARBECUE   Behind a protective reef at Maya Cove, you can enjoy the best ribs in the B.V.I., at least the equal of some of those served in Georgia and the Carolinas. This place has the look of an American sports bar, except for the covered porch that sprawls 30m (98 ft.) over the water. You can order from a selection of appetizers such as saltfish cakes and soups (including West Indian pumpkin). The famed barbecued Danish baby back ribs, served at both lunch and dinner, are marinated in Guinness and then perfectly grilled with the chef's

If you decide to navigate the roller coaster hills of the British Virgin Islands, head to **Cane Garden Bay,** one of the choicest pieces of real estate on the island, discovered long ago by the sailing crowd. Its white-sand beach with sheltering palms is the epitome of Caribbean charm.

Rhymer's, Cane Garden Bay (© 284/495-4639), is the place to go for food and entertainment. Skippers of any kind of craft like to stock up on supplies here, and you can order cold beer and refreshing rum drinks. If you're hungry, try the conch, lobster, black-bean gazpacho, or barbecued spareribs. The beach bar and restaurant are open daily from 8am to 9pm. Main courses cost $10 to $30. On Thursday night, a steel-drum band plays. Ice and freshwater showers are available for $3 per person (and you can rent towels). You can also rent a room here (p. 208).

secret sauce. They're so tender that the meat literally falls off the bone. If you don't want ribs for dinner, main courses include great catches from Anegada, not only lobster but also game fish, and steaks (including a juicy porterhouse) that will delight the Texan in you. For dessert, the pumpkin cheesecake is an unexpected delight.

Maya Cove, East End. © 284/495-1010. www.pussers.com/t-pussers-east.aspx. Reservations recommended. Main courses lunch $9–$16, dinner $18–$27. AE, MC, V. Daily 7am–10pm (later if business warrants it).

Pusser's Landing CARIBBEAN   This Pusser's location, opening onto the water in West End, is more desirably situated than the original Pusser's Road Town Pub. In this nautical setting, you can enjoy fresh grilled fish of the day cooked to your requirements. Begin with a hearty soup, perhaps pumpkin or freshly made seafood chowder. Many of the main courses have real island flavor, the most justifiably popular being the grilled chicken breast with fresh pineapple salsa. A classic is the curried shrimp over rice. Mud pie remains the choice dessert here, but the Key lime pie and mango soufflé beckon as well. Happy hour is daily from 5 to 7pm.

Frenchman's Cay, West End. © 284/495-4554. www.pussers.com/t-pussers-landing.aspx. Reservations required. Main courses $16–$35. AE, MC, V. Daily 11am–10pm.

Quito's Gazebo ★ 🍴 CARIBBEAN/INTERNATIONAL   This restaurant, owned by Quito Rymer, the island's most acclaimed musician, is the most popular of those located along the shore of Cane Bay. Quito himself performs after dinner several nights a week. The restaurant, which is designed like an enlarged gazebo, is set directly on the sand. Frothy rum-based drinks are the order of the day here (ask for the piña colada or the Bushwacker, made with four kinds of rum). Lunch includes sandwiches, salads, and platters. Evening meals might feature conch or pumpkin fritters, mahimahi with a wine-butter sauce, chicken roti, and steamed local mutton served with a sauce of island tomatoes and pepper. On Wednesday, for only $15, you can enjoy a buffet of barbecue ribs, chicken roti, johnnycakes, and more, from 3:30 to 5pm.

In Quito's Ole Works Inn (p. 208), Cane Garden Bay. © 284/495-4837. www.quitorymer.com. Main courses $18–$32; lunch platters, sandwiches, and salads $6–$14. AE, MC, V. Tues–Sun 11am–3pm and 6:30–9pm. Bar Tues–Sun 11am–midnight.

The peaceful Taíno Indians were the first settlers on Tortola. Perhaps they saw Columbus sail by in 1493 on his second voyage to the New World, but he didn't come ashore. Even though Sir Frances Drake arrived on the shores in 1595, it wasn't until the late 17th century that British claimed the islands. The seat of the British colony moved from Virgin Gorda to Tortola in 1741.

Inexpensive

Jolly Roger ★ SEAFOOD/INTERNATIONAL   This open-air bar and restaurant is a local favorite, and popular with sailors. Diners come for the stewed and cracked conch, unique pizzas, and great burgers, but the best thing about the Jolly Roger is the staff. Just stick your head into the kitchen and ask Wanda for one of her great omelets for breakfast (she's here for lunch, too). The house specialty is homemade Key lime pie—don't miss it. Check the schedule or call to ask about the weekend Caribbean barbecue and live entertainment, put on several nights a week.

In the Jolly Roger Inn (p. 207), West End. ✆ **284/495-4559.** www.jollyrogerbvi.com. Main courses $12–$25; pizzas from $12. AE, DISC, MC, V. Daily 8am–10pm. Closed Aug–Sept.

Sebastian's Seaside Grill INTERNATIONAL   Sebastian's is a good choice if you're in the West End area for lunch. The wooden tables and rush-bottomed chairs here are scattered, Polynesian-style, beneath a rustic yet comfortable pavilion a few feet from the waves. Sun lovers sit within the open courtyard nearby. Choices include hot sandwiches, West Indian fritters, a homemade soup of the day, and burgers—nothing special, but it's all satisfying. At night, dishes have more flair and flavor. Your best bet is the fresh fish of the day, which can be pan fried, grilled, or blackened, and is served with a choice of sauces, including a local blend of seasonings and spices. You might also try the Jamaican jerk chicken or vegetable casserole. Weekends there is a live band at dinner.

In Sebastian's on the Beach (p. 206), West End. ✆ **284/495-4212.** www.sebastiansbvi.com. Reservations required for dinner. Main courses lunch $5–$13, dinner $18–$38. AE, DISC, MC, V. Daily 7am–10:30pm.

Beaches

Tortola's wide sandy beaches are rarely crowded on Tortola, unless a cruise ship is in port. The best beaches are on the northern coast, especially Cane Garden Bay with its silky stretch of sand and gin-clear waters. Apple Bay is best for surfers, and Long Bay West is a dazzling strip of white sand running for a mile. Reached down a horrible road, riddled with pot holes, Smugglers Cove, with its palm-fringed beach, is worth the trouble to get there. **Note:** If you take a taxi to the sands, don't forget to arrange a time to be picked up.

Tortola's finest beach is **Cane Garden Bay** ★, on the aptly named Cane Garden Bay Road, directly west of Road Town. You'll have to navigate some roller-coaster hills to get there, but these fine white sands, with sheltering palm trees and gentle surf, are among the most popular in the B.V.I., and the lovely bay is many a yachtie's favorite. Outfitters here rent Hobie Cats, kayaks, and sailboards. Windsurfing is possible as well. There are seven places to eat along the beach, plus a handful of bars. Be prepared for crowds in the high season.

Surfers like **Apple Bay,** which is west of Cane Garden Bay along North Shore Road. The beach isn't very big, but that doesn't diminish activity when the surf's up. Conditions are best in January and February. After enjoying the white sands here, you can have a drink at the **Bomba Surfside Shack,** a classic dive of a beach bar at the water's edge (p. 221).

Smugglers Cove ★, known for its tranquillity and for the beauty of its sands, lies at the extreme western end of Tortola, opposite the offshore island of Great Thatch, and just north of St. John. It's a lovely crescent of white sand with calm turquoise waters. A favorite with locals, Smugglers Cove is also popular with snorkelers, who explore a world of sea fans, sponges, parrotfish, and elkhorn and brain corals. Beginning snorkelers in particular appreciate the fact that the reef is close to shore. The beach, sometimes called "Lower Belmont Bay," is located at the end of bumpy Belmont Road. Once you get here, even if you're a little worse for the wear, you'll find the crystal-clear water and the beautiful palm trees are worth the effort.

East of Cane Garden Bay, **Brewers Bay,** accessible via the long, steep Brewers Bay Road, is ideal for snorkelers and surfers. This clean, white-sand beach is a great place to enjoy walks in the early morning or at sunset. Or just sip a rum punch from the beach bar and watch the world go by. There is a campground here if you want to spend the night.

The 2km-long (1¼-mile) white-sand beach at **Long Bay West,** reached along Long Bay Road, is one of the most beautiful in the B.V.I. Joggers run along the water's edge, and spectacular sunsets make this spot perfect for romantic strolls. The Long Bay Beach Resort stands on the northeast side of the beach; many visitors like to book a table at the resort's restaurant overlooking the water.

If you'd like to escape from the crowds at Cane Garden Bay and Brewers Bay, head east along Ridge Road until you come to **Josiah's Bay Beach** on the north coast. This beach lies in the foreground of Buta Mountain. On most occasions we have found it either empty or with only a handful of bathers. If you visit in winter, beware: On many days there's a strong undertow, and there are no lifeguards.

At the very east end of the island, **Long Bay East,** reached along Beef Island Road across the Queen Elizabeth Bridge, is a great spot for swimming.

Exploring the Island

Travel Plan Tours, Romasco Place, Harbour House (P.O. Box 437), Road Town (**☏ 284/494-4000;** www.aroundthebvi.com), offers a 3½-hour tour that touches on

The B.V.I.'s Tropical Showcase

It's free and it's a gem. The **J.R. O'Neal Botanic Gardens,** Botanic Station (no phone), is a 1.6-hectare (4-acre) park in Road Town. It was created by the B.V.I. National Parks Trust and is run by local volunteers eager to show you around. The orchid house and a small rainforest are reached by crossing a charming lily pond, and other paths lead to a cactus garden and a palm grove. The aptly named flamboyant tree, with its brilliant scarlet flowers, is just one of the highlights here.

THE WRECK OF THE RHONE & OTHER TOP DIVE SITES

The one site in the British Virgin Islands that lures divers over from St. Thomas is **the wreck of the HMS _Rhone_ ★★**, which sank in 1867 near the western point of Salt Island. _Skin Diver_ magazine called it "the world's most fantastic shipwreck dive." The wreck teems with marine life and coral formations, and was featured in the 1977 movie _The Deep._

Although it's no _Rhone, **Chikuzen**_ is another intriguing dive site off Tortola. It's a 266-foot steel-hulled refrigerator ship, which sank off the island's eastern end in 1981. The hull, still intact under about 24m (79 ft.) of water, is now home to a vast array of tropical fish, including yellowtail, barracuda, black-tip sharks, octopus, and drum fish.

South of Ginger Island, **Alice in Wonderland** is a deep-dive site with a wall that begins at around 3.6m (12 ft.) and slopes gently to 30m (98 ft.). It abounds with marine life such as lobsters, crabs, rainbow-hued fan coral, and mammoth mushroom-shaped coral. **Spyglass Wall** is another offshore dive site dropping to a sandy bottom and filled with sea fans and large coral heads. The drop is from 3 to 18m (10–59 ft.). Divers here should keep an eye out for tarpon, eagle rays, and stingrays.

Blue Water Divers, Road Town (© **284/494-2847;** www.bluewater diversbvi.com), is a PADI outfitter that offers various dive packages, including one to the wreck of the _Rhone._ A resort course costs $105; a PADI open-water certification is $410.

the natural highlights of Tortola (a minimum of four participants is required). The cost is $32 to $45 per person. The company also offers 3-hour **snorkeling tours** for $64 per person (with snacks included). A full-day **sailing tour** aboard a catamaran that goes from Tortola to either Peter Island or Norman Island costs $165 per person; a full-day tour, which goes as far afield as the Baths at Virgin Gorda and includes lunch, costs $125 per person. And if **deep-sea fishing** appeals to you, book a half-day excursion, with equipment, for four fishermen and up to two "nonfishing observers" for $900, or a full-day excursion for $1,260.

A **taxi tour** of the island costs $65 for two passengers for 2 hours, or $85 for 3 hours. To call a taxi in Road Town, dial © **284/494-2322;** on Beef Island, it's © **284/495-1982.**

No visit to Tortola is complete without a trip to **Sage Mountain National Park ★**, rising to an elevation of 523m (1,716 ft.). Here, you'll find traces of a primeval rainforest, and you can enjoy a picnic while overlooking neighboring islets and cays. Covering 37 hectares (91 acres), the park protects the remnants of Tortola's original forests (those that were not burned or cleared during the island's plantation era). Go west from Road Town to reach the mountain. Before you head out, stop by the tourist office in Road Town and pick up the brochure _Sage Mountain National Park._ It has a location map, directions to the forest and parking, and an outline of the main trails through the park. From the parking lot at the park, a trail leads to the park entrance. The two main trails are the Rainforest Trail and the Mahogany Forest Trail.

Outdoor Activities

Visitors come to Tortola not for historic sights but to explore the island's natural scenery, with its rugged mountain peaks, lush foliage, and wide sandy beaches.

HORSEBACK RIDING   **Shadow's Ranch,** Todman's Estate ((C) **284/494-2262**), offers horseback rides through the national park or down to the shores of Cane Garden Bay. Call for details daily from 9am to 4pm. The cost is from $100 per hour.

SNORKELING   A good beach for snorkeling is **Brewers Bay** (p. 215). Snorkelers should also consider heading to the islet of **Marina Cay** (p. 223), or taking an excursion to or booking a room on **Cooper Island** (p. 203), across the Sir Francis Drake Channel. Limited ferry service is run by the hotel. **Blue Water Divers** (see the box "The Wreck of the *Rhone* & Other Top Dive Sites") leads expeditions to both sites. Or consider a trip to **Norman Isle** (p. 219), the fabled setting of *Treasure Island,* for its caves and protected pools.

YACHT CHARTERS   Tortola boasts the largest fleet of bareboat sailing charters in the world. The best place to get outfitted is the **Moorings,** Wickham's Cay ((C) **888/ 535-7289** in the U.S. and Canada, or 284/494-2331 in the B.V.I.; www.moorings.com). This outfit, along with a handful of others, makes the British Virgins the cruising capital of the world. You can choose from a fleet of sailing yachts, which can accommodate up to five couples in comfort and style. Depending on your nautical knowledge and skills, you can arrange a bareboat rental (with no crew) or a fully crewed rental with a skipper, staff, and a cook. Boats come equipped with a portable barbecue, snorkeling gear, dinghy, linens, and galley equipment. If you're going out on your own, you'll get a thorough briefing session on Virgin Island waters and anchorages.

If you'd like sailing lessons, consider **Steve Colgate's Offshore Sailing School** ((C) **800/221-4326**), which offers courses in seamanship year-round.

DRIVING TOUR: TORTOLA'S WEST END

START & FINISH: **Harbour Drive, in the center of Road Town.**

TIME: **2 hours, not counting stops.**

BEST TIME: **Any day before 5:30pm.**

WORST TIME: **Sunday, when many places are closed.**

This tour concentrates on Tortola's West End, site of some of the lovelier beaches and vistas. Along the north coast you'll find many of the least developed beaches, which boast such imaginative names as Apple Bay, Little Carrot and Great Carrot bays, and Ballast Bay. Stop at any of them to swim or snorkel wherever it looks safe; if in doubt, ask a local. See the "Tortola" map on p. 193.

1 Wickham's Cay

Here you'll find the densest concentration of shops and restaurants in Road Town. At first glance, Road Town seems to be a scattered sprawl of modern buildings that form a crescent along the harborfront and up the hillsides. At Wickham's Cay, however, some of the town's charm is more apparent, with its clapboard painted in bright pastel colors, shutters at the windows, and verandas gracing the facades.

6 | Driving Tour: Tortola's West End

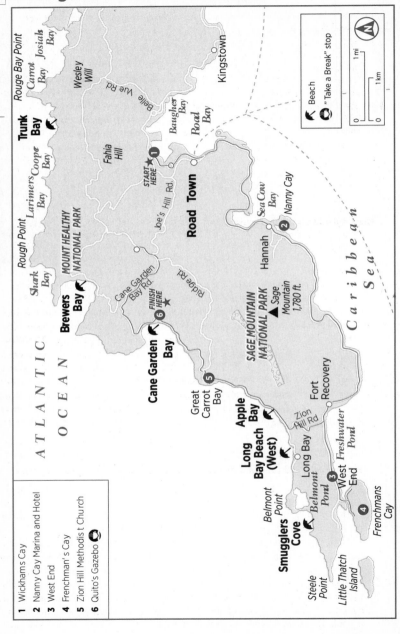

1 Wickhams Cay
2 Nanny Cay Marina and Hotel
3 West End
4 Frenchman's Cay
5 Zion Hill Methodist Church
6 Quito's Gazebo

Beach
"Take a Break" stop

ATLANTIC OCEAN

Caribbean Sea

Rouge Bay Point
Carrot Bay
Josials Bay
Wesley Will
Kingstown
Trunk Bay
Larimers Bay
Coope Bay
Rough Point
Fahia Hill
Baughers Bay
Road Bay
Belle Vue Rd.
START HERE
Road Town
Joe's Hill Rd.
Sea Cow Bay
Nanny Cay
Shark Bay
MOUNT HEALTHY NATIONAL PARK
Brewers Bay
Cane Garden Bay Rd.
Ridge Rd.
FINISH HERE
Hannah
Sage Mountain 1,780 ft.
SAGE MOUNTAIN NATIONAL PARK
Cane Garden Bay
Great Carrot Bay
Apple Bay
Fort Recovery
Long Bay Beach (West)
Long Bay
Zion Hill Rd
Freshwater Pond
West End
Belmont Point
Belmont Pond
Frenchmans Cay
Smugglers Cove
Steele Point
Little Thatch Island

1 mi
1 km

Across Drake Channel from Tortola lies **Norman Isle.** Although it used to be a pirate den with treasure ships at anchor in the 18th century, it is now deserted except by seabirds and small wild animals. Legend has it that Norman Isle was the inspiration for Robert Louis Stevenson's *Treasure Island,* first published in 1883. You can row a dinghy into the southernmost cave of the island—with bats overhead and phosphorescent patches—where Stevenson's Mr. Fleming supposedly stowed his precious treasure. Norman Isle has a series of other caves that are some of the best-known snorkeling spots in the B.V.I., teeming with spectacular fish, small octopuses, squid, and garden eels, and featuring colorful coral. Intrepid hikers climb through scrubland to the island's central ridge, Spy Glass Hill.

There is talk of making the island more accessible through regular transport, but nothing definitive has been decided. In the meantime, a private boat rental is the only way to reach Norman Isle. To cut costs, ask three or four other people to go with you. Contact **Moorings Limited,** P.O. Box 139, Road Town, Tortola (✆ **888/952-8420** or 284/494-2331; www.moorings.com). They rent 32- to 46-foot catamarans that range from $1,090 to $1,400 per day for a 3-day minimum rental. A skipper onboard is optional for an extra $200 a day. Or contact **Travel Plan Tours** (see above) about their sailing tour.

You can spend the good part of a day exploring a re-creation of a Caribbean town at Wickham's Cay II, with the West Indian–style buildings with red tin roofs. For lunch, there are various restaurants serving Caribbean cuisine and fresh seafood. Most of the activity centers on **Village Cay Center** (✆ **284/494-2711**), with slips for boats, ice for sale, a small spa, and various shops catering to yachties. From this point, sightseers can take day sails aboard the *White Squall II,* an 80-foot schooner that docks here. Also at the ferry dock is **Crafts Alive Village,** with a collection of small shops selling local crafts for the most part. There is also a colorful farmers' market every Saturday morning. Islanders sail in on boats from the neighboring islands to hawk home-grown farm products.

From Road Town, head southwest along the coastal road, passing the capital's many bars and restaurants. You'll also pass St. Paul's Episcopal Church (established in 1937) and the Faith Tabernacle Church. Less than 3.2km (2 miles) away on your left is the sandy peninsula containing:

2 Nanny Cay Marina and Hotel

There's an attractive restaurant here called **Pegleg Landing** (p. 212) and the opportunity to view some fine yachts bobbing at anchor.

Along the same road, 4km (2½ miles) southwest of Road Town, you'll get panoramic views of 8km-wide (5-mile) Sir Francis Drake Channel, which is loved by yachters throughout the world as the heart of sailing in the Virgin Islands. It is a beautiful stretch of water filled with some of the most expensive yachts in the Western Hemisphere. The white triangles of their sails against the incredible blue sea is one of the great scenic experiences in the Caribbean. Irregularly shaped islands (most of them uninhabited) appear on the south side of the channel, curving around like a pearl necklace. This expanse of uncluttered road is one of the loveliest on Tortola.

The crumbling antique masonry on the right side of the road (look through the creeping vegetation) is the ruins of a stone prison built by the English in the 18th century for pirates and unruly slaves. Lush St. John will appear across the distant channel.

Continuing on, you'll come to the unpretentious hamlet of:

3 West End

Here, you'll see the pier at Soper's Hole. Yachters and boaters report to the Immigration and Customs officer stationed here.

Turn left on the hamlet's only bridge to:

4 Frenchman's Cay

Enjoy the scenic view and, to the west, Little Thatch Island.

Retrace your route toward Road Town. At the first major intersection, turn left up Zion's Hill. Tucked into a hollow in the hillside is the:

5 Zion Hill Methodist Church

This church boasts a devoted local following, despite its rural isolation.

Continue on the road that runs along the island's northern coast, past some of its greatest beaches; you'll pass the Methodist Church of Carrot Bay and the Seventh-Day Adventist Church of Tortola.

6 Quito's Gazebo

Quito's Gazebo (p. 213; © 284/495-4837) is located at Cane Garden Bay, on the island's north coast. The owner is Quito Rymer, one of the island's best musicians. The place serves piña coladas (either virgin or laced with liberal quantities of local Callwood's rum) from an enlarged gazebo built almost directly above the waves.

Shopping

Most of Tortola's shops are on Road Town's Main Street. Unfortunately, the British Virgins have no duty-free shopping. British goods are imported without duty, though, and you can find some good buys among these imported items, especially in English china. In general, store hours are Monday to Saturday from 9am to 4pm.

You might start your shopping expedition at **Crafts Alive,** an open-air market lying in the center of Road Town and impossible to miss. It consists of a series of old-fashioned West Indian–style buildings that are stocked with crafts, ranging from Caribbean dolls to straw hats, from crocheted doilies to the inevitable B.V.I. T-shirts. Very few of these items, however, are made on the island; we noted that some, in fact, come from Panama.

In arts and crafts, you'll find higher-quality items at **Aragorn's Local Arts and Crafts Center** ★, Trellis Bay (© **284/495-1849;** www.aragornsstudio.com), a showcase for the most talented artisans on the island. "A lot of Europeans used to look down on Caribbean art," Aragorn Dick-Read once told the press. But he has worked to create a greater appreciation of Caribbean culture among visitors. Here you will find an array of copper sculptures, island prints, local art, and jewelry, including the island's best selection of handcrafted pottery. The finest of woodcarving and metalwork is also displayed here in a newly expanded studio.

Sunny Caribbee Spice Co., 119 Main St., Road Town (© **284/494-2178;** www.sunnycaribbee.com), in an old West Indian building, was the first hotel on Tortola. It's now a shop specializing in Caribbean spices, seasonings, teas, condiments, and handicrafts. With an aroma of spices permeating the air, this factory is an attraction in itself. You can buy two famous specialties here: the West Indian hangover cure and the Arawak love potion. A Caribbean cosmetics collection, Sunsations, includes herbal bath gels, island perfume, and sunscreens. There's a daily sampling of island products—perhaps tea, coffee, sauces, or dips.

Samarkand, Main Street, Road Town (© **284/494-6415**), is an unusually good bet for jewelry and other items. Look for an intriguing selection of bracelets, pins, and pendants in both silver and gold, and pierced earrings. Caribbean motifs such as palms and seabirds often appear in the designs of the jewelry.

Pusser's Company Store, Main Street and Waterfront Road, Road Town (© **284/494-2467;** www.pussers.com), has gourmet food items including meats, spices, fish, and a nice selection of wines. Pusser's Rum is one of the best-selling items here.

Arawak, on the dock at Nanny Cay (© **284/494-5240**), is known for its household furnishings, such as placemats and candleholders, but also sells sporty clothing for adults and kids, along with a selection of gifts and souvenirs.

Flamboyance, Waterfront Drive (© **284/494-4099**), is the best place to shop for perfume and upscale cosmetics.

If you've rented a villa or condo, or if your accommodations have a kitchenette, consider a visit to **Ample Hamper,** Villa Cay Marina, Wickham's Cay I, Road Town (© **284/494-2494;** www.amplehamper.com). This outlet stocks some of the best packaged food and bottled wines on the island. It also offers fresh fruit and a tasty selection of cheeses.

Philatelists from all over the world flock to the **British Virgin Islands post office,** Main Street, Road Town (© **284/494-3701,** ext. 4996), for its exquisite and unusual stamps in beautiful designs. Even though the stamps carry U.S. monetary designations, they can be used only in the B.V.I.

Tortola After Dark

Ask around to find out which hotel might have entertainment on any given evening. Steel bands and fungi or scratch bands (African Caribbean musicians who improvise on locally available instruments) appear regularly, and nonresidents are usually welcome. Pick up a copy of *Limin' Times,* an entertainment magazine that lists what's happening locally; it's usually available at hotels.

Bomba Surfside Shack, Cappoon's Bay (© **284/495-4148**), is the oldest and most memorable hangout on the island, sitting on the beach near the West End and attracting an uninhibited crowd. It's covered with Day-Glo graffiti, and odds and ends of plywood, driftwood, and abandoned rubber tires. Despite its makeshift appearance, the shack has the sound system to create a real party. Every month (dates vary), Bomba stages a full-moon party, with free house tea spiked with hallucinogenic mushrooms. (The tea is free because it's illegal to sell it, although you have to buy the cup.) Note that the drug in this tea could be dangerous to your body. If one consumes it, as hundreds of tourists do every year, it should be done with caution—or, better yet, not at all. This place is also wild on Wednesday and Sunday nights, when there's live music. It's open daily from 10am to midnight (or later, depending on business).

FOR THE island hopper

If you'd like to island hop, seeing as many of the different British Virgins as you can in a week, your best bet is to base yourself in Tortola and take day trips from there. Tortola offers the most convenient network of planes and boats for getting from one island to another.

After a couple of days spent exploring Tortola, its beaches, and nearby accessible islets, you can either fly or take the ferry over to the second-most-intriguing island of the B.V.I., Virgin Gorda, which many visitors find even more charming than Tortola. **Speedy's Fantasy** (see below), a ferry service, arrives on Virgin Gorda in time to spend a day at its fabulous Baths and returns to Tortola in the evening. A round-trip costs $30 for adults or $20 for seniors and children ages 5 to 15.

On yet another day, you can set out to explore the rugged, small, and remote island of Jost Van Dyke, taking the **New Horizons Ferry Service** (☎ 284/495-9278) from Tortola, a 25-minute trip. Spend the day at the beach and lunch at one of the local eateries, such as Foxy's, before returning to Tortola.

The final island that merits a trip is Anegada, the most northerly of the Virgins, lying 48km (30 miles) east of Tortola. Once on the island, you can visit a bird sanctuary, indulge in uncrowded beaches, and have a lobster lunch at **Cow Wreck Beach Bar & Grill** (p. 242). Instead of a ferry service (there isn't any), go by private boat or take a short flight with **Fly BVI** (☎ 284/495-1747; www.fly-bvi.com), winging to the island from the Tortola airport.

Of course, you could spend months exploring other hidden islets and tiny islands in the B.V.I. Many of these are accessible only by a private yacht or rented boat. Don't despair if you're boatless or don't have the budget to rent a yacht—if you've seen Tortola, Virgin Gorda, Jost Van Dyke, and Anegada, you will have experienced the very best of the B.V.I.

The bar at the **Moorings/Mariner Inn,** Wickham's Cay II (p. 197; ☎ 284/494-2333; www.bvimarinerinnhotel.com), is the preferred watering hole for upscale yacht owners. Interestingly, drink prices are low. Open to a view of its own marina, and bathed in a dim and flattering light, this place has a relaxed atmosphere.

Adjacent to the previously recommended Spaghetti Junction, and run by the same people, the **Bat Cave Bar** (☎ 284/494-4880; www.spaghettijunction.net/batcave.htm) is located at Baughers Bay and has a 93-sq.-m. (1,000-sq.-ft.) disco.

Other places worth a stop on a barhopping jaunt include the **Jolly Roger,** West End (p. 207; ☎ 284/495-4559; www.jollyrogerbvi.com), where you can hear local or sometimes American bands playing everything from reggae to blues. In the same area, visit **Stanley's Welcome Bar,** Cane Garden Bay (☎ 284/495-9424), where a rowdy frat-boy crowd gathers to drink, talk, and drink some more. Finally, check out **Sebastian's,** Apple Bay (p. 214; ☎ 284/495-4212), especially on Sunday, when you can dance to live music under the stars, at least in winter.

Rhymer's, on the popular stretch of beach at Cane Garden Bay (p. 208; ☎ 284/495-4639), serves up cold beer or tropical rum concoctions, along with a casual menu of ribs, conch chowder, and more. The beach bar and restaurant is open daily 8am to 9pm.

A Nearby Island: Marina Cay

Marina Cay is a private 2.4-hectare (6-acre) islet near Beef Island. It was the setting of the 1953 Robb White book *Our Virgin Island,* which was later filmed with Sidney Poitier and John Cassavetes. For 20 years after White's departure, the island lay uninhabited, until its hotel (see below) opened. That hotel was recently taken over by Pusser's, the famous Virgin Islands establishment.

The island is only 5 minutes by launch from Tortola's Trellis Bay, adjacent to Beef Island International Airport. The ferry running between Beef Island and Marina Cay is free of charge. There are no cars here. Nonguests are welcome to visit.

WHERE TO STAY & DINE

Pusser's Marina Cay Resort ★ This small cottage hotel attracts the sailing crowd—the resort can be reached only by boat. Guests stay in simply furnished double rooms, all of which overlook a reef and the islands of Sir Francis Drake Channel. Each room has a private balcony. Accommodations are set on a bluff, which provides privacy and cool breezes. There is no air-conditioning, but ceiling fans help keep the rooms cool. There's casual dining in the beachside restaurant, with a cuisine that features Continental and West Indian dishes. Activities include snorkeling, Hobie Cat sailing, scuba diving (with certification courses taught by a resident dive master), castaway picnics on secluded beaches, and kayaking.

Marina Cay (P.O. Box 626), Road Town, Tortola, B.V.I. www.pussers.com. ✆ **284/494-2174.** Fax 284/494-4775. 6 units. Winter $250 double, $525 villa; off season $185 double, $375 villa. Rates include full breakfast. AE, MC, V. **Amenities:** Restaurant; 2 bars; watersports equipment/rentals; Wi-Fi (free in courtyard). *In room:* Ceiling fans, fridge, hair dryer.

VIRGIN GORDA ★★★

The second-largest island in the British cluster, Virgin Gorda is 16km (10 miles) long and 3.2km (2 miles) wide, with a population of some 1,400 people. It's located 19km (12 miles) east of Tortola and 41km (25 miles) east of St. Thomas.

In 1493, on his second voyage to the New World, Christopher Columbus named the island Virgin Gorda, or "Fat Virgin," because the mountain on the island looked (in his opinion) like a protruding stomach.

Virgin Gorda was a fairly desolate agricultural community until Laurance Rockefeller established the resort of Little Dix here in the early 1960s, following his success with Caneel Bay on St. John in the 1950s. He envisioned a "wilderness beach," where privacy and solitude reigned. Other major hotels followed in the wake of Little Dix, but seclusion is still highly guarded and respected.

Essentials

GETTING THERE

BY BOAT **Speedy's Fantasy** (✆ 284/495-5240; www.speedysbvi.com) operates a ferry service between Road Town, on Tortola, and Virgin Gorda. Monday to Saturday, at least four ferries a day leave from Road Town; three ferries make the trip on Sunday. The cost is $20 one-way or $30 round-trip. There is also service from St. Thomas to Virgin Gorda three times a week (on Tues, Thurs, and Sat), costing $40 one-way or $70 round-trip.

You'll also find that the more luxurious resorts have their own boats to take you from the airport on Beef Island to Virgin Gorda.

GETTING AROUND

BY BUS Independently operated open-sided **safari buses** run along the main road. Holding up to 22 passengers, these buses charge upwards of $3 to $5 per person to transport a passenger, say, from the Valley to the Baths.

BY CAR If you'd like to rent a car, try one of the local firms, including **Mahogany Rentals,** the Valley, Spanish Town (✆ **284/495-5469**), across from the yacht harbor. This company has the least expensive rentals on the island, beginning at around $55 daily for a Suzuki Sidekick. Road conditions on Virgin Gorda range from good to extremely poor. *Remember:* Drive on the left.

An aerial view of the island shows what looks like three bulky masses connected by two very narrow isthmuses. The most northeasterly of these three masses (which contains two of the most interesting hotels) is not even accessible by road at all, requiring ferryboat transit from the more accessible parts of the island.

One possibility for exploring Virgin Gorda by car is to drive from the southwest to the northeast along the island's rocky and meandering spine. This route will take you to the **Baths** (in the extreme southeast), to **Spanish Harbour** (near the middle), and eventually, after skirting the mountainous edges of **Gorda Peak,** to the most northwesterly tip of the island's road system, near **North Sound.** Here, a miniarmada of infrequently scheduled ferryboats departs and arrives from Biras Creek and the Bitter End Yacht Club.

[FastFACTS] VIRGIN GORDA

American Express The local American Express representative is **Travel Plan,** Virgin Gorda Yacht Harbour (✆ **284/494-6239**).

Banks **First Caribbean Bank** (✆ **284/495-5217**) is located in Spanish Town at the Virgin Gorda Shopping Centre. It has the only ATM on the island.

Dentists & Doctors Contact **Medicure Health Center** at Spanish Town (✆ **284/495-5479**).

Drugstore Go to **Island Drug Centre** at Spanish Town (✆ **284/495-5449**).

Emergencies Call ✆ **999** or **911.**

Internet Access Go to the **Chandlery,** Yacht Harbour Marina (✆ **284/495-5628**), where the cost is $5 for the first 10 minutes, 50¢ per minute thereafter. You can also pay a flat fee of $20 per hour.

Laundry **Stevens Laundry & Dry Cleaning,** near the Virgin Gorda Yacht Harbour (✆ **284/495-5525**), is open daily 8am to noon and 1 to 9pm.

Police There is a station in the Valley at Spanish Town (✆ **284/495-7584**).

Tourist Information The island's tourist office is in Virgin Gorda Yacht Harbour, Spanish Town (✆ **284/495-5181**).

Where to Stay

The best agency for a villa rental is **Virgin Gorda Villa Rentals Ltd.,** P.O. Box 63, Leverick Bay, Virgin Gorda, B.V.I. (✆ **800/848-7081** or 284/495-7421; www.virgingordabvi.com). This company manages villas throughout the island, most of which are quite expensive. A 5-night minimum stay is required in the off season, and a 7-night minimum stay is requested in winter. The cheapest weekly rentals in winter are $850 weekly, dropping to $725 per week in summer. Most accommodations have

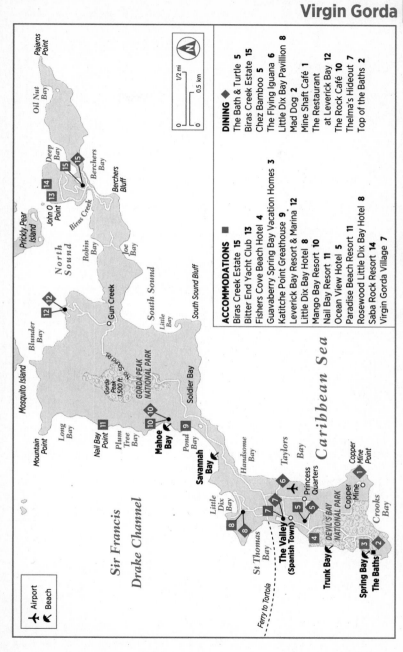

DINING ◆
The Bath & Turtle **5**
Biras Creek Estate **15**
Chez Bamboo **5**
The Flying Iguana **6**
Little Dix Bay Pavillion **8**
Mad Dog **2**
Mine Shaft Café **1**
The Restaurant
 at Leverick Bay **12**
The Rock Café **10**
Thelma's Hideout **7**
Top of the Baths **2**

ACCOMMODATIONS ■
Biras Creek Estate **15**
Bitter End Yacht Club **13**
Fishers Cove Beach Hotel **4**
Guavaberry Spring Bay Vacation Homes **3**
Katitche Point Greathouse **9**
Leverick Bay Resort & Marina **12**
Little Dix Bay Hotel **8**
Mango Bay Resort **10**
Nail Bay Resort **11**
Ocean View Hotel **5**
Paradise Beach Resort **11**
Rosewood Little Dix Bay Hotel **8**
Saba Rock Resort **14**
Virgin Gorda Village **7**

access to an outdoor pool, dining facilities, a spa, tennis courts, and extensive water-sports. Wi-Fi is free in most rentals, but not available in all locations.

VERY EXPENSIVE

Biras Creek Resort ★★★   Stay at this sophisticated, relaxing hideaway if you want to retreat from the world. You can reach the resort only by boat. This private, romantic property is the classiest place on the island. Biras Creek stands at the northern end of Virgin Gorda on a 60-hectare (148-acre) estate with its own marina, and occupies a narrow neck of land flanked by the sea on three sides. All the attractive, tropically decorated units, all suites, have well-furnished bedrooms, private patios, and garden showers. There are no TVs in the rooms, but who needs TV when you have the luxury of an oceanview veranda? Guests get their own bikes for their stay, and there are lots of hiking trails near the property. The fitness center and restaurant have also received upgrades, as well as the available watersports equipment. The resort now has several Boston Whalers boats free for guests to take for 2-hour snorkeling trips to remote coves and beaches nearby.

The hotel restaurant (p. 230) is a longtime favorite, and the open-air bar is quietly elegant. There's always a table with a view. The food has won high praise, and the wine list is excellent. A barbecued lunch is served on the beach.

North Sound (P.O. Box 54), Virgin Gorda, B.V.I. www.biras.com. ✆**877/883-0756** or 284/494-3555. Fax 284/494-3557. 31 units. Winter $850–$2,500 suite; off season $700–$1,950 suite. Rates include all meals (no drinks). Ask about packages. AE, MC, V. Take the private motor launch from the Beef Island airport, $95 per person round-trip. No children age 7 and under. **Amenities:** Restaurant; bar; babysitting; exercise room; pool (outdoor); spa; 2 tennis courts (lit); watersports equipment/rentals. *In room:* A/C, ceiling fan, TV, TV/DVD, fridge, hair dryer, MP3 docking station, Wi-Fi (free).

Bitter End Yacht Club ★★★ ☺   This place is the liveliest of the B.V.I. resorts, and is even better equipped than the more exclusive Biras Creek. It's the best sailing and diving complex in the British chain, opening onto an unspoiled, secluded deepwater harbor, accessible only by boat. Guests have unlimited use of the resort's million-dollar fleet and a complimentary introductory course at the Nick Trotter Sailing and Windsurfing School. The Bitter End has informal yet elegant accommodations in either a hillside chalet or a well-appointed beachfront or hillside villa overlooking the sound. All villas have two twins, two queen-size, or a king-size bed, plus a shower with sea views and a patio or veranda.

For something novel, stay aboard a 30-foot yacht, yours to sail, complete with dockage and daily maid service, meals in the Yacht Club dining room, and overnight provisions. Each yacht has a shower and can comfortably accommodate four.

First-rate meals are available in the Clubhouse Steak and Seafood Grille, the English Carvery, and the Pub, and entertainment is provided by a steel-drum or reggae band.

John O Point, North Sound (P.O. Box 46), Virgin Gorda, B.V.I. www.beyc.com. ✆**800/872-2392** in the U.S. for reservations, or 284/494-2746. Fax 284/494-4756. 85 units, 5 yachts. Winter (double occupancy) $700–$1,840 beachfront villa, suite, yacht, or hillside villa; off season (double occupancy) $500–$1,360 all units. Rates include all meals. AE, MC, V. Take the private ferry from the Beef Island airport, $30 per person one-way. **Amenities:** 3 restaurants; pub; babysitting; exercise room; pool (outdoor); watersports equipment/rentals. *In room:* A/C (in some), ceiling fan (in some), TV/VCR, fridge, Wi-Fi (free).

Katitche Point Greathouse ★★★ 🛍   Designed by British architect Michael Helm, this luxurious and spacious great house serves the needs of the most discerning travelers. Affording total privacy, it can be rented as a complete villa for up to 13 people, with more than 185 sq. m (1,991 sq. ft.) of living space. Sometimes six couples or one or even two families share the villa like a first-class commune. It is also possible to rent just one of the suites or the master bedroom. The villa lies just above a panoramic sweep of Mahoe Bay and its beach. This luxury vacation spot has an infinity pool, four suites, and one master bedroom, which is secluded and set apart from the rest of the villa. The main structure of the villa is shaped like a pyramid, rising three floors. All the beds are made of handcrafted teak, and are furnished with a king-size, anti-allergic mattress. A steel ladder leads to the tallest point of the villa, a "Crow's Nest" at the top of the pyramid on the third level.

Plum Bay Rd., the Valley, Virgin Gorda, B.V.I. www.katitchepoint.com. © **284/495-6274.** Fax 284/495-6275. 5 units. Year-round $5,100 double, $7,500 quad. Rates are for 3 nights. MC, V. **Amenities:** Bar; pool (outdoor); watersports equipment/rentals. *In room:* A/C, TV, hair dryer, Internet (free).

Rosewood Little Dix Bay ★★ ☺ This palace of low-key luxury is scattered along a .8km (½-mile) crescent-shaped, white-sand beach and private bay, on a 200-hectare (494-acre) preserve. Many guests find this resort too pricey and stuffy; we ourselves prefer the more casual elegance of Biras Creek Resort and the Bitter End Yacht Club, though Little Dix Bay does have an undeniably lovely setting, fine service, and an unmistakable elegance.

All rooms are surrounded by forest, and boast private terraces with views of the sea or gardens. Trade winds come through louvers and screens, and units also have ceiling fans and air-conditioning. Some units are two-story rondavels (think Tiki huts) raised on stilts to form their own breezeways. The furnishings and fabrics evoke Southeast Asia—beautiful wicker or reed furniture, bamboo beds, Balinese boxes and baskets, and ceramic objets d'art. The hotel has added two villas on an isolated stretch of white beach, each with dazzling white interiors, private pools, and alfresco dining pavilions.

The **Little Dix Bay Pavilion** (p. 231) is a romantic dinner spot on Virgin Gorda.

1km (⅔ mile) north of Spanish Town (P.O. Box 70), Virgin Gorda, B.V.I. www.littledixbay.com. © **888/767-3966** in the U.S., or 284/495-5555. Fax 284/495-5661. 100 units. Winter $725–$950 double, from $1,200 suite; off season $380–$775 double, from $875 suite. Extra person $75. AE, DISC, MC, V. Take the private ferry from the Beef Island airport, $85 per person round-trip. **Amenities:** 3 restaurants; 2 bars; babysitting; children's programs; exercise room; room service; 7 tennis courts (lit); watersports equipment/rentals. *In room:* A/C, ceiling fan, TV, TV/DVD, movie library, hair dryer, Wi-Fi ($20 per day).

EXPENSIVE

Leverick Bay Resort & Marina Set at the southern edge of the sheltered waters of Virgin Gorda's North Sound, this establishment offers a well-designed row of town house–style units on a white-sand beach. The bedrooms are pastel colored, breezy, and filled with original art. All have seafront balconies or verandas. A quartet of condo units is set in modern, red-roofed hexagons flanked on four sides by wraparound porches. The site contains a food market, an art gallery, and two small beaches (a larger beach at Savannah Bay is within a 10-min. drive). The **Restaurant at Leverick Bay** (p. 230) serves local, fresh fish at their light lunch and satisfying dinner.

North Sound (P.O. Box 63), Virgin Gorda, B.V.I. www.leverickbay.com. © **800/848-7081** in the U.S., 800/463-9396 in Canada, or 284/495-7421. Fax 284/495-7367. 14 units, 4 condos. Winter $2,023–$2,499 suite for 2 (by the week only); off season $1,666–$2,023 suite for 2 (by the week only). Extra person $36 in winter, $24 off season. AE, MC, V. **Amenities:** Restaurant; bar; pool (outdoor); tennis court (lit); watersports equipment/rentals. *In room:* A/C, ceiling fan, TV, CD player, fridge, Wi-Fi (in some; free).

Nail Bay Resort ★   Near Gorda Peak National Park, and a short walk from a trio of usually deserted beaches, this resort enjoys an idyllic position. You can enjoy some of the best sunset views of Sir Francis Drake Channel and the Dog Islands from this 59-hectare (146-acre) site. Room options are wide ranging, from deluxe bedrooms to suites, apartments, or villas. The villa community has a core of a dozen units in two structures on a hillside, with sitting areas amid old sugar mill ruins. Almost all the villas have their own pools. The most modest units are hotel-style bedrooms in the main building.

At night, Nail Bay evokes a luxury property in Asia, its landscaping highlighted by meandering stone walkways. One devotee told us that when she found the resort, it had the "terra-ultima exclusivity of Mustique, without that island's elitism."

Nail Bay (P.O. Box 69), Virgin Gorda, B.V.I. www.nailbay.com. ⓒ **800/871-3551** in the U.S., 800/487-1839 in Canada, or 284/494-8000. Fax 284/495-5875. 45 units. Winter $240–$495 double; off season $180–$395 double. AE, DISC, MC, V. **Amenities:** Restaurant; swim-up bar; babysitting; Jacuzzi; pool (outdoor); watersports equipment/rentals. *In room:* A/C, TV, DVD/VCR, hair dryer, kitchen or kitchenette, MP3 docking station, Wi-Fi ($5 per hr.).

Virgin Gorda Village ★★   This place has some of the most up-to-date accommodations on the island—a choice of luxury studios; one-, two-, and three-bedroom apartments; and two-bedroom town houses ranging from small to spacious. Surrounded by lush foliage, the complex faces the ocean, but the top floor has the most expansive views. Wide, breezy porches on each unit are another allure. The nearest and best beach lies at Savannah Bay, a 1.6km (1-mile) drive away. On-site is the Village Cafe, serving breakfast and lunch, and a commissary where you can purchase groceries.

The Valley, Virgin Gorda, B.V.I. www.virgingordavillage.com. ⓒ **284/495-5544.** Fax 284/495-5986. 26 units. Winter (minimum 2 nights) $250 studio, $265–$295 1-bedroom, $310–$425 2-bedroom, $485 3-bedroom; off season (minimum 2 nights) $180 studio, $190–$210 1-bedroom, $225–$250 2-bedroom, $320 3-bedroom. MC, V. **Amenities:** Restaurant; bar; babysitting; children's playground; health club and spa; watersports equipment/rentals; Wi-Fi (free at bar). *In room:* A/C, ceiling fans, TV, TV/DVD, hair dryer, kitchen.

MODERATE

Fischer's Cove Beach Hotel   You can basically swim from your doorstep at this group of units nestled near the sandy beach of St. Thomas Bay. Be sure to ask if the oceanfront cottages are available, as some smaller rooms are situated within a garden. Made of native stone, each of the eight cottages is self-contained, with one or two bedrooms and a combination living/dining room with a kitchenette, plus a small bathroom with a shower stall. There are also 12 pleasant but simple rooms with views of Drake Channel. Each has its own private balcony. You can stock up on provisions at a food store near the grounds.

The Valley (P.O. Box 60), Virgin Gorda, B.V.I. www.fischerscove.com. ⓒ **284/495-5252.** Fax 284/495-5280. 20 units. Winter $90–$125 double, $190–$315 studio cottage; off season $90 double, $125–$205 studio cottage. MAP (breakfast and dinner) $40 per person extra. AE, MC, V. **Amenities:** Restaurant; bar; babysitting; children's playground; watersports equipment/rentals; Wi-Fi (free in lounge). *In room:* A/C (in some), ceiling fans (in some), TV, fridge, kitchenette, no phone (in cottages).

Guavaberry Spring Bay Vacation Homes ★   Staying in one of these hexagonal, white-roofed redwood houses, all of which are built on stilts, is like living in a tree house. Screened walls with wooden blinds let in sea breezes. Each unique home has one, two, or three bedrooms with a full kitchen, dining area, and private bathroom. Each also has an elevated sun deck overlooking Sir Francis Drake Passage.

Within a few minutes of the cottage colony is the beach at Spring Bay, and the Baths. The Yacht Harbour Shopping Centre is 2km (1¼ miles) away.

Spring Bay (P.O. Box 20), Virgin Gorda, B.V.I. www.guavaberryspringbay.com. © 284/495-5227. Fax 284/495-5283. 18 units. Winter $235 1-bedroom house, $300 2-bedroom house; off season $150 1-bedroom house, $200 2-bedroom house. Extra person $25. No credit cards. **Amenities:** Babysitting; watersports equipment/rentals; Wi-Fi ($2 per half-hour). In room: A/C (in some), ceiling fans, fridge, kitchen, no phone.

Mango Bay Resort ★ 🦐   This compound of eight villas is set on lushly landscaped grounds overlooking the scattered islets of Drake's Channel, on the island's western shore. You get good value for your money here. The accommodations are the most adaptable on the island—doors can be locked or unlocked to divide each villa into as many as four independent units. Costs vary with the proximity of your unit to the beach. Interiors are stylish yet simple, often dominated by the same turquoise as the seascape in front of you. There are also two large villas, with four or five bedrooms available only on a weekly basis.

Mahoe Bay (P.O. Box 1062), Virgin Gorda, B.V.I. www.mangobayresort.com. © 284/495-5672. Fax 284/495-5674. 26 units. Winter $195–$355 studio, $275–$595 1-bedroom unit, $415–$995 2-bedroom unit, $645–$1,150 beachfront suite, $695 2-bedroom beachfront villa; off season $150–$220 studio, $205–$360 1-bedroom unit, $310–$580 2-bedroom unit, $440 beachfront suite, $580 2-bedroom beachfront villa. MC, V. **Amenities:** Restaurant; bar; pool (private villas only); limited watersports. In room: A/C, kitchen.

Saba Rock Resort ★ 🏨   This is an idyllic retreat, perched on its own small cay and reached by a free ferry. Yachties arrive on their private vessels. It is the ultimate escapist retreat. Built by local craftsmen, the island was owned for 3 decades by Bert Kilbride, the Caribbean's most legendary diver. Queen Elizabeth herself named him "Receiver of Wrecks," because he discovered some 90 shipwrecks in and around the B.V.I. His scuba-diving "resort course," created in the 1960s, is now taught around the world. Bert died in 2008 at the age of 93, and the island's new owners decided to turn his former private island into this rather luxurious compound of 1- and 2-bedroom suites.

Just under .4 hectares (1 acre) in size, this laid-back boutique hotel offers tranquillity and privacy in an area ideal for swimming, sailing, or exploring. Furnishings are minimal and tasteful, with a breakfast of island fruits and fresh-baked pastries served in an "over-the-water" dining room. Honeymooners prefer the Mustique House set in the back of the island. You can dine on-site, sampling steaks grilled to order, succulent pastas, and local seafood. Saba Rock has its own nautical museum with shipwreck artifacts accumulated by Bert.

P.O. Box 67, Saba Rock, North Sound, Virgin Gorda, B.V.I. www.sabarock.com. © 284/495-7711. Fax 284/495-7373. 9 units. Year-round $175–$225 double, $195–$375 quad. DC, MC, V. **Amenities:** Restaurant; bar; watersports equipment/rental. In room: A/C, TV, fridge, kitchenette (in some), MP3 docking station, Wi-Fi (free).

INEXPENSIVE

Ocean View Hotel ☺   This cinder-block building is definitely no frills, although it is conveniently located near a shopping center and the Virgin Gorda Marina, and is only a 15-minute walk from the beach. The rooms are clean and simply furnished, often done in pastels with two single beds or a double bed. All are equipped with a small bathroom. Children are welcome, and babysitting can be arranged. The rooms are on the second floor, with a long porch, and downstairs is an inexpensive restaurant. There's also a garden in back.

Spanish Town, across from the marina. ☎ **284/495-5230.** Fax 284/495-5262. 12 units. Winter $85–$100 double; off season $75–$90 double. DISC, MC, V. **Amenities:** Restaurant; bar; babysitting, Internet (free). *In room:* A/C, ceiling fan, TV.

Where to Eat

Many of the island's best restaurants are located in secluded resorts, accessible only by boat or resort ferry. Be sure to call ahead to find how to reach your desired table.

VERY EXPENSIVE

Biras Creek Resort ★★ INTERNATIONAL   With even better cuisine than that of Little Dix Bay Pavilion (see below), this hilltop restaurant is our longtime island favorite, and for good reason. The resort hires the island's finest chefs, who turn out superb cuisine based on quality ingredients. The prix-fixe menu changes every night, but the panoramic view of North Sound doesn't. A recent sampling of the appetizers turned up such delights as five-spice duck salad, followed by a main course of pan-seared salmon wrapped in Parma ham in a lentil-cream sauce, and grilled grouper with an herby couscous. The chef's special, grilled lobster, is featured Sunday and Wednesday nights. Desserts are prepared fresh, and are likely to range from a chilled green-apple parfait to a choice of sorbets served with a chilled cantaloupe soup.

In Biras Creek Resort (p. 226), North Sound. ☎ **284/494-3555.** www.biras.com. Reservations required. Fixed-price dinner $85–$125. AE, MC, V. Seatings daily 6:30–9pm.

EXPENSIVE

Chez Bamboo ★ 🎁CAJUN   This is the closest approximation to a New Orleans supper club in the B.V.I. Located within a 5-minute walk north of the yacht club, the building features a big veranda. Inside, there's a wraparound mural showing a jazz band playing within a forest of bamboo; bamboo artifacts continue the theme. Owner Rose Giacinto and Chef Joyce Rodriguez concoct superb dishes, including conch gumbo, Nassau grouper *en papillote*, and New Orleans–style strip steak covered with a creamy Worcestershire sauce. Desserts such as apple *crostini* and crème brûlée are among the very best on the island. Live music, usually blues or jazz (of course), is presented every Friday night on the terrace.

Next to the Virgin Gorda Yacht Harbour, Spanish Town. ☎ **284/495-5752.** Reservations recommended. Main courses $23–$46. AE, MC, V. Daily 4–10pm.

The Restaurant at Leverick Bay CONTINENTAL   A combined restaurant and beach bar, this is today's version of the old Pusser's, which now operates only a store here. During the day, you can enjoy all sorts of light meals for reasonable prices, including croissant sandwiches, burgers, fried snapper, and pizza. There's also a children's menu. At night, the menu is more ambitious, featuring such intriguing appetizers as roasted pumpkin soup made with island-grown pumpkins and a splash of truffle oil. The chicken satay served with a spicy peanut dipping sauce is also enticing. The chef's specialty is a tender and slow-roasted prime rib of beef with mashed potatoes and fresh vegetables. The ahi tuna, with a tangy wasabi-and-sweet-soy sauce, is full of aromatic flavor. If it's featured, you might opt for the grilled wahoo, caught in local waters, marinated in lime, and served with West Indian rice and fresh vegetables.

In the Leverick Bay Resort (p. 227), North Sound. ☎ **284/495-7154.** www.therestaurantatleverickbay.com. Reservations recommended. Lunch $9–$19; pizzas from $16; dinner $25–$50. MC, V. Daily 9am–midnight.

Moderate

The Flying Iguana WEST INDIAN   The owner of this place, Puck (aka Orling-ton Baptiste), studied his craft in Kansas City, with the Hilton Group, before setting up this amiable restaurant overlooking the airport's landing strip and the sea. Potted hibiscus and lots of effigies of iguanas, stuffed and carved, ornament a room that's a celebration of West Indian mystique. The house drink is the Iguana Sunset, a concoc-tion whose secret ingredients change according to the whim of the bartender. What-ever the recipe, it usually produces a lightheaded effect that goes well with the carefully conceived cuisine. Examples are not limited to combinations of fresh fish and shellfish, including calamari, shrimp, scallops, and conch: You'll also find steak, chicken, and lamb, seasoned in a way that evokes both the Caribbean and the Medi-terranean. Happy hour is from 4 to 6pm daily.

The Valley, at the airport. ✆ **284/495-5277.** www.flyingiguanabvi.com. Reservations recommended. Main courses breakfast $7–$15, lunch and dinner $12–$36. MC, V. Daily 6:30am–9pm.

Little Dix Bay Pavilion ★ INTERNATIONAL   The most romantic of the dining spots on Virgin Gorda, this pavilion is our preferred choice at this deluxe resort, which also operates Sugar Mill Restaurant. Guests (most middle-aged and well heeled) sit under a large thatched roof as trade winds breeze in through open doors. The chefs change the menu daily. Although many of the ingredients are shipped in frozen, especially meats, there is much that is fresh and good. The seafood keeps us return-ing again and again. Specialties include grilled halibut, seared snapper, and broiled lobster served with steamed broccoli in butter sauce with roasted almonds. Most dishes are at the lower end of the price range.

In Rosewood Little Dix Bay hotel (p. 226), 1km (⅔ mile) north of Spanish Town. ✆ **284/495-5555.** www.littledixbay.com/dine2.cfm. Reservations required. Main courses $20–$36. AE, MC, V. Daily 8–10:30am, noon–3pm, and 6–9:30pm.

Mine Shaft Café AMERICAN   Near Copper Mine Point, this little bistro draws diners who like a panoramic view, affordable prices, and well-prepared food. Count yourself lucky if you arrive for one of those all-you-can-eat Caribbean-style barbecues staged at least once a month. Locals flock to the cafe on those nights for a riotous party time. The catch of the day is usually your best bet, and it can be grilled to your specifications. The chef also turns out succulent steaks and some zestily flavored baby back ribs. Fresh lobster is also a feature, as is grilled shrimp. Throughout the day you can drop in for sandwiches and juicy burgers.

Copper Mine Point, the Valley. ✆ **284/495-5260.** http://mineshaftbvi.com. Reservations not needed. Sandwiches and burgers $7–$16; main courses $19–$34. AE, DC, MC, V. Mon–Thurs 5–10pm; Fri–Sun noon–10pm.

The Rock Café ★ ITALIAN/CARIBBEAN   Nestled among the rocks between the Baths and Spanish Town, this cafe with an adjoining piano bar is the place to go if you want to make an evening of it. The restaurant opens onto a big open terrace for moonlit dining. The chef cooks authentic Italian cuisine, and the food is superb in spite of the reliance on a lot of imported ingredients. Fresh locally caught fish is your best bet. Start with the tropical lobster salad with fresh fruit and grated ginger, or yellow fin tuna carpaccio with citrus vinaigrette. If it's featured, go for the fresh baked lobster brought in from the neighboring island of Anagada and served with cognac butter. Other mains include grilled swordfish in a basil sauce or some of the best pasta dishes in the B.V.I., especially the *fettuccine al salmon,* in a creamy sauce flavored with red pepper, parsley, and vodka. The island's best pizzas emerge piping hot from the oven, including a white pie with four different types of cheeses.

At the Mango Bay Resort (p. 229). ☏ **284/495-5482.** www.bvidining.com. Reservations recommended. Main courses $21–$39; pizzas $18–$26. AE, MC, V. Daily 4pm–9am.

Top of the Baths CARIBBEAN   This aptly named green-and-white restaurant overlooks the famous Baths, and has a patio with a swimming pool. Locals gather here to enjoy the food they grew up on. At lunch, you can order an array of appetizers, including conch fritters, sandwiches, and salad plates. At night, the kitchen turns out good home-style fresh fish, lobster, chicken, steaks, and West Indian dishes. Look for one of the daily specials. And save room for a piece of that rum cake. Live steel bands perform on Sunday, and you're invited to swim in the pool either before or after dining.

The Baths. ☏ **284/495-5497.** Dinner $23–$40; sandwiches and salads $12–$18. AE, MC, V. Daily 9am–10:30pm.

INEXPENSIVE

The Bath & Turtle INTERNATIONAL   At the end of the waterfront shopping plaza in Spanish Town sits the most popular pub on Virgin Gorda, packed with locals during happy hour, from 4:30 to 6:30pm. There are indoor and courtyard tables. Even if you're not hungry, you might want to join the regulars over midmorning mango coladas or peach daiquiris. If you're hungry, you can order fried fish fingers, tamarind-ginger wings, very spicy chili, or daily seafood specials such as conch fritters. There's live music every Wednesday and Friday night.

Virgin Gorda Yacht Harbour, Spanish Town. ☏ **284/495-5239.** Reservations recommended. Breakfast $7–$16; main courses lunch $10–$19, dinner $10–$24. AE, MC, V. Daily 7am–9pm.

Mad Dog SANDWICHES   This is the most skillful and charming reconstruction of a West Indian cottage on Virgin Gorda. The wide veranda and the brightly painted 19th-century wooden timbers and clapboards create a cozy and convivial drink-and-sandwich bar. The piña coladas are absolutely divine. The founder of this laid-back place was London-born Colin McCullough, a self-described "mad dog" who sailed the British Virgin Islands for almost 30 years before establishing his domain here. He has since departed for Mad Dog heaven, but his little dive still flourishes.

The Baths, the Country. ☏ **284/495-5830.** Sandwiches $5–$8.50. No credit cards. Daily 10am–6pm.

Thelma's Hideout ★ 🏠 CARIBBEAN   Mrs. Thelma King, one of the most outspoken grande dames of Virgin Gorda (who worked in Manhattan for many years before returning to her native B.V.I.), runs this convivial gathering place for the island community. It's located in a concrete house with angles softened by ascending tiers of verandas. Food choices include steamed and grilled fish, fish filets, and West Indian stews of pork, mutton, goat, or chicken. Limeade and *mauby* are available, but many stick to rum or beer. Live music is presented on Saturday nights in winter, and every other Saturday off season. You have to call ahead to see if they are doing dinner.

The Valley. ☏ **284/495-5646.** Reservations required prior to 3pm for dinner. Main courses lunch $8–$12, dinner $18–$25. No credit cards. Daily 8:30–10am, 11:30am–2:30pm, and 6:30–8pm. Bar daily 8am–9pm.

Exploring the Island

The northern side of Virgin Gorda is mountainous, with Gorda Peak reaching 417m (1,368 ft.), the highest spot on the island. In contrast, the southern half of the island is flat, with large boulders appearing at every turn.

If you're over for a day trip, the best way to see the island is to call **Andy Flax** at the Fischer's Cove Beach Hotel. He runs the **Virgin Gorda Tours Association** (© 284/495-5252; www.virgingordatours.com), which will give you a tour of the island from $55 to $220 for one or two persons, adding $15 to $30 per person more depending on the group size. You can be picked up at the ferry dock if you give 24-hour notice.

FUN IN THE SURF & SAND

HITTING THE BEACH   The best beaches are at the **Baths** ★★, where giant boulders form a series of tranquil pools and grottoes flooded with seawater. Nearby snorkeling is excellent, and you can rent gear on the beach. Scientists think the boulders were brought to the surface eons ago by volcanic activity. The Baths and surrounding areas are part of a proposed system of parks and protected areas in the B.V.I. The protected area encompasses 273 hectares (675 acres) of land, including sites at Little Fort, Spring Bay, and Devil's Bay on the east coast.

Devil's Bay National Park can be reached by a trail from the Baths. A 15-minute walk through boulders and dry coastal vegetation ends on a secluded coral-sand beach.

Neighboring the Baths is **Spring Bay,** one of the best of the island's beaches, with white sand, clear water, and good snorkeling. **Trunk Bay** is a wide, sandy beach reachable by boat or along a rough path from Spring Bay.

Savannah Bay is a sandy beach north of the yacht harbor, and **Mahoe Bay,** at the Mango Bay Resort, has a gently curving beach with neon-blue water.

DIVING   **Kilbrides Sunchaser Scuba** is located at the Bitter End Yacht Club at North Sound (© 800/932-4286 in the U.S., or 284/495-9638; www.sunchaser scuba.com). Kilbrides offers the best diving in the British Virgin Islands, at 15 to 20 dive sites, including the wreck of the ill-fated HMS *Rhone*. Prices range from $100 to $110 for a two-tank dive on one of the coral reefs. A one-tank dive in the afternoon costs $75. Equipment, except wet suits, is supplied at no charge. Hours are 7:45am to 5:30pm daily.

HIKING   Consider a trek up the stairs and hiking paths that crisscross Virgin Gorda's largest stretch of undeveloped land, the **Gorda Peak National Park.** To reach the best departure point for your uphill trek, drive north of the Valley on the only road leading to North Sound for about 15 minutes of very hilly driving (using a four-wheel-drive vehicle is a very good idea). Stop at the base of the stairway leading steeply uphill. There's a sign pointing to the Gorda Peak National Park.

It will take between 25 and 40 minutes to reach the summit of Gorda Peak, the highest point on the island, where views out over the scattered islets of the Virgin Islands archipelago await you. There's a tower at the summit, which you can climb for even better views. Admire the flora and the fauna (birds, lizards, and nonvenomous snakes) en route. Because the vegetation you'll encounter is not particularly lush, wear protection against the sun. Bring a picnic—tables are scattered along the hiking trails.

Shopping

There isn't much here. Your best bet is the **Virgin Gorda Craft Shop** at Yacht Harbour (© 284/495-5137), which has some good arts and crafts, especially straw items. Some of the more upscale hotels have boutiques, notably the Bitter End Yacht Club's **Reeftique** (© 284/494-2745), with its selection of sports clothing, including sundresses and logo wear. You can also purchase a hat here for protection from the sun. You might also check out **Island Silhouette in Flax Plaza** (no phone), located in Flax Plaza near Fischer's Cove Beach Hotel (p. 228), which has a good selection of resort-style clothing that's been hand-painted by local artists. **Pusser's Company Store,** Leverick Bay (② 284/495-7369), sells rum products, sportswear, and gift and souvenir items. **Tropical Gift Collections,** the Baths (② 284/495-5380), is a good place to shop for local crafts. Here you'll find island spices, bags, T-shirts, wraps, jewelry, maps, and pottery on sale at good prices.

Virgin Gorda After Dark

There isn't a lot of action at night, unless you want to make some of your own. **The Bath & Turtle** pub, at Yacht Harbour (p. 232; ② 284/495-5239), brings in local bands for dancing in the summer on Wednesday and Friday at 8:30pm. **The Bitter End Yacht Club** (② 284/494-2746; www.beyc.com) has live music on Fridays. Accessible only by boat, this is the best bar on the island. With its dark wood, it evokes an English pub and even serves British brews. Call to see what's happening at the time of your visit, and see p. 226 for more on the resort.

Andy's Chateau de Pirate, at the Fischer's Cove Beach Hotel, the Valley (p. 228; ② 284/495-5252), is a sprawling, sparsely furnished local hangout. It has a simple stage, a very long bar, and huge oceanfront windows, which almost never close.

JOST VAN DYKE

This 10-sq.-km (4-sq.-mile) rugged island (pop. 150) on the seaward (west) side of Tortola was named after a Dutch settler. In the 1700s, a Quaker colony settled here to develop sugar-cane plantations. (One of the colonists, William Thornton, won a worldwide competition to design the Capitol in Washington, D.C.) Smaller islands surround this one, including Little Jost Van Dyke, the birthplace of Dr. John Lettsom, founder of the London Medical Society.

On the south shore are some good beaches, especially at **White Bay** and **Great Harbour.** The island has a handful of places to stay but offers several dining choices, as it's a popular stopover point not only for the yachting set but also for many cruise ships. Jost Van Dyke is very tranquil, but only when cruise ships aren't in port.

Essentials

GETTING THERE   Take the ferry to White Bay on Jost Van Dyke from either St. Thomas or Tortola. (**Be warned:** Departure times can vary widely throughout the year, and often don't adhere very closely to the printed timetables.) Ferries from St. Thomas depart from Red Hook Friday, Saturday, and Sunday, usually twice daily. A round-trip is $40, while one-way is $30. More convenient (and more frequent) are the daily ferryboat shuttles from Tortola's isolated West End. The latter depart five times a day for the 25-minute trip, and the round-trip cost is $20 for adults, $10 for children 12 and under. Call the **New Horizon Ferry Service Paradise Express** (② 284/495-9278; www.bestofbvi.com) for information about departures from any of the above-mentioned points. If all else fails, negotiate a transportation fee with one of the handful of privately operated water taxis on Tortola. Fees start around $100 one-way.

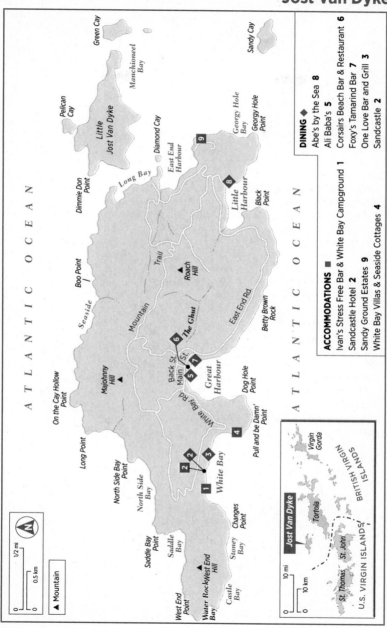

DINING ◆

Abe's by the Sea 8
Ali Baba's 5
Corsairs Beach Bar & Restaurant 6
Foxy's Tamarind Bar 7
One Love Bar and Grill 3
Sandcastle 2

ACCOMMODATIONS ■

Ivan's Stress Free Bar & White Bay Campground 1
Sandcastle Hotel 2
Sandy Ground Estates 9
White Bay Villas & Seaside Cottages 4

In His Footsteps: William Thornton (1759–1828)

This multitalented architect and inventor was also a painter, an author of medical books (especially on methods to teach the deaf to read), and a fervent abolitionist. But he is remembered best as the designer of the U.S. Capitol Building in Washington, D.C.

o **Birthplace:** Jost Van Dyke, B.V.I.
o **Residences:** Jost Van Dyke, B.V.I.; London, England; and Washington, D.C.
o **Resting Place:** Congressional Cemetery, Washington, D.C.

GETTING AROUND   To get around the island, call **Bun Taxi** at © **284/495-9281.** Only two places on Jost Van Dyke rent jeeps—**Abe's by the Sea** (© **284/495-9329**) at $65 to $80 per day and **Paradise Jeep Rentals** (© **284/495-9477**) at $55 to $70 per day.

FAST FACTS   In a medical emergency, call **VISAR (Virgin Islands Search and Rescue)** at © **284/494-4357;** you can be flown to Tortola. There are no banks, ATMs, or drugstores on the island. Stock up before you arrive here.

Where to Stay

Ivan's Stress Free Bar & White Bay Campground   A seventh-generation native of Jost Van Dyke, Ivan Chinnery runs this campground, featuring a choice of campsites, equipped tent sites wired for electricity, and one-room "cabins" made of plywood and furnished with screens, ceiling fans, refrigerators, large beds, and access to showers and flush toilets. Amenities include food service, a communal kitchen, drinking water, picnic tables, and a public phone. Located on the east end of White Bay Beach, this place is simplicity itself, but it's also the most happening place on the island. Locals and yachties gather in Ivan's Stress Free Bar at happy hour, enjoying sundowners as the wafting aroma of dinner emerges from the communal kitchen. Evening sing-alongs are a tradition. The big jam night is Saturday; Thursday is the well-attended barbecue night. Ivan, who plays guitar in the Ever Changing All Star International Band (the house band), is the island's top guitar player. Visiting musicians often drop in—yes, even Keith Richards or Jimmy Buffet.

White Bay Beach, Jost Van Dyke, B.V.I. www.ivanscampground.com. © **284/495-9358.** 8 cabins, 15 campsites, 5 tents. Year-round $65–$75 cabin, $40 tent, $20 bare site, $150–$260 studio. MC, V. **Amenities:** Food service. *In room:* TV (in some), TV/DVD (in some), fridge (in some), no phone, Wi-Fi ($10).

Sandcastle Hotel   A retreat for escapists who want few neighbors and absolutely nothing to do, these six cottages are surrounded by flowering shrubbery and bougainvillea, and have panoramic views of a white-sand beach. Bedrooms are spacious, light, and airy, furnished in local art, rattan furnishings, daybeds, and king-size beds. Two units are air-conditioned, while the others have ceiling fans. You mix your own drinks at the beachside bar, the Soggy Dollar, and keep your own tab. Visiting boaters often drop in to enjoy the beachside informality and order a drink called the Painkiller. The restaurant (see below) is an old standard on the island and presents a candlelit beachside dinner on Saturdays. A line in the guest book proclaims, "I thought places like this only existed in the movies."

White Bay Beach, Jost Van Dyke, B.V.I. www.soggydollar.com/sandcastlehotel. © **284/495-9888.** Fax 284/495-9999. 6 units. Winter $265–$295 double; off season $190–$230 double. Extra person $35–$45.

3-night minimum. Children 15 and under not permitted. MC, V. **Amenities:** Restaurant; bar; watersports equipment/rentals. *In room:* A/C (in some), ceiling fan, no phone, Wi-Fi (free).

Sandy Ground Estates   These self-sufficient apartments are along the edge of a beach on a 7-hectare (17-acre) hill site on the eastern part of Jost Van Dyke. The complex rents two- and three-bedroom villas. One of the best accommodations is constructed on a cliff, and seems to hang about 25m (82 ft.) over the beach. The airy villas, each privately owned, are fully equipped with refrigerators and stoves. The interiors vary widely, from rather fashionable to bare bones, but all have ceiling fans. The living space is generous, and extras include private balconies or terraces. The managers help guests with boat and watersports rentals. Diving, day sails, and other activities can be arranged, and there are dinghies available. The rates quoted are for 1 week.

Sandy Ground Estate, Jost Van Dyke, B.V.I. www.sandyground.com. ℂ **284/494-3391.** Fax 284/495-9379. 7 units. Winter $1,950 villa for 2; off season $1,400 villa for 2. Extra person $500 per week in winter, $350 off season. MC, V. Take a private water taxi from Tortola or St. Thomas. **Amenities:** Watersports equipment/rentals. *In room:* Ceiling fan, kitchenette, no phone, Wi-Fi (free).

White Bay Villas & Seaside Cottages ★ 🎒   With its panoramic view of the sea and ready access to the beach, this is a real discovery for couples or larger groups seeking a first-rate, secluded retreat. Perched above the sea, all the cottages were built by owner John Klein, who first visited the island in 1976. He fell in love, as most do, and built his own villa here. Eventually, Klein expanded the property to include several different accommodations options ranging from one- to two-bedroom houses to a three-bedroom, three-bathroom villa accommodating up to eight guests. The most desirable is the Plantation Villa, the largest in the complex, with a great room and kitchen decorated with original murals depicting the island's culture.

Sandy Ground Estate, Jost Van Dyke, B.V.I. www.jostvandyke.com. ℂ **800/778-8066** or 410/571-6692. Fax 410/571-6693. 3 villas, 7 cottages. Weekly rates: winter $1,995 1-bedroom, $3,045 2-bedroom, $4,095 3-bedroom; off season $1,595 1-bedroom, $2,435 2-bedroom, $3,275 3-bedroom. No credit cards. *In room:* Ceiling fan, TV, kitchen.

Where to Eat

Abe's by the Sea WEST INDIAN   Sailors are satisfied with a menu of fish, lobster, conch, ribs, and chicken at this local bar and restaurant. Prices are low, and it's money well spent. With each main course you also get peas, rice, and coleslaw.

Little Harbour. ℂ **284/495-9329.** Reservations recommended for groups of 5 or more. Dinner $24–$50; nightly barbecue $30. MC, V. Daily 9am–11pm.

Ali Baba's ★ 🎒 CARIBBEAN   Built of rustic-looking beams and unvarnished planks, this restaurant welcomes diners and drinkers to a breeze-flooded veranda near the edge of the harbor, immediately adjacent to the Customs house. Inside, you're likely to meet Ali Baba himself (a member of the Baba family). Menu items focus on fresh grilled wahoo, kingfish (served with butter and braised onions), tuna, and snapper. Other dishes include lobster, West Indian conch, lime-garlic shrimp, and barbecued ribs or chicken. Drinks of choice include Painkillers and rum punches, but lots of the boat owners who come here seem to prefer beer—the colder, the better. If you're on the island in time for breakfast, drop in to join the locals for a tasty wake-up meal and what one visitor called "damn good coffee."

Great Harbour. ℂ **284/495-9280.** Breakfast from $10; main courses lunch $9–$12, dinner $18–$22. AE, DISC, MC, V. Daily 9am–11pm.

The answer to your problem might be the famous Painkiller, which got its start at the Soggy Dollar Bar and has gone on to greater glory at all Pusser's outlets. An Englishwoman, Daphne Henderson, is said to have invented the drink in the 1980s, which is an orange-colored blend of island rum, orange juice, pineapple juice, cream of coconut, and a scraping of nutmeg on top. Today the Painkiller is probably the most popular drink among sailors in the B.V.I.

Corsairs Beach Bar & Restaurant TEX-MEX/CARIBBEAN   Instead of the usual catch of the day, this convivial beach bar offers zesty Tex-Mex dishes as well as savory pizzas. You can order the island's heartiest breakfast here, hang out in the bar all day, and still be around for a rib-sticking dinner after happy hour. Many boaters anchor right on the beach and drop in here, and those who dare order absinthe or "voodoo juice.". Every Sunday and Tuesday night, the barbecue grill sends the aroma of meat cooking into the night. Start with conch fritters in a goat-cheese sauce, followed by seared tuna with a spicy mango-rum sauce or lobster Thai style in a coconut-and-pumpkin sauce. Four pastas, including fettuccine shrimp al pesto, are featured nightly.

Great Harbour. ✆ **284/495-9294.** www.corsairsbvi.com. Lunch from $15; dinner main courses $25–$39. MC, V. Daily 8:30am–2pm and 6:30–9pm.

Foxy's Tamarind Bar ★★ WEST INDIAN   Arguably the most famous bar in the B.V.I., this mecca for yachties and other boat people is built entirely around sixth-generation Jost Van Dyke native Philicianno "Foxy" Callwood. He opened the place in the late 1960s, and guests have been coming back ever since. A songwriter and entertainer, Foxy is part of the draw. He creates impromptu calypso—almost in the Jamaican tradition—around his guests. If you're singled out, he'll embarrass you, but it's all in good fun. He also plays the guitar and takes a profound interest in preserving the environment of his native island.

Thursday through Saturday nights, a live band entertains. On other evenings, it's rock 'n' roll, reggae, or soca. The food and drink aren't neglected, either—try Foxy's Painkiller Punch. During the day, flying-fish sandwiches, rotis (West Indian burritos), and the usual burgers are served; evenings might bring freshly caught lobster, spicy steamed shrimp, or even grilled fish, depending on the catch of the day. They also have a big barbecue on the weekends.

Great Harbour. ✆ **284/495-9258.** www.foxysbar.com. Reservations recommended. Lunch $10–$15; dinner $18–$35. AE, MC, V. Daily 9am–11pm.

One Love Bar and Grill CARIBBEAN   The oldest son of Foxy (see previous recommendation) operates one of the most popular flotsam-and-jetsam bar and grills on the island. Seddy Callwood and his wife, Raquel, have a loyal following of yachties combined with come-and-go day-trippers from Tortola and St. Thomas. The house policy of "No Shoes, No Shirt, No Problem" inspired Kenny Chesney's hit song of the same title. After you've downed a Bushwhacker (or more than one), you can order from a menu that includes the catch of the day, wraps, kabobs, and tangy ribs. One

Love features live music Thursday to Sunday afternoon, but when the sun sets, Seddy locks up and goes home.

White Bay. ℂ **282/495-9829.** www.onelovebar.com. Main courses $10–$15. MC, V ($25 minimum). Daily 11am–sunset.

Sandcastle INTERNATIONAL   This hotel restaurant often serves food that has been frozen, but even so, the flavors remain consistently good. Lunch is served in the open-air dining room, while lighter fare and snacks are available at the Soggy Dollar Bar, which specializes in a lethal Painkiller. Dinner features four courses, including mahimahi Martinique (marinated in orange-lemon-lime juice and cooked with fennel, onions, and dill). Sandcastle hen is another specialty likely to appear on the menu: It's a grilled Cornish hen that's been marinated in rum, honey, lime, and garlic. But we'd skip all that for the sesame snapper, if available. Meals are served with seasonal vegetables and fresh pasta, along with a variety of salads. The homemade desserts are luscious, including such treats as Key lime pie, Irish whiskey cheesecake, and mango mousse. If you dine on Saturday night, you'll be treated to a candlelit dinner on the beach.

At the Sandcastle Hotel (p. 236), White Bay. ℂ **284/495-9888.** www.soggydollar.com. Reservations required for dinner by 4pm. Lunch main courses $10–$15; fixed-price dinner $22–$33. MC, V. Daily 9am–3pm and 1 seating at 7pm.

Dive Sites

Increasingly, Jost Van Dyke attracts divers. They are drawn in particular to the north coast of Little Jost Van Dyke, with its twin towers, a pair of rock formations jutting up some 27m (90 ft.). The best dive operator is **Jost Van Dyke Scuba and BVI Eco-tours,** Great Harbour (ℂ **284/495-0271;** www.bvi-ecotours.com). A one-tank dive goes for $85, a two-tank dive for $115. You can also arrange rentals here for snorkel gear, scuba equipment, kayaks, surfboards, windsurfers, small boats, or fishing equipment. You can also book boat excursions to nearby islands, costing $880 for 1 day for up to four passengers, including the services of a captain.

ANEGADA ★

The most northerly and isolated of the British Virgins, located 48km (30 miles) east of Tortola, Anegada has a population of about 250, none of whom has found the legendary treasure from the more than 500 wrecks lying off notorious Horseshoe Reef. This is a remote little corner of the Caribbean: Don't expect a single frill, and be prepared to put up with some hardships, such as mosquitoes.

Anegada is different from the other British Virgins in many ways. First, it's a coral-and-limestone atoll, flat, with an airstrip. Its highest point reaches 8m (26 ft.), and it hardly appears on the horizon if you're sailing to it. At the northern and western ends of the island are some good white-sand beaches, which might be your only reason for coming here. Second, most of the island has been declared off limits to settlement and is reserved for birds and other wildlife. The B.V.I. National Parks Trust has established a flamingo colony, which is also the protected home of several varieties of heron, ospreys, and terns. The Trust has also designated much of the interior of the island as a preserved habitat for Anegada's animal population of some 2,000 wild goats, donkeys, and cattle. Among the endangered species being given a new lease on

Any trip to Anegada has to include a visit to the fantastic beach and reef at Loblolly Bay. If you're taking a day trip from Tortola, make sure you call **Tony's Taxis** (*②* **284/495-8027**) ahead of time; Tony Smith will take you across the island to the bay, with one quick stop to see the legendary pink flamingos en route. Once you pull up at Loblolly Bay, stake out a place on the beach and enjoy some of the most spectacular snorkeling in the B.V.I. Break for lunch at Big Bamboo, and have a drink at the small thatched-roof bar where scrawled signatures on the bar and roof supports are from Cindy Crawford, Brooke Shields, and Andre Agassi (the bartender swears they're real).

life here is the rock iguana, a fierce-looking but quite harmless reptile that can grow to a length of 2m (6½ ft.). Although rarely seen, these creatures have called Anegada home for thousands of years.

Slowly, ever so slowly, the modern world is coming to Anegada. The government has paved the main road here and installed a fire department and even a little library.

Essentials

GETTING THERE   Fly BVI (*②* **284/495-1747;** www.fly-bvi.com) operates a private charter/sightseeing service between Anegada and Beef Island off Tortola. The one-way cost is $175 per person.

You can also take a day excursion to Anegada by charter boat from Tortola. **Smith's Ferry** (*②* **340/775-7292;** www.smithsferry.com) goes from Road Town, Tortola, to Anegada twice a day on Monday, Wednesday, and Friday. It costs $52 round-trip (from St. Thomas to Tortola) or $30 one-way (from one location to the other).

Dive BVI (*②* **284/495-5513;** www.divebvi.com) travels from Virgin Gorda to Anegada on Tuesdays and Fridays for $80 one-way.

GETTING AROUND   Limited taxi service is available on the island—not that you'll have many places to go. **Tony's Taxis** (*②* **284/495-8027**), which you'll easily spot when you arrive, will take you around the island for $35 for one to three people. It's also possible to rent bicycles at **Little Bit Cash and Carry** (*②* **284/495-9932**) at Sutton Point across from Anegada Reef.

FAST FACTS   Anegada has a small fire department and a little library, but it has no banks, ATMs, or drugstores. Make adequate arrangements for supplies before coming here.

Where to Stay

Guests who stay on this remote island are basically hiding out. The accommodations below are bare-bones, but great for those seeking tranquillity.

Anegada Beach Campground   Despite its isolated setting on one of the least developed islands in the B.V.I., this property boasts excellent amenities. It lies near

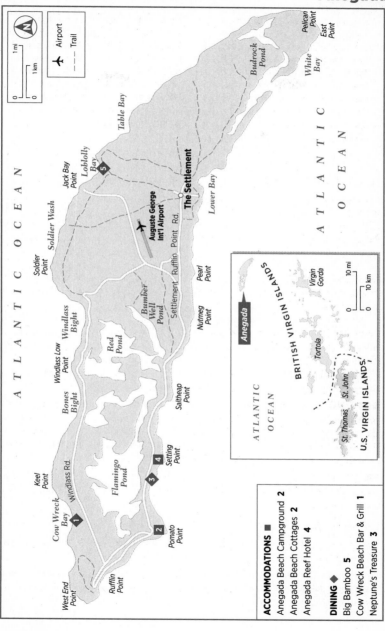

waters that are great for snorkeling, at the edge of about 19km (12 miles) of secluded beachfront. There's also access to cookout areas for budgeters who want to barbecue, flush toilets, and outdoor showers whose privacy is ensured by artfully woven palm fronds. Lodging comes in the form of seven breezy beach cottages, all equipped with private kitchenettes and bathrooms. The campground no longer rents tents or bare sites.

Anegada, B.V.I. ℂ **284/495-9466.** 7 units. Winter $200 cottage; off season $170 cottage. MC, V. *In room:* Kitchen, no phone.

Anegada Beach Cottages A true hideaway, this property consists of three spread-out and well-furnished cottages standing on 2 hectares (5 acres) of beach-front. Each of the cottages, equipped with a full bathroom, lies about 15m (49 ft.) from the water. The cottage cluster opens onto a long curving beach of white sands. During the day, guests lounge about, snorkel, or go bonefishing. It's the lazy life.

Pomato Point, Anegada, B.V.I. www.anegadabeachcottages.com. ℂ **284/495-9234.** 4 units. Year-round $175–$275 double. 2-night minimum stay. MC, V. *In room:* Kitchen, no phone.

Anegada Reef Hotel ★ The only major hotel on the island is 5km (3 miles) west of the airport, right on the beachfront. Standing on the site of a resort built in the 1970s that never opened, this is one of the most remote places covered in this guide, and a favorite of the yachting set, who enjoy the hospitality of the owners who built the complex by hand. The hotel offers motel-like, very basic rooms with private porches and either garden or ocean views, plus small bathrooms. Come here for tranquillity, not for pampering.

You can arrange to go inshore fishing, deep-sea fishing, or bonefishing (there's a tackle shop). In addition, you can set up snorkeling excursions and secure taxi service and jeep rentals. There's a beach barbecue nightly; the house specialty is lobster, and many attendees arrive by boat. If you're visiting the island for the day, you can use the hotel as a base. Call and they'll have a van meet you at the airport.

Setting Point, Anegada, B.V.I. www.anegadareef.com. ℂ **284/495-8002.** Fax 284/495-9362. 16 units. Winter $265–$400 double; off season $240–$365 double. Rates include all meals. MC, V. **Amenities:** Restaurant; bar; babysitting; Internet ($5 per 15 min.). *In room:* A/C, no phone.

Where to Eat

Big Bamboo CARIBBEAN On the crescent-shaped Loblolly Bay, this is one of the best known of the local beach bars and restaurants. If you're cast away on this island, chances are you will make your way here. Arriving either in a yacht or in a small boat, day-trippers sample the famous fresh Anegada lobster as well as locally caught conch. Red snapper and grouper also appear in the day's catch, or you can order baby back ribs and spicy barbecue chicken. Desserts range from their cheese-cake to Key lime pie. After all this food and drink, you can chill out in a nearby ham-mock under a palm.

Loblolly Bay. ℂ **284/499-1680.** Reservations recommended for large groups. Main courses $16–$40 lunch, $22–$45 dinner. MC, V. Daily 9am–9pm.

Cow Wreck Beach Bar & Grill ★ 🍴 WEST INDIAN This laid-back, family-run, and definitely funky joint is a coveted address among yachties anchoring at Anegada. Ice-cold beer and the best lobster in the B.V.I. keep patrons coming back.

The crustaceans are kept in a cage underwater, until they are summoned to the grill. Diners sit on a terrace under a straw roof, at rough-hewn wooden tables that feature a view of the water. If you go for lunch, you can tie in a visit with a snorkel trip. At night, this is the most popular place on the island for a sundowner. Other standard dishes appear on the menu, but we've never known a guest to order anything but lobster for a main course.

Lower Cow Wreck Beach. ☏ **284/495-8047.** www.cowwreckbeach.com. Reservations required for dinner. Main courses $18–$53. MC, V. Daily 7am–6pm; dinner at 6pm but they can accommodate later reservations. Closing time for bar "when the last customer departs."

Neptune's Treasure 🍴 INTERNATIONAL   Set near its own 24-slip marina, near the southern tip of the island in the same cluster of buildings that includes the high-priced Anegada Reef Hotel, this funky bar and restaurant usually hosts a mix of yacht owners and local residents. The spacious indoor dining area features a bar and lots of nautical memorabilia. The drink of choice is a Dark and Stormy, composed of ginger beer and rum. The Soares family serves platters of swordfish, lobster, fish fingers, chicken, steaks, and ribs; dispenses information about local snorkeling sites; and maintains order in something approaching a (low-key) party atmosphere.

The restaurant also offers nine simple bedrooms with air-conditioning. Depending on the season, rooms (with a private bathroom) rent for $129 to $371 per double. Discounts are offered for stays of a week or more.

Btw. Pomato and Saltheap points, Anegada, B.V.I. ☏ **284/495-9439,** or shortwave channel 16. www. neptunestreasure.com. Reservations for dinner must be made by 4pm. Breakfast $8–$12; main courses lunch $12–$32, dinner $18–$49. MC, V. Daily 8am–10pm.

PETER ISLAND ★

Half of this island, boasting a good marina and docking facilities, is devoted to the yacht club. The other part is deserted. A gorgeous beach is found at palm-fringed Deadman's Bay, which faces the Atlantic but is protected by a reef. All goods and services are at the one resort (see below).

The island is so sparsely populated that except for an occasional mason at work, about the only company you'll encounter will be an iguana or a feral cat whose ancestors were abandoned generations ago by shippers (the cats are said to have virtually eliminated the island's rodent population).

A complimentary, hotel-operated ferry, **Peter Island Ferry** (☏ **284/495-2000**), departs Tortola from the pier at Trellis Bay, near the airport. Other boats depart six or seven times a day from Baugher's Bay in Road Town, on Tortola. Passengers must notify the hotel 2 weeks before their arrival so transportation can be arranged.

Where to Stay & Eat

Peter Island Resort ★★★   This 720-hectare (1,779-acre) tropical island is solely dedicated to Peter Island Resort guests and to yacht owners who moor their crafts here. The island's tropical gardens and hillside are bordered by five gorgeous private beaches, including Deadman's Beach (in spite of its name, it's often voted one of the world's most romantic beaches).

The resort contains 32 rooms facing Sprat Bay and Sir Francis Drake Channel, and 20 larger rooms on Deadman's Bay Beach. There are also several (less desirable) garden-view rooms. Designed with a casual elegance, all the rooms have a balcony or terrace. The least desirable rooms are the smallest, housed in two-story, A-frame structures next to the harbor. Bathrooms range from standard motel-unit types to spectacularly luxurious offerings, depending on your room assignment. The Crow's Nest, a luxurious four-bedroom villa, overlooks the harbor and Deadman's Bay, and features a private swimming pool. The Hawk's Nest villas are three-bedroom villas situated on a tropical hillside.

The resort has two restaurants. For the day-tripper, the **Deadman's Beach Bar and Grill** is the more casual of the two, although reservations are recommended. Set right on the beach, it enjoys a secluded setting in the midst of sea-grape trees and towering palms. The restaurant has a wood-fired pizza oven and an expansive salad bar buffet, which also includes freshly made desserts. At lunch, expect an array of sandwiches, even one made from a big portobello mushroom. Other selections include Jamaican jerk chicken, tuna tartare, and roti. Dinner includes the fresh catch of the day, succulent lamb kabobs, and other enticing dishes. On Sunday afternoons, a live steel-drum band plays; on Monday nights, there's a West Indian buffet.

Peter Island (P.O. Box 211), Road Town, Tortola, B.V.I. www.peterisland.com. © **800/346-4451** in the U.S., or 284/495-2000. Fax 284/495-2500. 52 units. Winter $680–$1,595 double, $3,100–$5,900 3-bedroom villa, $11,000 4-bedroom villa; off season $360–$1,280 double, $3,100 3-bedroom villa, $6,200 4-bedroom villa. Rates include all meals. AE, MC, V. **Amenities:** 2 restaurants; 2 bars; babysitting; health club and spa; pool (outdoor); 4 tennis courts (lit); watersports equipment/rentals; Wi-Fi (free in lobby and clubhouse). *In room:* A/C, hair dryer, minibar.

GUANA ISLAND ★

This 340-hectare (840-acre) island, a nature preserve and wildlife sanctuary, is one of the most private hideaways in the Caribbean. Don't come here looking for action; rather, consider vacationing here if you want to retreat from the world. This small island, right off the coast of Tortola, offers seven virgin beaches, plus nature trails ideal for hiking. Unusual species of plant and animal life abound, including iguana, red-legged tortoise, the Caribbean roseate flamingo, and rare species of orchids. Arawak relics have also been discovered here. You can climb 242m (794-ft.) Sugarloaf Mountain for a panoramic view. It's said that the name of the island comes from a jutting rock that resembles the head of an iguana.

The Guana Island Club will send a boat to meet arriving guests at the Beef Island airport (trip time is 10 min.).

Where to Stay & Eat

Guana Island Club ★★　Guana Island was bought in 1974 by Henry and Gloria Jarecki, dedicated conservationists who run the resort as a nature preserve and wildlife sanctuary. Upon your arrival, a Land Rover will meet you and transport you up one of the most scenic hills in the region, in the northeast of Guana.

The cluster of white cottages was built as a private club in the 1930s, on the foundations of a Quaker homestead. The stone cottages never hold more than 30 guests (and have only two phones), and because the dwellings are staggered along a flower-dotted ridge overlooking the Caribbean and the Atlantic, the sense of privacy is almost absolute. The entire island can be rented by groups of up to 35. Renting North Beach cottage, the most luxurious of the accommodations, is like renting a private home complete with a pool. The panoramic sweep from the terrace is spectacular, particularly at sunset. There are seven beaches, some of which require a boat to reach.

Guests will find a convivial atmosphere at the clubhouse; casually elegant dinners are served by candlelight on the veranda.

P.O. Box 32, Road Town, Tortola, B.V.I. www.guana.com. ℂ **800/544-8262** in the U.S., or 284/494-2354. Fax 284/442-2050. (For reservations, write or call the Guana Island Club Reservations Office, 10 Timber Trail, Rye, NY 10580; ℂ 800/544-8262 in the U.S., or 914/967-6050.) 15 units. Winter $1,250–$1,550 double, $2,325–$2,850 cottage, $4,329–$8,100 villa; off season $695–$950 double, $1,535–$2,165 cottage, $4,325–$6,500 villa. Rent the island for $19,585–$33,975 per day. Rates include all meals and drinks served with meals. MC, V. Closed Sept–Oct. Call ahead to see if children are being accepted. **Amenities:** Restaurant; self-service bar; babysitting; 2 tennis courts (lit); watersports equipment/rentals. *In room:* Ceiling fan, Internet (free), no phone.

PLANNING YOUR TRIP TO THE VIRGIN ISLANDS

7

I f you live on the East Coast of the U.S., getting to the U.S. Virgin Islands is as easy as flying to Florida. If you plan to visit the B.V.I., you'll probably have to make a transfer in lieu of a direct flight. If you live elsewhere, you might have to fly to New York and then transfer to a flight going to the Virgin Islands. Those who reside in the U.K., Australia, or Canada often fly first to Miami or San Juan.

If you're an American citizen, visiting the U.S. Virgin Islands is relatively easy and hassle-free, as it is part of the U.S. territory. Those from other countries should read "Visas" and "Passports," later in this chapter.

A little advance planning can go a long way. In this chapter, we will give you all the information you need to know before you go.

GETTING THERE
By Plane

The bigger islands, like St. Thomas, have regularly scheduled air service on North American carriers, and the smaller islands are tied into this network through their own carriers. If you're coming from the United Kingdom, you'll likely fly first to Miami and then take another flight to your final destination. There are no direct flights from North America or Europe to any of the B.V.I. You will most likely make a connection in St. Thomas, St. Croix, or San Juan in Puerto Rico after first connecting in the mainland U.S.

The major airports in the Virgin Islands are the **Cyril E. King Airport** (© 340/774-5100; www.viport.com/airports.html; airport code STT) in St. Thomas and the **Henry E. Rohlsen Airport,** Estate Mannings Bay (© 340/778-1012; airport code STX), on St. Croix. From these airports, you can take ferries or smaller planes onto your destination in the Virgin Islands.

For more information on how to reach each island, see the "Getting There" sections in the individual island chapters. To find out which airlines travel to the Virgin Islands, see "Airline Websites," p. 264.

Be Ready for Airport Security

Because of increased security measures, the Transportation Security Administration has made changes to the prohibited-items list. All liquids and gels—including drinks, shampoo, toothpaste, perfume, hair gel, suntan lotion, and all other items with similar consistency—are allowed in carry-on baggage only if they are packed in 3-ounce containers and sealed in a quart-size, ziplock plastic bag. If you don't want to limit the amount of liquids you bring on your trip, pack these items in your checked baggage. Carrying liquids of any sort to the screening checkpoint will cause you delays, and if it's not properly packed, it will be confiscated.

With the ever-changing security measures, we recommend that you check the **Transportation Security Administration**'s website, **www.tsa.gov**, as near to your departure date as possible to make sure that no other restrictions have been imposed. Speed up security by **not wearing metal objects** such as big belt buckles. If you've got metallic body parts, a note from your doctor can prevent a long chat with the security screeners.

By Cruise Ship

A high percentage of Caribbean cruises make at least one stop in the Virgin Islands. Charlotte Amalie in St. Thomas is the most popular port, followed by historic Frederiksted in St. Croix and Road Town in Tortola. Miami is the cruise capital of the world, but ships also leave from San Juan, New York, Port Everglades, and other points. Most cruise ships travel at night, arriving the following morning at ports of call, where passengers can go ashore for sightseeing and shopping.

THE CRUISE LINES

Once you've decided that a cruise to the Virgin Islands is right for you, you'll need to choose your cruise line. Two helpful resources for choosing a cruise line are *Frommer's Cruises & Ports of Call* (Wiley Publishing, Inc.) and *Cruise Vacations for Dummies* (Wiley Publishing, Inc.). Below you'll find a rundown of various ships cruising the Virgin Islands.

Carnival Cruise Lines (℃ 888/CARNIVAL [227-6482]; www.carnival.com) offers affordable vacations on some of the biggest and most brightly decorated ships afloat. It's the richest, boldest, brashest, and most successful mass-market cruise line in the world. Its boats leave from Miami, Tampa, New Orleans, Mobile, Port Canaveral, and San Juan, and stop over at selected ports throughout the eastern and western Caribbean, including St. Thomas, St. Lucia, San Juan, St. Martin, Barbados, Martinique, Grand Cayman, and Jamaica. Most of its cruises offer good value, last from 4 to 8 days, and feature nonstop activities, lots of glitter, and the hustle and bustle of armies of passengers and crew members embarking and disembarking at every port.

Celebrity Cruises (℃ 877/202-4345; www.celebrity-cruises.com) maintains 10 medium to large ships offering cruises of between 7 and 11 nights to such ports as Key West, San Juan, Grand Cayman, St. Thomas, Ocho Rios, Antigua, and Cozumel, Mexico, among others. The line is unpretentious and classy (several notches above mass market), but offers pricing that's nonetheless relatively competitive.

Travel in the Age of Bankruptcy

Airlines go bankrupt, so protect your-self by **buying your tickets with a credit card**, as the Fair Credit Billing Act guar-antees that you can get your money back from the credit card company if a travel supplier goes under (and if you request the refund within 60 days of the bankruptcy). **Travel insurance** can also help, but make sure it covers against "carrier default" for your spe-cific travel provider. And be aware that if a U.S. airline goes bust midtrip, a 2001 federal law requires other carriers to take you to your destination (albeit on a space-available basis) for a fee of no more than $25, provided you rebook within 60 days of the cancellation.

Accommodations are roomy and well equipped, and the cuisine is among the most refined on the seas.

Princess Cruises (© **800/PRINCESS** [774-6237]; www.princess.com) places more emphasis on luxury living on a mass scale than any other line afloat. The company's ships usually carry fewer passengers than similarly sized vessels on other lines. Cruises last between 7 and 15 days, and include stops at such islands as Aruba, Barbados, Caracas, Dominica, Grenada, St. Lucia, St. Martin, St. Kitts, and St. Thomas.

Royal Caribbean International (© **866/562-7625**; www.royalcaribbean. com) leads the industry in the development of megaships. This mainstream, mass-market cruise line encourages a restrained house-party atmosphere that's some-how a bit less frenetic than that of other "party-style" cruise lines. Though accommodations and accouterments are more than adequate, they are not upscale, and cabins aboard some of the line's older vessels tend to be a bit more cramped than the industry norm. Using Miami, San Juan, or Fort Lauderdale as their home ports, Royal Caribbean ships call regularly at such ports as St. Thomas, San Juan, Ocho Rios, St. Martin, Grand Cayman, St. Croix, and Curaçao. Most of the company's cruises last for 7 days, although some weekend jaunts from San Juan to St. Thomas are available for 3 nights.

Seabourn Cruise Line (© **800/929-9391**; www.seabourn.com) is an upscale, expensive outfit known for luxurious, small-scale ships. Its deluxe *Seabourn Legend* and *Seabourn Pride* spend from 10 to 14 days sailing the eastern Caribbean, leaving from Fort Lauderdale. There are more activities than you'd expect aboard such relatively small ships (10,000 tons), and an absolutely amazing amount of onboard space per passenger. Cuisine is superb, served within a dining room that's unapologetically formal.

GETTING AROUND
By Plane

Travelers can fly between St. Thomas and St. Croix, and between St. Thomas and Tortola. St. John doesn't have an airport; passengers usually land first at St. Thomas, then travel to St. John by boat.

By Boat

Ferry service is a vital link between St. Thomas and St. John; private water taxis also operate on this route. Launch services link Red Hook, on the East End of St. Thomas, with both Charlotte Amalie in St. Thomas and Cruz Bay in St. John. **Seaborne Airlines** (© 866/359-8784; www.seaborneairlines.com) makes the trips between St. Thomas and St. Croix.

In the B.V.I., ferries and private boats link Road Town, Tortola, with the island's West End; there's also service to and from Virgin Gorda and some of the smaller islands, such as Anegada and Jost Van Dyke. However, on some of the really remote islands, boat service may be only once a week. Many of the private islands, such as Peter Island, provide launches from Tortola.

You can travel by ferry from Charlotte Amalie, on St. Thomas, to West End and Road Town on Tortola, a 45-minute voyage. Boats making this run include **Native Son** (© 284/495-4617; www.nativesonferry.com) and **Smith's Ferry Service** (© 284/495-4495; www.smithsferry.com). **Inter-Island Boat Services** (© 284/495-4166) brings passengers from St. John to the West End on Tortola.

For details on specific ferry connections, including sample fares, see the "Getting Around" sections of the individual island chapters.

By Car

A rented car is often the best way to get around each of the Virgin Islands. Just remember the most important rule: In both the U.S. and the British Virgin Islands, *you must drive on the left.*

All the major car-rental companies are represented in the U.S. Virgin Islands, including **Avis** (© 800/331-1212; www.avis.com), **Budget** (© 800/626-4516; www.budget.com), and **Hertz** (© 800/654-3131; www.hertz.com); many local agencies also compete in the car-rental market (for detailed information, see the "Getting Around" sections in individual island chapters). On St. Thomas and St. Croix, you can pick up most rental cars at the airport. On St. John, there are car-rental stands at the ferry dock. Cars are sometimes in short supply during the high season, so reserve as far in advance as possible.

Parking lots in the U.S. Virgin Islands can be found in Charlotte Amalie, on St. Thomas, and in Christiansted, on St. Croix (in Frederiksted, you can generally park on the street). Most hotels, except those in the congested center of Charlotte Amalie, have free parking lots.

In the British Virgin Islands, many visitors don't even bother renting a car, mainly because taxi service is adequate, but also because they'll have to drive on the left along roads that can be hairy when they exist at all—some of the roads are like roller-coaster rides. To rent a car on the B.V.I., you must purchase a local driver's license for $10 from police headquarters or a car-rental desk in town; and you must be at least 25 years old. Major U.S. companies are represented in these islands, and there are many local companies as well. ***Note:*** There are no car-rental agencies at the airports on Tortola or Virgin Gorda. Vehicles come in a wide range of styles and prices, including Jeeps, Land Rovers, mini mokes, and even six- to eight-passenger Suzukis. Weekly rates are usually slightly cheaper.

GASOLINE There are plenty of service stations on St. Thomas, especially on the outskirts of Charlotte Amalie and at strategic points in the north and in the more congested East End. On St. Croix, most gas stations are in Christiansted, but there

saving money ON A RENTAL CAR

Car-rental rates vary even more than airfares. The price you pay will depend on the size of the car, the length of the rental period, how far you drive it, whether you purchase insurance, and a host of other factors. You can save hundreds of dollars by asking a few key questions, including these: Are special promotional rates available? Are weekend rates lower than weekday rates? Is a weekly rate cheaper than the daily rate? Is it cheaper to pick up the car at the airport compared to another island location? How much does the rental company charge to refill your gas tank if you return with the tank less than full?

Don't forget that if you're a member of AARP, AAA, a frequent-flier program, or a trade union, you may well be entitled to car-rental discounts of up to 30%. Also, many package deals include airfare, accommodations, and a rental car with unlimited mileage. To see if a package might offer a good deal, compare the prices of packages with the cost of booking airline tickets and renting a car separately.

are also some along the major roads and at Frederiksted. On St. John, make sure your tank is filled up at Cruz Bay before heading out on a tour of the island.

Gas stations are not as plentiful on the British Virgin Islands. Road Town, the capital of Tortola, has the most gas stations; fill up here before touring the island. Virgin Gorda has a limited but sufficient number of gas stations. Chances are you won't be using a car on the other, smaller British Virgin Islands.

Taxes are already included in the printed price. One U.S. gallon equals 3.8 liters or .85 imperial gallons.

BREAKDOWNS   All the major islands, including St. Thomas, St. John, St. Croix, Tortola, and Virgin Gorda, have garages that will tow vehicles. Always call the rental company first if you have a breakdown. If your car requires extensive repairs because of a mechanical failure, a new one will be sent to replace it.

By Taxi

Taxis are the main mode of transport on all the Virgin Islands. On **St. Thomas,** taxi vans carry up to a dozen passengers to multiple destinations, and smaller private taxis are also available. Rates are posted at the airport, where you'll find plenty of taxis on arrival. On **St. John,** both private taxis and vans for three or more passengers are available. On **St. Croix,** taxis congregate at the airport, in Christiansted, and in Frederiksted, where the cruise ships arrive. Many hotels often have a "fleet" of taxis available for guests. Taxis here are unmetered, and you should always negotiate the rate before taking off.

On the **British Virgin Islands,** taxis are sometimes the only way to get around. Service is available on Tortola, Virgin Gorda, and Anegada, and rates are fixed by the local government.

By Bus

The only islands with recommendable bus service are **St. Thomas** and **St. Croix.** On St. Thomas, buses leave from Charlotte Amalie and circle the island; on St. Croix, air-conditioned buses run from Christiansted to Frederiksted. Bus service elsewhere is highly erratic; it's mostly used by locals going to and from work.

TIPS ON ACCOMMODATIONS

Resorts and hotels in the Virgin Islands offer package deals galore, and though they have many disadvantages, the deals are always cheaper than rack rates. It's always best to consult a reliable travel agent to find out what's available in the way of land-and-air packages before booking accommodations.

There is no rigid classification of hotel properties on the islands. The word "deluxe" is often used, or misused, when "first class" might be more appropriate. "First class" itself isn't always what it's touted to be. For that and other reasons, we've presented fairly detailed descriptions of the properties so that you'll get an idea of what to expect. However, even in the deluxe and first-class properties, don't expect top-rate service and efficiency. Life here moves pretty slowly, and that can have its disadvantages.

The facilities available at hotels in the Virgin Islands vary widely. All the big, first-class hotels have swimming pools and are usually located on or near a beach. If you book at less expensive accommodations, you can often pay a small fee to use the facilities of a larger, more expensive resort.

The good news: During the **off season** (mid-Apr to mid-Dec) hotels slash prices 25% to 50%.

Renting Your Own Villa or Vacation Home

Looking for something a little different? You might decide to rent a villa, condo, apartment, or cottage for your Virgin Islands vacation.

Private apartments and cottages are more no-frills options than villas and condos. Most can be rented with or without maid service. Cottages usually contain a simple bedroom with a small kitchen and bathroom. Many open onto a beach, while others are clustered around a communal swimming pool. If you're planning your trip for the high season, reservations should be made at least 5 to 6 months in advance. Sometimes local tourist offices will advise you on vacation home rentals, if you write or call them directly.

Dozens of agencies throughout the United States and Canada offer rentals in the Virgin Islands. **At Home Abroad,** 405 E. 56th St., Ste. 6H, New York, NY 10022 (© **212/421-9165;** www.athomeabroadinc.com), has a roster of private homes, villas, and condos for rent in St. Thomas, St. John, Tortola, and Virgin Gorda; maid service is included in the price. **Hideaways International,** 767 Islington St., Portsmouth, NH 03801 (© **800/843-4433** or 603/430-4433; www.hideaways.com), has rentals ranging from cottages to villas to entire islands. In most cases, you deal

---

The West Indian Guesthouse

Most Caribbean natives stay in guesthouses when they travel to the Virgin Islands. Many of these lodgings are comfortable, with private bathrooms in each room, air-conditioning or ceiling fans, and swimming pools. Don't expect the luxuries of a first-class resort, but for the money the guesthouse can't be beat. The guesthouses we've recommended in this book are clean and comfortable.

Veteran travelers usually carry some essential items to make their trips easier. Following is a selection of handy online tools to bookmark and use.

- **Virgin Islands Now** (www.vinow.com)
- **Virgin Islands Daily News** (www.virgin islandsdailynews.com)
- **B.V.I. Online Travel Guide** (www. b-v-i.com)
- **St. John Beach Guide** (www.stjohn beachguide.com)
- **GoToStJohn.com** (www.gotost john.com)
- **GoToStCroix.com** (www.gotost croix.com)

- **Airplane Food** (www.airlinemeals.net)
- **Airplane Seating** (www.seatguru.com and www.airlinequality.com)
- **Maps** (www.mapquest.com)
- **Travel Warnings** (http://travel.state. gov, www.fco.gov.uk/travel, www.voyage. gc.ca, and www.dfat.gov.au)
- **Visa ATM Locator** (www.visa.com), **MasterCard ATM Locator** (www. mastercard.com)
- **Weather** (www.intellicast.com and www.weather.com)

directly with the owners. The company also arranges specialty cruises, yacht charters, airline tickets, rental cars, and hotel reservations. Annual membership is $195. **Villas of Distinction,** P.O. Box 55, Armonk, NY 10504 (© **800/289-0900;** www. villasofdistinction.com), offers "complete vacations," including car rental and domestic help. Its private villas have one to six bedrooms, and almost every villa has a swimming pool.

In the U.K., browse the options offered through **Holiday Rentals** (© **020/8846-3441;** www.holiday-rentals.co.uk).

Island Villas, 340 Strand St., Frederiksted, St. Croix, U.S.V.I. 00840 (© **877/788-0361** or 340/718-0361; www.stcroixislandvillas.com), offers some of the best properties on St. Croix, specializing in villas, condos, and private homes, many of which are on the beach. One- to seven-bedroom units are available, with prices from $1,000 to $15,000 per week.

Renting Your Own Island

Extremely well-heeled escapists can look into renting a private island in the British Virgin Islands. Here's what's up for grabs (and see chapter 6 for more details):

- **Guana Island** (© **800/544-8262;** www.guana.com): For a negotiable fee, up to 35 guests can take over this privately owned, 344-hectare (850-acre) island, the sixth largest of the British Virgin Islands. Guana Island is a nature sanctuary with seven pristine beaches and a network of hiking trails.

- **Necker Island** (© **212/994-3070;** www.neckerisland.virgin.com): This 30-hectare (74-acre) hideaway is enveloped by its own unpolluted coral reef. It's owned by Richard Branson (of Virgin Atlantic Airways), who is well acquainted with its trio of sugar-white beaches. When he's not around, he leases the entire island to friends like Eddie Murphy. At the core of the island is a 10-bedroom villa, surrounded by three one-bedroom guesthouses. Sun pours into the lush tropical garden, which has a private freshwater pool and Jacuzzi. The daily rate is $22,500 to $36,000, depending on the number of guests, and includes food, drinks, and activities (tennis, snorkeling, windsurfing, boating, and sea kayaking, to name a few) for up to 26 people.

GETTING MARRIED IN THE VIRGIN ISLANDS

The U.S. Virgin Islands are increasingly popular as a wedding venue. Each island boasts wedding consultants who work hand in glove with resort hotels, and take care of everything from airline tickets to flowers. Although there are some independent small consultants, we have found that the best deals are arranged by a specialist at one of the resort hotels. Our favorites include **Vera Payne** at Caneel Bay on St. John (© 340/776-6111), **Luza Gutierrez** at Frenchman's Reef & Morning Star Marriott Beach Resort on St. Thomas (© **800/FOR-LOVE** [367-5683]), and **Candy McGinley** at the Buccaneer on St. Croix (© **800/255-3881** or 340/773-2100).

Marrying in the U.S. Virgin Islands

No blood tests or physical examinations are necessary, but there is a $50 license fee, a $50 notarized application, and an 8-day waiting period, which is sometimes waived, depending on circumstances. Civil ceremonies before a judge of the territorial court cost $200 each; religious ceremonies performed by clergy are equally valid. Fees and schedules for church weddings must be negotiated directly with the officiate. More information is available from the **U.S. Virgin Islands Department of Tourism,** 1270 Avenue of the Americas, New York, NY 10020 (© **800/372-USVI** [372-8784] or 212/332-2222; www.usvitourism.vi). The guide *Getting Married in the U.S. Virgin Islands* is distributed by U.S.V.I. tourism offices; it gives information on all three islands, including wedding planners, places of worship, florists, and limousine services. It also provides a listing of island accommodations that offer in-house wedding services.

Couples can apply for a marriage license for St. Thomas or St. John by contacting the **Superior Court of the Virgin Islands,** P.O. Box 70, St. Thomas, U.S.V.I. 00804 (© **340/774-0640**). For weddings on St. Croix, contact the **Territorial Court of the Virgin Islands,** Family Division, P.O. Box 929, Christiansted, St. Croix, U.S.V.I. 00821 (© **340/773-1130**).

Marrying in the British Virgin Islands

There's no requirement of island residency, but a couple must apply for a' license at the attorney general's office, and stay in the B.V.I. for at least 3 days while the paperwork is processed. You'll need to present a passport or an original birth certificate and photo identification, plus certified proof of your single marital status, including any divorce or death certificates pertaining to former spouses. Two witnesses must accompany the couple. The license fee is $110. Local registrars will perform marriages, or you can choose your own officiate. For information and an application for a license, contact the **Registrar's Office,** P.O. Box 418, Road Town, Tortola, B.V.I. (© **284/494-3701** or 494-3492).

COMMITMENT CEREMONIES FOR gay & lesbian TRAVELERS

When there's a request for a commitment ceremony on St. Croix, all eyes turn to **the Palms at Pelican Cove** (p. 150), a former "gay but straight-friendly" resort which, under new owners, still thoughtfully maintains an open attitude among its diverse guests.

Ceremonies are usually performed at sunset, on a photogenic stretch of white-sand beach. From there, it's an easy walk to the bar and restaurant for after-ceremony celebrations. The Palms has access to three or four spiritualists/theologians, one of whom is a sea captain. The commitment ceremonies are not legally binding, and their legalities have not yet been tested in the courts.

[FastFACTS] THE VIRGIN ISLANDS

Area Codes   The area code for the U.S.V.I. is **340;** in the B.V.I., it's **284.** You can dial direct from North America; from outside North America, dial 001, plus the number for the U.S.V.I., and 011-44 plus the number for the B.V.I.

Automobile Organizations   Motor clubs will supply maps, suggested routes, guidebooks, accident and bail-bond insurance, and emergency road service. The **American Automobile Association (AAA)** is the major auto club in the United States. If you belong to a motor club in your home country, inquire about AAA reciprocity before you leave. You may be able to join AAA, even if you're not a member of a reciprocal club; to inquire, call AAA (✆ **800/222-4357;** www.aaa.com). AAA has a nationwide emergency road service telephone number (✆ **800/AAA-HELP** [222-4357]).

Business Hours   See "Fast Facts" in individual island chapters for information on business hours.

Car Rental   See "Getting Around," above.

Crime   See "Safety," later in this section.

Customs   Every visitor to the U.S.V.I. 21 years of age or older may bring in, free of duty, the following: (1) 1 liter of wine or hard liquor; (2) 200 cigarettes, 100 cigars (but not from Cuba), or 3 pounds of smoking tobacco; and (3) $100 worth of gifts. These exemptions are offered to travelers who spend at least 72 hours in the United States and who have not claimed them within the preceding 6 months. It is altogether forbidden to bring into the country foodstuffs (particularly fruit, cooked meats, and canned goods) and plants (vegetables, seeds, tropical plants, and the like). Foreign tourists may carry in or out up to $10,000 in U.S. or foreign currency with no formalities; larger sums must be declared to U.S. Customs on entering or leaving, which includes filing form CM 4790. For details regarding U.S. Customs and Border Protection, consult your nearest U.S. embassy or consulate, or **U.S. Customs** (✆ **800/232-5378;** www.cbp.gov).

Visitors to the B.V.I. can bring in food, with the exception of meat products that are not USDA-approved. Visitors can bring up to $10,000 in currency and 1 liter of alcohol per person.

Australian Citizens: A helpful brochure available from Australian consulates or Customs offices is *Know Before You Go*. For more information, call the **Australian Customs Service** at ✆ **1300/363-263,** or log on to **www.customs.gov.au.**

Canadian Citizens: For a clear summary of Canadian rules, write for the booklet *I Declare,* issued by the **Canada Border Services Agency** (✆ **800/461-9999** in Canada, or 204/983-3500; www.cbsa-asfc.gc.ca).

New Zealand Citizens: Most questions are answered in a free pamphlet available at New Zealand consulates and Customs offices: *New Zealand Customs Guide for Travellers, Notice no. 4.* For more information, contact **New Zealand Customs Service,** the Customhouse, 17–21 Whitmore St., Box 2218, Wellington (✆ **04/473-6099** or 0800/428-786; www.customs.govt.nz).

U.K. Citizens: From the B.V.I., U.K. citizens can bring back (duty-free) 200 cigarettes (250g of tobacco), 2 liters wine, 1 liter strong liquor, 60cc perfume, and £145 of goods and souvenirs. Larger amounts are subject to tax. For further information, contact **HM Revenue & Customs** at ✆ **0845/010-9000** (from outside the U.K., 020/8929-0152), or consult their website at **www.hmce.gov.uk.**

U.S. Citizens & Residents: From the U.S.V.I., U.S. citizens can bring back 5 liters of liquor duty-free, plus an extra liter of rum (including Cruzan rum) if one of the bottles is produced in the Virgin Islands. Goods made on the island are also duty-free, including perfume, jewelry, clothing, and original paintings; however, if the price of an item exceeds $25, you must be able to show a certificate of origin.

Be sure to collect receipts for all purchases in the Virgin Islands, and beware of merchants offering to give you a false receipt—he or she might be an informer to U.S. Customs. Also, keep in mind that any gifts received during your stay must be declared. For the most up-to-date specifics on what you can bring back **from the B.V.I.** and the corresponding fees, download the invaluable free pamphlet *Know Before You Go* online at **www.cbp.gov.** (Click on "Travel," and then click on "Know Before You Go.") Or contact the **U.S. Customs & Border Protection (CBP),** 1300 Pennsylvania Ave. NW, Washington, DC 20229 (✆ **877/287-8667**), and request the pamphlet.

Disabled Travelers

For the most part the accessibility of hotels and restaurants in the U.S.V.I. remains far behind the progress made on the mainland, and you must take this into account if you're planning a vacation here. Of the U.S. Virgins, St. Thomas and St. John, because of their hilly terrain, remain the most unfriendly islands to those who are wheelchair bound. Because it is flat, St. Croix is an easier place to get around.

Some resorts on **St. Thomas** and **St. Croix** have made inroads in catering to persons with disabilities; St. John and all of the British Islands lag far behind in this regard. As of this writing, about a third of the major resorts (and none of the cheaper guesthouses or villas) in St. Thomas or St. Croix have the facilities to accommodate vacationers who have disabilities. Of all the hotels in the U.S.V.I., the **Ritz-Carlton, St. Thomas** (p. 65), is the most hospitable to persons with disabilities. It maintains "accessible rooms"—rooms that can be reached without navigating stairs—in every price category. The Ritz also offers beach wheelchairs (resting on balloon tires). Most hotels in the Virgin Islands, however, have a long way to go before they become a friend of a person with disabilities. If you're planning a vacation in the Virgin Islands, you should contact a travel agent or call the hotel of your choice to discuss your requirements.

Accessible Adventures (✆ **340/344-8302;** www.accessvi.com) is a tour operator in St. Thomas that offers a land-based tour of St. Thomas in a wheelchair-accessible trolley. Originating from Wico Dock at Havensight or Crown Bay at the Sub Base, tours stop Magens Bay, Drakes Seat, Skyline Drive, and Mountain Top, and cost $34 per person.

Doctors Finding a good doctor in the Virgin Islands is not a problem. If you do get sick, you may want to ask the concierge at your hotel to recommend a local doctor—even his or her own physician. See "Fast Facts" in individual island chapters for information on doctors.

Drinking Laws In the U.S. Virgins, the legal age for purchase and consumption of alcoholic beverages is 18. Proof of age is required and often requested at bars, nightclubs, and restaurants, so it's always a good idea to bring ID when you go out.

Do not carry open containers of alcohol in your car or any public area that isn't zoned for alcohol consumption. The police can fine you on the spot. Don't even think about driving while intoxicated. Although 18-year-olds can purchase, drink, and order alcohol, they cannot transport bottles back to the United States with them. If an attempt is made, the alcohol will be confiscated at the Customs check point. The same holds true for the B.V.I.

In the B.V.I., the legal minimum age for purchasing liquor or drinking alcohol in bars or restaurants is 18. Alcoholic beverages can be sold any day of the week, including Sunday. You can have an open container on the beach, but be careful not to litter or you might be fined.

Driving Rules In both the U.S.V.I. and the B.V.I., you must drive on the left. See "Getting Around," earlier in this chapter.

Electricity The electrical current in the Virgin Islands is the same as on the U.S. mainland and Canada: 110 to 120 volts AC (60 cycles), compared to 220 to 240 volts AC (50 cycles) in most of Europe, Australia, and New Zealand. Downward converters that change 220 to 240 volts to 110 to 120 volts are difficult to find in the United States, so bring one with you.

Embassies & Consulates There are no embassies or consulates in the Virgin Islands. If you have a passport issue, go to the local police station, which in all islands is located at the center of government agencies. Relay your problem to whomever is at reception, and you'll be given advice about which agencies can help you.

Emergencies Call ✆ **911** in the U.S.V.I. or **999** in the B.V.I.

Family Travel Most of the Virgin Islands, both U.S. and British, are family-friendly. **St. Thomas** and **St. Croix** have the most facilities and attractions for families. The British Virgin Islands have significantly fewer family-oriented activities, and some of the smaller and less developed islands don't cater much to children, although families who love spending whole days on the beach will probably have a great time. When compared with some of the other major destinations in the Caribbean (such as Jamaica, where crime is high), the U.S. Virgins are generally safe, and the British Virgin Islands are even safer. To locate accommodations, restaurants, and attractions that are particularly kid-friendly, refer to the "Kids" icon throughout this guide.

Gasoline Please see "Getting Around," earlier in this chapter, for information.

Healthy Travels to You

The following government websites offer up-to-date health-related travel advice:

○ **Australia:** www.smarttraveller.gov.au

○ **Canada:** www.hc-sc.gc.ca/index_e.html

○ **U.K.:** www.dh.gov.uk/en/policyand guidance/healthadvicefortravellers

○ **U.S.:** wwwn.cdc.gov/travel

Health   Other than the typical tropical environment health concerns, like sun exposure and sea sickness (see below), there are no major health concerns in the Virgin Islands.

St. Thomas has the best hospital in the U.S. Virgin Islands (Roy Lester Schneider Hospital; p. 54). St. Croix also has good hospital facilities (Governor Juan F. Luis Hospital & Medical Center; p. 145). There is only a health clinic on St. John; more serious cases are transferred to the hospital on St. Thomas.

Medical facilities in the B.V.I. are very limited. In very serious cases, patients are transported to Puerto Rico. There is only one small general hospital, Peebles Hospital (p. 196) on Tortola. There are one public and one private clinic on Virgin Gorda. Both islands are served by ambulances with paramedics. There is a very small clinic with a government nurse on both Jost Van Dyke and Anegada, but no clinics on the other islands. There is also no hyperbaric chamber in the B.V.I. Patients requiring treatment for decompression illness are transferred to St. Thomas.

It is not difficult to get a prescription filled or find a doctor on St. Thomas, St. Croix, and Tortola. You should get your prescriptions filled before heading to the other islands, where it's sometimes tricky and complicated to get prescriptions from the mainland refilled. Often it requires a phone call from the U.S.V.I. to a stateside pharmacy or to the doctor who prescribed the medicine in the first place. CVS and Wal-Mart are the best for contacting a stateside branch of those chains, if your prescription is on a computer file. To avoid possible hassles and delays, both in the B.V.I. and the U.S.V.I., it is best to arrive with enough medication for your entire vacation.

o   **BUGS & BITES**   **Mosquitoes** do exist in the Virgin Islands, but they aren't the malaria-carrying mosquitoes that you might find elsewhere in the Caribbean. They're still a nuisance, though. **Sand flies,** which appear mainly in the evening, are a bigger annoyance. Screens can't keep these critters out, so carry your bug repellent.

o   **DIETARY RED FLAGS**   If you experience **diarrhea,** moderate your eating habits, and drink only bottled water until you recover. If symptoms persist, consult a doctor. Much of the fresh water on the Virgin Islands is stored in cisterns and filtered before it's served. Delicate stomachs might opt for bottled water.

o   **SEASICKNESS**   The best way to prevent **seasickness** is with the scopolamine patch by Transderm Scop, a prescription medication. Bonine and Dramamine are good over-the-counter medications, although each causes drowsiness. Smooth Sailing is a ginger drink that works quite well to settle your stomach. You might also opt for an acupressure wristband available at drugstores (www. sea-band.com). We find that a ginger pill taken with a meal and followed by Dramamine an hour before boating also does the job.

o   **SUN EXPOSURE**   The Virgin Islands' sun can be brutal. To protect yourself, consider wearing sunglasses and a hat, and use **sunscreen** (SPF 15 and higher) liberally. Limit your time on the beach for the first few days. If you overexpose yourself, stay out of the sun until you recover. If your sunburn is followed by fever, chills, a headache, nausea, or dizziness, see a doctor.

Hospitals   The largest hospital in St. Thomas—and the only emergency room on the island—is the **Roy Lester Schneider Hospital** (p. 54). Islanders from St. John also use this hospital, which is about a 5-minute drive from Charlotte Amalie. The other major hospital is the **Governor Juan F. Luis Hospital & Medical Center** on St. Croix (p. 145). The payment of Medicare and Medicaid operates as it does in the United States. If you walk into a hospital without any coverage or insurance, you are expected to pay.

On Tortola, in the British Virgin Islands, the main hospital in the little country is **Peebles Hospital** (p. 196). If you are on one of the out islands, you are generally taken to Tortola for treatment. In addition to these hospitals, there are a number of private doctors' offices throughout the islands, charging higher rates than the hospitals.

Insurance   For information on traveler's insurance, trip-cancellation insurance, and medical insurance while traveling, visit www.frommers.com/planning.

Internet & Wi-Fi   There is limited Internet access on the major islands in the Virgin Islands chain. The best chances for Internet access are found in St. Thomas, less so in St. Croix, and even less so in St. John. On some of the more remote islands, you may be completely out of luck. Your hotel remains the best bet for Internet or Wi-Fi access, as there aren't many Internet cafes in the Virgin Islands. In Charlotte Amalie, you will find a few small cafes that will let you use an Internet-ready computer for the price of a coffee. Throughout the British Virgin Islands, it is difficult to find places where you can use the Internet. Increasingly, Tortola and Virgin Gorda have Internet access, but it is still very rare in the out islands of the B.V.I.

If your hotel is small and doesn't have Internet access, see the "Fast Facts" section of each island chapter for specific recommendations of where to go.

Language   English is the official language of both the U.S. and British Virgin Islands.

Legal Aid   While driving, if you are pulled over for a minor infraction (such as speeding), never attempt to pay the fine directly to a police officer; this could be construed as attempted bribery, a much more serious crime. Pay fines by mail, or directly into the hands of the clerk of the court. If accused of a more serious offense, say and do nothing before consulting a lawyer. In the U.S.V.I., the burden is on the state to prove a person's guilt beyond a reasonable doubt, and everyone has the right to remain silent, whether he or she is suspected of a crime or actually arrested. Once arrested, a person can make one telephone call to a party of his or her choice.

LGBT Travelers   The Virgin Islands, along with Puerto Rico, are some of the most gay-friendly destinations in the Caribbean. However, discretion is still advised in some parts. Islanders tend to be very religious and conservative, and displays of same-sex affection, such as hand holding, are frowned upon.

St. Thomas is the most cosmopolitan of the Virgin Islands, but it is no longer the "gay paradise" it was in the 1960s and 1970s. Most gay vacationers now head for Frederiksted, in St. Croix, which has more hotels and other establishments catering primarily to the gay market, none better than the **Sand Castle on the Beach** (p. 155) or the **Palms at Pelican Cove** (p. 150). In Charlotte Amalie, on St. Thomas, the most boisterous gay nightlife takes place in the Frenchtown section of the city. On Thursday, Friday, and Saturday nights beginning at around 11pm, gay men and women flock to **Stereo,** Frenchtown Mall, 24-A Honduras, in Frenchtown (✆ **340/774-5348**), which is upstairs over the Epernay Bistro.

The B.V.I., however, still remain uptight and closeted toward gay visitors. Sometimes when a gay man wants to let loose, he takes the boat to Charlotte Amalie.

Mail   At press time, U.S. domestic postage rates were 28¢ for a postcard and 44¢ for a letter. For international mail, a first-class letter of up to 1 ounce costs 98¢; a first-class postcard costs the same as a letter. For more information, go to **www.usps.com**. Always include zip codes when mailing items in the U.S. If you don't know your zip code, visit **www.usps.com/zip4**.

If you aren't sure what your address will be in the U.S. Virgin Islands, mail can be sent to you, in your name, c/o General Delivery at the main post office of the city or region where you expect to be. (Call ✆ **800/275-8777** for information on the nearest post office.) The addressee must pick up mail in person and must produce proof of identity (driver's license, passport, and so on). Most post offices will hold your mail for up to 1 month, and are open Monday to Friday 8am to 6pm, and Saturday 9am to 3pm.

Postal rates in the British Virgin Islands to the United States or Canada are 35¢ for a postcard (airmail), and 50¢ for a first-class airmail letter (½ oz.). Mailing a postcard to the U.K. costs 50¢ and a first-class letter via airmail costs 75¢ (½ oz.).

Medical Requirements   Unless you're arriving from an area known to be suffering from an epidemic (particularly cholera or yellow fever), inoculations or vaccinations are not required for entry into the U.S. Virgin Islands or the British Virgin Islands.

If you have a medical condition that requires **syringe-administered medications,** carry a valid signed prescription from your physician; syringes in carry-on baggage will be inspected. Insulin in any form should have the proper pharmaceutical documentation. If you have a disease that requires treatment with **narcotics,** you should also carry documented proof with you—smuggling narcotics aboard a plane carries severe penalties in the U.S.

For **HIV-positive visitors,** requirements for entering both the U.S.V.I. and B.V.I. are somewhat vague and change frequently. Anyone who does not appear to be in good health may be required to undergo a medical exam, including HIV testing, prior to being granted or denied entry. For up-to-the-minute information, contact **AIDSinfo** (© **800/448-0440** or 301/519-0459 outside the U.S.; www.aidsinfo.nih.gov) or the **Gay Men's Health Crisis** (© **212/367-1000;** www.gmhc.org). Also see "Health."

Mobile Phones   **In the U.S. Virgin Islands:** The two largest cellphone operators in the U.S.V.I. include Sprint PCS (www.sprint.com) and AT&T Wireless (www.att.com/wireless), which is still referred to by some locals as Cingular. Phones operating in the mainland U.S. under those plans will usually operate seamlessly, and without any excess roaming charges, in the U.S.V.I. If your phone presently operates through some other carrier, it's wise to call them before your departure about signing up (at least temporarily) for one of their international plans, which will save you money on roaming charges during the duration of your trip. If your cellphone is not equipped for reception and transmission in the U.S.V.I., consider renting (or buying) a cheap cellphone for temporary use, or, less conveniently, head for a Sprint PCS or AT&T sales outlet (each maintains offices on all three of the U.S.V.I.'s major islands) for a substitute SIM card, a key operating component that can be inserted into your existing phone, making it operational. Throughout the U.S.V.I., the electrical system is the same as within the U.S. mainland (115 volts and female sockets which accept the U.S.-style "flat" plugs), so most U.S. residents won't need any special transformers or adaptors.

In the British Virgin Islands: The two largest cellphone operators in the B.V.I. include CCT Global Communications (www.cctwireless.com) and Digicell BVI (www.digicelbvi.com), both with offices in Road Town and on Virgin Gorda. Other than that, the cellphone situation is roughly equivalent to what's described immediately above in the U.S.V.I. The electrical system in the B.V.I. is the same as that within the U.S.V.I. and the mainland U.S. (115 volts), so British and European visitors may want to bring adaptors and transformers.

What Things Cost in St. Thomas	US$
Taxi from airport to Charlotte Amalie	$15.00
Double room, moderate	$140.00
Double room, inexpensive	$100.00
Three course dinner for one, no wine, moderate	$24.00
Cup of coffee in a cafe	$2.75
Bottle of beer	$3.50

Hotels in the B.V.I. often have the appropriate adaptors, and in some cases, those adaptors are physically built directly into the wall sockets.

Money & Costs

THE VALUE OF THE U.S. DOLLAR VS. OTHER POPULAR CURRENCIES

US$	Can$	UK£	Euro (€)	Aus$	NZ$
$1.00	C$1.30	£0.73	1.50€	A$1.50	NZ$2.00

The U.S. Virgin Islands and the British Virgin Islands both use the **U.S. dollar** as the form of currency. Frommer's lists exact prices in the local currency. The currency conversions quoted above were correct at press time. However, rates fluctuate, so before departing consult a currency exchange website such as **www.oanda.com/currency/converter** to check up-to-the-minute rates.

Banks on the islands are your only option if you need to **exchange currency.** These rates can be expensive, and additional charges are often tacked on; it is best to change money before you arrive.

There seems to be no shortage of **ATMs** in the Virgin Islands, all of which dispense U.S. dollars. They are everywhere—on the downtown streets of Charlotte Amalie, within the large resorts, and in shopping arcades—making it easy to get quick cash. ATMs are most prevalent in Charlotte Amalie on St. Thomas, and in Christiansted on St. Croix. They are also available in Cruz Bay on St. John, and in the British Virgin Islands on Tortola and Virgin Gorda. The other islands do not have ATMs, so if you're planning a visit, be sure to visit an ATM to get some cash first. Each machine charges around $2 to $3 for a transaction fee. Nearly all of the machines are operated by three banks: **Scotiabank** (www.scotiabank.com), **FirstBank** (www.firstbankvi.com), and **Banco Popular** (www.banco popular.com/vi).

Many establishments in the Virgin Islands, including most of those recommended in this guide, accept **credit cards.** MasterCard and Visa are widely accepted on all the islands that cater to visitors, especially Virgin Gorda, Tortola, St. John, St. Croix, and, of course, St. Thomas. In the past few years, there has been a tendency to drop American Express because of the high percentage it takes from transactions with shopkeepers.

However, visitors should not rely solely on credit cards, as many establishments in the Virgin Islands accept only **cash.** Often, villas and condos or small inns will only accept cash or personal checks in advance. You will also want to arm yourself with cash while browsing the small boutiques and curio shops throughout the islands, as most do not take credit cards.

Beware of hidden credit card fees while traveling. Check with your credit or debit card issuer to see what fees, if any, will be charged for overseas transactions. Recent reform legislation in the U.S., for example, has curbed some exploitative lending practices. But many banks have responded by increasing fees in other areas, including fees for customers who use credit and debit cards while out of the country—even if those charges were made in U.S. dollars. Fees can amount to 3% or more of the purchase price. Check with your bank before departing to avoid any surprise charges on your statement.

For help with currency conversions, tip calculations, and more, download Frommer's convenient Travel Tools app for your mobile device. Go to www.frommers.com/go/mobile and click on the "Travel Tools To Go" icon.

Newspapers & Magazines   Daily U.S. newspapers are flown into St. Thomas, St. Croix, Tortola, and Virgin Gorda. For local papers, see "Fast Facts" in individual island chapters. The B.V.I. have no daily newspaper, but the *Island Sun,* published Wednesday

DEAR VISA: I'M OFF TO CHARLOTTE AMALIE!

Some credit card companies recommend that you notify them of any impending trip so that they don't become suspicious when the card is used numerous times in an unusual destination and block your charges. Even if you don't call your credit card company in advance, you can always call the card's toll-free emergency number if a charge is refused—a good reason to carry the phone number with you. But perhaps the most important lesson here is to carry more than one card with you on your trip; a card might not work for any number of reasons, so having a backup is the smart way to go.

and Friday, is a good source of information on local entertainment, as is the *BVI Beacon,* published on Thursday. *Standpoint* is another helpful publication that comes out on Monday and Saturday. You can find these in most supermarkets and shops.

Packing   For helpful information on packing for your trip, download our convenient Travel Tools app for your mobile device. Go to www.frommers.com/go/mobile and click on the "Travel Tools To Go" icon.

Passports   If you're a U.S. citizen and you travel directly to the U.S.V.I. and do not visit the British Virgin Islands, you do not need a passport—but you are highly encouraged to carry one. If you return to the mainland U.S. from the U.S.V.I. through another country (Mexico or Bermuda, for example), you will need a passport to get back home. For non-U.S. citizens, visiting the U.S. Virgin Islands is just like visiting the mainland United States: You need a passport and visa.

A passport is necessary for *all* visitors to the British Virgin Islands (including citizens of the U.K.).

For information on how to get a passport, contact your passport office (see below). Allow plenty of time before your trip to apply for a passport; processing normally takes 3 weeks but can take longer during busy periods. And keep in mind that if you need a passport in a hurry, you'll pay a higher processing fee. When traveling, safeguard your passport in an inconspicuous, inaccessible place like a money belt, and keep a copy of the critical pages with your passport number in a separate place. There are no foreign consulates in the Virgin Islands, so if you lose your passport, go to the local police station.

Passport Offices

○ **Australia Australian Passport Information Service,**   R.G. Casey Building, John McEwen Crescent, Barton ACT 0221 (✆ **131-232;** www.passports.gov.au).

○ **Canada Passport Office,** Department of Foreign Affairs and International Trade, Ottawa, ON K1A 0G3 (✆ **800/567-6868;** www.ppt.gc.ca).

○ **Ireland Passport Office,** Setanta Centre, Molesworth Street, Dublin 2 (✆ **01/671-1633;** www.foreignaffairs.gov.ie).

○ **New Zealand Passports Office,** Department of Internal Affairs, 47 Boulcott St., Wellington, 6011 (✆ **0800/225-050** in New Zealand or 04/474-8100; www.passports.govt.nz).

○ **United Kingdom**   Visit your nearest passport office, major post office, or travel agency or contact the **Identity and Passport Service (IPS),** 89 Eccleston Square, London, SW1V 1PN (✆ **0300/222-0000;** www.ips.gov.uk).

o **United States** To find your regional passport office, check the U.S. Department of State website (travel.state.gov/passport) or call the **National Passport Information Center** (© **877/487-2778**) for automated information.

Petrol Please see "Getting Around," earlier in this chapter for information.

Pets To bring your pet to the U.S.V.I., you must have a health certificate from a mainland veterinarian and show proof of vaccination against rabies. Very few hotels allow animals, so check in advance. If you're strolling with your dog through the national park on St. John, you must keep it on a leash. Pets are not allowed at campgrounds, in picnic areas, or on public beaches. Both St. Croix and St. Thomas have veterinarians listed in the Yellow Pages.

Your dog or cat is permitted entry into the B.V.I. without quarantine, if accompanied by an Animal Health Certificate issued by the Veterinary Authority in your country of origin. This certificate has a number of requirements, including a guarantee of vaccination against rabies.

Police Dial © **911** for emergencies in the U.S.V.I. In the B.V.I., the main police headquarters is on Waterfront Drive near the ferry docks on Sir Olva Georges Plaza (© **284/494-3822**) in Tortola. There are also police stations on Virgin Gorda (© **284/495-9828**) and on Jost Van Dyke (© **284/495-9345**). See individual island chapters for more detailed information.

Safety The Virgin Islands are a relatively safe destination. The small permanent populations are generally friendly and welcoming. That being said, **St. Thomas** is no longer as safe as it once was. Crime against tourists has been on the rise, and muggings are frequent. Wandering the island at night, especially on the back streets of Charlotte Amalie (particularly on Back St.), is not recommended. For a town of this small size, there is an unusually high crime rate. Guard your valuables or store them in hotel safes if possible.

The same holds true for **St. Croix** and the back streets of Christiansted and Frederiksted. Although these areas are safer than St. Thomas, random acts of violence against tourists in the past, even murder, have been known to happen. Know that most crime on the island is petty theft aimed at unguarded possessions on the beach, unlocked parked cars, or muggings (rarely violent) of visitors at night. Exercise the same amount of caution you would if you were traveling to an unfamiliar town on the mainland. Whether on St. Thomas or St. Croix, always take a taxi home after a night out.

St. John is a bit different, because there is no major town and most of the island is uninhabited. Muggings and petty theft do happen, but such occurrences are rarely violent. You are most likely to find your camera stolen if you leave it unattended on the beach.

The **British Virgin Islands** are very safe. Crime is practically nonexistent on these islands. Minor robberies do occur on Tortola, with less trouble reported on Virgin Gorda.

In general, the Virgin Islands' steep, curvy roads are often poorly lit at night. St. Croix's road network is particularly poor and is composed of rocky, steep dirt roads through the interior. As a result, car-rental insurance is higher on this island than the others. For those travelers who are unaccustomed to driving on the left, we suggest leaving the night driving up to a taxi driver. Do not attempt the most rural roads at night, as cellphone service is spotty at best and breakdowns or robberies are an all-too-perfect way to ruin your Virgin Islands vacation; see "Getting Around," earlier in this chapter.

Student Travel St. Thomas has the most youth-oriented scene of any of the Virgin Islands, British or American. Some areas of St. Thomas are more popular than others with young people, especially the bars and restaurants around Red Hook. The major resorts at

Flamboyant Point and the East End of St. Thomas cater mainly to a middle-age or senior crowd. Many young people who visit St. Thomas stay in the guesthouses in and around Charlotte Amalie. Beyond St. Thomas, the island of St. Croix attracts a large array of young, single travelers, mainly to the inns in and around Christiansted and Frederiksted.

Taxes   For the U.S. Virgin Islands, the United States has no value-added tax (VAT) or other indirect tax at the national level. The U.S.V.I. may levy their own local taxes on all purchases, including hotel and restaurant checks and airline tickets. These taxes will not appear on price tags.

In the British Virgin Islands, there is a departure tax of $5 per person for those leaving by boat or $20 if by airplane. Most hotels add a service charge in the $5 to $18 range; some restaurants will also tack on a 10% surcharge if you pay by credit card. There's also a 7% government tax on hotel rooms, but no sales tax.

Telephones   In the Virgin Islands, hotel surcharges on long-distance and local calls are usually astronomical, so you're better off using your **cellphone** or a **public pay telephone.** Many convenience stores, groceries, and packaging services sell **prepaid calling cards** in denominations up to $50; for international visitors these can be the least expensive way to call home. Many public pay phones at airports now accept American Express, MasterCard, and Visa credit cards. **Local calls** made from pay phones in most locales cost either 25¢ or 35¢ (no pennies, please). Many of the most rural or expressly private resorts and hotels in the Virgin Islands do not provide phones in the rooms, but have phones in their lobbies or common areas.

To make calls within the United States, including the U.S. Virgins, and to Canada, dial 1 followed by the area code and the seven-digit number. **For other international calls,** dial 011 followed by the country code, city code, and the number you are calling.

You can **call the British Virgins** from the United States by just dialing **1,** the area code **284,** and the number; from the U.K. dial **011-44,** then the number. **To call the U.S. from the B.V.I.,** just dial 1 plus the area code and the number; **to call the U.K. from the B.V.I.,** dial 011-44-, then the number.

Calls to area codes **800, 888, 877,** and **866** are toll-free. However, calls to area codes **700** and **900** (chat lines, bulletin boards, "dating" services, and so on) can be very expensive—usually a charge of 95¢ to $3 or more per minute, and they sometimes have minimum charges that can run as high as $15 or more.

For **reversed-charge or collect calls,** and for person-to-person calls, dial the number 0, then the area code and number; an operator will come on the line, and you should specify whether you are calling collect, person-to-person, or both. If your operator-assisted call is international, ask for the overseas operator.

For **local directory assistance** ("information"), dial 411; for long-distance information, dial 1, then the appropriate area code and 555-1212.

Time   The Virgin Islands are on Atlantic Standard Time, which is 1 hour ahead of Eastern Standard Time. However, the islands do not observe daylight saving time: so in the summer, the Virgin Islands and the East Coast of the U.S. are on the same time. In winter, when it's 6am in Charlotte Amalie, it's 5am in Miami; during daylight saving time it's 6am in both places.

Tipping   In hotels, tip **bellhops** at least $1 per bag ($2–$3 if you have a lot of luggage) and tip the **chamber staff** $1 to $2 per day (more if you've left a disaster area for him or her to clean up). Tip the **doorman** or **concierge** only if he or she has provided you with some specific service (for example, calling a cab for you or obtaining difficult-to-get theater tickets). Tip the **valet-parking attendant** $1 every time you get your car.

In restaurants, bars, and nightclubs, tip **service staff** and **bartenders** 15% to 20% of the check, tip **checkroom attendants** $1 per garment, and tip **valet-parking attendants** $1 per vehicle.

As for other service personnel, tip **cabdrivers** 15% of the fare; tip **skycaps** at airports at least $1 per bag ($2–$3 if you have a lot of luggage); and tip **hairdressers** and barbers 15% to 20%.

Toilets   You won't find public toilets or restrooms on the streets, but they can be found in hotel lobbies, bars, restaurants, museums, department stores, bus stations, and service stations. Large hotels and fast-food restaurants are often the best bet for clean facilities. Restaurants and bars in resorts or heavily visited areas may reserve their restrooms for patrons.

Visas   Non-U.S. visitors to the **U.S. Virgin Islands** should have a U.S. visa; those visitors may also be asked to produce an onward ticket. In the **British Virgin Islands,** visitors who stay for less than 6 months don't need a visa if they possess a return or onward ticket.

For information about U.S. visas, go to **http://travel.state.gov** and click on "Visas." Or go to one of the following websites:

Australian citizens can obtain up-to-date visa information from the **U.S. Embassy Canberra,** Moonah Place, Yarralumla, ACT 2600 (✆ **02/6214-5600**), or by checking the U.S. Diplomatic Mission's website at **http://canberra.usembassy.gov/visas.html**.

British subjects can obtain up-to-date visa information by calling the **U.S. Embassy Visa Information Line** (✆ **09042-450-100** from within the U.K. at £1.20 per min.) or by visiting the "Visas to the U.S." section of the American Embassy London's website at **http://london.usembassy.gov/visas.html**.

Irish citizens can obtain up-to-date visa information through the **U.S. Embassy Dublin,** 42 Elgin Rd., Ballsbridge, Dublin 4 (✆ **1580-47-VISA** [8472] from within the Republic of Ireland at €2.40 per minute; http://dublin.usembassy.gov).

Citizens of **New Zealand** can obtain up-to-date visa information by contacting the **U.S. Embassy New Zealand,** 29 Fitzherbert Terrace, Thorndon, Wellington (✆ **644/462-6000;** http://newzealand.usembassy.gov).

Visitor Information   You can surf the **U.S.V.I. Division of Tourism**'s website at www.visitusvi.com. The **British Virgin Islands Tourist Board** can be found at www.bvi tourism.com.

In the U.S.: Before you take off for the U.S. Virgin Islands, you can get information from the **U.S. Virgin Islands Division of Tourism,** 1270 Avenue of the Americas, New York, NY (✆ **800/372-8784** or 212-332-2222); 225 Peachtree St., N.E., No. 760, Atlanta, GA (✆ **404/688-0906**); 122 S. Michigan Ave., No. 1270, Chicago, Il., (✆ **312-670-8784**); 900 17th St., Ste. 500, Washington, DC 20006 (✆ **202/293-3707**); 2655 Le Jeune Rd., Ste. 907, Coral Gables, FL 33134 (✆ **305/442-7200**); and 3450 Wilshire Blvd., Ste. 1202, Los Angeles, CA 90010 (✆ **213/739-8931**). For details on the British Virgin Islands, get in touch with the **British Virgin Islands Tourist Board** at 3450 Wilshire Blvd., Ste. 1202, Los Angeles, CA 90010 (✆ **213/736-8931**).

In the U.K.: Information for the British Virgin Islands is available at the **B.V.I. Information Office,** 15 Upper Grosvenor St., London W1K 7PS (✆ **020/7355-9585**).

Water   Many visitors to both the U.S. and British Virgins drink the local tap water with no harmful effects. To be prudent, especially if you have a delicate stomach, stick to bottled water.

Wi-Fi   See "Internet & Wi-Fi," earlier in this section.

Women Travelers   St. John and the British Virgin Islands have a low crime rate, while St. Thomas and St. Croix have the highest crime rate against women in the archipelago. However, you are far safer in the Virgin Islands than you would be walking the streets of any major U.S. city. Some of the local men (those who have not had sensitivity training) still regard a single woman as an object to hassle with unwanted attention, but such encounters happen in the Virgin Islands no more often than in most urban U.S. areas. Follow the usual precautions that you'd follow in any major U.S. city.

AIRLINE WEBSITES

MAJOR AIRLINES

American Airlines
www.aa.com

Continental Airlines
www.continental.com

Delta Airlines
www.delta.com

Jet Blue
www.jetblue.com

Spirit Airlines
www.spirit.com

United Airlines
www.united.com

US Airways
www.usairways.com

LOCAL AIRLINES

Air Sunshine
www.airsunshine.com

Bohlke Airlines
www.bohlke.com

Cape Air
www.flycapeair.com

Caribbean Wings
www.bvi-airlines.com

Fly BVI
www.fly-bvi.com

Island Birds
www.islandbirds.com

LIAT Airlines
www.liatairline.com

Seaborne Airlines
www.seaborneairlines.com

Vieques Airlink
www.viequesairlink.com

Index

Restaurants